Emerging Powers in Global Governance

Studies in International Governance is a research and policy analysis series from the Centre for International Governance Innovation (CIGI) and Wilfrid Laurier University Press. Titles in the series provide timely consideration of emerging trends and current challenges in the broad field of international governance. Representing diverse perspectives on important global issues, the series will be of interest to students and academics while serving also as a reference tool for policy-makers and experts engaged in policy discussion. To reach the greatest possible audience and ultimately shape the policy dialogue, each volume will be made available both in print through WLU Press and, twelve months after publication, accessible for free online through the IGLOO Network under the Creative Commons License.

CIGI

The Centre for International
Governance Innovation
Centre pour l'innovation dans
la gouvernance internationale

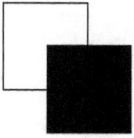

Emerging Powers in Global Governance
Lessons from the Heiligendamm Process

Andrew F. Cooper and Agata Antkiewicz, editors

Wilfrid Laurier University Press
[WLU]

Wilfrid Laurier University Press acknowledges the financial support of the Government of Canada through its Book Publishing Industry Development Program for its publishing activities. Wilfrid Laurier University Press acknowledges the financial support of the Centre for International Governance Innovation. The Centre for International Governance Innovation gratefully acknowledges support for its work program from the Government of Canada and the Government of Ontario.

Library and Archives Canada Cataloguing in Publication

Emerging powers in global governance : lessons from the Heiligendamm process / Andrew F. Cooper and Agata Antkiewicz, editors.

(Studies in international governance)
Co-published by: Centre for International Governance Innovation.
Includes bibliographical references and index.
ISBN 978-1-55458-057-6 (pbk).— ISBN 978-1-55458-194-8 (pdf).
— ISBN 978-1-55458-659-2 (epub)

1. International organization. 2. International cooperation. 3. International relations. 4. Group of Eight (Organization). 5. G8 Heiligendamm Process. I. Cooper, Andrew F. (Andrew Fenton), [date] II. Antkiewicz, Agata III. Centre for International Governance Innovation IV. Series.

JZ1318.E43 2008   341.2   C2008-905844-5

Co-published with the Centre for International Governance Innovation.

© 2008 The Centre for International Governance Innovation (CIGI) and Wilfrid Laurier University Press

Cover images from iStockphoto <http:www.istockphoto.com>. Cover design by David Yoon and Scott Lee. Text design by Catharine Bonas-Taylor.

Contents

THE EVOLVING ARCHITECTURE OF CHANGE

Foreword

The ongoing tectonic power shifts in the global system have become the paramount topic for academic reflection and political strategies in international affairs. A group of rising powers from the global South is effectively challenging western predominance, the hallmark of the global order over the last two centuries. Different labels and analytical categories are used in identifying the new powerhouses, such as Asian drivers of global change, anchor countries, and now the B(R)ICSAM constellation of Brazil, Russia, India, China, South Africa, and Mexico, introduced by the Centre for International Governance Innovation (CIGI) in Waterloo, Canada. This highly innovative think tank has been at the forefront of systematic research on global governance arrangements that would be capable of addressing the survival issues of sustainable development and equity. CIGI's research is built on long-term transnational networking that brings together high-ranking scholars from the industrialized and the developing worlds.

The volume at hand is an excellent example of the timeliness and inclusiveness that characterize CIGI publications. It takes a comprehensive view of the Heiligendamm Process (HP) established in 2007 by German chancellor Angela Merkel, then G8 host. This outreach effort of the leading industrialized countries toward those five emerging powers provides a new framework for issue-based informal exchanges on crucial aspects of global policy making. Due to end in 2009, the HP has come half the way in trying to build trust and identify common approaches to pressing problems. It remains to be seen if it can open the gate to a formal expansion of the G8 or if it, rather, represents yet another makeshift exercise without positive impact for summit reform.

The contributions to this volume cover a wide range of analytical and policy issues related to the HP and to the current global order in a broader sense. They highlight the multiple motivations and interests of participating nation-states and ask for the implications of G8 reform for the global governance system. Of particular relevance are the perspectives of rising powers, which are introduced through detailed country profiles of each of the five dialogue partners. An article on the Association of South East Asian Nations (ASEAN) complements the section on the developing world and an article on the Organisation of Economic Cooperation and Development (OECD) offers an institutional context for the HP. With regard to industrialized countries, the United States, Russia, and Germany (as initiator of the HP) receive special attention. The insights of these excellent contributions will be of lasting benefit to scholars and practitioners alike as they grapple with the turbulent reshaping of global affairs of which the HP is a small but significant element.

Dirk Messner
Director, German Development Institute (DIE)
Bonn, August 2008

Preface

This is a book on the role of big emerging powers in the workings of the Group of Eight. It considers a number of global issues that bother states and organizations at the high diplomatic table and the strategies used to address them. The contributions here certainly deliver—in detail and with sophistication—to this important discussion, given the fact that the area is new.

The editors set the stage in the introductory chapters by stating their interest in structure over causation. But the compulsion of life—even at the level of global abstraction—pushes analysis further, toward interests and changing strategies in an emerging multi-polar world. The interface between this analytical discourse and the descriptive and normative aspects of structure is the true strength of this book. It recognizes that no neat formulas are available to explain certain developments and that some formulas fall by the wayside as states manoeuvre their own interest through different structural organizations.

The analysis, however, has substantive content, since the global aspects of issues emerging again and again are compelling. At the structural level, the authors examine institutional alternatives. They bring out the relationship between ideas, economic strategy, performance, and diplomatic leverage. This is a fascinating book, and it will be read widely by students of international affairs and used in diplomatic training.

The question that will follow—and one hopes that Andrew F. Cooper and Agata Antkiewicz will use some of their unbounded energy to pursue further—is this: Why did some of the earlier outreach initiatives not go as far as designed? Progress toward the laudable leaders' 20 (L20) initiative, as promoted by former Canadian prime minister Paul Martin, was started but never matured to Martin's original design.

We need to push the analysis of mistakes made, for, as the contributors rightly bring out, the world is different now and the cost of making mistakes is much higher. The G8 has struggled to develop an effective strategy of engaging the big emerging powers from the global South, and can be seen as ill equipped to face the reality of emerging global problems. There is, for example, an unerring similarity with the outcomes of the special Committee on Agriculture of the World Trade Organization (WTO), in its different roles since the 2001 Doha ministerial. Modalities drafts are changed at the last minute with almost expected consequences.

In terms of structures, there is one major finding and there are two issues. The finding is that it is early hours yet and each structural profile has positive and negative points, from very practical ones such as the Outreach Five (O5) to the normative ones advanced by Colin I. Bradford. The urge for clarity can in this context be neurotic; the actual outcomes will vary. Abdul Nafey talks about states using concentric circles of influence as strategy and methods—an idea developed by Rajiv Gandhi—to pursue their objectives, and expanding the G8 will be only one such method. It needs to be strengthened, since normatively it is an attractive solution.

Yet there are two riders. The first is the networks available at present are not strong enough to bring global ideas to the fore in a business-like manner such that the current format of the G8 Plus Five—that is, including Brazil, China, India, Mexico, and South Africa—addresses them in compelling terms for solutions. The WTO is not discussed here as an alternative in any meaningful way. And second, although the initiatives of self-help groups were taken by the G8 in 2005 at the Gleneagles Summit, this discussion leaves out most of the big global financing reform issues and the national policies on empowerment of organizations of the poor, on rural development, and on agricultural growth. The energy initiative fell short. China engaged, but was skeptical; it was new and pursued the art of following its national interest and championing the developing world simultaneously. India was skeptical, with its prime minister saying that he was not coming to petition but to solve the problem, and the structure does not provide for it. The force of Brazil in opening up world markets has not yet been fully unleashed. Mexico occupies a strategic position geographically but also as a bridge to the Organisation for Economic Co-operation and Development (OECD). South Africa and its revolutionary concepts of egalitarian change (coining the expression of solidarity) do not get a hearing. On the sixty-first anniversary of Indian independence, the South Africans are a very refreshing presence, for they remind us of the early years of independence, as we here in India celebrate the National Day in a jaded manner.

When I wrote in *Reforming from the Top: A Leaders' 20 Summit* that in addition to the sherpas we also need the coolies, I was quite serious. Anne-Marie Slaughter has elegantly described the need for networks to buttress the G8 Plus Five or any other arrangements. This book is an important part of that process. Change will be incremental, but the preparations for it must be inclusive. Paul Martin's idea that personal interaction among leaders is necessary in solving difficult problems remains a powerful one, for if the language of the other is not known or understood, progress is impossible.

"Alagh's law" states that the next generation is smarter than mine. The future will inexorably build on experiences of the present. This collection assembled by the Centre for International Governance Innovation draws out the next few steps on which future encounters and battles will take place. This book is recommended to all those interested in the future of the world.

Yoginder K. Alagh
Chairman, Institute of Rural Management, Anand, Chancellor, Nagaland University, and former Minister of Power, Planning and Science and Technology, India
Ahmedabad, August 2008

Acknowledgements

This volume highlights the evolution of the BRICSAM project, a set of research activities undertaken at The Centre for International Governance Innovation (CIGI) designed to identify and analyse key emerging economies. The initial concentration of this project was economic, focusing on the BRICSAM countries—Brazil, Russia, India, China, South Africa and Mexico—with a view to determine long-term trends shaping the sustainability of their individual and collective economic growth. Over time, however, the research agenda of BRICSAM project has expanded in depth, scope and policy orientation. In addition to looking at the impact of the processes and policies of these rising states on the global economy, CIGI has sought to focus on the Economic Diplomacy of the BRICSAM countries.

The main attraction of undertaking an in-depth examination of the Heiligendamm Process (HP) was in its privileging of the BRICSAM countries—or in this area more appropriately B(R)ICSAM, with Russia already a G8 member—as the core ingredients of a G8 "outreach" agenda. This configuration allowed the HP to be used as both a targeted and novel case study of the shifting global order, with special attention accorded to how this form of extended dialogue reflects the influential role of emerging powers in the reshaping of global governance. Nonetheless, the lessons derived from the HP are not only located in the mirroring of structural change. What jumps out from this collection is the divergence, as well as convergence, among the BRICSAM countries. For all their common attributes and ambition, these rising states retain very distinctive diplomatic profiles and personalities, characterised in their specific responses towards the HP.

CIGI's International Advisory Board of Governors has provided great encouragement and intellectual guidance for study in this area, placing emerging economies at the top of our research agenda. Board member and leading Indian thinker Yoginder Alagh has provided instrumental direction from the beginning of the BRICSAM project and we thank him for contributing the Preface to the volume. Complementing the front-end of the book, we are very pleased to have a Foreword by German opinion-maker and policy-shaper Dirk Messner, who has prompted us to consider the future of the HP.

Of course, the collection would not exist without the unwavering dedication of our many contributors. Our heartfelt thanks go to them and the discussants who participated in either of the preparatory workshops in Canada and Mexico, including Barry Carin, Tony Payne, Ariel Buria, Yuen Pau Woo and Rafael Fernández de Castro. The level of discussion at these sessions was impressive and is keenly reflected in the pages of this book.

Our thinking on the subject matter was also shaped by a number of experts. We want to thank Ulrich Benterbusch for his ongoing support, Ramesh Thakur for his organizational and conceptual contributions, Manmohan Agarwal for his substantive and editorial comments on earlier drafts, as well as a select group of senior Canadian government officials for constructive discussions.

The production of the book benefited from the diligence of many individuals. In particular, Madeline Koch took on much of the heavily lifting as copy-editor, smoothing out the style and syntax. Meagan Kay, Thomas Agar, Joe Turcotte and Deanne Leifso assisted with reference checking and page proofing. David Yoon shared his talents once more to create an attractive cover design. Max Brem provided spirited guidance throughout the publication process.

The Events Team at CIGI provided logistical support for our two workshops. In particular, Briton Dowhaniuk has our thanks for her never-ending willingness to help and prompt response to requests, no matter the time of day. On the research side, Anne-Marie Sánchez ensured ongoing activities were supported while we completed work on this volume.

As the Economic Diplomacy research area has grown, Andrew Schrumm has taken on many responsibilities in support of our efforts. He has kept up with our ongoing requests with patience and enthusiasm. And even though she has left CIGI to pursue a new career, Kelly Jackson has had a lasting influence on the development of this work after framing many of its main research questions.

As in all projects, CIGI's Executive Director John English created an environment amenable to productive research. In his role this year as Acting Executive Director, Daniel Schwanen has provided strong ongoing support and intellectual leadership towards this and many related projects.

CIGI was founded in 2002 by Jim Balsillie, co-CEO of RIM (Research In Motion), and collaborates with and gratefully acknowledges support from a number of strategic partners, in particular the Government of Canada and the Government of Ontario.

Le CIGI a été fondé en 2002 par Jim Balsillie, co-chef de la direction de RIM (Research In Motion). Il collabore avec de nombreux partenaires stratégiques et exprime sa reconnaissance du soutien reçu de ceux-ci, notamment de l'appui reçu du gouvernement du Canada et de celui du gouvernement de l'Ontario.

The final thanks are for Brian Henderson, Rob Kohlmeier and Heather Blain-Yanke, the publishing professionals of Wilfrid Laurier University Press who have shown us patience and grace despite demanding deadlines. Working together with this team on the Studies in International Governance series has developed a lasting, fruitful partnership.

Andrew F. Cooper and Agata Antkiewicz
Waterloo, August 2008

Abbreviations and Acronyms

ABC	Brazilian Agency of Cooperation (Agência Brasileira de Cooperación)
ALADI	Latin American Integration Association (Associação Latino-Americana de Integração)
ANC	African National Congress
APEC	Asia-Pacific Economic Cooperation
APT	ASEAN Plus Three (China, Japan, and Korea)
ASEAN	Association of Southeast Asian Nations
ASEAN+4	**ASEAN plus Indonesia, Malaysia, Philippines, and Thailand**
ASEM	Asia Europe Meeting
ASGISA	Accelerated and Shared Growth Initiative for South Africa
AU	African Union
BCIM	Bangladesh, China, India, and Myanmar
BDI	Federation of German Industries (Bundesverband der Deutschen Industrie e.V.)
BMZ	Ministry for Economic Cooperation and Development, Germany (Bundesministerium für wirtschaftliche Zusammenarbeit und Entwicklung)
BNDES	Brazilian Development Bank (O Banco Nacional de Desenvolvimento Econômico e Social)
BRICs	Brazil, Russia, India, and China
B(R)ICSAM	Brazil, Russia, India, China, South Africa, and Mexico
BUKO	Bundeskoordination Internationalismus
CAF	Andean Development Corporation (Corporación Andina de Fomonto)

CASA	South American Community of Nations (Comunidade Sul-Americana de Nações)
CASS	Chinese Academy of Social Sciences
CfA	Commission for Africa
CFGS	Centre for Global Studies, University of Victoria
CIA	Central Intelligence Agency (of the United States)
CICIR	China Institute of Contemporary International Relations
CIDE	Centro de Investigación y Docencia Económicas (Center for Teaching and Research in Economics)
CIGI	Centre for International Governance Innovation
CIS	Commonwealth of Independent States
CLMV	Cambodia, Laos, Myanmar, and Vietnam
CO_2	carbon dioxide
COMEXI	Consejo Mexicano de Asuntos Internacionales (Mexican Council on Foreign Relations)
COSATU	Congress of South African Trade Unions
DAC	Development Assistance Committee (of the Organisation for Economic Co-operation and Development)
DGB	Confederation of German Trade Unions (Deutscher Gewerkschaftsbund)
DGVN	German United Nations Association (Deutsche Gesellschaft für die vereinten Nationen e.V.)
DIHK	German Chambers of Industry and Commerce (Deutschen Industrie- und Handelskammertages)
DRC	Democratic Republic of Congo
EAEC	East Asian Economic Caucus
ECOSOC	United Nations Economic and Social Council
FAO	Food and Agriculture Organization
FARC	Revolutionary Armed Forces of Colombia (Fuerzas Armadas Revolucionarias de Colombia)
FDI	foreign direct investment
FOCAC	Forums on China-African Cooperation
FSF	Financial Stability Forum
FTAA	Free Trade Agreement of the Americas
G5	Group of Five—see Outreach Five
G7	Group of Seven (Canada, France, Germany, Italy, Japan, the United Kingdom, and the United States)
G8	Group of Eight (G7 plus Russia)
G20 Finance	Group of Twenty finance ministers and central bank governors (G8 plus Argentina, Australia, Brazil, China, India, Indonesia, Mexico, Saudi Arabia, South Korea, and Turkey)

G20	Group of Twenty developing countries, led by Brazil, India, and South Africa, formed to challenge trade issues at the 2003 Cancun ministerial meeting of the World Trade Organization
G77	Group of Seventy-Seven (developing countries)
GATT	General Agreement on Tariffs and Trade
GDP	gross domestic product
GEAR	Growth, Employment, and Redistribution
HP	Heiligendamm Process
IADB	Inter-American Development Bank
IAEA	International Atomic Energy Agency
IBSA	India–Brazil–South Africa (Dialogue Forum)
IEA	International Energy Agency
IFIs	international financial institutions
IIRSA	Initiative for Integration of Regional Infrastructure in South America
ILO	International Labour Organization
IMF	International Monetary Fund
IMFC	International Monetary and Financial Committee (of the International Monetary Fund)
IPCC	Intergovernmental Panel on Climate Change
IPO	initial public offering
IPR	intellectual property rights
ISI	import substitution industrialization
IT	information technology
ITO	International Trade Organization
L20	Leaders Twenty (proposed grouping of the G20 [finance ministers and central bank governors] at the leader's level)
LDC	least developed country
MDG	Millennium Development Goal
MDIC	Ministério do Desenvolvimento (Ministry of Public Works and the Economy, Brazil)
MEM	Major Economies Meeting on Energy Security and Climate Change
MINUSTAH	United Nations Stabilization Mission in Haiti
MNC	multinational corporation
N11	Next Eleven
NAM	Non-Aligned Movement
NAMA	non-agricultural market access
NAFTA	North American Free Trade Agreement
NATO	North Atlantic Treaty Organization
NEPAD	New Partnership for Africa's Development

NGO	nongovernmental organisation
NPT	Non-Proliferation Treaty
NSAAsP	New Asian-African Strategic Partnership
NSG	Nuclear Suppliers Group
O5	Outreach Five (Brazil, China, India, Mexico, and South Africa)
OAS	Organization of American States
OAU	Organization of African Unity
ODA	official development assistance
OECD	Organisation for Economic Co-operation and Development
OEEC	Organisation for European Economic Co-operation
OMC	other major countries
OPEC	Organization of the Petroleum Exporting Countries
OSCE	Organization for Security and Cooperation in Europe
P5	Permanent Five (members of the United Nations Security Council)
P21	Partnership 21
PEMEX	Petróleos Mexicanos
PPP	purchasing power parity
PRC	People's Republic of China
PRI	Partido Revolucionario Institucional
PT	Workers' Party (Partido dos Trabalhadores)
RICs	Russia, India, and China
ROSCs	Reports on the Observance of Standards and Codes
SACP	South African Communist Party
SACU	Southern African Customs Union
SADC	South African Development Community
SAFTA	South American Free Trade Area
SCO	Shanghai Cooperation Organisation
SPP	Security and Prosperity Partnership
TRIPS	Trade-Related Aspects of Intellectual Property Rights
UNCTAD	United Nations Conference on Trade and Development
UNDP	United Nations Development Programme
UNEP	United Nations Environment Programme
UNFCCC	United Nations Framework Convention on Climate Change
UNSC	United Nations Security Council
UPA	United Progressive Alliance
USR	United States respondents
VSTO	Eastern Siberia–Pacific Ocean (pipeline)
WHO	World Health Organization
WIPO	World Intellectual Property Organization

WMD	weapons of mass destruction
WP3	Working Party Number 3 on Policies for the Promotion of Better International Payments Equilibrium (of the Organisation for Economic Co-operation and Development)
WSF	World Social Forum
WTO	World Trade Organization

1

The Heiligendamm Process
Structural Reordering and Diplomatic Agency

Andrew F. Cooper

The question of how to deal with emerging powers in a manner that buttresses the architecture—and rule-making—of the international system rests at the core of global governance. Fundamental rearrangements of the global order have taken place historically via post-conflict settlements. New forms of institutional structures—and representational privileges—are one of the main outcomes emanating from massive disruptions in the status quo. The distinctiveness of these rearrangements (post-1815, post-1918, and post-1945) is in how they were constituted as specific frameworks, not the causation of their making.

Bringing big emerging powers into global governance as a means to temper conflict is far more novel, whether conflict is interpreted in a classic geopolitical fashion or stretched out to include economic rivalry. If the potential benefits of such an effort can be readily understood, the challenges to such an ambitious design are formidable. Operationally, the crucial test hinges on a degree of anticipation. If the template for dealing with structural reordering follows the traditional path, the process of reorganization will only come when the old system breaks down amidst strategic and commercial turmoil. Breaking with orthodoxy before this stage is reached takes far more imagination with regard to the capacity for responsiveness to balance order and innovation.

Normatively, the design sets a higher bar than in the past. On the one hand, it points toward some greater collective responsibility in an array of functional areas. On the other hand, it necessitates some serious redistribution of powers and status with respect to diplomatic agency. Order must be joined with some attributes of governance, at the very least in terms of the multipolarity of power and the addition of key new institutional ingredients. At the same time as the established interstate hierarchy is reconfigured (Clark 1991; Ikenberry 2001; Hurrell 2007), the character of the rule-making processes deepens in tandem with the heightened range of issues on the policy agenda.

Because of the centrality of emerging powers—as both drivers of structural change and claimants for elevated diplomatic recognition—there is a selective, even exclusive quality to the design of the new global architecture. From this perspective, there is some degree of continuity built into the process. Akin to earlier formulas, the benefits *vis-à-vis* a fundamental reordering of the international system was highly inequitable. This was as true of the 19th century concert of power as it was of the post–Second World War architecture, as witnessed in the creation of the Bretton Wood system and the United Nations Permanent Five (P5) members of the Security Council (UNSC).

The experience of the G8 club of rich northern industrial countries, with the Atlantic hub supplemented by Japan, reveals both the strengths and weaknesses of the established order as it evolved over time. Faced with the severe economic shocks associated with the oil crisis of the Organization of the Petroleum Exporting Countries (OPEC) and deep-set stagflation, the creation of the club was proof that imaginative leadership could be produced without the requirement of war. Its record also illustrated a number of success stories. In terms of its functional reach, the G8 was able to extend its ambit from its original economic focus to a wider set of geo-political and social or environmental concerns. In terms of its membership, the willingness of the G8 to move beyond its initial composition in a dramatic although still awkward fashion, (in comparison to the earlier integration of Italy and Canada) was signalled by the entry of Russia following its post–Cold War political transformation.

Increasingly, though, the G8 faces an accentuated double crisis of legitimacy and efficiency (see English et al. 2005; Cooper 2007a; Hajnal 2007, Introduction). The group's under-representation of emerging powers from the global South erodes its ability to set priorities for the international community. It detracts as well from its credibility as an institution that cannot only mediate or broker solutions to pressing global problems, but also act as a conduit between different constituencies within the international system.

The functional deficit that comes with holding onto the post-1975 order extends right across the policy continuum. The issue that jumps out in starkest fashion, nonetheless, has been the acknowledgement that the G8 is incapable of creating a relevant strategy for climate change without the participation of major carbon dioxide emitters, such as India or China, or leading alternative energy suppliers, such as Brazil. In the blunt assessment of Timothy Garton Ash (2008): "It makes no sense at all to tackle an issue like climate change without the world's largest growing carbon emitters ... at the table."

The legitimacy or credibility deficit is more amorphous, but is intimately wrapped up with issues of authority without representation. It is one thing for the G8 (or G7) to try to function as a body coordinating the practices of its own membership. As Robert Putnam (1988), among others, described a long time ago, this role was performed in a dualistic fashion: with a keen eye on both the one big G7/8 table and another on the individual domestic tables back at home. It is another thing altogether to try to extend this authority over other actors in the international system. This is especially the case in terms of emerging powers. The G8 cannot simply dictate to these countries on a policy-specific basis. It must engage with the "upstarts" in the system if a new type of order is to be constituted.

Beyond Big Bang Enlargement

The starting point for any new design hinges on the sense of robustness. The scale of change serves as one dimension. Is the change meant to be of a grand design, or a big bang nature, or, alternatively, to come out in an incremental format? The constellation of change forms another dimension. Does the process of change target a single country or a number of emerging powers?

Recipes for big-bang shape shifting have dominated the initial stage of debate about how the G8 should be reformed. As rehearsed in a number of publications, the most prominent of designs along these lines is the one put forward by former Canadian prime minister Paul Martin (2004; 2005) to create a new Leaders' 20 (L20) forum.

In terms of membership, the debate goes right across the spectrum. Martin's idea was for a diffuse type of membership that replicated the initiative of the G20 finance ministers and central bank governors. Other G8 countries have been tempted by a far more discrete formula, picking (or leaving out) specific countries on an ad hoc basis. The main source of controversy comes on the status of China. For many observers or participants, how to handle China remains the only true test of whether the international system can adjust or manage change in a creative manner. China is the emerging power reminiscent of past historical cycles, a rising state with both massive economic power and geo-political ambition. China needs to be brought in, this logic would have it, at the core of the international system before it is either unwilling or incapable of being drawn in via this sort of approach.

For others, China is as much the problem as the solution. It is simply too different or too big to be managed. Normatively, China dilutes the democratic or pluralistic solidarity of the G8 in a way that other emerging powers that have solid democratic credentials do not. Any G8-Plus club must retain some sense of the like-mindedness that animated its original conception. Operationally, through a similar lens, China hurt rather than helped on the effectiveness scale. China might be far more economically integrated (and in some ways institutionally interdependent, as witnessed in its membership of both the international financial institutions [IFIs] and the World Trade Organization [WTO]), but it simply lacked "we-ness." Its world view on core issues made it an outlier, as did its diplomatic style in the informal atmosphere of the G8 club.

What is fascinating about the so-called Heiligendamm Process (HP) is that it offers some possibility of opening up a middle path for initiating change in the international system. In terms of intensity, it shifts the onus from a grand or big bang approach—transforming the global structure at the apex of authority—to a more diplomatic incremental process. In terms of membership, it balances the claims of China as the largest and most challenging emerging power with those of India, Brazil, South Africa, and Mexico as additional (if uneven) emerging powers and robust democracies.

This process, it must be acknowledged, is still often overshadowed by more impromptu calls for change—via an explicit agenda of G8 enlargement—coming from a variety of sources. What is nonetheless clear is that the theme of both incrementalism and a targeted membership remains built into these declarations. An excellent illustration of this perspective comes out in one of the frequent references to G8 reform made by French president Nicolas Sarkozy (2007):

> The G8 must continue its slow transformation, which got off to a good start with the Heiligendamm process. The dialogue conducted during recent summits with the top leaders of China, India, Brazil, Mexico and South Africa should be institutionalized and scheduled for an entire day. The G8 can't meet for two days and the G13 for just two hours. That doesn't seem fitting, given the power of these five emerging countries. I hope that bit by bit, the G8 becomes the G13.

Moreover, although the L20 and other more ambitious proposals are still in play in terms of policy championship as well as in terms of some considerable intellectual engagement, it is the HP that is a tangible entity. Enlargement may not have been on the agenda in Heiligendamm, but the future of the relationship between the world's most industrialized and key emerging countries was the major output at the 2007 summit. In recognition of their stature as major economic and diplomatic players, China, India, Brazil, South Africa, and Mexico (termed by the G8, the Outreach Five or O5) were invited to participate in a structured forum for ongoing dialogue with the G8 over the following two years. The HP was established to focus on four topics: the promotion of innovation, the enhancement of free investment and corporate social responsibility, common responsibilities in respect to African development, and knowledge exchange on technologies to fight climate change (G8 2007).

Reconfiguring the G8 Club through Incrementalism

At one level, this book traces the HP as an initiative designed to reconfigure the international order as it exists in the 21st century. As such, it is an attempt to gauge the success of an effort that is both technically orientated and highly anticipatory. If appearing far less dramatic and comprehensive than the well-known narratives surrounding previous attempts at historical reorders, it is a testimony to the desire to expand the habits and mechanisms of co-operation, at least at the upper tier of the international system. Although premature to accord any definitive conclusions about the actual delivery of results, the book provides conceptual and practical lessons on both the reach and the limits of innovation as played out in a chronologically and issue-defined initiative.

If institutions matter, so do the individual members who make up those institutions. Special treatment is given in this book to the capacities and diplomatic identities of the emerging powers that have been on the outside looking in at the G8. These emerging powers have been termed in G8 parlance either the O5 or dialogue partners. The emerging powers themselves have preferred the term the G5. Although not officially endorsed, the favoured terminology in the book is B(R)ICSAM. This phrase avoids the paternalism as well as the lack of specificity of the O5/dialogue partners—"outreach" being a term that is used not only in connection to states but also by civil society and even celebrities such as Bono and Bob Geldof (Cooper 2007b)—while exaggerating the image of the emerging powers acting as a collective entity. Although the latter scenario remains an open possibility, it is blurred by a number of other forms of interaction taking place in and beyond the O5. From within the best-known grouping is IBSA, encompassing India, Brazil and South Africa. Extending beyond the so-called BRICs has taken on some tangible diplomatic shape, with meetings between Brazil, India, China, and Russia. B(R)ICSAM privileges those five emerging powers at the core of the HP while at the same recognizing the connection between the big three of that grouping with Russia—the most recent country to enter into the G8. All continue to have some elements of their diplomatic character shaped by their sense of discontent with the established international system. At the same time, all have long records of diplomatic agency that highlights their own very own distinctive national personalities. Besides tracing the actual HP as an initiative, therefore, the book aims to map out what the B(R)ICSAM countries want in term of a reordered world and how they are prepared to push for those alternative objectives.

At still another level, the book puts the process of reform and the upward drive of the B(R)ICSAM into the wider national/international perspective. Unlike past reorderings, the HP has been initiated without winners and losers decided by direct conflict. This process of reform can still only be a partial mode of adaptation, notwithstanding the G8's institutional claims—or analytical acceptance—to be the centrepiece or pivot of global governance (for very different interpretations of this role see Kirton 1999, 46; Payne 2008, 534–535). If in some ways anticipatory, it is also in some ways reminiscent of other specific forms of institutional reform that took place after the end of the Cold War, most notably the transition of the General Agreement on Tariffs and Trade (GATT) to the World Trade Organization (WTO). Without a significant rupture, across-the-board transformation was not an option. Yet, as the WTO case demonstrates, space could be made of significant institutional innovation. Indeed, in parallel with the trajectory of the HP, one of the most significant outcomes from the creation of the WTO has been the increased role for rising economic powers.

The international context becomes thoroughly intertwined with national conditions. Through a domestic-oriented set of lens, the motivations of both the champions and resisters to reform must be factored in. Why do some countries buy into an agenda of change, either enthusiastically or grudgingly, and others stay on the sidelines or attempt to push back the initiative? If viewed through an international institutional lens, questions of partnership (or ownership) come to the fore. The G8 has continued to be at the core of the reordering process. However, much of the work of the HP has been outsourced via a partnership with the Organisation for Economic Co-operation and Development (OECD). The merits of this move were supported by a logic of rationality, as the OECD possesses organizational assets (both in terms of technical and secretariat support) unavailable to the G8. But this partnership contained considerable elements of risk as well. If the HP flourishes, which organization takes the credit? And if it flounders, which takes the blame?

Although part of the intent here is to provide an account of the operational mode of the HP, the book speculates as well about some of the larger implications of the initiative in terms of global order and governance. Awareness of complex forms of diplomatic agency goes hand-in-hand with an appreciation of structural forces as determining both change and continuity. Is the process of accommodation *vis-à-vis* emerging powers within the G8 confined to the workings of that particular club? Or can the HP act as a catalyst for a wider range of reforms? In either case, the lessons garnered from the HP possess value well beyond a case specific basis.

Bringing in the B(R)ICSAM

As noted above, the origin of B(R)ICSAM countries being treated as a collective partner to the G8 was in some part a function of their individual identification as big carbon emitters and energy suppliers. Situationally, the B(R)ICSAM group was originally invited as an entity by British prime minister Tony Blair to participate at a discussion on climate change and energy security at the 2005 Gleneagles Summit, in contradistinction to African representation on debt relief and development assistance. Yet, as the chapter by Timothy M. Shaw, Agata Antkiewicz, and Andrew F. Cooper showcases, the logic of bringing in the B(R)ICSAM goes deeper than this functional rationale.

At the heart of the drive for restructuring the G8 has been a recognition that the global balance of power is in the process of changing. By what criteria and to what stage this change has occurred is still very much open to debate. Popular phrases and acronyms abound to explain or brand the constellation of emerging powers. "Rising China" targets the country with the quintessential profile—a large population with a rapidly growing economy in terms of global trade, investment, and foreign exchange reserves—of an emerging power coming through the ranks within the international system. The terms "Chindia" (Lloyd and Turkeltaub 2006) and the "Asian drivers" (Kaplinsky and Messner 2008) add India, the country with the closest structural similarities to China (albeit with an economy with a strikingly different character). Goldman Sachs's "BRICs" adds Brazil and Russia, countries that have little in common in terms of economic profile except sheer size of territory, population, and resources (Wilson and Purushothaman 2003). "B(R)ICSAM" goes further in adding South Africa, Mexico, and possibly Indonesia (via the Association of Southeast Asian Nations [ASEAN]). All combine abundant natural and material strengths as well as weaknesses (notably pollution, including, in the case of Brazil and Indonesia, massive deforestation).

On criteria such as gross domestic product (GDP) and growth rates, nonetheless, the B(R)ICSAM group brought into the Gleneagles Summit, and formalized through the HP, is as striking for its members differences as for their similarities. To privilege them as a distinct entity, therefore moves the rationale beyond not only functional, but also attributes of a structural nature. Economic diplomatic characteristics—what Denise Gregory and Paulo Roberto de Almeida in their chapter term the "diplomatic GDP"—are the glue that puts and holds the B(R)ICSAM group together.

Again, in some part, these diplomatic characteristics merge with classic geo-political power resources. In pushing forward the notion of a G8 Plus Five at the 2007 World Economic Forum, at a panel themed "The Shifting Power Equation," Tony Blair (2007) justified the move on the grounds that it would provide (in his often-cited words) an important "forum for agreement between the most powerful nations with a true modern global reach."

The fixation on geo-political concerns, however, was almost exclusively placed on China as part of a wider strategy of enmeshment through an adaptive institutional design. Alone among the emerging powers, China is judged not only on its economic attributes, but also by its strategic intentions. The stark question was, in the words of John Ikenberry (2008), "will China overthrow the existing order or become a part of it?"

This exceptional conception (and apprehension) of China merits fuller treatment about the motivations and behaviour of that country *vis-à-vis* the HP. But it also reinforces the need to look more closely at the specific details of the diplomatic GDP of the other members of the B(R)ICSAM. Indeed, it is the rich variety of these attributes that inform the country-specific chapters that make up the middle section of the book.

First, however, the diplomatic attributes of the HP itself must be brought out. John Kirton explores this theme in his historically sensitive chapter that locates the HP as part of longer and larger dynamic around the "need to develop a new centre of global governance." His survey of how and when the

G8 has sought inclusion of the official O5 includes snapshots of the G7/8's relationship with China, the formation and activities of the G20, and the role of the finance ministers.

In looking more closely at the HP, Kirton focuses on its distinctive character. The sense of precedent or social trust is given due attention, as after having three consecutive summits to which the B(R)ICSAM countries were invited, it was hard to let them go. The blend of incrementalism and intensity is also featured as integral to the "structured dialogue" within the HP. The unique traits of particular leaders (above all, German chancellor Angela Merkel) come to the fore. But the technical orientation of the process allows sherpas and other state officials to shine as well. In Kirton's reading of the future trajectory of the HP, this bias toward bureaucratic skills is unlikely to go away, and there is a big incentive to expand the mandate of the process into other issue areas such as macroeconomic management, trade, and infectious diseases.

A Collective Entity or Individual Diplomatic Actors?

The shared diplomatic characteristics of the B(R)ICSAM countries should not be overlooked. All continue to have a good deal of their international identity shaped by their position either as a developing country or in solidarity with the global South. Gregory Chin's elaborate analysis of China and the HP gives pride of place to this ideational notion. He reaffirms that one of the basic points of reference behind China's cautious stance is its desire to maintain its links to and status with the developing world, despite its material condition as the world's factory. As Abdul Nafey, Denise Gregory and Paulo Roberto de Almeida, and Brendan Vickers are at pains to portray, the same is true of India, Brazil, and South Africa, respectively. All value highly the part of their diplomatic identity that links them to the non-West. Indonesia, as Paul Bowles describes, is somewhat different in the sense that so much of its diplomatic identification is concentrated on ASEAN, but Indonesia has as one of its paramount diplomatic legacies the founding conference of the Non-Aligned Movement in Bandung.

Mexico, as Duncan Wood denotes, is the exception that proves the rule. Alone among the B(R)ICSAM countries, Mexico has explicitly shaken its identity as a developing country, exiting from the G77 when it entered the OECD. If not diplomatically a part of the South, however, Mexico continues to identify itself very much as a bridge between North and South.

While important, these collective attributes should not be exaggerated. Each of the countries has a special and highly nuanced diplomatic identity of their own. It is this separate identity that dominates their behaviour toward the HP. China's position is shaped by its unique mix of diplomatic attributes in the form of confidence and patience, allowing it to play the long game with respect to the G8. But as Chin argues, this mix does not mean passivity. China has engaged the HP both to block and to promote initiatives.

India's strategic capabilities are in many ways as formidable as its economic strengths, not least because of its nuclear status. But neither of these attributes have translated into realized—as opposed to potential—diplomatic prowess. Not only does India live in a tough neighbourhood, but it has also fallen short of its major diplomatic goal of obtaining UNSC membership. These sensitivities spill over into the debate about the HP (Baruah 2008b; Chaulia 2008). Is this dynamic a means of compensating for other diplomatic difficulties? Or, as Nafey notes in great detail, will India's role in the HP fade because of symbolic shortfalls, with the process exacerbating not soothing a sense of status deprivation?

Brazil's behaviour mirrors some of the Indian sensibilities, a commonalty that extends into their role in IBSA and the G20 of developing countries whose focus is on trade and agriculture. It is differentiated, nonetheless, on a number of counts. For one thing, Brazil has a number of potent images or identities that it can project, a list that includes an innovative energy superpower and the hub of Mercosur. For another, in President Luiz Inácio Lula da Silva it possesses a personalistic leader with a global reach. Amidst these choices, Gregory and Almeida remain cautionary about Brazil's capability and commitment to move beyond an issue-specific focus to a grander ambition concerning the G8.

As neither South Africa nor Mexico have the economic structural strengths of China, India, or Brazil, their reliance on diplomacy is far more pronounced. As laid out by Vickers, South Africa's diplomatic network is impressive for its breadth, with a set of institutional connections (and leadership stature) that few other countries can match. The basic deficiency for South Africa goes back to another form of legitimacy: whether it can be seen as the authentic representative voice for Africa in the HP.

Mexico's institutional links are more concentrated than South Africa's. By using these links strategically, however, Mexico has been able to ratchet up its role in the HP. Its position inside the OECD was used in particular to leverage its position within the B(R)ICSAM grouping. Not only did

Mexico organize a caucus meeting of the group, but it also hosted the first formal meeting within the HP. Diplomatic location and skill allowed advantages for Mexico that the other more materially endowed countries were unable or unwilling to take on.

Indonesia's relationship to the HP is more amorphous. Still, even though it is not a formal member, its potential role merits discussion. In large part, the argument for inclusion is a default option. Without representation from a Muslim country, or a country from ASEAN, Indonesia has become an attractive choice over other candidates. Both a vibrant democracy at home and an increasingly high-profile diplomatic actor on a selective basis (the UN Bali process on climate change, for example), Indonesia in principle seems a good fit. The question that mars this enthusiasm, as Bowles reminds us, is whether there is any more instrumental logic for bringing Indonesia in to the HP.

Champions and Blockers

It has been the robust champions of G8 reform that have grabbed most of the attention. Statements by French president Nicolas Sarkozy (2007), at the Fifteenth Ambassadors' Conference, showed outward support for the eventual transformation of the G8 into a G13. And he explicitly repeated this call on several other occasions, including a press conference setting out the major themes of the French presidency of the European Union Council in the second half of 2008, and on a trip to India in January 2008. In the former, he said that: "France will do all in its power to make the G8 into the G13" ("Nicolas Sarkozy Champions a Protective Europe" 2008). In the latter context, he reinforced the impression that expanding the G8 into a G13 forms part of his international priorities (Baruah 2008a).

To a greater and lesser degree of enthusiasm, other voices supporting an expanded G8 have been heard as well. Gordon Brown, Tony Blair's successor as the UK's prime minister, noted that: "The G8+5 meets on a regular basis but only for a small amount of time ... Now there are proposals to extend the relationship and to broaden it so that India, China, South Africa, Mexico, and Brazil are part of these discussion and that's something we favour also" ("Brown Backs Sarkozy Plan for Expanding G8" 2008).

At the operational rather than declaratory level, however, it has been Angela Merkel and the German coalitional government that have ramped up the project for an institutionalized dialogue with the emerging powers. Thomas Fues and Julia Leininger provide a valuable account not only of the motivations behind this initiative, but also how this ownership has both helped and limited what became known as the Heiligendamm Process. What stands out in this account is the degree to which this initiative was improvised—with some high degree of creativity—using the prerogatives of the hosting function during Germany's G8 presidency. Deep-set divisions within the coalition government—and anxiety about Germany's own global position—shaped the initiative in accordance to an incremental script. And, notwithstanding the national financial and human resources used to launch the process, German ownership is hard to retain as other countries take up the G8 presidency (Japan in 2008, Italy in 2009, and Canada in 2010), hence the re-relocation of the diplomatic initiative not in Germany but at the OECD.

The OECD has been tasked with facilitating the HP over a two-year period. As Richard Woodward makes clear in his chapter, this approach contains elements of both continuity and adaptation, as it builds on the OECD's experience as a "pre-negotiation forum," albeit in a very different context. The basic operational structure has been outlined with the HP Support Unit's work being governed politically by a high-level steering committee, with more technical discussions occurring within special working groups (Benterbusch and Seifert 2008). As Woodward astutely shows, the OECD-G8 connection rests on a number of strong pillars, including the OECD's own enhanced engagement with the big emerging powers, the established culture of utilizing working groups, the range of its ambit in issue-specific terms, and a new mode of entrepreneurial leadership at the top of the organization via Angel Gurría, the OECD's secretary general.

If Germany and the OECD fall into the category of champions, the blockers come in far more diffuse form. Apart from France and the UK, the other G8 members remain ambivalent to the dialogue process or staunchly opposed. In the latter camp, most notable is the 2008 host Japan, which has no interest in seeing its longtime rival, China, join the club. Even Japan, however, acknowledges that there is an efficiency justification for including the emerging countries on specific issues, as in the case of emissions targets for all major greenhouse gas producers. Prime Minister Yasuo Fukuda made this point clear in remarks he made in January 2008 at Davos: "As chair of the G8 summit, I am resolved to take on responsibilities, in working towards the establishment of a framework in which all major emitters participate" ("Japan to Press for Emissions Targets at G8: PM" 2008b).

It is the attitudes of the more ambivalent countries that this collection showcases. One of these countries is Russia, the missing R in the B(R)ICSAM grouping. Although Russia was reluctant to invite the group of emerging powers in 2006, when it hosted the G8 in St. Petersburg, in declaratory terms at least, the Russian position has evolved into a more positive stance. Mikhail Kamynin (2007), a spokesperson for the Russian foreign ministry, suggested robust support for post-Heiligendamm G8 reform, deeming expansion "a natural trend."

In her chapter on Russia, Victoria Panova draws a more nuanced picture. Panova certainly notes the principled support by Russia of the HP. She also suggests, however, that Russia is playing a waiting game, allowing the HP to "slowly unravel." Support for a collective solution is subordinated to an alternative strategy that acknowledges some firm similarities between Russia and most other of the B(R)ICSAM countries, especially the important subset of the BRICs. It is the bilateral relations with these emerging powers that will continue to be accented.

Colin I. Bradford's chapter is more normative and speculative in tone. It acknowledges that the United States would not be a leader in G8 reform during the administration of George W. Bush, despite sporadic attempts to engage the big emerging powers on specific issues (most notably Bush's conference bringing together the biggest 16 emitting countries). The bigger question, then, is whether there will be an appetite for such reforms in the post-Bush years. From an ideational angle, Bradford's confirms that such an appetite exists in the U.S. In his survey, the U.S. respondents were as enthusiastic for a reform agenda as those from the rest of the world. The need is judged to be a function of both symbolism (pluralism in the global system) and instrumentalism (innovative problem solving).

Still, on a practical note, Bradford is left wondering how the 2008 presidential election campaigns will endorse or discount the notion of G8 reform. Republican John McCain's approach takes an "us versus them" attitude—as applied through democratic like-mindedness—as the essence of the G8 (with a push to bring India and Brazil into the club at the expense of not only China but Russia as well). Democrat Barack Obama so far at least sees institutional reform in functional terms, with an emphasis on new coalitions designed to tackle energy and environmental issues. Significantly, however, Obama privileges the G8 Plus Five for the creation of the Global Energy Forum.

What Sort of Reordering?

In the past, structural reorderings have featured emerging powers claiming new powers of authority and voice in massive convulsions of the international system. Yet, even with the degree of coercion attached to these decisive breaks with the status quo, huge amounts of uncertainty remained about the new order in terms of its institutional make-up and rules of the game. What Ian Clark (1991, 10) terms the "regulative and allocative principles of the global system," remained marked (and marred) by ambiguity, fragility, and the need for reassurance. Accentuated by its voluntary, diplomatic, and *ad hoc* or incremental nature, the HP reflects a high degree of contestation as even a partial resettlement to a new order—never mind a new system of global governance. If space has been allowed for opening up to an innovative form of engagement between the members of the old pivotal club of the North and the new elite of powers emerging from the South, questions abound whether these countries even want to be part of an enlarged club. The B(R)ICSAM countries held their own strategic meeting in Berlin prior to the June 2007 Heiligendamm Summit and there is a distinct possibility of the alternative of a separate caucus of the G5 (as the emerging powers prefer to be called). The HP could encourage as much as stymie this possibility.

In the months following the Heiligendamm Summit, stories began to emerge about the B(R)ICSAM countries' unhappiness, both with their treatment at the summit and with the OECD's involvement in the HP. The *Financial Times* reported that the O5 leaders felt snubbed by the announcement of the communiqué, which proclaimed the HP's establishment prior to the group joining the G8 meetings (Williamson 2007). Indian prime minister Manmohan Singh voiced his displeasure to the media about the limited role that the O5 was given, arguing that these countries had much to offer in terms of addressing a wider array of global governance challenges than those on the summit agenda: "I said [to the G8] 'We have come here not as petitioners but as partners in a ... fair management of the global community of nations'" (Bidwai 2007). Indeed, India's international club options continue to be manifold, having received an invitation from Brazil to join a prospective (South–South) G5 and having membership in the (North-South) WTO G4, which includes the U.S., the EU, and Brazil.

Other B(R)ICSAM countries voiced their hesitation to the OECD's significant involvement in the HP, given the perception of the OECD as a club for the rich nations. Brazil specifically expressed concern that its individual dealings with the organization could be (negatively) affected by the launch of the HP. Civil society in South Africa has had a mixed reaction, with some claiming that membership in a G13 would compromise the country's historic position "as a proponent of South–South cooperation" (Hazelhurst 2007). China's foreign ministry responded positively to Sarkozy's statements on G8 expansion, affirming its willingness "to strengthen dialogue and cooperation with the G8 and work together to establish a new win-win North–South development partnership based on equality and mutual benefit" ("China Positive on Sarkozy's G8 Proposal—Foreign Ministry" 2007). Still, China has been more guarded in response to the HP itself. The role appointed to the OECD may trigger previous anxieties over the G8 Outreach program being seen by the G8 members as a means of exerting pressure on developing countries (Feng 2007).

Instead of embracing the G8 overtures, the B(R)ICSAM countries may eventually distance themselves from the HP. As one respected journalist, Philip Stevens (2008), lays out this scenario in a more generalized observation: "New powers might be accommodated in a reformed system or they might choose to shun it."

One outcome thus might be a consolidation of the bilateral relations between the B(R)ICSAM countries and some greater sense of enmeshment among members of the group. If the sherpas of the G8 and the collection of B(R)ICSAM countries meet together on a regularized basis, there are signs of a concerted engagement between key members of this group. In October 2007, the trio of foreign ministers from China, Russia, and India met in Harbin, China, and in May 2008 the foreign ministers of the BRIC countries met in Yekaterinburg, Russia.

Additionally, all of these countries have increasingly diverse options beyond this sort of constellation, including championing the traditional sense of solidarity with the wider developing world, both on functional issues and on emerging regional associations. In the context of the WTO, meetings of the G4 and the G20 developing countries continue to provide opportunity for a number of B(R)ICSAM countries. The strength of IBSA continues to grow both in terms of diplomatic influence in the United Nations and the group's combined economic weight. China has been the pivot of the Shanghai Cooperation Organisation (SCO), to give just one illustration of its own global reach.

If the HP is as full of ambiguity, fragility, and the need for reassurance as previous big-bang structural reorderings, it also contains an enormous amount of novelty in terms of diplomatic agency. The shock of the new brings with it not only complex obstacles, but also a rich promise as a voluntary and anticipatory means of dealing with issues relating to the distribution of power.

To tease out the full extent of this conundrum, the framework of analysis must be cast in much wider fashion, as this book is designed to do. The structural implications of the G8's engagement with the collective of big emerging powers in a sustained fashion are recognized here, but it is the mapping of the diplomatic agency beyond the established club members to the role of B(R)ICSAM countries in global governance through this initiative that animates this volume, and provides it with its own unique mix of order and innovation.

References

Ash, Timothy Garton (2008). "One Practical Way to Improve the State of the World: Turn G8 into G14." *Guardian*, 24 January.

Baruah, Amit (2008a). "Sarkozy, Brown Push for India in G13." *Hindustan Times*, 2 February.

Baruah, Amit (2008b). "Sarkozy Wants India in Expanded G8." *Hindustan Times*, 24 January.

Benterbusch, Ulrich and Juliane Seifert (2008). *The Heiligendamm Dialogue Process: Joining Forces to Meet the Challenges of the World Economy*. Dialogue on Globalization, Fact Sheet No. 3. Berlin: Friedrich Ebert Foundation. library.fes.de/pdf-files/iez/global/05310.pdf (May 2008).

Bidwai, Praful (2007). "India's Clumsy Balancing Act." *Inter Press Service*, 26 June.

Blair, Tony (2007). "Speech at Davos." 27 January. www.number-10.gov.uk/output/Page10858.asp (May 2008).

"Brown Backs Sarkozy Plan for Expanding G8." (2008). *Agence France Presse*, 8 January.

Chaulia, Sreeram (2008). "India, China Hold G8 Options." *Asia Times*, 29 April.

"China Positive on Sarkozy's G8 Proposal—Foreign Ministry." (2007). *AFX International Focus*, 31 August.

Clark, Ian (1991). *The Post–Cold War Order: The Spoils of Peace*. Oxford: Oxford University Press.

Cooper, Andrew F. (2007a). "The Logic of the B(R)ICSAM Model for G8 Reform." CIGI Policy Brief No. 1. Waterloo ON: Centre for International Governance Innovation. www.cigionline.org : Publications : Policy Briefs (May 2008).

Cooper, Andrew F. (2007b). *Celebrity Diplomacy*. Boulder: Paradigm Publishers.

English, John, Ramesh Thakur, and Andrew F. Cooper (2005). *Reforming from the Top: A Leaders' 20 Summit*. Tokyo: United Nations University.

Feng Chen (2007). "G8 Not Platform for Exerting Pressure." 4 June, Beijing. Government of the People's Republic of China. www.gov.cn/misc/2007-06/04/content_636224.htm (May 2008).

G8 (2007). "Growth and Responsibility in the World Economy." 7 June, Heiligendamm. www.g8.utoronto.ca/summit/2007heiligendamm/g8-2007-economy.html
(May 2008).

Hajnal, Peter I. (2007). *The G8 System and the G20: Evolution, Role, and Documen-
tation*. Aldershot: Ashgate.

Hazelhurst, Ethel (2007). "Sarkozy's Proposal to Include SA in G8 Meets Mixed
Response." *The Star (South Africa)*, 28 August.

Hurrell, Andrew (2007). *On Global Order: Power, Values, and the Constitution of
International Society*. Oxford: Oxford University Press.

Ikenberry, G. John (2001). *After Victory: Institutions, Strategic Restraint, and the
Rebuilding of Order after Major Wars*. Princeton: Princeton University Press.

Ikenberry, G. John (2008). "The Rise of China and the Future of the West: Can the
Liberal System Survive?" *Foreign Affairs* 87(1). www.foreignaffairs.org/
20080101faessay87102/g-john-ikenberry/the-rise-of-china-and-the-future-of
-the-west.html (May 2008).

"Japan to Press for Emissions Targets at G8: PM." (2008b). *Agence France Presse*,
26 January.

Kamynin, Mikhail (2007). "Russia Supports French President's Idea of G8 Enlargement." Text of report by Russian Ministry of Foreign Affairs website reported by
BBC Monitoring Former Soviet Union, 28 August.

Kaplinsky, Raphael and Dirk Messner (2008). "The Impact of Asian Drivers on the
Developing World." *World Development* 36(2): 197–209.

Kirton, John J. (1999). "Explaining G8 Effectiveness." In *The G8's Role in the New
Millennium*, edited by M.R. Hodges, J.J. Kirton, and J.P. Daniels, 45–68. Aldershot: Ashgate.

Lloyd, John and Alex Turkeltaub (2006). "India and China Are The Only Real Brics
in the Wall." *Financial Times*, 4 December, 17.

Martin, Paul (2004). "Address by Prime Minister Paul Martin on the Occasion of His
Visit to Washington DC." 29 April, Washington DC. epe.lac-bac.gc.ca/100/205/301/
prime_minister-ef/paul_martin/05-10-06/www.pm.gc.ca/eng/news.asp@id=192
(May 2008).

Martin, Paul (2005). "A Global Answer to Global Problems." *Foreign Affairs* 84(3): 2–6.

"Nicolas Sarkozy Champions a Protective Europe." (2008). *Agence Europe*, 9 January.

Payne, Anthony (2008). "The G8 in a Changing Global Economic Order." *International Affairs* 84(3): 519–533.

Putnam, Robert (1988). "Diplomacy and Domestic Politics: The Logic of Two-Level
Games." *International Organization* 42(3): 427–460.

Sarkozy, Nicolas (2007). "Fifteenth Ambassadors' Conference: Speech." 27 August,
Paris. www.ambafrance-uk.org/President-Sarkozy-s-speech.html?var_recherche
=Fifteenth%20Ambassadors%20Conference%20Speech (May 2008).

Stevens, Philip (2008). "Clever Conceits Cannot Hide the World's Jagged Edges." *Financial Times*, 2 May.

Williamson, Hugh (2007). "Emerging Powers Flex Muscles to Push for More Power in the G8." *Financial Times*, 4 July.

Wilson, Dominic and Roopa Purushothaman (2003). "Dreaming with BRICs: The Path to 2050." Global Economics Paper No. 99, October. New York: Goldman Sachs. www2.goldmansachs.com/ideas/brics/book/99-dreaming.pdf (May 2008).

2

The Logic of the B(R)ICSAM Model
for Global Governance

Timothy M. Shaw, Agata Antkiewicz,
and Andrew F. Cooper

The BRICs story is not just about developing country growth success. What makes the BRICs special is that they have the scale and the trajectory to challenge the major economies in terms of influence on the world economy.
—*Jim O'Neill, Dominic Wilson, Roopa Purushothaman,*
and Anna Stupnytska, Goldman Sachs

In the "club model" of diplomacy, diplomats meet only with government offi-cials ... in the world of the 21st century, the "club model" of diplomacy has given way to a flatter, less hierarchical "network model" in which diplomats engage a vastly larger number of players in the host country ...   —*Jorge Heine*

Introduction

The model of Brazil, Russia, India, and China (BRICs), developed by Go-ldman Sachs in *Dreaming with BRICs: The Path to 2050* at the start of the new century, has attracted considerable attention (Wilson and Purushothaman 2003). From an economic perspective, the model has enormous appeal in focusing attention on four countries that are dynamic global motors of growth. On the basis of gross domestic product (GDP) and purchasing power parity (PPP), these countries rank among the dozen largest economies of the world: China (4), India (6), Russia (9), and Brazil (11) (Central Intel-ligence Agency 2008).

Yet, if one looks beyond material resources to diplomatic logic and on to forms of soft power, such as public diplomacy and cultural exports, the utility of this model declines considerably. This group is highly differentiated in terms of their positioning in the international arena. It contains a member of the Permanent Five (P5) members of the United Nations Security Council (UNSC), one entrant into the Group of G8, and two traditional champions of the global South as expressed through the G77 and other forums.

This overview chapter—which juxtaposes several overlapping literatures, including global governance, emerging economies, diplomatic styles, and development—seeks to place a number of shared perspectives and discourses into a context relevant to both global governance and the BRICs, or, if South Africa and Mexico are included, B(R)ICSAM (with the parenthesis around Russia given its position as a member of both the BRICs and the G8).[1] It pays special attention to whether different formulations—combinations of states and partnerships—in the B(R)ICSAM orbit have the most salience. In particular, it begins to examine whether the BRICs and B(R)ICSAM encourage their members to focus upward toward the G8 or the Organisation for Economic Co-operation and Development (OECD), or to reach downward toward their traditional allies in the global South of the G77 (Shaw et al. 2007). It also contrasts the debate over the interrelated club diplomacy versus network diplomacy—the degree to which such states talk only to each other or the degree to which they broaden their reach to a more diverse range of non-state actors, such as private companies and civil society, in homogenous or heterogeneous, hierarchical or flat partnerships (Heine 2006, 5). It thus talks to the "varieties of capitalism" perspectives, especially the rise of multinational corporations (MNCs) from the South, particularly in the BRICs (Goldstein 2007). Indeed, such matters are inseparable from issue area, level of interaction—regional or global, time period, and so on.

Thus, whether the BRICs/B(R)ICSAM are defined more narrowly or broadly matters to their formulation of and contribution to global governance, particularly G8 reform. So the subsequent mid-decade revisionism from Jim O'Neill and his colleagues (2005) at Goldman Sachs about the N11—Next Eleven—influences international relations as well as the global economy. Importantly and controversially, in asking how solid the BRICs are, they excluded South Africa and also cautioned that, of the N11, "only Mexico and perhaps Korea have the capacity to become as important globally as the BRICs" (4). But, as this analytical framework suggests, economic importance, especially if limited by inter-state club diplomacy, may differ from political and strategic, cultural and diasporic network diplomacy (Cooper and Legler 2006, esp. 120–139; Heine 2006). The Heiligendamm

Process initiated during the German presidency of the G8 may serve as a response to such debates and definitional difficulties.

One reaction to the seemingly unwieldy nature of both BRIC and B(R)ICSAM constellations is to narrow the focus by privileging "Chindia"; that is to say, by restricting the catalysts to the two massive Asian drivers of the global economy, China and India (Enderwick 2007; Lloyd and Turkeltaub 2006). Even this reductionist approach, though, has its conceptual deficiencies. The economic strengths of these two countries are quite different. China has been the recipient of far more foreign direct investment (FDI), and is better connected to global supply chains. Its growth is based mainly on the trade in goods. By contrast, India's growth has been more internally generated thanks to its large services trade.

And from the traditional perspective of club diplomacy, China and India have as many dissimilar characteristics as they have features in common. To provide one obvious example, India has campaigned as part of the so-called Group of Four along with Brazil, Germany, and Japan to break into the UNSC. By way of contrast, China has exhibited the prerogatives of a status quo–minded member of the P5 along with the United States, Russia, the United Kingdom, and France. Furthermore, in terms of club versus network diplomacy, India's democratic, anglophone traditions equip it to advance heterogeneous network diplomacy rather than limited club diplomacy, whereas China has little capacity to transcend its club preoccupations (Cooper and Legler 2006; Heine 2006).

B(R)ICSAM for Global Governance?

The argument of this overview is that, instead of contraction from BRICs to Chindia, the former might be expanded to encompass the B(R)ICSAM group. This would allow coverage of not only the core BRIC countries but also Mexico, South Africa, and, potentially, a member of the Association of Southeast Asian Nations (ASEAN)—specifically Indonesia. To be sure, the economic logic of this extended model is not strong, as Mexico is ranked 15 in terms of PPP, Indonesia 17, and South Africa 24. But this slack is more than compensated by the convincing diplomatic-cum-regionalist or strategic logic for focusing on the B(R)ICSAM group.

All of the B(R)ICSAM members have demonstrated a global (if not yet quite globalist) reach in terms of their diplomatic profile, shifting from club to network diplomacy. The stretch of China's international influence has been well documented. For example, Beijing's concerted "charm offensive" toward Africa has been conducted not only bilaterally, but also multilaterally through the convening of the impressive Forum on China-Africa Cooperation in November 2006. Similarly, New Delhi hosted the first ever India-Africa Summit in April 2008. India has become a hub of diplomatic interaction—network as well as club diplomacy—as representatives of India's old and new friends vie for attention and deals, particularly reflecting its recent strategic partnership with the United States. Prime Minister Manmohan Singh was chosen to speak on behalf of the South in Bandung, Indonesia, on the 50th anniversary of the creation of the Non-Aligned Movement (NAM). Brazil, under President Luis Inácio Lula da Silva, has run with a number of high-profile diplomatic initiatives, ranging from leadership on the G20 developing countries via the World Trade Organization (WTO), the proposal for a global fund against hunger, and the recent push on biofuel diplomacy using its sugar cane–based ethanol production. South Africa shares an innovative partnership with India and Brazil—the India–Brazil–South Africa (IBSA) Trilateral—as well as playing a strong role in the G77, the African Union (AU), and the New Partnership for Africa's Development (NEPAD). And Mexico has combined its membership in the North American Free Trade Agreement (NAFTA) with an ascendant role in the OECD.

Of more instrumental purpose for this conceptual paper, this cluster of countries coincides with the so-called G5 outreach countries that have been gradually, albeit unevenly, incorporated into the G8 summit process. The value of using the term B(R)ICSAM, therefore, is that it recognizes the individuality of each member of this group of countries while minimizing the sensitivities of hanging onto terms such as "outreach"—terms that are problematic from the perspective of the global South, mainly due to their condescending connotation.

Nevertheless, the selection of this core group is certainly not without its own diplomatic limitations. By the standards of some ambitious conceptualizations of G8 reform, this model is a step down. The best known of these initiatives was the one pushed by the former Canadian prime minister Paul Martin for a Leaders' Twenty, or L20. This builds on the success of the G20 of finance ministers and central bank governors developed as a consequence of the Asian financial crisis of 1997–99 (Bradford Jr. and Linn 2007). As in the case of the G20 finance, the L20 was intended to act as a bridge between the G8 positioned in the global North and selective representatives from the global South. Another model of similar scope has been the proposal by Klaus Schwab, the executive chair of the World Economic Forum, for Partnership 21 (P21) along the lines of the UNSC-P5.

B(R)ICSAM is also complicated by the presence of Russia in its midst. As mentioned above, there is a rationale for putting Russia in the group, although it may not be entirely of the group. Unlike the other members of B(R)ICSAM, Russia is already an established member of the G8 at the political level, as witnessed by its role as host of the 2006 St. Petersburg Summit. Yet, this insider position should not be exaggerated. Russia still is excluded from the key economic discussions within the G7/8 process, including those on currency matters.[2] It is still more accurate in some instances to talk of a hybrid G7/8.[3]

Normatively, the addition of Russia complicates the element of "we-ness" contained in the traditional club model of the G7. On the one hand, it puts the onus on socializing from within, nudging and cajoling Russia to become a sustained champion of democracy. This was the justification for the G7 to extend membership to Boris Yeltsin's Russia in the late 1990s. On the other hand, with the turn of Vladimir Putin's Russia toward managed democracy, the need for this criterion for membership lessened. At St. Petersburg Russia took centre stage not on the basis of its democratic credentials but because of its role as an energy superpower.

Consequently, the question is opened up about whether Russia is (and should be) exceptional or not. If democracy is no longer the criterion for we-ness, should this criterion be replaced by other measures? One such possibility is economic bigness—that is to say, simply adjusting the G8 to a G13 or even an L20 simply by economic ranking (based on GDP/PPP or some other measure). *The Economist* ("There Were Seven in the Bed ..." 1993), for example, championed reform of the G8 along these lines many years ago (with the replacement of some existing members by countries with bigger economies). Another measure would be a more subjective one of diplomatic weight, focusing less on structure and more on behaviour or agency.

The attraction of a limited, stable, and status equivalent group suggested in the B(R)ICSAM model is reinforced by its simplicity. Procedurally, this model cuts out much of the debate about membership for the L20 beyond a core grouping. Calls for rotational membership, or some form of delegation, are made moot. There are also benefits to sticking to small numbers, in that consensus on complex issues (hard enough with a G13) would increase with an L20. The ability to solve crises—as the UN has often found out—is not enhanced by simply building a more inclusive decision-making process.

Operationally, the case for the inclusion of these core countries can be made on grounds of both efficiency and legitimacy. As noted at the outset, all of the core B(R)ICSAM members of the L20 configuration fit the profile of classic, big, emerging markets or regional powerhouses, all of which are becoming increasingly integrated into the world economy (Wilson and Purushothaman 2003). And in B(R)ICSAM the still-statist regimes of China and Russia, with their communist origins, constitute a distinct minority: one of club rather than network inclination, given their limits on non-state private capital and civil society.

This structural strength goes hand in hand with diplomatic prowess. As suggested by John Humphrey and Dirk Messner (2005, 2) in their innovative work on what they term "anchor countries," the size of the economies of these hub countries must be blended with their capacity to "actively participate in global dialogue" that is crucial for this analysis.

Responding to the Crisis of Legitimacy and Efficiency: A Diffuse Pattern of Outreach

The legitimacy of the G7/8 has long been questioned. The greatest source of weakness (as well as, paradoxically, of strength in terms of club cohesion) has been its self-selected and un-elected status. To outsiders, especially in the global South, it is precisely this feature that has demarked the G8 as an illegitimate body in contrast to the universal form of multilateralism via the UN system, with all its formalism.

What has made these tensions about a democratic deficit escalate into a crisis has been the increased inability of the G8 to be effective on an issue-specific basis. With regard to many of its traditional economic concerns, the G8 has shown itself to be stronger on words than on deeds, exhorting action from China on currency re-valuation with little or no impact. The same is true on foreign and security issues, with declarations on the Middle East but no tangible results. At the same time, however, the G8 has continued to expand its agenda. And it must be acknowledged that many of its perceived successes have come in the area not of economics or security affairs but on social and development issues such as debt relief and the creation of the Global Fund to Fight AIDS, Tuberculosis, and Malaria.

Still, rather than ameliorating the need for reform, these successes increase the normative need and procedural momentum for reform. A strong argument can be made that the global economy can no longer be managed—or globalization reshaped—without the presence of the B(R)ICSAM countries embedded in the G8 process. But this governance gap is magnified on the developmental and social arena. As India, China, Brazil, and South Africa extend their own functional reach in these domains, is it ethical or practical to leave the B(R)ICSAM out?

After all, different scenarios now predict that in less than 40 years the B(R)ICSAM economies will be bigger than those of the G7 in U.S. dollar terms (Wilson and Purushothaman 2003; Antkiewicz and Whalley 2005). All G7 countries are currently ranked within the top 10 largest economies of the world. By 2050, China will lead the ranks, the U.S. will be the second largest followed closely by India and Japan; the UK and Germany will be closing the top-10 list, pushed down by Brazil, Mexico, Russia, and Indonesia (Goldman Sachs Economic Group 2007, 140). It is expected that Vietnam will overtake both Canada and Italy, while France will fall behind Nigeria. Certainly, the world economy and global governance will have changed radically by then.

Whatever configuration of rising powers is used within the context of global governance, it is difficult not to start the discussion with their apparent economic emergence. As Anthony Payne (2008, 526) noted, many discussions of emerging economies do not offer an explanation "from what they are supposedly emerging or at what point they began visibly to emerge, or indeed what it means to emerge." In the context of this conceptual chapter, the "emergence" of the B(R)ICSAM is based on a common perception of their becoming more like the rich industrialized nations and less representative of the rest of the global South. In essence, they create a new triangular formation in the world (Cooper et al. 2007). In other words, they form a distinctive post-bipolar triad of state types: a "first world" club of highly industrialized nations of the North, a "second" tier world of emerging economies, and an extensive and heterogeneous "third world" (previously the G77) of the rest—a new three-world structure (see "Perspectives on Emerging Would-Be Great Powers" 2006, with a special section on emerging economies or emerging powers).

In this framework, the emergence of the B(R)ICSAM countries started with their ever deeper engagement in a globalized world, especially when it came to economic issues. Popular perceptions often present this as a recent occurrence, since the beginning of the 21st century at best. It is worth noting, however, an examination of individual economic profiles of the B(R)ICSAM countries in a historical perspective reveals that this view is often not correct.

Starting in Asia, China's economic success has its roots in the adoption of agricultural reforms in the mid-1970s, supplemented in the 1990s with large increases of FDI in manufacturing.[4] The average growth rate in China since late 1970s stands at approximately 9.4 percent (with only two years' growth below 5 percent, in 1989 and 1990). While the Chinese growth performance before the agricultural reforms was volatile and not as strong as in the post-reform period, contrary to popular views it was not weak. Average annual growth in China between 1965 and 1978 is estimated to have been over 7 percent. In the case of India, major policy reforms in the late 1980s and early '90s seem to have triggered a higher growth, although the high growth occurred more slowly than in China. Once the "Hindu growth" of the first three economically disappointing decades after independence was overcome, India has experienced a sustained, high GDP growth of 4 percent to 8 percent annually with an average of 5.8 percent over the past 20 years (with a drop to 0.91 percent in 1991 caused by a currency crisis and domestic political instability). The features of growth in India and China are often juxtaposed: growth led by the services sector in India, rather than manufacturing relying on FDI inflows in China. It is important to note here that the economic growth of both China and India favours the urban areas and fuels growing divergence among Indian states and Chinese provinces. Economic growth in the ASEAN region over the past two decades averaged at 5 percent annually. Indonesia, Thailand, and Malaysia grew at anywhere between 6 and 13 percent annually since the mid-1980s, until the Asian financial crisis of the late 1990s. The ASEAN nations have recovered remarkably fast following the crisis, adopting important monetary policies, reducing non-performing loans, increasing their foreign exchange reserves, and boosting intra-regional trade. Current growth rates in the region are at a more modest average of 4 percent to 6 percent; however, they seem to be more stable than their pre-crisis numbers. It is hard to generalize across the diverse experiences. Nonetheless, the main triggers of the high growth rates in ASEAN seem to be Japanese investment in electronics production in the 1970s and then a sharp increase of FDI and speculative capital inflows as of the 1980s and 1990s.

The Russian case differs sharply from other B(R)ICSAM members, with a sharply negative growth in the immediate post-Soviet period. Its recovery came only after the Asian-turned-global financial crisis with growth rates averaging at 6.8 percent (from 1999 to 2004). Immediately after the crisis, political stabilization and structural reforms helped the growth revival in Russia. However, the main reason for Russia's economic recovery was the sharp ruble devaluation of 1998, after which import substitution ensued and helped strengthen domestic production. The more recent growth exceeding 7 percent annually is driven by energy exports and high world oil prices.

In the Americas, Mexico's elevated growth originated from trade flows and FDI inflows through the linkage to the U.S. in the years following the establishment of NAFTA in 1994. Even though increases in trade and inward FDI were proportionally larger than in many Asian countries, growth performance was not as successful. Historically, Mexico has experienced sustained economic growth since the 1940s at approximately 6 percent in each decade until the early 1980s, when the almost autarkic period caused much volatility and the growth dropped below 4 percent. On the other hand, Brazil also enjoyed strong growth at approximately 7 percent annually from 1940 until the debt crises of the 1980s. Its "lost decade" began in the aftermath of the oil shocks in the 1970s. As in the case of ASEAN, the crises were followed by economic reforms that resulted in more openness of the economy both in trade and investment and led to privatization. Further adjustments followed with a stronger growth in the mid 1990s, only to slow down again by the end of the decade with yet another currency crisis. Economic growth in Brazil remains on the low side and is volatile, although export growth in agriculture and natural resources promise a revival in the coming years.

Finally, the historical perspective is not as favourable to South Africa as it is to other B(R)ICSAM countries. The country is unstable and highly sensitive to political instability and social unrest, such as the Soweto uprising in 1976 and the economic sanctions of 1985. Its downward trend lasted until the post-apartheid period. Since then, extensive structural reforms—including land reform trade and capital flows liberalization, privatization, and changes in the tax system—allowed for a gradual recovery from a protected, closed economy to a more globally integrated open economy.

In general, the common features of the B(R)ICSAM countries generally include large populations accounting collectively for more than 50 percent of world's total, with a rapid increase of urban dwellers, low wage rates, episodes of high growth, growing inflows and outflows of FDI, high rates of growth of trade and, consequently, fast accumulation of foreign exchange reserves, growing domestic demand as a result of increases in individual incomes and overall economic development, fast growing demand for energy, and an image of regional hubs. There is often a substantial variation in these indices between different countries of this group. For example, China's long-standing high economic growth stands in contrast with Mexico, South Africa, and Brazil, where the growth of economies is more episodic and volatile. While the growth rates of the emerging powers tend to be unstable, they are, for the most part, significantly higher than those of the G7 and match or surpass the world average. In population size, although

China is still leading the group, India's high population growth will mark this country as the largest in the world within the next two decades. On the other side of the scale, Russia and South Africa are struggling with their populations shrinking in the recent years. Over the past 20 years, China as well as Indonesia have seen an average 20 percent decrease in their rural population.

Differences notwithstanding, it seems clear that the economic and social transformation in the B(R)ICSAM countries is tied to their development paths, from economies based on agriculture and communal incentives rather than individual, to a modern model of economies focused more on high-end technologies in manufacturing, large service sectors, and highly efficient agriculture. This transformation bears similarities to the industrial revolution in Europe discussed by Karl Polanyi (1944), but seems to be taking less time. Longer episodes of high growth are not without precedent: Korea and Japan may serve as examples. However, the economic prowess of the B(R)ICSAM members combined with their large populations, as well as diplomatic and political rise, underpins the ever more visible shift in the global balance of power and calls for changes in the current global order.

On average (and generalizing across cases), the emerging economies enjoy significantly higher economic growth than the G7 and the global economy as whole (see Figure 2-1). In fact, the combined weight of the BRIC economies alone (not including South Africa, ASEAN, or Mexico) currently accounts for 15 percent of the global economy (Goldman Sachs Economic Group 2007, 5). The G7 still accounts for more than half of world's GDP, however, a decline of 8 percent suggests an important shift in the global economy (see Table 2-1, sec. C). A quick analysis of the relative size of the B(R)ICSAM economies based on GDP at PPP rates, which is based on standardized set of international prices (as opposed to current exchange rates), offers an even more remarkable picture (see Table 2-1, sec. D). The difference between the B(R)ICSAM and the G7 in terms of the share of world's GDP is now only 7 percent, down from 22 percent in 1995. A direct comparison of both groupings shows that the combined size of B(R)ICSAM is more than 80 percent that of the G7. It is conceivable that the B(R)ICSAM will overtake the G7 by the mid 2010s (on a PPP basis). It is true that these simplistic projections do not take into account many factors that can potentially hinder the pace of economic growth of B(R)ICSAM. Nevertheless, it seems increasingly problematic for the G7 to discuss the global economy without any participation from the emerging powers at the table.

Figure 2-1

Growth Rates for B(R)ICSAM, G7, and the World, selected years (percent)

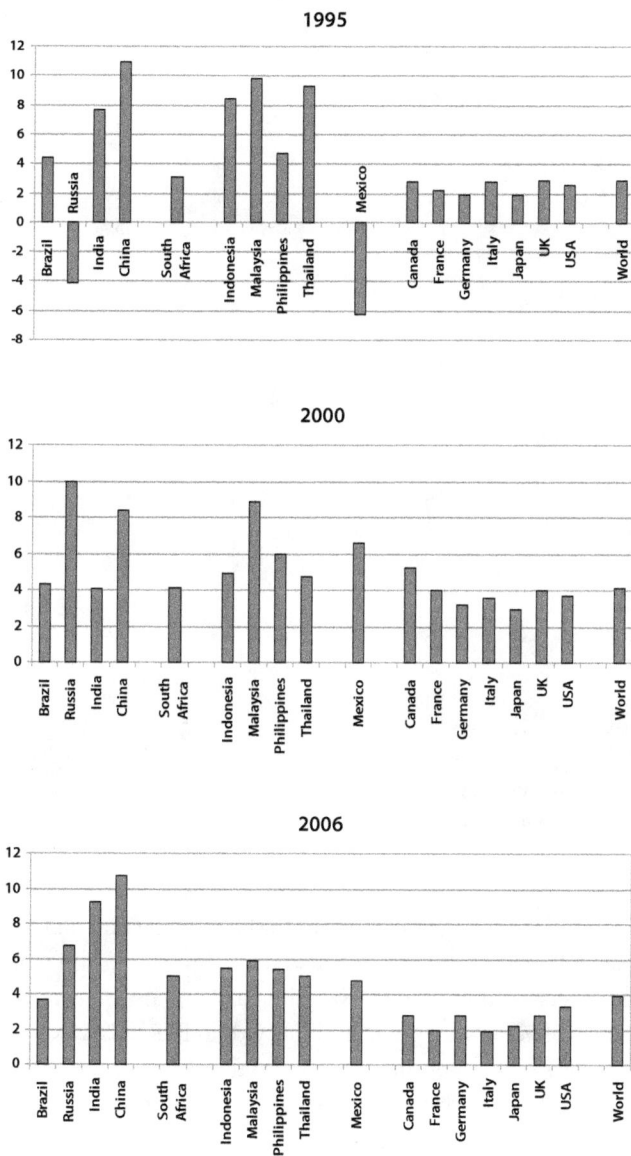

Source: World Bank, World Development Indicators online.

Table 2-1

B(R)ICSAM Indices Relative to G7 and World, selected years

	1995	2000	2005	2006
A. Merchandise Exports				
BRICSAM/World	12%	14%	18%	19%
BRICSAM/G7	24%	31%	46%	50%
G7/World	49%	46%	39%	38%
B. Merchandise Imports				
BRICSAM/World	11%	12%	15%	16%
BRICSAM/G7	24%	25%	35%	37%
G7/World	47%	49%	44%	43%
C. GDP (current US$)				
BRICSAM/World	11%	12%	14%	16%
BRICSAM/G7	16%	18%	24%	27%
G7/World	66%	66%	60%	58%
D. GDP, PPP (current international$)				
BRICSAM/World	25%	27%	32%	33%
BRICSAM/G7	54%	60%	76%	81%
G7/World	47%	46%	41%	40%
E. FortEx Reserves				
BRICSAM/World	18%	21%	34%	38%
BRICSAM/G7	56%	68%	137%	172%
G7/World	31%	30%	25%	22%

Source: World Bank, World Development Indicators online and World Trade Organization database online, authors' calculations.

The extraordinary increase of world trade in the second half of the 20th century has allowed the G7 to increase its influence on the world.[5] The emerging powers are no different. Notwithstanding the internal differences of the sources of economic growth in individual B(R)ICSAM countries, it is clear that their ever closer integration into the global economy has played a major role in their economic success. China's exports are second only to those of Germany, already exceeding U.S. exports by between $50 billion and 80 billion (according to the WTO 2007). Regarding imports, China has overtaken five of the G7 members, Germany and the U.S. being the last two exceptions (WTO 2007, 12). The B(R)ICSAM's combined share in world's exports is 7 percent higher now than it was in the mid 1990s. During the same period, the G7 share fell by 11 points. Furthermore, B(R)ICSAM merchandise exports are currently half of those of the G7, double that of 1995 (see Table 2-1, sec. A). Similar comparisons can be made for imports (see Table 2-1, sec. B).

Growing out of increasing exports, the foreign exchange reserves of B(R)ICSAM are also a clear indication of their weight in global economy (see Table 2-1, sec. E). Their combined reserves exceed those of the G7 by over US$800 billion and account for almost 40 percent of world's total. One consequence of such a significant rise of reserves over the first half of this decade is the recent ascent of state-owned sovereign wealth funds (even if tempered by falling equity prices as happened when China bought a 10 percent share of the U.S. investment company Blackstone in 2007). *The Economist* points out that their increasing involvement on global and national financial markets may give them "a bigger direct stake in capitalism's future" ("The Invasion of the Sovereign-Wealth Funds" 2008). This might bring the dominance of the U.S. dollar to an end, tipping the balance in the global economy further yet.

Any discussion of the economic successes of the B(R)ICSAM countries cannot omit questions regarding the sustainability of the economic growth in these countries. Here it is worthwhile to point to, among other factors, potential risk of financial crises, slower growth of FDI inflows, insufficient diversification of economies, limits on exports, and rising energy prices. Social issues may also impede the projected economic growth, for example growing inequality, aging societies, gender imbalance, or increasing health issues.

Apart from economic indices and forecasts, environmental constraints will present a major challenge to the sustained growth and fast economic development of the emerging powers. It is becoming clear that B(R)ICSAM are increasingly important when it comes to issues related to environment, pollution, and climate change. China, for example, is expected to overtake the U.S. as the world's largest carbon dioxide (CO_2) emitter in nominal terms within the next decade. Indeed, looking at the CO_2 emissions per capita for selected G7 and B(R)ICSAM countries, it is clear that the B(R)ICSAM emissions will, on average, grow faster than those of the G7. However, by 2030 China and most other B(R)ICSAM countries will still be behind the biggest G7 emitters in per capita terms (see Figure 2-2). However, as long as the emerging economies' growth is concentrated in energy-intensive industrial sectors and transportation, their energy-related emissions

Figure 2-2

Carbon Dioxide Emissions per capita, selected countries, 2004 and 2030

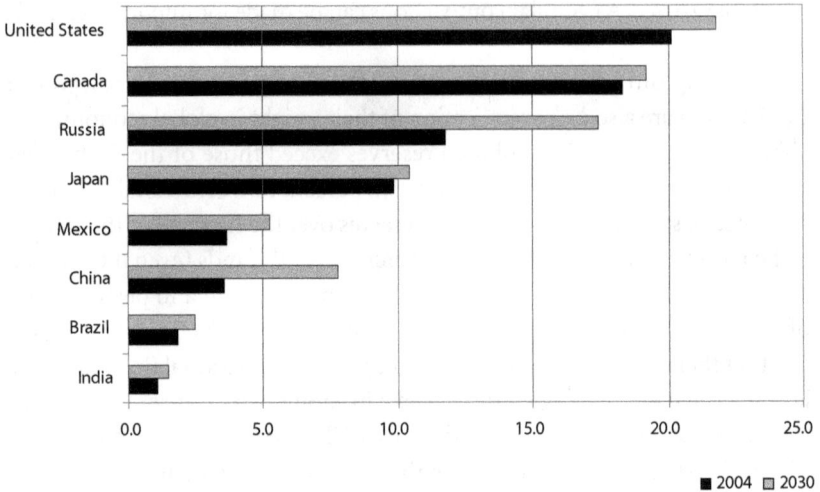

■ 2004 ▢ 2030

Source: Energy Information Administration, *International Energy Outlook 2007.*

will increase more rapidly than the G7 countries (see Figure 2-3). This increase is to be expected given the stage of the development of the B(R)ICSAM countries, and any suggested measures of curbing the CO_2 emissions will have to take this into account. Clearly, no discussion within the G7 forum (or any other governance forums) related to environmental protection can take place without B(R)ICSAM representatives at the table.

Indeed, the BRICs/B(R)ICSAM have permeated the public domain, becoming synonymous with economic growth, opportunities, and change. Widely accepted as increasingly important drivers of global economic growth, the emerging economies attract the attention of politicians, diplomats, economists, investors, and civil society alike. The response by the G8 has been an opening up through a diffuse pattern of outreach. At the Evian Summit in 2003, France chose to showcase members of B(R)ICSAM—with the leaders from China, India, and Brazil (along with those from other L20 potential members including Mexico and Saudi Arabia). At Gleneagles in 2005, the UK, with a similar model in mind, invited the same core countries (albeit without Middle East representation) to discuss climate change.

Figure 2-3

Average Annual Growth in Energy-Related Carbon Dioxide Emissions, selected countries, 2004–2030, percent/year

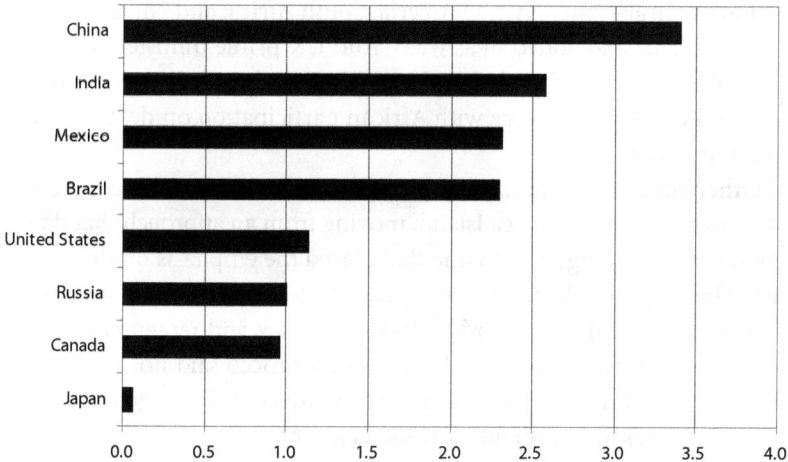

Source: Energy Information Administration, *International Energy Outlook 2007*.

A similar framework was used in key ancillary bodies. Most noticeably, the G7 forum of finance ministers has been opened up to the upper echelon of the B(R)ICSAM group. The finance ministers from China and India attended the two 2005 meetings, in St. Petersburg and London.

So entrenched has this hub approach become that it operates with little critical comment. At the societal level, protestors have targeted many aspects of the G8 for criticism, but the outreach component has slid under the radar. The main focus for reproach has not been because of the inclusion of these countries, but when this core group has appeared to have been excluded. French president Jacques Chirac (2004) publicly rebuked the United States, most obviously, for not being more inclusive to these regional hubs at the 2004 Sea Island Summit: "We cannot discuss major economic issues nowadays without discussing these issues with China, with India, Brazil, South Africa."

If inviting the B(R)ICSAM appears to have become a habit at the generalized level, it has not been so at a more specific level. Italy and Canada took what might be termed an Afro-centric approach. At the G8 summits they hosted—in Genoa in 2001 and Kananaskis in 2002 respectively—they picked a form of representation that emphasized the attendance of leaders from the African continent and the implementation of the New Partnership for Africa's Development (NEPAD) agenda. Japan at the 2000 Okinawa Summit took a similar line, inviting Algeria, South Africa, and Nigeria into the mix (with Thailand added in as well). And UK prime minister Tony Blair played the African card as well at Gleneagles, combining B(R)ICSAM participation on climate change with African participation on debt relief and development assistance.

Other countries have taken a divergent track. As mentioned, the U.S. did things its own way at Sea Island, moving from an approach that downplayed outreach altogether, to one that placed the emphasis on the Middle East. The response rate, however, proved mediocre for this invitation: Afghanistan, Bahrain, Iraq, Jordan, Tunisia, Turkey, and Yemen said yes. But Saudi Arabia, Kuwait, Pakistan, Egypt, and Morocco said no. So the Bush administration scrambled in the last six months to bring together a blend of African states to Sea Island (Atwood et al. 2004).

Notwithstanding all its limitations, the B(R)ICSAM has a good number of advantages over the other models, not only in terms of economics, but also with regard to diplomacy. The behavioural or functional range of each of B(R)ICSAM member on the diplomatic axis is far greater than the other potential members of the L20. For example, the G20 finance ministerial that was established by the G7 in the aftermath of the financial crisis in 1997–99 included most of the potential members of the L20, although a few more could be added on. Yet the diplomatic status among the G20 countries was not equitable. Some countries (most notably Argentina and Turkey) were included less because they were seen as problem solvers, and more because they were themselves problem cases. Another (Indonesia) was chosen not on its own merits but because another candidate (Malaysia) had imprisoned its former finance minister. And still other countries, although not without impressive economic assets (Saudi Arabia and South Korea), are commonly judged not to possess the geographical or functional range of diplomatic credentials held by the B(R)ICSAM countries.

Confirmation of the elevated status accorded the B(R)ICSAM countries has come out in the rotation of the presidency of the G20. India was tasked with this role in 2002, Mexico in 2003, China in 2005, and South Africa in 2007, with Brazil taking over in 2008. A top tier of countries with the G20 constellation has thus been credentialized, with ongoing implications for the G8 summit.

If attractive by design, there are also benefits by default, as the B(R)ICSAM model provides the most appropriate form of compensation for failure in reforming the UN, which for many observers is the first best option. Almost all the leading non-G8 candidates for a permanent seat on the UNSC would be accommodated in this model (most notably, India and Brazil). Likewise, there is room for a number of alternative UNSC possibilities (Indonesia, for example) and for some strong blockers (above all, Mexico which opposed Brazil's bid to join the UNSC).

Targeting the B(R)ICSAM as the G7/8 Plus

The refinement of the diffuse pattern of outreach has been pushed by both the UK government of Tony Blair, in the aftermath of its presidency of the G8, and by members of the coalition German government, in the lead-up to Heiligendamm in June 2007. Blair (2007) made his call for G8 reform at the 2007 World Economic Summit at Davos specifically targeting what he termed the "Outreach Five" or "O5." A number of negatives associated with Blair's initiative cannot be ignored. In terms of language, Blair's call signalled the limits as much as the boundary-spanning dynamics of the initiative, for offering outreach status was still very different than equitable partnership via the enlargement or expansion model. In terms of operation, it still left the modalities of this outreach up in the air. Would this core group be invited simply for breakfast or lunch on an ongoing basis? If so, the asymmetrical nature of the G8 plus would be emphasized, not reduced (Martin 2006).

In other ways, it is the positives that stand out. If not completely novel, the Blair initiative advanced the reformist drive in terms of both process and selection. With regard to the previous outreach model, it is the differentiation between the G8 and the G8 Plus group—that is, the G8 plus invited countries—that stands out. Some G8 watchers, such as Nicholas Bayne, had long recommended that leaders should maintain the practice, begun at Okinawa in 2000, of inviting a group of leaders from developing countries to meet them before the summit proper (Bayne 2001, 2004). He has argued that the admission of new members to the G8 itself, however, should be approached with caution. He characterizes the G8's great merit as the fact that "it is small and compact enough for the leaders to have a direct exchange around the table. This quality would be lost if extra members were added in the interest of making the G8 more widely representative" (quoted in Kirton 2002).

In terms of membership, Blair's initiative makes a clear choice on a permanent outreach group very different from the *ad hoc* approach adopted since 2000. He does not make explicit his rationale for picking what is effectively the B(R)ICSAM. But one close observer suggests that the pick was made on as much diplomatic as economic criteria: "There is a general consensus concerning the regional and global role of China, India, and Brazil. South Africa gets the nod because of its active global-governance policy … although there are major reservations on the continent of Africa concerning South Africa's claim to a leading role. Mexico's claims are less obvious. Presumably US interests come into play here: the USA wishes to provide its neighbor with a leading position in the global hierarchy. Having said that, by virtue of its OECD and NAFTA membership Mexico is suitable for a bridging role between North and South and in addition has strategic significance as a major oil exporter" (Fues 2007, 16–17).

Germany's approach for its Heiligendamm Summit in 2007 was more fragmented. Chancellor Angela Merkel's own view at the outset of the German presidency was that the G8 summit should be a "back to basics" summit in terms of site, agenda, and participation (Morgan 2006). This perspective has been twisted out of shape by both international and domestic circumstances. At the international level, several of the original agenda items pushed by the Germans have proved an awkward fit with the G7/8 process, most notably initiatives on hedge fund reform. Here, it is worth noting the ever more popular BRIC funds offered by a host of asset management companies (from HSBC to Goldman Sachs to Schroders) present prospects of high returns despite their often volatile nature. For example, the Templeton BRIC fund reported that an investment made at the beginning of 2006 would have grown by 51 percent at year end as compared to 5 percent in 2005 (Franklin Templeton Investments 2007, 9). Many, however, question the recent BRIC fund euphoria, pointing to the lack of economic cohesion of the grouping and the arbitrary exclusion of other emerging markets such as Mexico and Indonesia (Foster 2007).

Alternatively, developmental and social issues reminiscent of Gleneagles have proved to be attractive. This widening-out approach has, in turn, reinforced the need for outreach, especially with the B(R)ICSAM countries. The most noticeable characteristic of the G8 process in 2007 has been the embedded nature—and high level of participation—of the relationship between the G8 members and the B(R)ICSAM countries. Within the framework of the G8, all of these countries were invited to the meeting of finance ministers meeting at Essen, Germany, in February. And the sherpas for the

G8 summit have closely engaged their counterparts from the B(R)ICSAM countries including on developing issues. To reinforce this point, Bernd Pfaffenbach (2007), State Secretary in the Germany's Ministry of Economics and Labour, and Merkel's sherpa, put into the public domain the planned permanent integration of the B(R)ICSAM members into the G8 process, namely the Heiligendamm Process.

Domestically, the coalition nature of the German government has been an important source of fragmentation. Finance minister Peer Steinbrueck, a member of the Social Democratic Party, has been a vocal champion of G8 reform to extend the summit to include selected members from the North and South. After making his views known at the November 2006 G20 finance ministerial in Melbourne Australia, Steinbrueck repeated them to a home (and increasingly attentive) audience at the Essen meeting of G7/8 finance ministers ("G20 warnt vor steigender Inflation; Industrie- und Schwellen-länder aber nicht einig über Rezepte" 2006).

As in the case of the Blair initiative, Steinbrueck's shift was not entirely unanticipated. With the push by Paul Martin for an L20, Hans Eichel (a key actor with Martin in the establishment of the Finance G20 and Germany's finance minister in 2004), expressed some sympathy: "There is a need to reinforce the growing sense of responsibility of all members for their respective regions and for the world economy as a whole. On this basis policy co-operation could be broadened as well. This applies both to the number and frequency of meetings and to the division of labour by subject matter. If the G20 continues to develop along these lines and becomes even more effective, I think we could in theory expect to see a G20 comprising the Heads of State and Government set up at some time in the future."[6]

The fundamental distinction between the two German finance ministers was on timing. Whereas Eichel was still looking well into the future, Stein-bruck urged that the G8 be reformed "not next year, but in two or three years" ("G20 warnt" "G20 warnt vor steigender Inflation; Industrie- und Schwellenländer aber nicht einig über Rezepte" 2006, authors' translation).

Constraints on the B(R)ICSAM Model for G8 Reform

If there is an opening for the B(R)ICSAM countries to be the model for G8 reform, there continue to be severe obstacles to progress along these lines, whether compatible with either club or network diplomacy genres. Inside the G8, there remains some considerable opposition to any major reform. One of the major functional initiatives of the UK government during its presidency was the creation of a "G8 Plus Five" process to connect the ministers of energy and environmental ministers of the G8 and the G5 outreach group. The potential of this initiative is still ready to be captured. However, Russia, during its time as president of the G8, did not nurture this process, marginalizing it at the St. Petersburg Summit in 2006.

Japan has also downplayed the role of the G5 outreach group during its presidency in 2008. Japan highly values its participation in the G8, and is unlikely to place pressures for greater legitimacy over its club mentality. This bias is reinforced—in a similar manner to the U.S.—by the sense that democracy is essential to "we-ness." On this premise, the candidateship of China (by economic as well as diplomatic criteria at the top of the list for entry into the G8) is nixed: novel network diplomacy is still overshadowed by more established club forms.

Outside the G8, one main type of resistance comes from the principle that any move toward reinforcing the legitimacy and efficiency of this self-selective group is detrimental to universalism as embodied by the UN. Another comes from selectivity. The presence of South Africa as the sole African member of B(R)ICSAM remains controversial. The notion of its involvement has begun to grab some positive attention in South Africa (Vickers 2006). However, as the UNSC contest revealed (in that three African countries— South Africa, Nigeria, and Egypt vied openly for two potential spots), this ownership will not be uncontested.

The other point of controversy is the absence of a single Islamic country. This mode of participation was at the core of the U.S.'s approach to outreach at the 2004 Sea Island Summit. Even with the dual approach of the Blair government—with both core B(R)ICSAM and African representation—the UK found itself in a position where it had no major Islamic representation at Gleneagles (a missing element that was made more glaring by the London bombings on 7 July 2005).

Notwithstanding these deficiencies, there are solid counterarguments why the model of G8 reform should not be stretched too far to gain additional representativeness. Paul Martin contemplated adding either Egypt or Nigeria, or both, to the L20 model. But the concept that he was convinced was right built on the G20 model, with Indonesia and Saudi Arabia along with Turkey in and Nigeria and Egypt out. On the basis of diplomatic logic, Indonesia would appear to be the best country to add to B(R)ICSAM, in that it is a large majority Islamic country, a member of the Organization of the Petroleum Exporting Countries (OPEC) with an emergent democratic culture, as expressed well through its support for democratic values through the new ASEAN charter, and a long-standing member of the NAM and the G77. In addition, by 2030 Indonesia will most likely be the sixth largest economy in the world and the largest Islamic country. If Indonesia engaged more with the other Islamic countries (especially those in the Middle East), it could potentially play an active role of a Muslim bridge builder ("Indonesia: Muslim Bridge-Builder?" 2008).

The remaining flaws of the B(R)ICSAM model appear to pale as well by contrast with those offered in alternative designs. The International Task Force on Global Public Goods (2006) suggests an expanded version of the L20 that, if commendable in other ways, is overcrowded with a Global 25. Such a large group also has the deficiency of tilting the balance toward legitimacy at the expense of efficiency.

The Way Forward

Paul Martin (2004) laid out his model of the L20 for all to see. This was highly commendable as a model of global governance. The intellectual endorsement of this approach is impressive. Yet, in terms of an immediate diplomatic impact, this initiative has fallen short of its ambitious aims.

Incrementalism—if far less attractive as a normative device for reform—appears under current circumstances to be a far more productive vehicle. It allows different champions, whether Tony Blair or Angela Merkel, for example, to hand off some elements of ownership as they move out and in of the presidency of the G8. It also avoids direct confrontation with the resisters. Instead of trying to address all of the detailed issues of modalities, the focus is a neo-functional one with an emphasis that reform is required for the major questions of the day (be they energy, climate change, health, development, or global economic imbalances).

If incrementalism does continue to progress, it seems predictable that the B(R)ICSAM countries will be the big winners. The L20 has many advantages over this more parsimonious option, not the least because it encompasses the G20 model. But parsimony has it virtues from a diplomatic perspective. It is very difficult to argue that any of the B(R)ICSAM countries do not belong in a reformed G8 on diplomatic grounds, notwithstanding their political and economic differences. All of these countries are necessary ingredients for unblocking issues both as constructive *demandeurs* and as countries that have been blockers themselves.

The top-down orientation of this dynamic of multilateral reform will linger as a basic feature of this type of reform process. Nonetheless, the means of bringing about changes in the G8 will at least in governmental terms bubble up from below. The sherpa process is an important component of this dynamic. For example, will sherpas of the B(R)ICSAM countries be invited to the G8 preparatory meetings as a club, or will they be invited by the individual country that holds the presidency? On top of this question there is the issue of if and how ministers from B(R)ICSAM countries will be involved in the elaborate web of ministerial and official-level meetings associated with the G8. Here, as in the case of the meetings of energy and environmental ministers, the barometer will be on how seamless this process becomes.

There are, of course, other possibilities both for reform and of rejection. Still, the B(R)ICSAM model for G8 reform seems to have become the best bet for movement. It allows a sizable degree of reform without either tipping the balance away from the G8 or raising the bar of expectations too far for other countries. An adjustment will in all likelihood be added sometime in the future, perhaps with another African country or an Islamic country, but the core group has been established. The increasingly strong impulse toward enhancing legitimacy and efficiency at the heart of the global governance architecture brings with it a recognition that the B(R)ICSAM countries are an integral—if not complete or exclusive—means to this end. We return in conclusion to the revisionism of Jim O'Neill and his colleagues at Goldman Sachs (2005, 3), who coined the BRIC acronym very early this century:

> Since we began analysing these countries, each has grown more strongly than our initial projections. Our updated forecasts suggest that the BRICs economies can realise the "dream" more quickly than we thought in 2003. The case for including this group directly in global economic policymaking in a systemic way is now overwhelming.

Likewise, it is crucial that the concept of the B(R)ICSAM, along with parallel discourses about types of diplomacy and varieties of capitalism, be brought into the theory and practice of studies in the disciplines of international relations, international political economy, and development. Alas, there is still considerable reluctance to so recognize and include this field of study, even on the eve of the second decade of the 21st century (Shaw 2004; Shaw et al. 2007).

Notes

1 For the purposes of this chapter only, the term includes Russia.
2 It is because of this exclusion that China has been reluctant to become a member of the so-called G9 (Yu 2005).
3 However, for the purposes of this discussion, unless referring to the G7 without Russia, the term G8 is used throughout.
4 The country overview here and the ones that follow draw on Antkiewicz and Whalley (2006).
5 World exports increased tenfold since 1960s (World Bank 2007, 30).
6 The authors are grateful to Thomas Fues, of the Deutsches Institut für Entwicklungspolitik, for providing this information.

References

Antkiewicz, Agata and John Whalley (2005). "Shifting Economic Power: From OECD to B(R)ICSAM." Mimeo. Waterloo ON: Centre for International Governance Innovation.

Antkiewicz, Agata and John Whalley (2006). 'The Sustainability of Growth in the B(R)ICSAM Countries.' Paper presented at the 2nd annual Conference on International Governance Innovation. Waterloo ON.

Atwood, J. Brian, Robert S. Brown, and Princeton Lyman (2004). *Freedom, Prosperity, and Security: The G8 Partnership with Africa, Sea Island 2004 and Beyond.* New York: Council on Foreign Relations. www.cfr.org/content/publications/attachments/G8Africa.pdf (May 2008).

Bayne, Nicholas (2001). "Concentrating the Mind: Decision-Making in the G7/G8 System." Paper prepared for the conference on Promoting Conflict Prevention and Human Security: What Can the G8 Do? 16 July, Rome. www.g8.utoronto.ca/conferences/2001/rome/bayne-conflict.pdf (May 2008).

Bayne, Nicholas (2004). "Prospects for the 2005 G8 Gleneagles Summit." 22 November, Toronto. G8 Research Group. www.g8.utoronto.ca/speakers/bayne2004.htm (May 2008).

Blair, Tony (2007). "Speech at Davos." 27 January. www.number-10.gov.uk/output/Page10858.asp (May 2008).

Bradford Jr., Colin I. and Johannes F. Linn (2007). "Summit Reform: Toward an L20." In *Global Governance Reform: Breaking the Stalemate*, edited by C.I. Bradford Jr. and J.F. Linn, 77–86. Washington DC: Brookings Institution Press.

Central Intelligence Agency (2008). "Rank Order—GDP (Purchasing Power Parity)." World Factbook, Washington DC. www.cia.gov/library/publications/the-world-factbook/rankorder/2001rank.html (May 2008).

Chirac, Jacques (2004). "Press Briefing by French President Jacques Chirac." 9 June, Sea Island. www.g8.utoronto.ca/summit/2004seaisland/chirac040609.html (May 2008).

Cooper, Andrew F. and Thomas Legler (2006). *Intervention without Intervening? The OAS Defence and Promotion of Democracy in the Americas.* New York: Palgrave Macmillan.

Cooper, Andrew F., Agata Antkiewicz, and Timothy M. Shaw (2007). "Lessons from/for B(R)ICSAM about South-North Relations at the Start of the 21st Century: Economic Size Trumps All Else?" *International Studies Review* 9(4): 673–689.

Enderwick, Peter (2007). *Understanding Emerging Markets: China and India.* New York: Routledge.

Foster, Lauren (2007). "Brics: Coherent Strategy or Catchy Name?" *Financial Times,* 9 October. us.ft.com/ftgateway/superpage.ft?news_id=fto100920070131407372 (May 2008).

Franklin Templeton Investments (2007). *Semi-Annual Management Report of Fund Performance.* Toronto. www.franklintempleton.ca/ca/retail/en/pdf/downloads/literature/legaldoc/mrfp/semi_annual/340.pdf (May 2008).

Fues, Thomas (2007). "Global Governance Beyond the G8: Reform Prospects for the Summit Architecture." *International Politik und Gesellschaft*(2): 11–24. www.fes.de/ipg/arc_07_set/set_02_07e.htm (May 2008).

"G20 warnt vor steigender Inflation; Industrie- und Schwellenländer aber nicht einig über Rezepte." (2006). *Frankfurter Allgemeine Zeitung,* 20 November.

Goldman Sachs Economic Group (2007). "BRICs and Beyond." www2.goldmansachs.com/ideas/brics/book/BRIC-Full.pdf (May 2008).

Goldstein, Andrea (2007). *Multinational Companies from Emerging Economies.* London: Palgrave Macmillan.

Heine, Jorge (2006). "On the Manner of Practising the New Diplomacy." Working Paper No. 11, October. Waterloo ON: Centre for International Governance Innovation. www.igloo.org/cigi/Publications/workingp/ontheman (May 2008).

Humphrey, John and Dirk Messner (2005). "The Impact of the Asian and Other Drivers on Global Governance." Paper prepared for the conference on Institutions and Development: At the Nexus of Global Change. 18–19 January 2006, St. Petersburg. www.ids.ac.uk/UserFiles/File/globalisation_team/asian_driver_docs/AsianDriversGovernancepaper05.pdf (May 2008).

"Indonesia: Muslim Bridge-Builder?" (2008). 28 February. BBC News Online. news.bbc.co.uk/2/hi/asia-pacific/7269017.stm (May 2008).

International Task Force on Global Public Goods (2006). *Meeting Global Challenges: International Cooperation in the National Interest.* International Task Force on Global Public Goods. Stockholm. www.globalpolicy.org/socecon/gpg/2006/09globalchallenges.pdf (May 2008).

Kirton, John J. (2002). "Canada's Kananaskis G8 Summit: What Can and Should Be Done?" *Canadian Foreign Policy* 9 (June): 31–48.

Lloyd, John and Alex Turkeltaub (2006). "India and China Are The Only Real Brics in the Wall." *Financial Times,* 4 December, 17.

Martin, Paul (2004). "Address by Prime Minister Paul Martin on the Occasion of His Visit to Washington DC." 29 April, Washington DC. epe.lac-bac.gc.ca/100/205/301/ prime_minister-ef/paul_martin/05-10-06/www.pm.gc.ca/eng/news.asp@id=192 (May 2008).

Martin, Paul (2006). "Speaking Notes for the Annual Meeting of the Development and Peace Foundation." 8 June, Dresden. www.paulmartin.ca/speech-20060608 -1.html (May 2008).

Morgan, Simon (2006). "Germany Wants G8 to 'Go Back to Roots,' to Tackle World's Economic Problems." *Agence France Presse*, 28 December.

O'Neill, Jim, Dominic Wilson, Roopa Purushothaman, *et al.* (2005). "How Solid Are the BRICs?" Global Economics Paper No. 134, 1 December. New Delhi: Goldman Sachs. www2.goldmansachs.com/hkchina/insight/research/pdf/BRICs_3_12-1-05 .pdf (May 2008).

Payne, Anthony (2008). "The G8 in a Changing Global Economic Order." *International Affairs* 84(3): 519–533.

"Perspectives on Emerging Would-Be Great Powers." (2006). Special issue. *International Affairs* 82(1): 1–94.

Pfaffenbach, Bernd (2007). "Germany and Africa: Partners at Work." Speech on the occasion of the German Weltbank Forum, 22 May, Berlin. www.bmwi.de/English/ Navigation/Press/speeches-and-statements,did=204548.html (May 2008).

Polanyi, Karl (1944). *The Great Transformation: The Political and Economic Origins of Our Time*. New York: Farrar and Rinehart.

Shaw, Timothy M. (2004). "International Development Studies in the Era of Globalization ... and Unilateralism." *Canadian Journal of Development Studies* 25(1): 17–24.

Shaw, Timothy M., Andrew F. Cooper, and Agata Antkiewicz (2007). "Global and/or Regional Development at the Start of the 21st Century: China, India and (South) Africa." *Third World Quarterly* 28(7): 1255–1270.

"The Invasion of the Sovereign-Wealth Funds." (2008). *Economist*, 17 January, 386. (May 2008).

"There Were Seven in the Bed..." (1993). *Economist*, 72.

Vickers, Brendan (2006). "Heading toward the G8 St. Petersburg Summit: What's In It for Africa?" *Global Insight*(63): 1–4.

Wilson, Dominic and Roopa Purushothaman (2003). "Dreaming with BRICs: The Path to 2050." Global Economics Paper No. 99, October. New York: Goldman Sachs. www2.goldmansachs.com/ideas/brics/book/99-dreaming.pdf (May 2008).

World Bank (2007). *Global Economic Prospects 2007: Managing the Next Wave of Globalization*. Washington DC: World Bank go.worldbank.org/6PT7IQPSP2 (May 2008).

World Trade Organization (2007). *International Trade Statistics 2007*. Geneva: World
   Trade Organization. www.wto.org/english/res_e/statis_e/its2007_e/its2007_e.pdf
   (May 2008).
Yu, Yongding (2005). "China's Evolving Global View." In *Reforming from the Top: A
   Leaders' 20 Summit*, edited by J. English, R. Thakur, and A.F. Cooper, 187–200.
   Tokyo: United Nations University Press.

3

From G8 2003 to G13 2010?
The Heiligendamm Process's
Past, Present, and Future

John Kirton

Should China, India, Brazil, South Africa, and Mexico join the G8? Some G8 leaders now think so. The club of major market democracies, whose leaders have been meeting annually since six of them first assembled in Rambouillet, France, in 1975, has expanded before, but only slowly, by adding one new member at a time. In January 2007, however, British prime minister Tony Blair (2007) boldly declared that "the G8 is already on its way into metamorphosis into G8+5. At G8+5, it can be a forum for agreement between the most powerful nations with a true modern global reach. But sooner or later the metamorphosis should be complete." Later that year, Blair's successor Gordon Brown and newly elected French president Nicolas Sarkozy both publicly backed Blair's call. And at the summit in Germany on 6–8 June 2007, all the G8 leaders agreed to join with their renamed Outreach Five (O5) partners to launch a two-year officials-level dialogue on investment, innovation, development, and energy.

Whether, when and how this burgeoning Heiligendamm Process (HP) culminates in a new G13 summit depends critically on the evolving attitude of the G8 leaders toward the value of fully accepting the Brazil, India, China, South Africa, and Mexico—the B(R)ICSAM partners, in this case excluding Russia as it is already a member of the G8—as equals in an expanded summit club. It also depends on whether these same O5 partners want to join the G8, on the terms presented, and transform it into a G13. Thus far, both sides appear open to the possibility of a closer association. This process began at the ministerial level, when the O5 joined the new G20 forum of finance ministers and central bank governors in 1999. It expanded when some O5 members started participating in the G7 finance ministers club in 2005. It was elevated to the leaders' level when the O5 came to the G8 summit in 2003 and then regularly from 2005 to 2007. The launch of the officials-level HP thus represents the latest major step forward in this process of partnership between established and emerging powers. Its performance will do much to determine if and how a new G13 summit is born and what form it will take. But, of equal importance will be the functional need to develop a new centre of global governance through this G13, as the global community confronts the growing challenges of a newly vulnerable world.

The few existing accounts of the HP have expressed cautious optimism about its prospects, highlighting the many obstacles it confronts (Kirton 2007a; Gnath 2007; Cooper and Jackson 2007). Yet, until now, none has examined in detail the HP's precursors, origins, negotiation, architecture, and early operation as a basis for judging how successful it could be in governing its existing agenda. And none has looked far enough ahead to chart how and why the grouping could and should grow into a new G13.

This chapter presents a detailed analysis of the past, present, and potential future of the HP and emerging G13 as a contributor to, and a centre of, global governance. It argues that the prospects for the HP to produce an eventual G13 are more promising than the existing analyses and early skeptical mood of G8 governors suggest. While the G8 has proven to be an effective centre of global governance, it increasingly needs the capabilities of the major emerging powers of B(R)ICSAM to cope with the many vulnerabilities the G8 and O5 countries and the global community commonly confront. The G8 has realized this logic and acted upon it by progressively reaching out in response to the shocks of the Asian-turned-global financial crisis that began in 1997. Both the G8 and O5 members have been willing (with varying degrees of enthusiasm) to participate in this ever closer association, including the reluctant United States and Japan.

The HP is now off to a promising start, if predictably slow. Its initial success may reinforce a strong case based on global demand and G13 supply to expand the dialogue process, at the leaders, ministers, and officials levels, to embrace the issues of trade, finance, climate change, and health. Should the O5 members continue to emerge as major powers and acquire global reach, responsibility, and political openness, the G8 will eventually be well positioned to take a great leap forward toward a G13. But there is still strong competition from alternative formulae for expansion, and it is too soon to tell if the G13 will eventually win.

This chapter first examines the G8's increasing inclusion of the O5 powers through the finance G20, finance G7, and other ministerial forums, and the G8 Plus Five summit process that began in 2003. It then analyses the conception, negotiation, emergence, and early operation of the HP created in 2007. It next identifies the HP's potential, G8 members' perspectives, and possible pathways toward a new G13 as a centre of global governance by the time of, or soon after, the Canadian-hosted G8 summit in 2010.

The Past: The G8's Inclusion of the Outreach Five

The Pattern

Since its 1975 start, the G8 has reached out incrementally to include as members Canada in 1976, the European Union in 1977, and Russia from 1991 through 1998 (as these members are now known). It invited the executive heads of multilateral organizations to participate in 1996 and has done so regularly since 2000 (see Appendix A). In 2000, it also started regularly to invite the leaders of individual countries to participate. Here the O5 countries and the African quartet of South Africa, Nigeria, Senegal, and Algeria have emerged as the regular partners of choice.

There are several strong patterns to this 34-year process of expansion that started early and has recently grown. First, all leaders of the new members and core participating partners have almost always accepted their invitations to attend or for increased participation. Second, none has ever been downgraded, phased out, or expelled, although short-term sabbaticals have sometimes occurred. Third, the first phase of one-at-a-time additions has been superseded with a handful-at-a-time additions, first with the multilateral organizations in 1996, then the African quartet in 2001, and finally the O5 in 2003. Fourth, among the country members and participants, there has been less of a premium placed on major power than on the principles of open democracy and global responsibility as the criteria for the invitation list. The combined result has been a G8-controlled, one-way street of ever greater expansion, especially in the 21st century, designed to deepen democracy throughout the world.

The G7/8's Relationship with China

Of particular importance in this process has been the G8's relationship with China, as the largest but least democratic of the participating non-member states and the B(R)ICSAM set. Over the past decade the G8 has made major moves to include China, even though the nature and wisdom of this closer association have remained matters of debate (Kirton 2001b; Martinez-Diaz 2007). Among G8-focused scholars engaged in the early debate, one school of thought treated China as an outside object, warranting no institutionalized association with the G7 (Bayne 1995; Sachs 1998; Kirton 1999a). A second school viewed China as a worthy associate, although one lacking at present and, perhaps for some time, a legitimate claim for full membership (Whyman 1995; Hodges 1999; Baum and Shevchenko 2001). A third school regarded China as a legitimate member of some or all of the G7/8 system (Jayarwedna 1989; Smyser 1993; Haq 1994; Commission on Global Governance 1995; Brezinski 1996; Bergsten 1998; "Welcome to China, Mr. Clinton" 1998; Desai 2006). This debate largely ignored key issues, notably the particular form any association should take, the rationale and ultimate objective for association, and, above all, the process of moving toward a system in which China, without or with others, had a mutually comfortable, meaningful place in the G8.

A detailed analysis of the G8's treatment of China from 1975 to 2000 shows the G8 increasingly embracing China (Kirton 1999b, 2001b). China's responsible role in the 1997–98 financial crisis, its like-minded approach to international financial system reform on some core issues, and its contributions to the G22 finance ministers (the precursor to the G20 finance forum), to the G20, and to the Financial Stability Forum (FSF) justified a move toward association with the G8 at the leaders level itself. The proper move for the G8 in 2000 seemed to be to invite China's leader to join G8 leaders for a pre-summit dinner dialogue, a strategy that Japanese prime minister Keizo Obuchi embraced in part as he prepared to host his summit at Okinawa that year (Kirton 2001b). Greater participation or even full membership in the G7 finance ministers forum, where not all participating individuals are democratically and popularly elected, seemed appropriate as well (Kirton 2001b; Desai 2006). Since that time, the closer association between the G8 and China has emerged through the G20 finance ministers since 1999, G7 finance ministers since 2004, and the G8 summit itself starting at French-hosted Evian in 2003 and continuing at the European-hosted summits from 2005 to 2007.

The G20

The G8's first major move to embrace the emerging powers came immediately after the first member of the B(R)ICSAM, Russia, was welcomed as a permanent, if not quite full, member of the now G8 summit in 1998. By 1999, the financial crisis had produced the G20 finance ministers' forum, with Brazil, India, China, South Africa, and Mexico—the full B(R)ICSAM group—along with several systematically significant middle powers, and these were treated as equal members from the very start. There is a rich debate about the performance of this group, especially over its role in empowering the emerging economy members. But careful analyses conclude that the G20 has increasingly become a valuable and valued balanced centre of global governance across an increasingly wide range of fields (Kirton and von Furstenberg 2001; Kirton 2001a, 2005b; Martinez-Diaz 2007).

A consequence of American, Canadian, German, and then G8 leadership, the G20 was created as a consensus-oriented club of significant countries with a mission to prevent financial, economic, and related crises, and to institute the social protections that would make globalization work for all. With a strong start in its first two years, it evolved during its first half-decade from a largely deliberative forum to one that set new normative directions, took collective decisions, and developed global governance by broadening its own agenda, thickening its own structure, and working in conscious interdependence with other multilateral organizations and the G8.

The G20 has had an increasingly autonomous impact in bridging differences between and within its developed and emerging country components, and in hastening agreement on "constitutional" issues in outside governance forums. Essential to its success has been its pattern of working closely in tandem with the similarly constructed, much more experienced, and much more cohesive G8, in support of the principles of transparency, openness, democracy, social advancement, and equity that the G8 has at its institutional core. Its success has supported the case that a leaders-level summit (or Leaders 20 [L20]), composed of the same members, should be created, through a strengthening of the G8 Plus Five process that emerged after 2003 (Kirton 2004a, 2004b; Cooper 2007).

The strength of the G20 platform can be seen in several ways. The first is the growing breadth of the agenda that the G20 has discussed. It has gone well beyond financial stability to embrace trade, other economic issues, and a wide range of matters extending into the security sphere. The second is the general rise in the number of commitments, amidst great annual variation, that each autumn meeting has produced. The third is the move toward rotating the chair, generally alternating between a G8 or developed country member and a non-G8 or developing country one. In the lead among this latter constituency have been the O5 powers of India in 2001 (although the location of the meeting was changed due to the September 11 terrorist attacks), Mexico in 2003, China in 2005, South Africa in 2007, and Brazil in 2008

(Cooper 2007). Beyond the G8, the B(R)ICSAM are thus in the lead within the G20.

Since its Canadian-hosted meeting in 2000, the G20 has made many collective decisions on the key economic and development issue of trade. Its performance peaked at five trade commitments made in 2005, when China held the chair. Here the G20 went beyond traditional multilateral trade liberalization measures to embrace South–South trade, trade and investment, and trade for development. G20 commitments on trade and other subjects in 2003 seemed to induce compliance from its developed and developing country members alike. Trade also appears to be an area where the G20, in balanced fashion as a forum of equals, sides with the positions of neither the G7 nor the G24 (Martinez-Diaz 2007, 11). The G20 has also come to play a role in crisis prevention in finance. The central banks of the U.S., EU, Britain, and Canada, with support from Japan, agreed at the G20 meeting in Cape Town in November 2007 to take coordinated action to stem the global inter-bank lending credit crunch. There it also acted to advance the needed reforms of "voice and vote" at the International Monetary Fund (IMF) and World Bank.

G7 Finance Ministers

A second process of expansion came from the G7 finance ministers forum, where even Russia is not yet a full member of the club. The G7 finance club was born in 1973 with four, then soon five members. It became a seven-member club during the Japanese-hosted summit in 1986, after which the former G5 faded away. Russia became associated with it first in 1992 and more regularly as the 21st century began. China attended as an invited guest first in October 2004, and again in February, September, and December 2005, June 2006, February, May, and October 2007, and February 2008. It came alone in its first two appearances, but was joined in September 2005, following the Gleneagles G8 Summit, by the full slate of Plus Five countries. In December 2005, Mexico and South Africa were missing among the O5. In June 2006, Brazil did not attend, although G20 members South Korea and Australia did. For those times when China has been absent, no countries other than the G8 members have come. There is thus a variable geometry with a fixed order of precedence, with China first, India second, and Brazil third.

At the ministerial level beyond finance, the O5 were the founding members of the G8's Gleneagles Dialogue on Clean Energy, Climate Change, and Sustainable Development. This was created at British initiative at the G8 summit in 2005. Moreover, China, Brazil, and South Africa have each participated once in G8 ministerial meetings for foreign affairs, for environment, and for energy, while India has done so twice.

The Plus Five Process

The instinct to involve outsiders at the summit itself was led by France, first when it invited a large group of global leaders for what turned out to be a parallel dinner at its Paris summit in 1989, and then when it invited the heads of multilateral organizations for a post-summit lunch with the G7 at Lyon in 1996. In 2003, France invited a much larger collection of countries (Kirton and Panova 2007; Chirac 2004). After the interruption of the 2004 American-hosted G8, when no emerging economies were invited, the British invited the O5 and Africans to the Gleneagles Summit in 2005, where the O5 leaders produced a declaration of their own. The O5 came in the same configuration for Russia's G8 in 2006 at British insistence but the G8's engagement with the O5 was perfunctory (Aslund 2006; Vickers 2006). They came again to Germany's summit in 2007. Their inclusion appears to have encouraged them to comply with the G8's summit commitments, even if these commitments were made without their involvement.

The Present: The Heiligendamm Process

This now familiar G8 Plus Five group has demonstrated its value in addressing financial, social, environmental, and security issues. The G8 and O5 leaders recognized this benefit in the summer of 2007. For one of the major deliverables of their Heiligendamm Summit was the creation of the HP, allowing the O5 powers a more reliable, institutionalized involvement in the G8 than ever before. This innovation was seen by most observers as one of the key achievements of the summit (Kirton 2007a; Gnath 2007; Cooper and Jackson 2007). A detailed examination of its evolution from its initial appearance as an idea of one G8 leader to an institution accepted by the G8 and O5 members suggests the potential of this emerging G13.

Preparing the Heiligendamm Process

The process of producing the HP began at the last session of the 2006 St. Petersburg Summit. There, British prime minister Tony Blair proposed that the O5 countries be added to the G8 as full members. But while the ultimate goal of a full G13 had acquired a private expression and champion, Blair's partners were convinced that the G8 should remain capable of taking action. They thus decided to keep their club the way it was. They calculated that the bigger the group, the smaller the commonality among its members and thus the smaller its capacity for action.

From the start of their summit planning process for 2007, the German hosts proposed the alternative of a special relationship between the G8 and the O5. The O5—sometimes referred to by the Germans as the "threshold countries"—would not only be invited to their third G8 summit in a row but would have an additional association with the G8 as well. This approach proposed by the German sherpa team was approved by the German cabinet in mid October 2006. But it deliberately remained devoid of a defined concept or any details, for fear that any concrete proposal sent to and approved by Germany's coalition government was likely to leak. With the cabinet's approval, the German sherpa team developed a small paper in the fall, on which the German sherpa briefed his G8 counterparts orally.

Germany's G8 partners had few indications at the outset that the O5 countries would play any greater part in the G8 in the coming year. There was no mention of the term "Heiligendamm Process" in the initial papers prepared by the Germans and circulated to their G8 partners. Yet, to close observers, it was clear that the German hosts were now structuring the agenda to focus on those issues where the presence of the O5 would be appropriate, even necessary, on functional grounds.

At the first sherpa meeting, designed to set the summit agenda and produce a freewheeling discussion about it, the concept for outreach came up. No one objected to the direction the German's wanted to take, in part because all saw outreach as the prerogative of the G8 host every year. On the basis of this discussion, draft documents were prepared.

In February the sherpas collectively addressed how the G8 could best engage the O5. Blair (2007) had publicly stated at Davos the month before that he wanted the G8 to expand to a G13. The sherpas felt that the G8 would see the adaptation of its structure. Heiligendamm would be the third consecutive time their leaders would meet with the O5. Many within the group considered it hard not to invite the O5 if the G8 was to have any outreach at all. To them, the O5 or nothing seemed the only choice.

Beyond public prompting and institutional precedent lay power and purpose as compelling rationales for promoters of the O5/HP idea. They argued the G8 had to adapt to the evolving shifts in geopolitical and geo-economic power. The sherpas agreed that the core of the G8 focused no longer just on economics and markets but also on shared values and on sharing and broadening the benefits of globalization. The combined G8 did not represent the global strength it once did. Consequently, several issues no longer had a G8-only solution. Issues with a global impetus could no longer be discussed fully and dealt with satisfactorily without involving the O5.

This led to a consideration of issues that might be appropriate for such a shared discussion. One was climate change. Among the O5, China was about to surpass the U.S. as the world's number-one producer of greenhouse gas emissions. Brazil was already number four, with three quarters of its emissions resulting from deforestation, mostly in the Amazon.

Yet there was still some reluctance to give up the shared history of the G8. There was also a clear desire to carefully think through any possible expansion scenarios. It was crucial that the Americans participate. As a new broader representation developed, it must not create a forum for ganging up on the American "G1" (May 2005). Nor could it diminish the G8 or come at the expense of the candour, intimacy, and shared values of this forum, which gave impetus to other institutions. There also needed to be plans for continuity, particularly to preserve the sense of a G8 meeting with a G8 agenda and G8 documents, rather than one shared with the O5.

Another issue was participation beyond the O5. Some felt that an enlarged group should probably extend beyond five in order to ensure, for example, Muslim representation. This could be fulfilled by including Nigeria—the largest African country—or Saudi Arabia. This factor, among others, would make it difficult to demonstrate broad representation of an enlarged group with the addition of only five handpicked members.

The agenda was also a consideration. Here, the sherpas recalled that the G7 emerged in the aftermath of the oil crises of the early 1970s, the burning issue of the day. Inclusion in a wider group required a real issue to discuss and advance. They also concluded that they needed to be careful to find an issue that did not detract from other institutions that already had it in their mandate. It must be an issue that would allow for deliverables beyond the discussion stage. The G8's Heiligendamm agenda already included several items appropriate for a G8 Plus Five discussion, under the label of ensuring, sharing, and broadening the benefits of globalization. These topics were climate change, economic imbalances, and intellectual property protection, with the interrelated issues of funding new research and technologies to address climate change with effective shields for intellectual property rights. The question was how to pull these elements together into a robust agenda. Care needed to be taken to avoid overlap in developing a collective agenda among the G8 and the O5.

Amidst these differing perspectives on what to do and how to proceed, some saw a pragmatic opportunity to bring out the creative element of G8 leadership and take the evolution of its architecture to the next stage. While transformation would not be possible in time for the 2007 summit, the G8 was ready to take the next step through a more elaborate engagement at Heiligendamm. This attitude prevailed.

By April, the Germans had labelled their intended institutional innovation the Heiligendamm Process. They decided to hold two G8 and O5 encounters in their hosting year, where 13 or 14 participants would engage in an equal exchange. The first was on climate change. The Germans asked the environmental and climate experts of each country to come to a special meeting in Berlin on 4 May, and then another on 16 October.

After the first meeting, the Germans concluded that the way members of the G8 knew one another and their positions from their meetings was quite different from the dynamic between them and the O5. With new guests at the table, it was not always possible to see the articulation and evolution of positions. Discussions were more difficult; participants were more cautious; and progress was slower. Thus, this joint meeting showed the importance of intensifying the G8-O5 dialogue. It also implied that the industrialized countries must not expect too much from the threshold countries in the field of climate change.

The Germans also proceeded with their proposal for the HP—a structured, issue-specific dialogue on other subjects whose results would be submitted in an interim report to the Japanese-hosted summit in 2008 and in a final report to the Italian-hosted summit in 2009. Possible issues would focus on topics related to the world economy, of mutual interest to the threshold countries and the G8.

One such topic was innovation and its protection. Knowledge-based societies needed innovation and to promote it for the sake of growth and jobs in the G8. But there was also a need to protect innovation, through patents and copyright. The protection of intellectual property rights was deemed a priority where common solutions should be pursued.

Another potential issue was investment. It was important that the G8 countries themselves made it clear that they favoured open investment markets. This preference could no longer be taken for granted. The United Nations Conference on Trade and Development (UNCTAD) had found that in the 1990s national investment legislation contained protectionist rules covering about 3 percent of the economy. This had risen to 20 percent at the beginning of the 21st century (OECD 2007). Whatever one's position on globalization, the German chancellor and her sherpa were convinced of the danger of this protectionist path. They sought a declaration that supported freedom of investment. The more open markets become, the more necessary it is to agree on similar investment conditions with one's most important trading partners. This was thus a good issue for the O5.

Two other possible items fit the criteria. One was energy efficiency. Here, the debate on climate change was unavoidable. When asked practical questions about potential first steps, the Germans replied with the hope that the framework of the HP would produce reasonable results. However, the separate joint meeting, already scheduled for 16 October, would focus on climate change, outside the HP itself.

The other topic was development. The Germans were convinced that for Africa to embark on the path to much better development, good governance was needed. It was thus important for the international donor community to reach a consensus on governance. There were already several forums available. But the Germans wanted to discuss this issue with the O5 too.

The Germans' goal was a structured dialogue between the G8 and the O5. They felt that for global governance, the leaders of these threshold countries must become aware that with their growing economic weight came increased responsibility. They were only able to take on such responsibility against the background of preparing for the G8. On issues such as climate change, the O5 expected advanced steps to be taken by the G8. Although this was taken for granted by the Europeans, not all G8 partners agreed. The Germans were obliged to respond first within the G8, through its consensus-oriented process. They also had to find a way to sum it all up in documented form. At the end of May, the Germans were hopeful they would achieve this. With such dialogue and cooperation, a G13 could be possible in the end but its creation was by no means fore-ordained.

On the eve of the summit, all understood that the HP would be a major deliverable. However, this deliverable would extend beyond Germany's year in the chair. The Germans thus needed to negotiate with the Japanese, who would host in 2008, and with the Italians, who would do so in 2009. All wanted a higher degree of confidence in what the process entailed. The sherpas saw the HP as a logical way to address the obvious calls for the G8 to expand its dialogue. The agenda could be built collaboratively throughout the year. That said, options were kept open about the degree of formal institutionalization, right down to the selection of who the outreach participants would be. There was a desire to keep the communiqué wording flexible.

At the Summit

At the Heiligendamm Summit, German chancellor Angela Merkel's skills as a good chair were tested to attain agreement on the HP. The O5 leaders had been kept waiting for some time by themselves in a separate room, without even the German foreign minister to tend to them. The only G8 leader who visited the O5 was Russia's Vladimir Putin, who spent an hour with them. The G8 leaders' discussions went more smoothly and hence more quickly than anticipated, and the media was eager for news on the G8's achievements, especially on climate change, so the Germans publicly issued their comprehensive summit communiqué earlier than they had planned. It contained a passage announcing the creation of the HP. Because it was announced before the G8 leaders' meeting with the O5 had even taken place, at the subsequent outreach session with the O5, the Chinese, Indian, and South African leaders objected to what they felt was an inappropriate, premature announcement. Merkel managed their discontent smoothly, admitting that her officials had made mistakes. Emphasizing the importance of the process, she was able to bring all the O5 partners back on board.

At this session, Chinese president Hu Jintao presented a prepared statement outlining China's new, more forthcoming approach to climate change. This showed the G8 leaders that inclusion could bring the O5 along in a desirable way. But it also showed them that some O5 partners still had to learn how the flexible, freewheeling G8 game was played.

The innovative HP that emerged from the summit was a high-level, structured dialogue between the G8 and O5 on intellectual property, investment, development, and energy. It would start in the second half of 2007 and aim at producing tangible results in two years. The Organisation for Economic Co-operation and Development (OECD) was asked, at the suggestion of its executive head, Angel Gurría, to serve as a platform for the HP, helping prepare meetings on the chosen issues. It would not serve as a body for implementation or control. Although not all the participants, especially not those from the O5, supported this arrangement, the OECD's offer was eventually accepted. The closely affiliated International Energy Agency (IEA) would provide similar services in the field of energy efficiency. The German vision was fully realized, with the issue of energy efficiency included and the OECD given a supporting but limited role.

Through this institutionalized outreach, the G8 club expanded to embrace the rapidly rising, largely democratic threshold global powers of China, India, Brazil, Mexico, and South Africa. The HP extended the ongoing 2005 Gleneagles Dialogue on Clean Energy, Climate Change, and Sustainable

Development. The formula had already proven itself when the May 2007 meeting of the G8 and O5 sherpas had delivered the signal that developing countries would control their carbon dioxide emissions if America and its allies did. The HP showed again that the G8, like the OECD and the North Atlantic Treaty Organization (NATO), could expand to include rising powers, unlike the United Nations Security Council (UNSC), with its membership frozen at five permanent members, and unlike the executive boards of the Bretton Woods bodies still struggling with their divisive issues of voice and vote. But there was still an attempt to keep the summit outreach flexible. Its membership was not fixed. There was no certainty that the countries that had been invited for the previous five years would remain the same in the years ahead.

Follow-up

The follow-up to the Heiligendamm Summit was framed in response to French president Nicolas Sarkozy's public call for a new G13 to solidify (Kamynin 2007; Sarkozy 2007; Williamson 2007). Among the G8 members, questions remained about whether it would be the same five participants in the future, whether it would be the same agenda with the same overlap between the O5 and G8 issues, and whether the O5 leaders would come to the next summit to discuss the same issues the HP officials had. It was also unclear whether a summit agenda would be developed jointly between the G8 and O5.

Many felt that the O5 leaders warranted and would be granted a larger place in the process by the end of the year. But most also felt that the best part of the G8 summit was its informality, when the nine or ten leaders (including the EU leaders) talked frankly and openly about what it was like to be leaders of major market democracies, facing economic challenges as democratically elected leaders, amidst demanding media, legislatures, and judiciaries. At their exclusive part of the summit, they exchanged ideas about how to manage aspects of their common situations. Indeed, they set aside their prepared texts to engage in frank discussions about managing economies in today's difficult world. The opportunity to do so was what brought them back every year—it was what they enjoyed most about the G8 summit. In contrast, in the larger meeting at Heiligendamm with the O5 present, some G8 members felt that the Chinese leader had acted as though he were giving a speech at the UN. Others, in contrast, emphasized how at this summit he appeared much more spontaneous than ever before.

As this debate continued, the task of managing the HP and the O5 remained. The G8 had to be sure it had continued, effective, and valuable discussions with the O5. The role of the OECD remained somewhat controversial. With the exception of Mexico, O5 members were—like the G8's Russia—not members of the rich countries' OECD club. The Germans still had some work to do to make the HP's OECD connection acceptable to the O5.

Within the G8, one outstanding issue was whether the G8 Plus Five formula would induce the O5 to take real action on climate change. The reluctant Americans asked about the rationale for the 16 October G8-O5 meeting on climate as its long-known date approached. They were concerned because they had scheduled their own meeting of 16 major emitting countries on climate in Washington and feared duplication or competition. They reluctantly accepted the argument that it was important to show that the unity displayed at the Heiligendamm Summit on climate remained. They thus participated in the G8-O5 meeting. However, Indonesia, which had been invited in its capacity as the chair of the UN's Bali meeting, chose not to attend. The October session ended with a chair's statement that codified further G8-O5 convergence, if of a low-level sort.

A meeting of the HP steering committee on 17 October defined how the parallel HP would unfold. There would be two to three meetings a year among relatively senior, technical experts on each of the four HP topics. Some outreach countries still resisted anchoring the HP too deeply in the OECD, leading the G8 to look for a reasonable separation between the two. The G8 and O5 sherpas would constitute together a group of 13 or 14 individuals who could talk equally to one another. It was agreed that in addition to the issue-specific meetings there would also be an overall steering committee to provide direction to the process overall.

By this time, everyone was comfortable with the HP and taking it very seriously indeed. Even the initially resistant Japanese also appeared to be warming. At first they had accepted the HP as a German initiative that the Germans would implement on a separate track from the 2008 summit preparations. Now they indicated they might be willing to take over the HP's chair and steering committees after the German-hosted meeting in the spring of 2008. Media reports further suggested they might invite the O5 leaders to their summit in July ("Govt's G8 Priorities to Include Nuclear Nonproliferation" 2007). But the Japanese reserved the right to invite additional countries as well. Other G8 partners, notably France and Italy, said such flexibility was important to them too. It remained unclear, however, how the Japanese would structure their outreach at the summit itself.

In a number of areas, the G8 Plus Five formula was gathering momentum. At the end of December 2007, Germany, at its initiative, hosted a meeting for the heads of foreign policy planning for G8 and O5 countries for the first time. There was good representation from both the G8 and the O5. Officials from the EU and Portugal attended as well. The Americans sent their number two, while the Chinese sent Xu Bu, their deputy director general, who was senior in their system and had a reputation as a rising star. This full-day meeting discussed globalization in the morning and transformational diplomacy, based on shifting power patterns, in the afternoon. There were two guests: Uri Dadush, director of the International Trade Department of the World Bank, speaking on globalization in the morning, and Christoph Bertram, speaking on strategic transitional issues in the afternoon. It was a useful meeting, although not entirely informal, as some participants delivered set speeches.

By early March 2008, the HP had gotten off to a promising start. One working group meeting, on development was considered a successful introductory session. A second working group, on energy, met next, followed by those on investment and then innovation. Co-chaired by the British, the innovation group had intellectual property as its top agenda item. Britain's approach was to have an open dialogue, choosing not to focus exclusively on enforcement but rather on how intellectual property rights could be a driver for economic growth. They also sought to emphasize how intellectual property rights, if managed properly, could be a means for developing countries to access what they needed to facilitate their own development.

During the first semester of 2008, all four HP working groups held their meetings: development on 21 February and 18 May, energy on 18 March, investment on 25–26 March, and innovation and intellectual property rights on 3 April. All were attended by high-level delegates, most often director general–level specialists from the 13 dialogue partner countries and the EU. There they agreed on their work programs and the dates for their next meetings, as follows: development at the end of October in Mexico, energy on 26 September in Paris, investment on 25 June in Paris, and innovation on 19–20 June in the UK.

To provide balanced leadership, all groups had co-chairs from one G8 and one G5 country, as follows: France and South Africa for development, Canada and India for energy, the United States and Mexico for investment; and the United Kingdom and India for innovation. The sherpa-level Steering Committee to oversee the dialogue met on 17 October 2007 in Berlin, and was scheduled to do so again on 3 June in Versailles, France.

More broadly, however, the overall HP was still institutionally led by Germany and would be so until the Hokkaido Toyako Summit, after which Japan was due to take over. The interim report due at the Hokkaido Summit would indeed be delivered. But it was likely to be considered only as a *pro forma* item for the G8 leaders to take note of, rather than discuss and direct in any meaningful way.

The delivery of the formal, final report at the Italian-hosted in 2009, however, suggested that the O5 leaders would have to be at that summit together with their G8 colleagues, providing the possibility of a great Plus Five moment. But whether it would lead to expanded engagement remains in doubt.

The Spectrum of Opinion

As the process of preparing the Hokkaido Summit proceeded, different countries continued to approach the HP's format and substance in various ways. Some developed countries, with clear policy objectives, wanted to use it to address and push through certain issues. Others viewed it as an opportunity to institutionalize relationships among the G8 and the O5. And others continued on a cautious course. Despite their different approaches, most recognized that how well the HP worked over the next 18 months and its impact on the relationship between G8 and O5 would be important. If it generated concerted, helpful outputs in one or more of its four issue areas, it could have a significant influence on the willingness of G8 members to engage with the O5. If it became a standard confrontational "developed versus developing" country debate, then the prospects for a sustained and broader G8-O5 institutional relationship would dim.

Its outcome was all the more important given the differences among G8 countries on the broader issue of moving toward any G13. Here there was a spectrum of views. But there was also a defining divide between an enthusiastic European four and an opposed Pacific four, with Russia for this purpose privately a member of the reluctant Pacific power club.

Germany was a leading enthusiast of outreach. As the inventor, namesake, sponsor, and guardian of the HP, it favoured broader G8-O5 engagement. Former chancellor Helmut Schmidt had publicly endorsed a full G13, giving the concept broader bipartisan support nationally and internationally. But he along with the German government thought it should first take the form of an HP-like dialogue, in order to show that such a forum would add value and work.

France had quickly become the primary public promoter, after Sarkozy had made a strong public call for a G13 in July 2007. By calling for the G8 to become G13, over time and incrementally, he had made the idea respectable within the G8. He also provided a hook on which O5 members' own ambitions could be hung. As the Hokkaido Summit approached, he offered another initiative, suggesting that Egypt be added to a G14 on the grounds that a Muslin and Middle East country was needed in the new club.

Britain was also eager, if less enthusiastically and expansively than the French. Blair had made his public call while still in office. His successor, Gordon Brown, had followed, more cautiously, calling for a larger, more prominent role for the O5 at the summit. He had long ago accepted the analytical case for expansion when, as Tony Blair's finance minister, he had participated in the new finance G20 and chaired the newly created International Monetary and Finance Committee (IMFC) at the IMF (Kirton 2001a). The British government was very supportive of the HP and of ensuring that it was a genuinely open dialogue among equal partners. On the G13 itself, it had a strong commitment—reiterated by Brown at Guild Hall and during his visit to India—to the concept of a rules-based international system. It felt that in a globalizing world, challenges such as climate change, energy security, and migration were not susceptible to solutions by individual countries, but required collective action and collectively agreed responses. While those responses were best delivered through international institutions and multilateral organizations, their internal politics made it difficult to achieve the consensus required. This gave a role for a smaller group of countries that, on the basis of their economic weight, shared values, willingness to take on degree of responsibility for global action and for global leadership, would try to work together to identify solutions and ideas that could be folded back into multilateral system to help it address those challenges. This meant starting with a G8 that had proven its worth in this regard.

But the economic weight of its existing members was declining in relative terms, down to 62 percent of the global total. It would decline even more as major emerging economies became preponderant in the global economy. The challenge of climate change required engaging with India, China, and Brazil, with the largest rainforest in world. Global leadership required solutions infused with the perspective of developing countries as well as the developed ones. Meeting the challenges of Africa required the involvement of Africans. In the G8, outreach had been the answer, with a clear pattern set. But outreach was the prerogative of the presidency. A different set of countries were invited each year, according to the agenda at hand. However, South Africa (which had sometimes come on its own) and the O5 had emerged as the most frequent attendees. And while the German sherpa had

had separate meetings with the heads of the O5 in advance of the summit to prepare the discussion with the G8, the HP was agreed to as a process separate from the summit itself.

Italy's position had been the basic pro-European one but became uncertain after the decisive outcome of the Italian election in the spring of 2008. Its new leader, Silvio Berlusconi, was more sympathetic than his predecessor to lobbying from Washington on how the process should be managed. But how this approach fit with the pan-European position of Sarkozy, Merkel, and Brown still needed to be played out. As the 2008 Hokkaido Summit approached, Italy signalled that climate change and very probably African development would be high on the agenda for 2009. It would thus be likely that African leaders would attend, as well as the O5. The latter would also be there to receive the final HP report.

Russia had already publicly suggested a desire to move toward a G13. But privately it resisted, feeling that Russia's full inclusion in the full G8 system was a priority task. There was no change in this attitude when its new president, Dimitry Medvedev, was elected in early March and took office in May.

On the other side of the divide, Japan stood as the strongest opponent of an expanded summit among the Pacific powers. As March began, the Japanese had still not decided whether the O5 would be invited to Hokkaido. They persuaded the Americans to acquiesce to having the Americans' long-planned Major Economies Meeting (MEM), with 16 members associated with the summit, eventually in the form of the summit's last session on climate change. To dilute the O5/G13 formula they publicly invited Australia to the summit at the beginning of March, and later added South Korea and Indonesia.

Japan insisted that it understood the importance of expansion and that it did not have a fixed idea here. It knew there were a number of issues that the G8 could not address alone. Therefore, as a matter of principle, it would have outreach with a number of countries relevant to the subjects at the summit. But there were many ways to think of the type of outreach they would have. One was with the U.S., through its expanded dialogue on climate change with the MEM of the G8, O5, South Korea, Australia, and Indonesia.

Beyond this, Japan argued, accurately, that the summit was very important to them, especially when it hosted it only once every eight years. It very much liked the G8 as a smaller forum where leaders could establish relationships and talk frankly about their individual feelings. It saw eight (plus the EU) as a good number for this. It also emphasized the sense of responsibility, especially that which came from being a democracy, and asked how expansion could generate the democratic ideals and responsibility all desired. The G8 had already changed its character with Russia in, and would change again with a move to 13. Japan asked if the group would really miss the last country not added—perhaps a reference to South Africa whose incoming leader lacked the aura of Nelson Mandela and Thabo Mbeki. Japan was also reticent about the role of China in a G8 context. It vividly remembered that China had recently thwarted Japan's bid to secure a permanent seat on the UNSC.

Outsiders assessing Japan's position argued that there was little basis for a "UNSC-P Plus"–G13 trade in which China would let Japan into "its" Permanent Five (P5) on the UNSC and Japan would let China into "its" G8. The national interest–based positions of too many partners were too deeply held for objective reasons on the issue of UNSC reform. But this impasse did need not to stop G8 outreach. This could have its own self-sustaining dynamic, which all involved could have an interest in developing. Another obstacle was the value Japan placed on its role as the only Asian advocate in the G8, and its reluctance to share this with China and India. Still others argued that the Chinese economy and Japanese economy were rather complementary and shared some approaches to a social market economy, and that G8 inclusion would encourage China to take a more responsible approach to global governance.

The U.S. opposition was due to doubts about these sorts of summit consultations and the impact of larger numbers on their overall effectiveness. The Americans instinctively felt that HP/O5 dialogue was a waste of time. They asked how so many people in one place could produce so much paper that no one would read. If a larger number of leaders came to read prepared statements then the value of the meeting was lost. The G8 dialogue had to allow participants to test the realm of the possible. That was the G8's real value, and the core of its capacity for global leadership to meet global challenges. From this shared attitude the Americans raised the question shared by all G8 partners about the impact of institutionalizing HP/O5 dialogue on the effectiveness of the G8, and implicitly America's continued participation in the group.

In practice, the attitude of the new U.S. president inaugurated in January 2009 will be important. Republican candidate John McCain has already proposed on the campaign trail that Russia be dropped from and China added to the G8. But Barack Obama has suggested a new "E8" that would join the G8 to deal with climate change. His rival for the Democratic presidential nomination, Hillary Clinton, had a proposal along the same lines. Most G8 partners felt that Obama and even McCain himself would tilt toward multilateralism once elected president, and would explore the potential of the G8 here. If the new president found it wanting after the first few encounters, the future of the entire G8 would be in doubt. The experience at the 2009 and 2010 summits will thus be key. Making the G8 work for and with the U.S. was in the ultimate interest of all. At the same time, America's central interest in G8 outreach was with China. This could be achieved in a new G9 with China alone, in a G10 with an India that would soon be as important as China, or through a Sino–U.S. dialogue on their own.

Canada was reserved about expansion. As the G8's smallest country, it was cautious about diluting its speaking time at the summit, the attention its interventions would receive as listeners adjusted to the relative capability of the speaker, and Canada's chance to host the G8 every eight years. Its instinct was thus toward continuity, incremental expansion, and meeting the demand for expansion through other forums. Indeed, some of its G8 partners felt that Canada was the G8 member most adamantly opposed to expansion, on the grounds that any change such would call into question Canada's inclusion in the G8 or in any smaller new group that might spring up as a result of the G8 becoming too big.

The Future: Toward 2010

From this analysis, several conclusions emerge. Most immediate is that outreach is here to stay. It is difficult to demote those already involved. More importantly, outreach enhances the effectiveness and legitimacy of the G8. Both the G8 and O5 need it, if in a shifting balance and to different degrees. Over the next few years there will probably be greater interaction and more involvement of the O5 in summit preparations, as pushed forward by the HP. The intimacy, effectiveness, and impact of the current G8 will likely be compromised should this be necessary for the greater gain of getting China, India, and others responsibly to provide more global leadership as part of a more powerful, cohesive and central, if not monopolistic, emerging G13.

But this process, path, and destination is by no means inevitable. It could easily be derailed by several forces at work. The HP might fail as a dialogue of equals that helps solve pressing problems in the world. American doubts about its North America Free Trade Agreement (NAFTA) in particular and globalization in general could carry over into broader plurilateral forums such as the G8 Plus Five, where their next-door neighbours Canada and Mexico are also involved. Should Italy not mount a post-HP moment in 2009, and should Sarkozy not be as eager when he hosts in 2011, the sequence of summits hosted by the currently skeptical Pacific powers of Japan in 2008, Canada in 2010, and the U.S. in 2012 could break the momentum the O5 has acquired during its three-year pan-European run from 2005 to 2007. More broadly, as with the early estimate of an inevitably soaring Soviet Union in the mid 1970s when the G7 was born, the O5 may have its many great vulnerabilities erupt and exposed to replace its growing capabilities that get all the attention now. The same logic and path that brought a post-1989 Soviet Union–turned–Russian Federation into the G8 could then come to prevail.

The G13 formula has currently emerged as the most likely long-term winner, in the great competition among new numerical combinations claiming to be the formula for creating an effective and legitimate centre of global governance for the 21st century. It has been winning out over other groups with fewer, greater, and different numbers, at the level of leaders, ministers, and officials and across a wide range of policy domains (Bradford Jr. and Linn 2004; Carin and Smith 2005; Cooper et al. 2006; Cooper and English 2005; Fues 2007; Gurría 2005; Lesage 2007; Maddox et al. 2007; Martin 2006; Wilson and Purushothaman 2003). But it is doing so by only a very narrow margin and much uncertainty prevails. Indeed, the L20, which will arguably come to life in the form of the issue-specific MEM-16 summit at the 2008 G8 Hokkaido Summit could easily surpass the G13 formula. This is so especially if Barack Obama becomes president of the United States, if Nicolas Sarkozy continues to add candidates to the G13, and if Canada in 2010 adds its fellow Asia-Pacific powers of South Korea, Australia, and Indonesia again, perhaps with a few more G20 colleagues as well. Other countries and international organizations may be added to the G13, and sometimes Mexico and South Africa may be left off the G7 finance ministers list. But the G13 core will usually be there, even if China and India refuse invitations to attend a few G7/8 finance ministerials. Its coalescence means the G8 may even transcend its older pattern of adding new members one at a time, with India having been seen by some as the next logical choice (Kirton 2005a; Thakur 2007).

The major outstanding short-term question concerns the subjects on which the current HP and emerging G13 will and can prove there worth. On the existing HP agenda, it is easy to identify what the G8 wants of the O5, notably higher standards on intellectual property and investment protection, more money and standards for development, and more action to control climate change. It is harder to identify what the O5 want from the G8 beyond the standard demands of the North–South dialogue of old (Yu Yongding 2005; "China Positive on Sarkozy's G8 Proposal—Foreign Ministry" 2007; Feng 2007). Moreover, there are a large number of issues, such as finance, macroeconomic management, trade, infectious disease, and climate change on which the G8 and O5 share predominant global capability and a common fate, but which are not on the shared HP agenda in their own right (see Appendix B).

Here the issue of trade stands out. China ranks fourth as a global exporter, and the O5 collectively provide 10 percent of world exports now (see Appendix C). The G8's global share of trade capability, as measured by exports, is only 46 percent, but with its O5 partners added jumps to a global majority of 56 percent. The G8's once robust global trade governance has now slipped for several years. The G8 summit, its trade ministers quadrilateral, the new G20 trade forum, the G20 finance, and the WTO all acting separately have failed to bring the long overdue Doha Development Agenda to a successful end. The interdependence among the G8 and O5 members on trade has been rising fast (see Appendix D). The G13 possesses the overwhelming and internally balanced trade power in the world. As the HP is already moving ahead on investment, the most directly trade-related issue, the time could well be right for trade-dependent, international institution–building Canada to put trade on the agenda of an enhanced HP or even G13 encounter when it hosts the G8 in 2010.

A second compelling candidate for inclusion is finance. Here the G8 alone, as measured by IMF quota shares, has only 48 percent of the world's specialized capability, whereas with the O5 added it leaps to 57 percent. The ministerial-level G20 finance and G7 finance with China have proven their worth. And the G8's current finance and economic agenda, with macroeconomic management, energy, biofuels, and food-fuelled inflation, financial supervision of hedge funds, subprime mortgage, credit, and sovereign wealth funds added, has now acquired the breadth and interlinkages that only leaders can address (Subacchi 2007; Meredith 2007). The IMF's recent voice-and-vote reforms, and the finance G20's contribution at the ministerial level, make the relative-capability case for adding China and other O5 partners stronger still.

A third and even more compelling candidate is climate change, including both of its dual dimensions of greenhouse gas sources and sinks. As long ago as 2003 the G8 produced only 46 percent of the world's carbon emissions, while the addition of the O5 raised the total to a commanding majority of

74 percent. To be sure, the Gleneagles Dialogue has added value, should be continued, and likely will be in the form of a "Toyako Dialogue" dedicated to devising a low carbon society. But the urgency of the climate problem and its tight linkages with investment, innovation, development, and energy efficiency warrant its integrated place as a whole, with both sources and sinks, in the HP itself and at the leaders' level in a G13.

More broadly, it is striking that, at present, the G8 alone still contains global collective predominance, defined as a majority of the relevant specialized capabilities, necessary to solve the four global problems chosen for the HP agenda during its first two years. This supports for the moment the case for a two-tier G8-O5 annual summit for agenda items such as these. Moreover, there is a long list of issues, largely in the political-security sphere, that G8 leaders currently need to discuss all alone. Winning the war in Afghanistan leads this list. However, in the fields of trade, finance, climate, and health the G8 alone currently commands only a minority of the relevant global capabilities (or vulnerabilities in the case of climate and health). The addition of the O5 here would restore the new G13 to global predominance again and endow it with international equality due to Brazil and Indonesia's status as superpower sinks for climate control. This suggests a strong need to add these issues to the HP as soon as possible, and to make the O5 full partners at the G8-G13 summit where issues of trade, finance, health, and climate are discussed. An analysis of the web of overlapping memberships in international institutions suggests that at the critical leaders' level; it is only in a new G13 that this desired more equal association and effective action can emerge (see Appendix E). If the 2008 Hokkaido Summit proves to be a success, then its formula of the G8 alone, adding the O5 and others more occasionally for the most appropriate subjects, could set the pattern for the years ahead.

References

Aslund, Anders (2006). "Russia's Challenges as Chair of the G8." Policy Brief No. 06-3, March. Washington DC: Institute for International Economics. www.iie.com/publications/pb/pb06-3.pdf (May 2008).

Baum, Richard and Alexei Shevchenko (2001). "Bringing China In: A Cautionary Note." In *The New Great Power Coalition: Toward a World Concert of Nation*, edited by R. Rosecrance, 327–344. New York: Rowman and Littlefield.

Bayne, Nicholas (1995). "The G7 Summit and the Reform of Global Institutions." *Government and Opposition* 30: 497.

Bergsten, C. Fred (1998). "The New Agenda with China." Policy Brief 98-2, May. Washington DC: Institute for International Economics. www.petersoninstitute .org/publications/pb/pb.cfm?ResearchID=81 (May 2008).

Blair, Tony (2007). "Speech at Davos." 27 January, www.number-10.gov.uk/output/ Page10858.asp (May 2008).

Bradford Jr., Colin I. and Johannes F. Linn (2004). "Global Economic Governance at a Crossroads: Replacing the G7 with the G20." Brookings Institution Policy Brief 131. www.brookings.edu/~/media/Files/rc/papers/2004/04globaleconomics _colin%20i%20%20bradford%20%20jr/pb131.pdf (May 2008).

Brezinski, Zbigniev (1996). "Let's Add to the G7." *New York Times*, 25 June, A11.

Carin, Barry and Gordon Smith (2005). "Making Change Happen at the Global Level." In *Reforming from the Top: A Leaders' 20 Summit*, edited by J. English, R. Thakur, and A.F. Cooper, 25–45. Tokyo: United Nations University Press.

"China Positive on Sarkozy's G8 Proposal—Foreign Ministry." (2007). *AFX International Focus*, 31 August.

Chirac, Jacques (2004). "Press Briefing by French President Jacques Chirac." 9 June, Sea Island. www.g8.utoronto.ca/summit/2004seaisland/chirac040609.html (May 2008).

Commission on Global Governance (1995). *Our Global Neighbourhood: The Report of the Commission on Global Governance*. Oxford: Oxford University Press.

Cooper, Andrew F. and John English (2005). "Introduction." In *Reforming from the Top: A Leaders' 20 Summit*, edited by J. English, R. Thakur, and A.F. Cooper. Tokyo: United Nations University Press.

Cooper, Andrew F., Agata Antkiewicz, and Timothy M. Shaw (2006). "Economic Size Trumps All Else? Lessons from BRICSAM." CIGI Working Paper No. 12. Waterloo ON: Centre for International Governance Innovation. www.cigionline .org : Publications : Working Papers (May 2008).

Cooper, Andrew F. (2007). "The Logic of the B(R)ICSAM Model for G8 Reform." CIGI Policy Brief No. 1. Waterloo ON: Centre for International Governance Innovation. www.cigionline.org : Publications : Policy Briefs (May 2008).

Cooper, Andrew F. and Kelly Jackson (2007). "Regaining Legitimacy: The G8 and the 'Heiligendamm Process.'" *International Insights* 4(10): www.igloo.org/ciia/ Library/ciialibr/intern~1/internat (May 2008).

Desai, Seema (2006). "Expanding the G8: Should China Join?" January. London: Foreign Policy Centre. fpc.org.uk/fsblob/749.pdf (May 2008).

Economist (2006). *Pocket World in Figures*. London: Profile Books.

Economist (2008). *Pocket World in Figures*. London: Profile Books.

Feng Chen (2007). "G8 Not Platform for Exerting Pressure." 4 June, Beijing. Government of the People's Republic of China. www.gov.cn/misc/2007-06/04/ content_636224.htm (May 2008).

Fues, Thomas (2007). "Global Governance Beyond the G8: Reform Prospects for the Summit Architecture." *International Politik und Geselschaft* 2): 11–24. www.fes.de/ipg/arc_07_set/set_02_07e.htm (May 2008).

Gnath, Katharina (2007). "Beyond Heiligendamm: The G8 and Its Dialogue with Emerging Countries." *Internationale Politik* 8(3): 36–39. www.g8.utoronto.ca/scholar/IPGE_3_Gnath.pdf (May 2008).

"Govt's G8 Priorities to Include Nuclear Nonproliferation." (2007). *Daily Yomiuri*, 26 November.

Gurría, Angel (2005). "A Leaders' 20 Summit?" In *Reforming from the Top: A Leaders' 20 Summit*, edited by J. English, R. Thakur, and A.F. Cooper, 63–71. Tokyo: United Nations University Press.

Haq, Mahbub ul (1994). "The Bretton Woods Institutions and Global Governance." In *Managing the World Economy*, edited by P.B. Kenen, 409–418. Washington, DC: Institute for International Economic.

Hodges, Michael (1999). "The G8 and the New Political Economy." In *The G8's Role in the New Millennium*, edited by M.R. Hodges, J.J. Kirton, and J.P. Daniels, 69–74. Aldershot: Ashgate.

International Monetary Fund (2008). "IMF Members' Quotas and Voting Power, and IMF Board of Governors." Washington DC. www.imf.org/external/np/sec/memdir/members.htm (May 2008).

Jayarwedna, L. (1989). "World Economic Summits: The Role of Representative Groups in the Governance of the World Economy." *Journal of the Society of International Development* 4: 17–20.

Kamynin, Mikhail (2007). "Russia Supports French President's Idea of G8 Enlargement." Text of report by Russian Ministry of Foreign Affairs website reported by BBC Monitoring Former Soviet Union, 28 August.

Kirton, John J. (1999a). "Explaining G8 Effectiveness." In *The G8's Role in the New Millennium*, edited by M.R. Hodges, J.J. Kirton, and J.P. Daniels, 45–68. Aldershot: Ashgate.

Kirton, John J. (1999b). "The G7 and China in the Management of the International Financial System." Paper prepared for forum on China in the 21st Century and the World, sponsored by the China Development Institute, the China International Center for Economic and Technical Exchange, and the National Institute for Research Advancement, Japan, 11–12 November. Shenzen.

Kirton, John J. (2001a). "The G20: Representativeness, Effectiveness, and Leadership in Global Governance." In *Guiding Global Order: G8 Governance in the Twenty-First Century*, edited by J.J. Kirton, J.P. Daniels, and A. Freytag, 143–172. Aldershot: Ashgate.

Kirton, John J. (2001b). "The G7/8 and China: Toward a Closer Association." In *Guiding Global Order: G8 Governance in the Twenty-First Century*, edited by J.J. Kirton, J.P. Daniels, and A. Freytag, 189–222. Aldershot: Ashgate.

Kirton, John J. (2004a). "Getting the L20 Going: Reaching Out from the G8." Paper prepared for a workshop on 'G20 to Replace the G8: Why Not Now?,' sponsored by the Brookings Institution, Institute for International Economics, and the Centre for Global Governance, 22 September. Washington DC.

Kirton, John J. (2004b). "Toward Multilateral Reform: The G20's Role and Place." Paper prepared for a conference on "The Ideas-Institutional Nexus: The Case of the G20," sponsored by the Centre of International Governance Innovation, United Nations University, FLASCO, and the University of Waterloo, 19–21 May. Buenos Aires. www.g8.utoronto.ca/scholar/kirton2004/kirton_g20_2004.pdf.

Kirton, John J. (2005a). "The Future of the G8." In *G8 Summit 2005: Mapping the Challenges*, edited by M. Fraser. London: Newsdesk Publications.

Kirton, John J. (2005b). "Towards Multilateral Reform: The G20's Contribution." In *Reforming from the Top: A Leaders' 20 Summit*, edited by J. English, R. Thakur, and A.F. Cooper, 141–168. Tokyo: United Nations University.

Kirton, John J. (2007a). "G8: An Economic Forum of the Enlarged Western Alliance? The Record from Rambouillet 1975 through Heiligendamm 2007 to Canada 2010." Paper prepared for the North American European Summer Academy of Centre International de Formation Européenn and the Zentrum für Wissenschaft und Weiterbildung Schloss Hofen, 24 July. Lochau, Austria. www.g8.utoronto.ca/scholar/kirton2007/kirton-schlosshofen-070724.pdf (May 2008).

Kirton, John J. (2007b). *Canadian Foreign Policy in a Changing World*. Toronto: Thomson Nelson.

Kirton, John J. and Victoria Panova (2007). "Coming Together: The Evian Legacy." In *Corporate, Public and Global Governance: The G8 Contribution*, edited by M. Fratianni, P. Savona, and J.J. Kirton, 201–230. Aldershot: Ashgate.

Kirton, John J. and George M. von Furstenberg, eds. (2001). *New Directions in Global Economic Governance: Managing Globalisation in the Twenty-First Century*. Aldershot: Ashgate.

Lesage, Dries (2007). "Globalisation, Multipolarity and the L20 as an Alternative to the G8." *Global Society* 21(3): 343–361.

Maddox, Bronwen, David Charter, and Roger Boyes (2007). "G8: What It All Means and What Comes Next." *Times*, 9 June.

Martin, Paul (2006). "Speaking Notes for the Annual Meeting of the Development and Peace Foundation." 8 June, Dresden. www.paulmartin.ca/speech-20060608-1.html (May 2008).

Martinez-Diaz, Leonardo (2007). "The G20 After Eight Years: How Effective a Vehicle for Developing-Country Influence?" Global Economy and Development Working Paper No. 12. Washington DC: Brookings Institution.

May, Bernhard (2005). "The G8 in a Globalising World: Does the United States Need the G8?" In *New Perspectives on Global Governance: Why America Needs the G8*, edited by M. Fratianni, J.J. Kirton, A.M. Rugman, *et al.*, 67–82. Aldershot: Ashgate.

Meredith, Robyn (2007). "China and India: The New Global Players." In *G8 Summit 2007: Growth and Responsibility*, edited by M. Fraser, 203–207. London: Newsdesk Publications.

Organisation for Economic Co-operation and Development (2007). "OECD Global Forum for International Investment." Paris. www.oecd.org/daf/investment/gfii (May 2008).

Sachs, Jeffrey (1998). "Global Capitalism: Making It Work." *Economist*, 12 September, 23–25.

Sarkozy, Nicolas (2007). "Fifteenth Ambassadors' Conference: Speech." 27 August, Paris. www.ambafrance-uk.org/President-Sarkozy-s-speech.html?var_recherche =Fifteenth%20Ambassadors%20Conference%20Speech (May 2008).

Smyser, W. R. (1993). "Goodbye , G-7." *Washington Quarterly* 16 (Winter)(15–28.

Subacchi, Paola (2007). "Shaping a New Global Economic Order." In *G8 Summit 2007: Growth and Responsibility*, edited by M. Fraser, 28–31. London: Newsdesk Publications.

Thakur, Ramesh (2007). "India's Rising and Shining: Will It Prove a False Dawn?" CIGI Policy Brief No. 2. Waterloo ON: Centre for International Governance Innovation. www.cigionline.org : Publications : Policy Briefs (May 2008).

Vickers, Brendan (2006). "Heading toward the G8 St. Petersburg Summit: What's In It for Africa?" *Global Insight* 63): 1–4.

"Welcome to China, Mr. Clinton." (1998). *Economist*, 27 June, 17.

Whyman, William (1995). "We Can't Go On Meeting Like This: Revitalizing the G7 Process." *Washington Quarterly* 18(3):

Williamson, Hugh (2007). "Emerging Powers Flex Muscles to Push for More Power in the G8." *Financial Times*, 4 July.

Wilson, Dominic and Roopa Purushothaman (2003). "Dreaming with BRICs: The Path to 2050." Global Economics Paper No. 99, October. New York: Goldman Sachs. www2.goldmansachs.com/ideas/brics/book/99-dreaming.pdf (May 2008).

World Health Organization (2008). "Global Health Atlas." Geneva. www.who.int/ globalatlas (May 2008).

World Trade Organization (2008). "Trade Profiles." Geneva. stat.wto.org/Country Profile/WSDBCountryPFHome.aspx?Language=E (May 2008).

Yu Yongding (2005). "China's Evolving Global View." In *Reforming from the Top: A Leaders' 20 Summit*, edited by J. English, R. Thakur, and A.F. Cooper, 187–200. Tokyo: United Nations University Press.

Appendix A: International Organizations at Recent G8 Summits

1989 Paris (4)
Non-Aligned Movement: Senegal (Abdou Diouf), Egypt (Mohamed Hosni Mubarak), Venezuela (Carlos Andres Perez), and India (Rajiv Gandhi)

1993 Tokyo (1)
Non-Aligned Movement: Indonesia (Suharto)

1996 Lyon (4)
International Monetary Fund (Michel Camdessus)
United Nations (Boutros Boutros-Ghali)
World Bank (James Wolfensohn)
World Trade Organization (Renato Ruggiero)

2001 Genoa (4)
United Nations (Kofi Annan)
World Bank (James Wolfensohn)
World Health Organization (Gro Harlem Brundtland)
World Trade Organization (Renato Ruggiero)

2002 Kananaskis (1)
United Nations (Kofi Annan)

2003 Evian (4)
International Monetary Fund (Horst Köhler)
United Nations (Kofi Annan)
World Bank (James Wolfensohn)
World Trade Organization (Supachai Panitchpakdi)

2005 Gleneagles (6)
African Union (Alpha Oumar Konaré, Mali)
International Energy Agency (Claude Mandil)
International Monetary Fund (Rodrigo de Rato y Figaredo)
United Nations (Kofi Annan)
World Bank (Paul Wolfowitz)
World Trade Organization (Supachai Panitchpakdi)

2006 St. Petersburg (7)
African Union (Alpha Oumar Konaré, Mali)
Commonwealth of Independent States (Nursultan Nazarbayev, Kazakhstan)
International Atomic Energy Agency (Mohammed El Baradei)
International Energy Agency (Claude Mandil)
United Nations (Kofi Annan)
United Nations Educational, Scientific, and Cultural Organization (Koichiro Matsuura)
World Health Organization: (Anders Nordström)

2007 Heiligendamm (6)
African Union (Alpha Oumar Konaré, Mali)
International Energy Agency (Claude Mandil)
International Monetary Fund (Rodrigo de Rato y Figaredo)
Organisation for Economic Co-operation and Development (Angel Gurría)
United Nations (Ban Ki-Moon)
World Bank (Paul Wolfowitz)

Appendix B: G20 Specialized Capability

	GDP[a]	FDI (inflow, $ million)	FDI (outflow, $ million)	Innovation Property Protection[b]	Development[c]	Energy Efficiency[d]	Trade[e]	Finance[f]	Climate Change[g]	Health[h]
United States	14,305.702	99,443.00	–	84,958	27,622	2,325.90	11.89	17.09	4,816.20	1,200,000
Japan	4,552.204	–	45,781.00	109,823	13,147	533.20	5.56	6.13	1,231.30	17,000
China	3,713.301	72,406.00	11,306.00	5,913	i	1,609.30	5.95	3.72	4,143.50	650,000
Germany	3,414.629	32,663.00	45,634.00	12,804	10,082	3480.00	8.83	5.99	805.00	49,000
Britain	2,933.245	164,530.00	101,099.00	3,430	10,767	233.70	6.33	4.94	569.10	68,000
France	2,656.527	63,576.00	115,668.00	9,023	10,026	275.20	4.69	4.94	373.90	130,000
Italy	2,174.816	19,971.00	39,671.00	2,298	5,091	184.50	3.56	3.25	445.50	150,000
Canada	1,527.764	33,822.00	34,083.00	1,057	3,756	269.00	3.18	2.93	565.50	60,000
Spain	*1,524.903*	*22,987.00*	*38,772.00*	*1,432*	*3,018*	*142.20*	*2.22*	*1.40*	*211.80*	*140,000*
Russia	1,480.180	14,600.00	13,126.00	18,264	–	641.50	1.94	2.74	1,493.00	940,000
Brazil	1,450.011	15,066.00	–	676	–	204.80	0.93	1.40	298.30	620,000
India	1,249.439	–	–	695	–	572.90	1.10	1.91	1,273.20	5,700,000
South Korea	1,006.129	–	–	31,915	752	213.00	2.34	1.35	455.90	–
Australia	942.331	–	–	–	1,680	115.80	1.05	1.49	354.10	16,000
Mexico	939.289	18,055.00	–	–	–	165.50	1.60	1.45	415.90	180,000
Netherlands	*804.636*	*43,630.00*	*119,454.00*	*1,887*	*5,115*	*82.10*	*3.57*	*2.38*	*140.90*	*18,000*
Turkey	513.298	–	–	–	601	81.90	0.72	0.55	146.20	2000
Belgium	*467.721*	*23,691.00*	*22,925.00*	–	*1,963*	*57.70*	*2.56*	*2.12*	*102.80*	*14,000*
Indonesia	444.641	–	–	–	–	174.00	0.69	0.96	295.00	170,000
Saudi Arabia	407.033	–	–	–	1,734	140.40	–	3.21	302.30	–
Taiwan	*398.408*	–	–	*29,773*	*483*	–	*1.64*	–	–	–
South Africa	299.600	–	–	–	–	131.10	0.48	0.86	285.40	5,500,000
Argentina	279.528	–	–	–	–	63.70	–	0.97	127.50	130,000

	GDP[a]	FDI (inflow, $ million)	FDI (outflow, $ million)	Innovation Property Protection[b]	Development[c]	Energy Efficiency[d]	Trade[e]	Finance[f]	Climate Change[g]	Health[h]
Hong Kong	*216.267*	*35,897.00*	*32,560.00*	*–*	*–*	*–*	*1.00*	*–*	*–*	*–*
Singapore	*166.170*	*20,083.00*	*–*	*–*	*–*	*–*	*1.35*	*0.40*	*–*	*5500*
G8 total	33,045.07	428,605.00	395,062.00	241,657	80,491	7,943.00	45.98	48.01	10,299.50	2,614,000
G8 % world[j]	57.70	61.11	53.56	57.10	72.75	63.75	45.98	48.01	45.63	6.62
05 total	7651.64	105,527.00	11,306.00	7,284	i	2,683.60	10.06	9.34	6,416.30	12,650,000
05 % world[j]	13.36	12.47	15.39	2.28	i	21.54	10.06	9.34	28.42	32.03
G13 % world[j]	71.06	73.58	68.95	59.38	72.75[i]	85.29	56.04	57.35	74.05	38.69

Notes: GDP = gross domestic product; FDI = foreign direct investment. Countries in italics are not members of the G20.

a. GDP in current prices, percentage of world according to the International Monetary Fund.

b. Average number of patents granted from 2002 to 2004.

c. Aid donors in US$ million.

d. Energy consumption in 2004, measured by million tonnes oil equivalent.

e. Percentage of total world exports in 2007.

f. Percentage of total International Monetary Fund quota shares.

g. Million tonnes of carbon dioxide emissions in 2003.

h. Estimated number of people with HIV/AIDS in 2005.

i. China provides aid but does not disclose the amount.

j. Includes only numbers represented in table and thus do not reflect the entire group (i.e., G8, Outreach Five, or G13).

Sources: Economist (2008); International Monetary Fund (2008)
World Health Organization (2008).

Appendix C: Global Trade Power

	GATT Contributions 1994[a]	Merchandise Exports, 1997, (US$ billion)[b]	Merchandise Exports, 2004, (US$ billion)[b]	Merchandise Exports, 2005, (US$ billion)[b]	Exports, 2005[b]	Exports, 2007[b]
Euro area	–	–	–	17.15	17.48	16.36
United States	14.60	12.60	9.00	8.65	12.72	11.89
Germany	12.40	9.40	10.00	9.28	9.55	8.83
Britain	6.30	5.10	3.80	3.67	6.42	6.33
China	–	3.30	6.50	7.28	4.85	5.95
Japan	8.50	7.70	6.20	5.68	6.02	5.56
France	7.20	5.30	4.90	4.43	5.32	4.69
Netherlands	4.10	3.50	3.90	3.88	3.54	3.57
Italy	5.50	4.40	3.80	3.56	4.04	3.56
Canada	3.90	3.90	3.50	3.43	3.67	3.18
Belgium	3.40	3.10	3.40	3.19	2.77	2.56
South Korea	2.30	2.50	2.80	2.72	2.30	2.34
Spain	2.40	1.90	2.00	1.84	2.53	2.22
Russia	–	1.60	2.00	2.33	1.58	1.94
Taiwan	–	2.20	–	–	1.74	1.64
Mexico	–	2.00	2.10	2.04	1.75	1.60
Singapore	–	2.30	2.00	2.19	1.19	1.35
India	–	–	–	0.95	0.80	1.10
Australia	–	–	–	1.01	0.98	1.05
Hong Kong	3.10	3.40	2.90	2.79	1.06	1.00
Brazil	–	–	–	1.13	0.84	0.93
Turkey	–	–	–	0.7	0.70	0.72
Indonesia	–	–	–	0.82	0.67	0.69
South Africa	–	–	–	0.49	0.46	0.48
Saudi Arabia	–	–	–	1.73	0.99	–
Argentina	–	–	–	0.39	–	–

Notes: GATT = General Agreement on Tariffs and Trade.
a. By percentage, excluding any below 2 percent.
b. Percentage of world total.
Sources: John Kirton (2007b), *Economist* (2006; 2008); World Trade Organization (2008).

Appendix D: The G8 and China's Top Five Trade Partners

	Exporter									
Destination	China	Canada	France	Germany	Italy	Japan	Russia	Britain	United States	European Union
China		1.60	1.70	2.70	–	13.50	4.60	–	4.60	4.8
Canada	–		–	–	–	–	–	–	23.4	–
France	–	–		–	–	–	–	–	–	–
Germany	–	–	–		–	–	–	–	–	–
Italy	–	–	–	–		–	–	–	–	–
Japan	11.00	2.10	1.50	–	–		–	1.80	6.1	4.1
Russia	–	–	–	2.20	2.00	–		–	–	5.3
Britain	–	–	–	–	–	–	–		–	–
United States	21.40	83.90	7.20	8.80	8.00	22.90	–	14.70		23.5
European Union	18.90	5.70	65.00	63.40	58.80	14.70	44.90	46.60	20.60	37.70
Total	51.30	93.30	75.40	77.10	68.80	51.10	49.50	63.10	54.70	37.70

Notes: Percentage of total exports for top five trading partner within the G8 and China.
Source: World Trade Organization (2008).

Appendix E: International Institutional Membership

	United States	Japan	Germany	Britain	France	Italy	Canada	Russia	China	India	Brazil	Mexico	South Africa
Summit Level													
G8-O5	Y	Y	Y	Y	Y	Y	Y	Y	Y	Y	Y	Y	Y
OSCE	Y		Y	Y	Y	Y	Y	Y					
APEC	Y	Y					Y	Y	Y			Y	
Commonwealth				Y			Y			Y			Y
Francophonie					Y		Y						
European Council			Y	Y	Y	Y							
SPP	Y						Y					Y	
SCO								Y	Y				
Non-Summit Level													
UNSC P5	Y			Y	Y			Y	Y	Y*			
IMF Board	Y	Y	Y	Y	Y		Y	Y	Y	Y			
IMFC	Y	Y	Y	Y	Y	Y	Y	Y	Y	Y	Y		
OECD	Y	Y	Y	Y	Y	Y	Y					Y	
G20	Y	Y	Y	Y	Y	Y	Y	Y	Y	Y	Y	Y	Y
FSF	Y	Y	Y	Y	Y	Y	Y						
G24									Y*	Y	Y	Y	Y
G77									Y*	Y	Y		Y
ASEAN (+3)		Y							Y				
SOA	Y						Y				Y	Y	
ASEM		Y	Y	Y	Y	Y		Y	Y	Y			
TOTAL	11	9	9	11	11	8	12	9	9	8	6	7	5

Notes: APEC = Asia Pacific Economic Cooperation; ASEAN = Association of South East Asian Nations; ASEM = Asia Europe Meeting; FSF = Financial Stability Forum; IMF = International Monetary Fund; IMFC = International Monetary and Financial Committee; O5 = Outreach Five; OECD = Organisation for Economic Co-operation and Development; OSCE = Organization for Security and Co-operation in Europe; SCO = Shanghai Cooperation Organisation; SOA = Summit of the Americas; SPP = Security and Prosperity Partnership; UNSC P5 = Permanent Five members of the United Nations Security Council.

*Indicates observer state. Y indicates membership.

B(R)ICSAM CASE STUDIES

4

China's Evolving G8 Engagement
Complex Interests and Multiple Identity
in Global Governance Reform

Gregory T. Chin[1]

There is increasing recognition that key global issues can no longer be adequately managed and reshaped by the G8 without the major emerging powers being fully integrated into the process.[2] While the G8's legitimacy problems are a long-standing issue, the elite grouping has come face to face with the more urgent problem of effectiveness (Payne 2008, 527). Andrew F. Cooper (2007, 4) suggests that this "dual crisis" of the G8 has led to a governance gap in the international system. Thomas Fues (2007, 11, 13) highlights the "impending dysfunctionality" of the G8, and notes that leading developing countries are challenging the claim of the western industrialized countries to sole leadership in the world economy. The G8 appears unable to set priorities for the international community, which, in turn, further reduces its capacity to set the agenda and broker solutions to pressing global problems. This governance deficit is evident across the entire range of issues on which the G8 has tried to forge consensus and policy coordination, from its traditional focus areas of global financial and macroeconomic management and energy cooperation to more recent policy concerns such as global climate change and development assistance to Africa. The response of the G8 and its key ancillary bodies (for example, the G7 forum of finance ministers) has begun to selectively open their meetings for discussions with participants from the most influential developing countries.

The most serious test for the G8 and its reform agenda hinges on the status of China (see Chapter 1 in this volume). It is already *de facto* a great power and is still on the rise, both economically and diplomatically, although it is not a member of this elite grouping. The conventional response, for those who support both engaging with China and preserving the existing architecture of power, is that China needs to be brought into the core international power structure (Ikenberry 2008). For others, China is the actual problem rather than the solution, due to its normative differences and supposed unmanageability. Ultimately, the essential question is whether China can be brought in at all. The intention of the G8 is to move toward some type of new partnership with the major emerging economies. Whether this effort will succeed depends in large measure on the response of the Outreach Five (O5) countries—the five countries of Brazil, China, India, Mexico, and South Africa, which have been invited to the G8 summits since 2005. Does China even want to be part of an expanded "G" club? Or would it rather pursue options outside the G8, including championing the solidarity of the developing world or emerging regional associations? Will the combination of China's growing global economic weight and diplomatic capacities soon lead its leaders to decide that it need not bother with the G8 at all?

This chapter examines China's evolving engagement with the G8, including its involvement in the G8/O5 Heiligendamm Process (HP). It argues that China has maintained a cautious yet confident demeanour toward the G8, but that it has gradually become less cautious since 2003, and is evolving toward increasingly deeper engagement. The specifics of China's engagement with the G8 provide insight into the complexity of the country's emerging international interests, self-identification, and efforts to project a national image in terms of foreign policy. The chapter's main finding is that Beijing's positioning on international governance reform at the apex of the global system—specifically its engagement with the G8, and by extension the HP—continues to be shaped, in some significant ways, by its self-alignment with the developing world, even as its main priority is to secure its more individualized national interests as a *de facto* great power. In the latest stage of China's evolving relations with the G8, its strategic interests and ideological needs are served by putting concerted attention and resources into reaffirming its self-proclaimed status as a developing country and representative of the interests of the global South, despite having become the "world's factory" and now possessing dimensions of global power—both economic and political—that even many G8 members cannot claim. This desire to self-identify as a leading member of the global South has also encouraged Beijing to support a nascent process of collective identity formation among the leading developing countries, with one expression found in the G8-O5 dynamic.

China, the Shifting World Order, and Global Governance: Cautious Confidence

Beijing's reaction to the initial overtures from the G7 was stand-offish to say the least. China was first invited to attend the G7 in the 1999 by German chancellor Gerhard Schroeder, and was invited again at the 2000 G8 summit in Okinawa to have a dialogue with G8 members. It did not accept either invitation. On the eve of the 2002 summit in Kananaskis, Canada, the G8 again sent the message to Beijing, through various channels, that China should take part in meetings at the annual event. It was only in 2003, in Evian, France, that China's top leader, president and party general secretary Hu Jintao, participated in side meetings at the G8 summit.

China's approach to the G8, and to the reordering of the global economic architecture more broadly, is one that balances caution and confidence. The caution is a response to what Chinese leaders see as the basic ontology of world order that China is facing. Beijing's view is that it is dealing with a shifting structure of international power, but in which the United States continues to be the lone superpower. The current leadership sees China facing a world of "tremendous change and adjustment," in which "progress toward a multipolar world is irreversible, economic globalization is developing in depth," and both trends bring opportunities and conditions favourable to world peace and development (Hu Jintao 2007a). Nor has the current leadership reversed the verdict of the previous party leadership that "the old international political and economic order, which is unfair and irrational, has yet to be changed fundamentally" (Jiang Zemin 2002). It continues to hold that "hegemonism and power politics still exist." It adds that "imbalances in the world economy are worsening, the North–South gap is widening, and traditional and nontraditional threats to security are intertwined" (Hu Jintao 2007a).

All sides of the domestic Chinese debate also accept that the U.S. is still the world's sole superpower, and will continue to be for the foreseeable future. For example, Wang Jisi (2005), director of the Institute for International Strategy at the Central Party School and dean of the School of International Studies at Peking University, writes:

> Here is a Chinese view: in the long term, the decline of U.S. primacy and the subsequent transition to a multipolar world are inevitable; but in the short term, Washington's power is unlikely to decline, and its position in world affairs is unlikely to change … For a long time to come, the United States is likely to remain dominant, with sufficient hard power to back up aggressive diplomatic and military policies.

As a consequence of this basic *Realpolitik*, "in handling international affairs, [China] should observe and cope with all situations cool-headedly, adhere to the principle of mutual respect and seek common ground while shelving differences" (Jiang Zemin 2002). Such thinking also informs China's so-called "peace rise" doctrine (Zheng Bijian 2005).[3] This means that as China emerges as a great power, its continued development depends on world peace, a peace that it should seek to help reinforce. Zheng asserted that "China must not choose the road of aggression and expansion, which will ultimately fail." These thoughts were echoed by Premier Wen Jiabao during his 2004 visit to the U.S., when he stressed that China would develop peacefully, and in turn help to maintain a peaceful international environment. Beijing is aware that

> a pattern of cooperation and coordination among the world's major powers, institutionalized through the G8 ..., has taken shape, and no great change in this pattern is likely in the next five to ten years ... It would be foolhardy, however, for Beijing to challenge directly the international order and the institutions favoured by the Western world—and, indeed, such a challenge is unlikely (Wang Jisi 2005).

A Chinese read on the depth of the G8's "crisis" is reflected in the following from Wang Zaibang, vice-president of the China Institute for Contemporary International Relations (CICIR) and a respected strategist of China's international affairs:

> In recent years, the G8 summits have become a target of ridicule. Dialogue between the Group of 20 (G20) and the G8 can merely remedy defects in the coordination mechanism between world powers. It cannot solve the vital problems influencing the future and destiny of the G8 (Wang Zaibang 2006).

Wang (2006) adds:

> This demonstrates the profound inconsistencies between the new balance of power and the existing power structure and how difficult it is to redistribute power through peaceful means. These problems have gone beyond the Yalta System and the international relations established in the Cold War and set new demands. The handling of these problems will influence the world's stability, security and future.

China's leaders, however, are aware of China's growing systemic importance, and have drawn confidence from its increasing economic weight. They have likely also drawn confidence from their success in effectively managing and leveraging economic globalization for their country's developmental benefit (see Mittelman 2006; Chin forthcoming). This cautious confidence is reflected in a 2006 news article from China's national *People's Daily*, entitled, "China's Relations with the G8 Raise Body's Status":

> The G8 has been attracting criticism in recent years. On the one hand, the group is trying to have a bigger say in international affairs, with its agenda extending from exclusively economic matters to international politics and security. On the other hand, however, the G8, bringing together just eight countries, is not representative enough. As a result, its prestige has dropped.
>
> G8, in a bid to free itself from this plight, has started to strengthen its ties with the rest of the world. Promoting dialogue with the developing world marks one of the most salient features in the G8's switch to a new orientation ...
>
> In the course of accelerating economic globalization, a number of major developing nations have emerged as influential economies. Having dialogue with them has hence become an imperative for G8 in order to effectively address the issues of the world economy and development.

China's cautious attitude toward the G8 becomes even more apparent when contrasted to the lofty praise that Beijing gives to the United Nations, which it describes as having been "founded as a result of mankind's persistent efforts to seek peace and development" and which "embodies the lofty spirit of the world's people to 'save succeeding generations from the scourge of war'" and "carries the beautiful ideal of the international community to jointly promote economic and social development" (Hu Jintao 2005b). The importance the Chinese leadership attaches to the UN is explicitly noted in Hu Jintao's (2007a) *Report to the Seventh Party Congress*: "all countries should uphold the purposes and principles of the United Nations Charter, observe international law and universally recognized norms of international relations, and promote democracy, harmony, collaboration and win-win solutions in international relations." In his speech to the UN Summit in 2005, Hu (2005b) described the UN as playing "an irreplaceable role in international cooperation to ensure global security" and stressed that "such a role can only be strengthened and must not in any way be weakened." He pledged China's support to the "active and prudent reform of the UN," and emphasized the importance of "maintaining the authority of the UN, improving its efficacy and give better scope to its role so that it will be empowered to take on new threats and challenges." For Beijing, the UN is clearly a key intermediary variable in how it views and responds to the advances of the G8 and the latter's reform agenda.

Another important intermediating variable that conditions Beijing's approach to the G8, and a factor that predisposes the Chinese leadership to taking a cautious approach to G8 summitry, is the party's principle of collective leadership. One of the most important shifts in China's political system in the post-Mao period has been the reversal from "one-man leadership" back to collective leadership, allegedly as a corrective measure to the "mistakes" of the Mao era. Deng Xiaoping (1980) emphasized:

> Major issues must certainly be discussed and decided upon by the collective... In the process of taking decisions, it is essential to observe strictly the principle of majority rule and the principle of one-man-one-vote, a Party secretary being entitled to only to his single vote. That is, the first secretary must not take decisions by himself.

The procedural norm of collective decision making at the top of China's Communist Party leadership runs counter to what the G8 proponents see as the main strength of the informal diplomacy at the G8 summits: its effectiveness relative to the more broadly representational but procedurally cumbersome decision-making procedures of the UN. The need for Chinese leaders to consult with other senior party leaders on policy decisions of G8 magnitude further constrains China's engagement at G8 summits. There are political institutional and political-cultural gaps between the Chinese representatives and the existing club members in terms of the capacity or willingness to practise robust, on-the-spot, informal elite diplomacy.

Chinese analysts do acknowledge, however, that China's growing interaction with the international system already means that Beijing is bringing its force to bear on the existing structures of international governance, and Chinese officials now recognize more fully that integration also brings unsolicited international attention and growing scrutiny.[4] Pang Zhongying (2006b) stresses that China must give serious consideration to what role it should play in the world. Along a similar vein, Wang Zaibang (2004) strikes a more conciliatory note in ending his presentation to an European audience: "A successfully revived China will play a more important role in the reform of international institutions such as UN, IMF [International Monetary Fund] and World Bank, and have much more interest in keeping closer contact with G8 and NATO [North Atlantic Treaty Organization]." A more general commitment to international cooperation, downplaying differences, and responsible international stewardship appears to be emerging from Beijing. What is unclear, however, is how Beijing is sizing up the future prospects of the G8 versus the UN, at the apex of world governance.

China's Evolving View of the G8

Alongside the official behaviour and statements, the topics that elite foreign policy scholars in China discuss in less formal but public forums reveals another dimension of the Chinese positioning and debate on the issues considered in this chapter.[5] In these exchanges, which occur in academic and policy meetings on foreign policy making as well as in the pages of China's most influential international studies journals and academic presses, Chinese policy analysts have explored the issue of engagement with the G8, especially the pros and cons and the cost versus the benefit of joining.[6] While the exact link between the domestic Chinese academic debates and actual policy making is not always self-evident, it is tenable to suggest correlation, in which the former both reflects and informs the official positioning through a variety of channels and linkages. Within the academic discussion, there is a more comprehensive presentation of the range of strategic considerations that informs Beijing's evolving approach to the G8.

Before any examination of the evolution in Chinese views on the G8, it is useful to note that Beijing's positioning has been highly influenced, if not framed, by its understanding of the initial purpose of the G8. According to Yu Yongding (2005a, 194), director general of the Institute for World Economy and Politics at the Chinese Academy of Social Sciences (CASS), Chinese authorities see the G8 as a "forum—in a non-institutional sense—for leaders of like-minded countries or countries of common purpose and perceptions of the world order to get together to share their thoughts on problems concerning them, with an aim to achieve policy convergence and coordination on a voluntary basis."[7] It is a strong possibility that China's view of the G8 has also been conditioned by the G7's decision in 1989 to condemn and sanction China for the Tiananmen tragedy, after basically ignoring China for its first ten years. The basic understanding is that G7/8 is mainly a forum for managing the capitalist world economy, but that, in some instances, its reach exceeds economic issues and extends to political concerns.

China's attitude toward the G7/8 has gradually evolved. For the first ten years of the club's existence, the Chinese government largely watched the G7—without Russia yet as a member—from a distance, without being overly concerned about its activities. According to Yu Yongding (2005b, 9), it was seen as a "forum of the rich countries and not a global regime with legitimacy of enforcement that is recognized by the sovereign governments of the rest of the world." Beijing did not think it could influence the G7, and did not think the G7 could do anything to China either. Yu does add that

"China was not amused by the G7's lectures on China's domestic issues. However, China's reactions were largely conciliatory" (9). Moreover he emphasizes that, "China does not covet membership of the G7. As a developing country that is still in the process of transformation, China will and must continue to concentrate on its Herculean domestic problems" (9). While Hu Jintao's first handshake with the G8 at the 2003 Evian Summit is officially portrayed as a major breakthrough in Sino-G8 diplomacy, the basic sentiment that Beijing felt toward the G7 is reflected in the statement below:

> the Chinese government fully understands the importance of G7. China wants to develop its dialogue with the G7. China's leaders would like to utilize opportunities to meet with the heads of state of the G7 and establish friendly personal relationships with them. However, China sees no necessity to join in the G7 at this moment even if it were to be invited. China does not want to intrude into an exclusive club consisting of so-called like-minded people. ... China does not want to bear responsibility which it does not own (Yu Yongding 2005b, 10).

What is implied here is that the G8 needs China, whereas China does not need the G8.

Meet but Do Not Join

Very little was written on China and the G7/8 in the Chinese literature prior to Hu Jintao's handshake in Evian. One of the first pieces written was Yu Yongding's (2004) article "Rising China and the G7/G20," in which he describes how the G7/8 shifted from having little interest in China at the outset, and largely ignoring China for its first ten years, to then being intensely interested in China's role in world affairs. Subsequent writers, including Cao Lingjun (2003) of the Central Party School, followed this general line, emphasizing that the G7/8 membership reflected the structure of international power of the 1970s and the legacies of the Cold War: the G7/8 does not include developing countries and is thus unable to set priorities for the global community; it has limited capacity to broker solutions to pressing global problems; and it has only become interested in China because of its "staggering" global economic weight relative to that of its own members.

Cao (2003) argues that the end of the Cold War allowed the G8 to change its approach to China, and that there were four main reasons why the G8 became so interested in attracting China into the group. The chief reason is a desire to protect the G8 itself as an international institution and strengthen its capacity to meet global challenges; the other reasons are to enhance the legitimacy of the G8's efforts in "global administration," to protect the existing global distribution of wealth and structure of vested interests and to recognize China's new and growing international influence. In a short commentary, Zhang Jianjing (2006) similarly argues that the G8 wants China to be a part of the group so that it can "better legitimize itself, and so that it can be more effective in its policy coordination efforts on matters of relating to the stabilization of the international economy."

The consensus in the Chinese academic literature just prior to and immediately after Hu Jintao's discussions at the 2003 Evian Summit was that China should get closer to the G8 but definitely not join. The main reason was that if it joined, China would remove itself from the developing world and cease being a "socialist nation." The primary rationale was ideological. The idea of joining the G8 was seen as running counter to former leader Deng Xiaoping's view that China, as a socialist developing country, should never seek a leadership position in world affairs, especially not a hegemonic one; and even if it were to become wealthy, China should still self-identify with the developing world for political ideological reasons.

Cao (2006a) lists six reasons why it is not in China's short-term interest to join the G8. First, the G8 is not a democratic organization, and the G8 being a club of wealthy western countries conflicts with China's emphasis on "democracy" in the international system. Second, China must consider the costs to its independence that may result from joining the western system of international relations. Third, the G8 could render the United Nations hollow of its meaning and purpose (he cites such a trend since September 11), and a marginalized UN would have a major impact on China's global influence. Fourth, the renminbi is not yet fully convertible and G8 membership would likely come with the insistence that China accept greater currency coordination. This could "hit China hard, and too soon." Fifth, joining the G8 would affect China's status as a developing country, which is still a central policy position. Sixth, because the G8 "still looks at China through a Cold War lens," China should wait and let time erode such sentiments until there is a point when the G8 members accept that it is indeed a "democratic nation." For these reasons, Cao believes that would be "unrealistic" to see China joining the G8 in the short term.

Yu Yongding (2005b, 10) sums up the consensus in this initial period of hesitant engagement by suggesting that "China might finally join in the G7/8 and play a role that is proportional to its economic strength. However, that time has not yet come." The preference was for China to participate in "some mechanism that could help China to become familiar with the workings of the G7/8 and provide China's Ministers and Deputy Ministers with opportunities to acquaint themselves with their counterparts," and even more importantly, to learn more about the rules of the G8 game. The solution, for Yu, was the G20 finance ministers and central bank governors meetings, which he saw as a "timely gift for a Chinese government, which wishes to have closer cooperation with the G7/8 but does not want to be part of it for the time being" (12). Unlike its cautious attitude toward the G8, the Chinese government's attitude toward the G20 has been much more receptive, and Beijing even agreed to host the finance forum in 2005.

Consider Closer Engagement, Seek Leverage

A noticeable shift in the debate on China's positioning *vis-à-vis* the G8 appears to have taken place from 2005 onward, in which the exchange was no longer about whether to join the G8, but over the range of benefits from joining and why it is in China's national interests to participate more fully. The importance of this shift in the policy debate was drilled home by Gao Zugui (2006), deputy director of the CICIR's Institute of Security and Strategic Studies, who emphasized that while the G8's invitation to China to participate in a more substantial way is a good opportunity, "it's the engagement, stupid!" Gao argues that Chinese analysts should stop fixating on whether China is going to join tomorrow or some time in the future, and should instead focus on how such involvement can be turned into an opportunity for China to engage more actively in issues of major global concern and increase the opportunities for international coordination at the top of the system.

What changes occurred to catalyze this shift in the debate? There are several likely explanations: China's cumulative learning process from its participation in G20 meetings since 1999, its decision to host the 2005 G20 meeting, and the transition to a more accommodating position toward the G8.

Indeed, China's decision to chair the G20 marks a significant advance in China's involvement in the G8 process. In that year, the United Kingdom chaired the G7 finance meetings. The UK, as the chair of the 2005 G8 Gleneagles Summit, took a particularly active role in encouraging China to get more involved in the overall G8/G20 process. Beijing agreed to issue a joint statement with the UK (from the finance ministers of both countries) under the G7/G20 umbrella on 5 February 2005 in which the two countries publicly committed to "work together and address macroeconomic and structural vulnerabilities in the world economy" (HM Treasury 2005). Beijing also committed to "re-examining the strategic role of the IMF [International Monetary Fund] and the World Bank—in particular the importance of a more independent role for the IMF in the vital task of surveillance of the world economy." This collaborative policy exercise, between China's Ministry of Finance and the UK's Treasury, fed into setting the agenda for the spring meetings of the World Bank and IMF, the UN Millennium Review Summit in September, the G20 ministerial in October, and the Hong Kong ministerial of the World Trade Organization (WTO) in December of that same year. Beijing would have gained a clear sense of how it could influence the G7/8 mechanism from the inside, and how this would in turn to influence the process of setting the objectives, priorities, and agenda for the key meetings in the international power structure for managing the world economy, year by year.

In short, China gained a deeper experience of how its involvement in strategic partnerships inside the elite club could be used to manage the encounter with economic globalization. It is highly likely that, through taking such a leadership role in the G8/G20 process, China gained a better sense of how to both promote certain issues of concern to it (and to its developing country allies) and how to block certain G8 initiatives. The shifts in the academic debate likely followed this evolution in China's policy toward the G8/G20 and its actual engagement from that of hesitant limited engagement to deeper, comprehensive, multi-level engagement.

Pang Zhongying (2006a), professor of international studies at Renmin University China, draws attention to another shift in China's actual positioning with regard to the main institutions of global economic governance that China's leaders and international strategists would have also likely noticed. He argues that there has been an important change in the terms of engagement in China's relations with the major international economic organizations over most of the past two decades, which has emerged in the past few years. He notes that China had to request to rejoin the WTO, and it took more than 15 years of negotiations before it was finally admitted. However, "now, it is the G8 that is inviting China, and not China that is requesting entry." For Pang, the new dynamic "reflects a qualitative change in the perception of China's global position among the world's leading nations. This is a great opportunity for China to further solidify its position and voice in the global economy."

In this new phase, there are still voices that continued to stress that the G8 is a club of the rich countries that works behind the scenes to influence global politics and economics. For example, Ding Lei (2007), professor in the Zhou Enlai School of Government at Nankai University, argues that for all "its ideological flavour and big country thinking," the G8 has sought out China because it is "difficult to accept that the world's factory is not a member of this club, and that without China as a member, the legitimacy of the G8 along with its legal standing, representativeness, and effectiveness will be called into question." Ding adds that the G8 has no choice now but to deal with the "China factor" when it tries to coordinate any "grand policies" in the realms of international economics, politics, or security because of China's growing market and economic power. Nonetheless, the new debate that emerged after 2005 is about how best to leverage China's strengths and relations to protect and promote its interests—and those of the developing world—within an expanded G8 mechanism.

Realist scholars of international relations talk in terms of benefit for China, and why it is in China's national interests to participate more fully. There is an evolution in Cao's thinking as he begins to argue that—over the longer term—it is "indispensable" for China to join the G8. Cao (2003) earlier argued that it was unrealistic for China to join the G8 in the short term. However, he later provided the details behind his distinction between short- and longer-term calculations and scenarios (Cao Lingjun 2006b). He offered four reasons why it would be realistic for China to join the G8 in the longer run. First, it would allow China to build a "new important diplomatic platform." Second, it would enable China to attract more foreign investment and loans. Third, China would be able to "affect the G8's decisions from inside the G8." And fourth, more coordinated involvement in the G8 concurs with China's strategic considerations in managing "great power politics." These points reflect Beijing's growing confidence in its ability to influence the agenda of even this elite grouping, as well as multilateral forums, from the inside. Cao furthers added that if China maintains its distance from the G8, the G8 may attempt to contain China in the future. His advice was for China to begin by seeking official observer status in the G8, and continue attending the side meetings at the G8 summits, and "wait for a suitable opportunity to join the G8."

In a number of articles published immediately prior to 2007 G8 Heiligendamm Summit, Chinese scholars saw China joining the G8 as a greater certainty. Ding Lei (2007), for example, saw China joining as "simply a matter of time, especially given that by the end of 2005 China was already the world's fourth largest economy, surpassing both France and Britain, which are both G8 members. Ding also saw joining the elite grouping as helping

China to achieve its developmental objectives. Most importantly, he believed that "China's future development will not progress smoothly without continuing coordination with the other G8 members. Thus China also needs the support of the G8; and it would be easier for China to secure such support if it were a member as it would increase the level of understanding between the various parties, and allow them to deal with conflicts through personal senior-level dialogue. Similar to Cao, Ding also wrote that China's entry into the G8 would allow "it to influence the G8's policies from the inside, as well as enable China to receive economic benefit for its development such as increased inflows of foreign investment and loans." According to him, China's entrance to the G8 will have its costs, as did its entrance into the WTO, but, over the long term, the benefits will be significant.

The start of actual efforts by Chinese leaders to more openly influence the G8's agenda can be seen in Hu Jintao's speech in Heiligendamm, when he implicitly placed the onus on the United States and the European Union to undertake structural adjustments to help alleviate global macroeconomic imbalances. He highlighted the importance, as Beijing sees it, of international financial controls:

> An unbalanced world economy and an increase of unstable elements in international financial markets will increase risks in the world economy. The international community should share responsibilities, and actively promote a systematic adjustment of the unbalanced world economy through strategies such as stimulating domestic demand, lowering financial debt, accelerating structural adjustment, and deepening systems reform; strengthening the supervision of international financial markets, particularly over short term capital flows, and maintaining a stable exchange rate for major reserve currencies; supporting the multilateral trade regime, oppose protectionism, promote the Doha Round of trade talks to achieve complete and balanced results soon, and accomplish the goals of development (Hu Jintao 2007b).

As early as 2004, He Fan (2004), a CASS researcher, had written that China's leaders should "go beyond always raising issues of direct concern for China's domestic circumstances" and instead improve its "opportunities" to raise issues of global concern for discussion, including key issues such as how to reform the international financial regime, how to improve capital flows, and how to reform IMF lending practices and especially the issue of conditionality. With this shift in its priorities in the discussions, China would become a leader for international reform for all developing countries.

His line of argumentation draws attention to a broader set of foreign policy motivations—beyond great power *Realpolitik*—that continue to fuel China's desire to maintain its self-image and project a national image as a leader of the developing world. The advice is to link China's role in the discussions with the G8 to representing the interests of the developing world. He's ideas represent the beginning of the most recent line of thought that emphasizes that China must engage the G8 more closely, but that it must not go it alone in the process and must band together with its developing country allies.

China's Complex Interests and Multiple Identity

Beijing has been reconsidering its international identity and image as it goes about searching for "space" for its rise in the world. It is groping its way through a complex process of sorting through its multiple and sometimes competing international interests and identities, in which it projects a certain international image tailored for a particular situation, receives feedback from the receiver, and then responds by either maintaining its position or modifying its foreign policy identity and image (see Hongying Wang 2003). China is not alone as an emerging power, as it tiptoes its way through a maze of continuity and change and reformulates its foreign policy and international image. India is in a similar position as a result of its growing economy, nuclear arms capability, and diplomatic ambitions, but it also differs from China due its lack of formal great power status as a member of the UN Security Council (UNSC) (Cooper and Fues 2008). Brazil is also grappling with issues of its place and positioning as an international power and aspires to play a leading role in its region and the developing world more broadly (see Chapter 6); it has also been making forays into Africa as an aid donor.[8] Indeed, Brazil, India, and China are all trying to reconcile their identity as members of the global South and the developing world with their emerging power status—or *de facto* great power status, in the Chinese case. What is unique in the Chinese case is that Beijing's recasting of China's international image and foreign policy identity entails the reformulation of official state ideology, namely China's reworking of its sense of purpose as a "socialist nation."

Since coming to power in 2003, China's current "Fourth Generation" leadership has placed strong emphasis on fostering solidarity within the developing world, including closer ties and greater policy coordination and coherence among the most influential developing countries. Starting with

Brazil in 2004, Hu announced that China would always stay on the side of the developing countries, and the following year he met with the leaders Brazil, India, Mexico, and South Africa on the margins of the G8 Gleneagles Summit to discuss and outline, for the first time, what amounted to the beginnings of an O5 collective vision, in which he pledged that China would help build a partnership of the leading developing countries, so that they could coordinate their efforts in engaging the international community.[9]

At the meeting of the O5 at Gleneagles on the morning of 7 July 2005, Hu stated that "we should strengthen our coordination and collaboration to push for great progress on the issue of development, narrow down the North-South gap and achieve common development" (Ministry of Foreign Affairs of the People's Republic of China 2005). He then outlined the following suggestions for the group:

first, to unite and cooperate to safeguard the common interest of developing nations, take consistent actions to strengthen the participation and decision-making rights of developing nations in international affairs, and drive economic globalization toward a balanced and win-win direction of universal benefits; second, to seek common ground while putting aside differences and properly handle the differences … ; third, to widen our ways of thinking and deepen South-South co-operation … ; fourth, to improve the occasion to actively promote South-North dialogue … (Ministry of Foreign Affairs 2005)

Hu also expressed strong support for the New Partnership for Africa's Development (NEPAD), and Brazilian president Luiz Inácio Lula da Silva's initiative to eliminate poverty and hunger (see Hu Jintao 2005a). He advocated for resolving the resurgence of trade protectionism by the developed countries and called for carrying out effective and pragmatic cooperation in handling global climate change based on the principle of "common but differentiated responsibilities." Equally important, following these talks, China—along with the other five states—adopted a "common declaration" that emphasized that developing countries should deal with the challenge of globalization by strengthening South–South cooperation and safeguard the common interests of developing nations by focusing on priority areas and international participation strategy.

In the Report to the 17th Party Congress, Hu Jintao (2007a) reaffirmed Beijing's line on southern cooperation:

While securing our own development, we will accommodate the legitimate concerns of other countries, especially other developing countries. We will increase market access in accordance with internationally recognized economic and trade rules, and protect the rights and interests of our partners in accordance with the law. We support international efforts to help developing countries enhance their capacity for independent development and improve the lives of their people, so as to narrow the North–South gap. We support efforts to improve international trade and financial systems, advance the liberalization and facilitation of trade and investment, and properly resolve economic and trade frictions through consultation and collaboration. China will never seek benefits for itself at the expense of other countries or shift its troubles onto others.

He added:

For other developing countries, we will continue to increase solidarity and cooperation with them, cement traditional friendship, expand practical cooperation, provide assistance to them within our ability, and uphold the legitimate demands and common interests of developing countries. We will continue to take an active part in multilateral affairs, assume our due international obligations, play a constructive role, and work to make the international order fairer and more equitable.

Such South–South policy, based on the continuation of clear North–South distinctions, has translated into China's actual policy positioning at the G8. Hu Jintao appeared to continue to advance an O5 collective vision in his speech at the Heiligendamm Summit in 2007. He stressed that reform of the international economic system should adequately reflect changes in the world economic structure and increase the voice and representation of the developing countries (Hu Jintao 2007b). While giving priority to global macroeconomic management issues in the speech, he emphasized the importance of the G8 and the O5 working together to promote the balanced and stable development of the world economy, and wove a developing country perspective into the narrative by using the issue of strengthening international development collaboration as the focus for framing Beijing's suggestions for the G8-O5 dialogue process.

In his G8 speech, Hu identified global cooperation on international development as Beijing's second area of concern in engaging with the G8, and sustainable development as third issue. He emphasized the importance of a common future and the basic objectives and requirements of developing countries. Hu then dedicated more than two thirds of his speech to climate change, driving home the collective vision that China had worked out with its key developing country partners, India and Brazil.[10] Hu's points on climate change had been worked out in advance through a substantial amount of consultation with China's major partners and discussed with the other developing countries at the G8 meeting.

Most Chinese analysts who have written on the topic of China and the G8 since 2006 support China taking a cautious, collective, and incremental approach to joining the club of great powers, but taking a similar tack to its accession to the WTO, where it maintains its developing country status. Pang Zhongying (2006a) argues that it is important to recognize that China is still a developing country and, in reality, not yet be a part of the wealthy club that is the G8. He suggests that China should consciously maintain multiple images with regard to the G8. He believes that Chinese authorities recognize that entering the G8 will neither automatically help strengthen the solidarity among developing countries nor automatically enhance their coordination on matters of mutual interest. The most effective policy for China, according to Pang, is to continue to unite with other significant developing countries (that is, India, Brazil, Mexico, and South Africa) to enhance and strengthen these relationships while simultaneously improving their coordination with the G8 members. And he warns that China should not feel compelled to quickly heed the invitation for entrance to the G8 at this stage.

He Fan (2004) also believes that China's voice would be too weak if it joins the G8 alone. He warns that one of the reasons the G8 wants China to join is to gain leverage over China on issues that are of great concern for G8 members but have yet to be resolved through other channels, for example, in their efforts to convince China to revalue its currency. He sees entry into the G8 as bringing pressure onto China from the G8, on key areas of its foreign and domestic economic policy, and sees the G20 as a useful mediating organization between China and the G8 for countering policy pressure. He supports Yu Yongding's idea that closer coordination between the G20 finance agenda and the G8 discussions is a useful mechanism for bringing developing country issues to the G8 table, and further suggests that preparations for such dialogue among the developing countries would strengthen the level of coordination between developing country partners. He argues for a more narrow band of outreach partners than the O5, stating that it would be a positive development for China if a "G7+3" (China, India, and Brazil) mechanism is formally established.[11]

He Fan notes that the needs of the less developed members of the G20 do not always coincide with the larger developing nations. The justification for China allying with a more narrow band of the O5 is rooted here in an instrumental national economic interest rationale: to ally only with those major emerging economies that have the diplomatic clout and economic weight and national fortitude—a Chinese reading of the actual international capacity of the other so-called emerging powers—to partner with China in mediating pressure from the G8 members. In short, He sees Mexico and South Africa as either incapable or unwilling to seriously play such a mediating or risk-mitigating role, essentially as not being in the same diplomatic league as China, India, and Brazil.

The distinction drawn here highlights the differences in developmental priorities that exist even between the more powerful and less powerful members of the O5, as well as the differing priorities of the most advanced members of the G20 versus those of the less developed members in this group. The policy implication is for China, India, and Brazil, but not necessarily Mexico and South Africa, to join the G8. The complexities and tensions in this process of international interest and partnership recalibration and image rebuilding can be seen in more detail in China's participation in the Heiligendamm Process (see Chapter 1).

The Heiligendamm Process

Beijing's agreement to participate in the HP represents another major step in its partial but growing accommodation of the G8. A leading official in the "Heiligendamm Dialogue Process Support Unit" (housed in the Organisation for Economic Co-operation and Development [OECD] in Paris) notes that Beijing has sent "credible and qualified participants" to the HP meetings so far, and that it has "no complaints about the Chinese representatives that have been attending the meetings."[12] Closer analysis of China's approach in specific dialogue areas of the HP reveals, however, a pattern of behaviour that is better described as partial accommodation and hedging.

With respect to the sessions on donor coordination on development assistance to Africa, an issue area in which the G8 has shown particular interest in tackling since Gleneagles in 2005, a German diplomat in Beijing has noted that Chinese representatives have not been pushing this item on the HP agenda and do not seem to show "much ownership." This implies that Beijing has been largely going through the motions in this dialogue area in the HP. Broader sector analysis on China's positioning on donor coordination of foreign aid reveals that Beijing appears to place more stock in its newly formed bilateral dialogues with the other great powers rather than the HP. This means the new U.S.-China strategic dialogue on Africa, the new China-EU strategic dialogue on cooperation in Africa, and the other new bilateral dialogues that China has entered to address assistance to Africa (including France).

In terms of global institutions for common dialogue on African development, Beijing prefers to work through the UN system and, more recently, the World Bank rather than through the HP. With the support of the United Nations Development Programme (UNDP), China has taken the lead in initiating the China-Africa Business Forum and the China-Africa Business Council. And Beijing is now studying the results of its decision to deliver aid (on infrastructure projects) to Palestine through the UNDP as a pilot to determine whether it can adopt a similar approach for countries in Africa. China is now also involved in a number of policy advisory initiatives for Africa supported by the UN and other donors.

A China-Africa World Bank Trust Fund was established in 2007, managed by the World Bank, that aims to improve China's aid statistics, facilitate the reform of China's aid architecture, and support outreach to African policy makers and Chinese aid recipients on development effectiveness. Also in 2007, the World Bank signed a memorandum of understanding with China EXIM Bank, which has become a major lender to Africa, for training on environmental issues and co-financing projects. The World Bank has a number of policy research papers in the works on China-Africa issues including "Lessons from China for Africa" on China-Africa infrastructure projects (Dollar 2008) and a joint report between the World Bank and Tsinghua University on China's aid architecture. Furthermore, the World Bank Institute is working with the China Development Bank to provide training on micro-finance in Africa, and China's Ministry of Foreign Affairs to share experiences in assisting Africa. China's comfort level in working with the World Bank, as donors, is growing.[13] The HP is clearly only one track, and apparently not the preferred track, that China is following to pursue its aid policy for Africa. While China has not been obstructionist within the HP, it cannot be said to be taking a highly active role in promoting greater donor coordination between emerging and traditional donors through the HP mechanism.

Another area in which the G8 is particularly interested in advancing through the HP is climate change. A month before the 2007 Heiligendamm Summit, China, India, and Brazil banded together at the week-long session of the Intergovernmental Panel on Climate Change (IPCC) to pressure developed countries to "accept main responsibility for global warming" (Angleys 2007). Some international observers suspected that this was part of a long-term negotiating strategy by the world's three most influential developing countries to set the stage for the major international political events that followed later that year, first the G8 summit in June and then the UN climate change conference in Bali in December. At their meetings on the sidelines of the G8 summit, China and India "vowed" to strengthen their partnership to combat climate change, and together the two countries rejected the climate change deal reached among the G8 powers (Le Tian 2007; Spencer and Foster 2007).

China and India have both been adamant that they cannot take steps to control climate change that would retard their economic growth, or undermine their need to tackle their efforts to reduce domestic poverty, they have requested major technological and other support from the advanced industrialized countries of the West. Indian foreign secretary Shiv Shankar Menon explains:

> I think what is important is that the burden of the incremental costs of doing additional steps must be shared fairly and the principle of that is well known, it's agreed. The fact is, historical responsibilities, even in terms of present emission levels—it's quite clear who's responsible for this. Once our per capita emission levels reach the same as those of the industrialized countries, we'll be very happy to do our share too (cited in Majumder 2007).

When asked about how China would respond to pressure from the G7 and the German G8 presidency in 2007 to accept emissions caps, Ma Kai, the chair of China's powerful National Development Reform Commission, stated that Beijing's position remains that it will not accept any mandatory limits on emissions and that the developed world must take the lead in cutting pollution. Echoing his Indian counterpart, Ma added: "The consequences of restricting the development of developing nations will be much more serious than the consequences of global warming" (cited in Ingham 2007).

Having worked out their collective position prior to the Heiligendamm Summit in consultation with India and Brazil, Hu Jintao used his speech as a platform from which to voice Beijing's position, and that of its closest O5 partners, on climate change. Hu (2007b) stressed the importance of the problem but then flagged differences with the G8 on which countries should take greatest responsibility for shouldering the burden in addressing the problem, and which international institution would be the appropriate forum for addressing the problem:

> Climate change is an environmental problem, but at its root it is s developmental problem ... We have to follow the common but different responsibilities principle established by the United Nations Framework on Climate Change (UNFCCC) agreement. This principle not only reflects different

countries' economic development levels, historical responsibilities, current per capita emission level differences, but also serves as the foundation to maintain and develop future international collaboration.

Based on this principle, developed countries should meet the emission goals set by the Kyoto Protocol, provide assistance to developing countries, and continue to take responsibility for lower emissions by 2012. Recently the European Union agreed to reduce greenhouse gas emissions by 20% by 2020. We welcome this decision, and at the same time hope other developed countries can make similar promises.

Rather than accommodating the wishes of the German G8 presidency to advance a climate change agenda through the G8 process, China banded together with India and Brazil on the sidelines of the G8 to play the role of blocker (Spencer and Foster 2007). At his bilateral meeting with India on the margins of the summit, Hu Jintao declared that "Sino-Indian relations are on the fast track" and "that China hopes both sides can step up talks on the border issue in the spirit of peace and friendship, equal consultation as well as mutual respect and understanding to seek a mutually acceptable solution at the earliest" (cited in Le Tian 2007). Indian national security advisor M.K. Narayanan called China the "greatest neighbour," and stressed that India wanted the "strongest relationship" with Beijing and would do "everything possible' to cement ties.

For the HP, the fact that China, India, and Brazil agreed on a defensive agenda to block the G8's climate change proposal is not necessarily a negative outcome, if the main objective of the HP, over its time frame from 2007 to 2009, is to build a process of dialogue and exchange that fosters trust and confidence among the partners, rather than to pursue any particular negotiated outcome on any particular issues. The fact that the "Big Three" among the O5 were able to work out a common position on a specific issue and advance it within the process means that nascent forms of a collective identity exist, at least among certain groupings within the five countries. It means that new consultation networks are forming, through which the O5 members—or some of them—meet, discuss, establish priorities, set agendas, and reach consensus. This actually provides the basis for sustained and robust dialogue between the G8 and the O5, and possibly, eventually, for negotiations over G8 expansion.

There are, however, some fundamental differences in national interests among the O5 members, on all HP issue areas, that may ultimately constrain the formation of any collective identity. For example, with regard to climate change and environmental protection, India and China are both major consumers of imported natural resources and major carbon emitters, while Brazil is one of the world's largest sources of natural resources and the guardian of the Amazon rainforest—the "lungs of the world." These differences highlight the fact that it has so far been Brazil's willingness to sacrifice a degree of its national interests on environmental protection that has enabled the new coalition of "G3 emerging powers" to emerge on the climate change issue, and that there may be limits to how far these three countries will continue to ally as blockers on climate change within the G8-O5, as well as inside the HP discussions.

Conclusion

China has clearly been engaging with the G8 from a position of cautious confidence and quiet patience. Its basic approach is in response to the ontology of world order that it believes it is facing: in short, an international system undergoing a fundamental shift to a multipolar world, but in which the United States remains the dominant power and willing to use its capability to project its force. This means that it would be "foolhardy," to quote Wang Jisi (2005), for Beijing to challenge the pattern of coordination among the world's major powers, institutionalized through the G8—especially in the "near future." As Chinese authorities have developed a better understanding of the inner workings of the G8 and the G20 and have gained more confidence in engaging with the G8, Beijing has not only avoided resisting the institutionalized structure of international power but, as Wang Zaibang (2004) notes, has even shown increasing interest in "keeping closer contact with the G8." This shift and the rationale for the policy shift are reflected in the evolving debates in the Chinese academic literature. China has moved from a position of hesitation to one that is closer and more engaged, from a mindset of "meet, but don't join" to "it's the engagement, stupid!," and a desire to secure its interests through that involvement. Such a shift is underpinned by growing confidence in Beijing's abilities, but also by Beijing's perception of important changes in how the world's advanced industrialized countries see China.

Beijing is not, however, in any rush to resolve the G8's dual crisis. It is gradually building alliances and consulting with strategic partners before making decisions. Chinese leaders seem willing to accept a more structured dialogue at this point, rather than focusing on the formalities of accession, and may indeed prefer a slower approach of incremental engagement. Beijing is leveraging China's economic strength together with a nuanced mix of diplomatic skill and timely diplomatic interventions at the bilateral, regional multilateral, and global levels. It is moving incrementally to secure China's interests and its desired peaceful rise and, where possible, to foster arrangements that are collective gains for other developing countries in so doing.

This chapter has examined how China is grappling with its changing international profile, presence (conscious or otherwise), and weight in the world. In engaging with the G8, China—not unlike the other O5 members— exhibits elements of individual personality as well as emerging forms of collective behaviour. China's foreign policy identity continues to be shaped, in some significant ways, by its positioning and ideological solidarity with the developing world, even as it pursues more individual national interests as a *de facto* great power. Despite becoming the world's factory and now possessing forms of international power—both economic and political—that even many G8 members cannot claim, Beijing still has devoted attention and resources to maintaining and even expanding its actual linkages to the global South and to maintaining its self-proclaimed status as a developing country. This harkens to a reworking of the old Maoist Three Worlds Theory for the current international environment and China's contemporary needs.

This chapter has also started to map the type of reconfigured G8 that one leading emerging power, arguably the one great power not currently in the G8, would want to see. What does the preceding discussion indicate about what to expect from China if its current engagement with the G8 evolves along the current course, and if the HP leads the G8 to get more serious about expanding its current outreach, leading to discussion of creating a G11 or a G13? First, would China be willing to participate? Over the past four years, China has appeared increasingly willing to engage, and could possibly agree to join an enlarged G11 or G13, under the right conditions. This likely means Beijing championing the cause together with India and Brazil. It means the enlarged group would agree to work toward stabilizing the world economy through measures that are perceived by the "G3"—China, India, and Brazil—as being in the direction of a fair global economic system. It also likely means a G11 or G13 more attentive to concrete arrangements for cooperation on energy security and demographics, as well as to Bretton Woods reform. Another example is that China would likely be willing to discuss global climate change in an enlarged G8 if it is in the context of energy security and cooperation (coordinated supply and demand), as Chinese authorities have been doing with their regional neighbours at the annual East Asia Summit since 2005 and the Boao Forum for Asia.

Andrew F. Cooper and Kelly Jackson (2007) have noted that the G8 outreach process relies partially on how the G8 enlargement initiative fits into other complex negotiation processes through the UN and the WTO, as well as the IMF and World Bank. For China would be very hesitant to strengthen the G8 if it means weakening the UN, especially the role of the Security Council. There is also one other probable political condition not to be overlooked: basic acceptance from the G7/8 members of China's political characteristics. This requirement can be extrapolated from Hu Jintao's (2007b) emphasis on the need of the G7/8 to "negotiate democratically to appropriately resolve differences and conflicts" and his declaration that

> there is not a unitary model of development. The international community should respect the rights of individual countries to autonomously choose forms of social organization and development paths, and put forth effort to help developing countries to strengthen their own ability to develop.

It is clear that Chinese authorities would be highly attuned to attempts of the G7/8 to socialize China politically. But Chinese leaders may be somewhat less concerned with this issue for now, considering the meek response of G7 leaders to Russia's resistance to their criticisms of the troubling path that the Russian political system seems to be on.

Beijing is becoming more sensitive about being perceived as a blocker at the global elite forum. Such perception does not support its efforts to ensure its peaceful rise or its desire to be seen as promoting peaceful and harmonious world development. In this context, the response by a Chinese foreign ministry spokesperson to the suggestion that China would use its growing economic muscle to block initiatives at the Heiligendamm Summit is telling:

> I don't think China will be Mr. No at the G8. We want to be Mr. Cooperation or Mr. Partnership. As far as China is concerned, we are a developing country and will be for a fairly long time to come. But we hope in the future our cooperation with the G8 can be institutionalized and regular (cited in Ingham 2007).

In short, the fact that there have been significant shifts in Beijing's positioning toward the G8 opens up the possibility for further shifts, although such an outcome is by no means certain. Much also depends on how the G8 members approach China, both individually and as a club.

Future Research Agenda

First, the Chinese views and actual developments in the HP outlined above hint at tensions and cracks within the O5 and factors that limit the prospects of the G8's current outreach strategy of reaching out to the O5. The O5 concept may not be sustainable over time, and a more realistic approach may be to reach out to an "O3." Chinese officials may not speak openly about these internal tensions within the O5; however, it is likely that Mexico and South Africa will need to provide more reason than currently exists for China, and for India and Brazil, to support their continued involvement in the G8 outreach process.

China's leaders appear to be articulating a new collective vision both within their engagement with the G8 and beyond. Beijing has put considerable diplomatic effort into promoting new collective interests with China's main developing country partners. This nascent collective vision is most advanced in the defensive positioning of China, India, and Brazil on the climate change discussions, and it would be worth further examination whether a more constructive collective vision is also starting to come through on the broader range of issues in the O5 discussions that took place prior to the Heiligendamm Summit. China, for example, seems to see the G8 as most useful for dialoguing on energy cooperation, demographic issues, and Bretton Woods reform. It would be useful to analyze whether, and to what degree, China is willing to champion developing country concerns in its engagement with the G7/8 that conflict with its own economic interests.

Second, starting in early 2007, and after the gains made by the developing countries at the Bali climate change conference at the end of that year, China has made some accommodating gestures on global climate change (although only to a point). In early 2007, Hu Jintao had already begun to offer public reassurances that China will be a responsible country and will support international efforts to tackle climate change. Beijing has indeed shown greater willingness to address concrete measures since Bali. It will be useful to examine whether, and to what degree, Beijing is willing to address global climate change issues inside the G8-O5 mechanism at the 2008 Hokkaido Toyako Summit in Japan, and whether it shifts from being a blocker on the G8's climate change agenda.

Third, it is also important to note that, even while China is participating in the HP, it is at the same time pursuing a series of regional initiatives in Asia and in other regions throughout the global South (Ministry of Foreign Affairs 2008). China has backed up its South–South cooperation rhetoric with concrete steps to foster bilateral alliances and regional activities across the developing world. China has joined the Organization of American States (OAS) as an observer; it is an observer at the Inter-American Development Bank (IADB); and it signed an agreement on closer relations with the Andean Development Corporation (CAF) (Comunidad Andina 2008). In Africa, it is providing major support to the African Development Bank (AfDB) and to the African Union (AU). In Asia, China has joined ASEAN as a dialogue partner, plays a growing role in the ASEAN Regional Forum, established a regional free trade agreement with ASEAN (Chin and Stubbs 2008), and, as already mentioned, is deeply involved in the East Asian Summit and the Boao Forum for Asia. China created an Asian cooperation fund to help Chinese government agencies increase their cooperation with ASEAN countries, and Asian diplomats note that China has initiated far more joint projects with the ASEAN members than either Japan or the United States (Kurlantzick 2007, 51). Since 2005 China has increased its support of another set of Asian regional initiatives that have received less international attention, specifically the meetings of Bangladesh, China, India, and Myanmar (BCIM) and trilateral meetings of India, China, and Russia. These regional initiatives are anchored on India–China relations, with increasing interest from Russia, and while they started at the non-governmental level, since 2006, these annual meetings have been capped by senior meetings of their foreign ministers.[14]

China is also exploring new regional ground on the security front, for example, with the Shanghai Cooperation Organisation (SCO). It is, however, careful to emphasize the SCO is not Asia's version of the North Atlantic Treaty Organization (NATO), and not to overplay its role as the representative of the Asian region in its discussions with the G8, most likely because Japan is already a G8 member and China also has to be careful to avoid patronizing its ASEAN dialogue partners or South Asian allies by speaking on their behalf unless it has their clear consent to do so. How likely is China to take major steps to resolve the global versus regional question or privilege the global track over the regional track? Or does it see the situation in terms of either/or and will likely continue pursuing a different global strategy that is heavily regionally based?

Notes

1 The author thanks the participants of the workshops organized by the Centre for International Governance Innovation on "Re-Evaluating the B(R)ICSAM Concept: From Structure to Agency" (Royal Roads University, Victoria, Canada, August 2007) and "Beyond the B(R)ICSAM" (Cancun, Mexico, March 2008) for their comments,

especially Andrew F. Cooper, Timothy M. Shaw, Agata Antkiewicz, and Alan Alexandroff. Thanks also to Hongying Wang, Paul Evans, and Yuen Pau Woo for their comments, as well as Julia Bentley and Douglas Heath of Canada's Department of Foreign Affairs and International Trade, Karim Morcos and Kent Smith of the Canadian International Development Agency, and Christopher Swarat for their research support. Translations are by Christopher Swarat and Gregory Chin unless otherwise indicated.

2   There is a growing literature on the global impact of "emerging powers," "would-be great powers," Brazil, Russia, India, and China as the BRICs or, with South Africa and Mexico, the B(R)ICSAM" (see Hook 2001; Wilson and Purushothaman 2003; Hurrell 2006; Shaw et al. 2007; Cooper et al. 2006; Kaplinsky and Messner 2008; Subacchi 2008).

3   The term "peaceful rise" was first used by Zheng Bijian in public at the Boao Forum for Asia in late 2003, when he was vice-president of the Central Party School. Chinese premier Wen Jiabao then picked up the term at a meeting with the leaders of the Association of South East Asian Nations (ASEAN) and during a visit to the U.S. in 2004.

4   Interview with officials from China's Ministry of Foreign Affairs and Ministry of Commerce on the international reaction to China's growing role as a foreign aid donor, Beijing, April 2007. Discussions with foreign diplomats posted in Beijing, April, October 2007.

5   The term "elite foreign policy scholars" refers to the group of scholars affiliated with a short list of prominent party- and government-sponsored research institutes, think tanks, and universities within China that are involved with analyzing the country's foreign relations. This list includes the Institute for International Strategy in the Central Party School, the Research Office of the Central Committee of the Chinese Communist Party, the Institute of World Economy and Politics in the Chinese Academy of Social Sciences (CASS), the China Institute of International Studies under the Ministry of Foreign Affairs, the China Institute for Contemporary International Relations (CICIR), the Shanghai Institute of International Relations, and Peking University's Institute of International Relations. Allen Carlson (2004, 10) has referred to a similar grouping, minus the Chinese Communist Party think tanks, as the "foreign policy elite" in China.

6   It is interesting to note that the amount of attention given to the G8 in Chinese publications has been much less than the vast amount attention given to China and the World Trade Organization (WTO).

7   Yu Yongding is one of China's leading authorities on international monetary issues, and an influential observer of China's participation in the G20 finance ministers and central bank governors meetings. His work draws on the writings of his colleague Wang Yizhou (2003), who has explored the gradual convergence and mutual accommodation theory of China's engagement with the major international organizations.

8   The Brazilian Agency of Cooperation (Agência Brasileira de Cooperación [ABC] reports spending US$120 million around the world in 2007 on HIV/AIDS relief programs, vocational training, agricultural development, and ex-combatant rehabilitation.

ABC's biggest beneficiary is neighbouring Paraguay, followed by East Timor, Haiti, and the lusophone African states Mozambique, Angola, and Guinea-Bissau. See the ABC website at <www.abc.gov.br>.

9 The details of this O5 "common declaration" are reported by the Ministry of Foreign Affairs of the People's Republic of China (2005). See also Hu Jintao (2005a).

10 It was only in the final third of this speech that Hu referred to China's own situation to drive home the point of China's specific efforts in environmental management.

11 It is not clear where Russia fits into He's G7+3 formula.

12 Discussion with senior official in the Heiligendamm Dialogue Process Support Unit, Cancún, March 2008.

13 That Beijing's increased collaboration with the World Bank happens at the same time as a Chinese national, Justin Yifu Lin, has been appointed as chief economist and executive vice-president is likely not coincidental.

14 The author thanks M. Manoranjan Mohanty at the Developing Countries Research Centre of the University of Delhi for highlighting these cases.

References

Angleys, Emmanuel (2007). "China, India, Brazil Hold Up Climate Change Talks." *Terra Daily*, 2 May. <www.terradaily.com/reports/China_India_Brazil_Hold_Up_Climate_Change_Talks_999.html> (May 2008).

Cao Lingjun (2003). "Guanyu Zhongguo jujue jiaru Baguojituan de sikao." ["Thoughts on China's Refusal to Join the G8."] *Shantou Daxue Xuebao (renwen shehuikexue ban) [Journal of Shantou University, Humanities Edition]* (3): 10–16.

Cao Lingjun (2006a). "Cong yaoyuan zou xiang weilai—Baguo Jituan yu Zhongguo guanxi jiedu." ["Moving Toward the Future from a Great Distance: Interpreting Sino-G8 Relations."] *Zhenggong Yanjiu Dongtai [Trends in Governance Research]* (16).

Cao Lingjun (2006b). "Lun Zhongguo jiaru Baguojituan." ["Thoughts on China Joining the G8."] *Henan Gongye Daxue Xuebao [Henan Industry University Journal, Social Sciences Edition]* (3).

Carlson, Allen (2004). "Helping to Keep the Peace (Albeit Reluctantly): China's Recent Stance on Sovereignty and Multilateral Intervention." *Pacific Affairs* 77(1): 9–28.

Chin, Gregory T. and Richard Stubbs (2008). "ASEAN-China Free Trade Agreement and East Asian Regionalism." Paper presented at the International Studies Association convention, 26 March. San Francisco. <www.allacademic.com/meta/p250870_index.html> (May 2008).

Chin, Gregory T. (forthcoming). *China's Automotive Modernization: The Competition State and Rival Firms*. New York: Palgrave Macmillan.

Comunidad Andina (2008). "Common Foreign Policy: Asia." <www.comunidad andina.org/ingles/Exterior/asia.htm> (May 2008).

Cooper, Andrew F., Agata Antkiewicz, and Timothy M. Shaw (2006). "Economic Size Trumps All Else? Lessons from BRICSAM." *International Studies Quarterly* 9(4): 673–689.

Cooper, Andrew F. (2007). "The Logic of the B(R)ICSAM Model for G8 Reform." CIGI Policy Brief No. 1. Waterloo ON: Centre for International Governance Innovation. <www.cigionline.org : Publications : Policy Briefs> (May 2008).

Cooper, Andrew F. and Kelly Jackson (2007). "Controversy over 'Heiligendamm Process.'" 30 July. Centre for International Governance Innovation. <www.cigionline.org : cigi news> (May 2008).

Cooper, Andrew F. and Thomas Fues (2008). "Do the Asian Drivers Pull Their Diplomatic Weight? China, India, and the United Nations." *World Development* 36(2): 293–307.

Deng Xiaoping (1980). "On the Reform of the System of Party and State Leadership." 18 August. <english.people.com.cn/dengxp/vol2/text/b1460.html> (May 2008).

Ding Lei (2007). "Baguojituan yu Zhongguo waijiao de zhanlüe xuanze." ["The Group of Eight and the Strategic Decisions of China's Diplomacy."] *Tianjin Shifan Daxue Xuebao [Journal of Tianjin Normal University, Social Sciences Version]* (2): 6–10.

Dollar, David (2008). "Lessons from China for Africa." Research Working Paper No. 4531. Washington DC: World Bank. <papers.ssrn.com/sol3/papers.cfm?abstract_id=1098629> (May 2008).

Fues, Thomas (2007). "Global Governance Beyond the G8: Reform Prospects for the Summit Architecture." *International Politik und Gesellschaft* (2): 11–24. <www.fes.de/ipg/arc_07_set/set_02_07e.htm> (May 2008).

Gao Zugui (2006). "Dashiye xia kan Baguojituan fazhan." ["The G8 As Viewed from a Grand Perspective."] *Qiaowang [Outlook]* (29): 50–51.

He Fan (2004). "Zhongguo shifo xuyao jiru Qiguojituan?" ["Does China Need to Join the G7?"] *Guoji Jingji Pinglun [International Economic Review]* (5).

HM Treasury (2005). "Joint Statement by the Finance Ministers of China and the UK." 5 February. <www.hm-treasury.gov.uk/otherhmtsites/g7/news/g7_statement_jointchina.cfm> (May 2008).

Hongying Wang (2003). "National Image Building and Chinese Foreign Policy." *China: An International Journal* 1(1): 46–72.

Hook, Steven W., ed. (2001). *Comparative Foreign Policy: Strategies of the Great and Emerging Powers*: Prentice Hall.

Hu Jintao (2005a). *Working Together Towards a Common Future Through Win-Win Cooperation.* 7 July, Gleneagles. Beijing: Ministry of Foreign Affairs of the People's Republic of China. <www.fmprc.gov.cn/eng/wjdt/zyjh/t203660.htm> (May 2008).

Hu Jintao (2005b). "Build Towards a Harmonious World of Lasting Peace and Common Prosperity." Speech prepared for the High-Level Plenary Meeting of the

United Nations 60th Session, 15 September, New York. <www.fmprc.gov.cn/eng/wjdt/zyjh/t213091.htm> (May 2008).

Hu Jintao (2007a). "Hold High the Great Banner of Socialism with Chinese Characteristics and Strive for New Victories in Building a Moderately Prosperous Society in All Respects." Report to the 17th National Congress of the Communist Party of China, 15 October, Beijing. <news.xinhuanet.com/english/2007-10/24/content_6938749.htm> (May 2008).

Hu Jintao (2007b). "President Hu Jintao's Speech at the G8+5 Summit Meeting." 8 June, Heiligendamm.

Hurrell, Andrew (2006). "Hegemony, Liberalism, and Global Order: What Space for Would-Be Powers?" *International Affairs* 82(1): 1–19.

Ikenberry, G. John (2008). "The Rise of China and the Future of the West: Can the Liberal System Survive?" *Foreign Affairs* 87(1). <www.foreignaffairs.org/20080101faessay87102/g-john-ikenberry/the-rise-of-china-and-the-future-of-the-west.html> (May 2008).

Ingham, Richard (2007). "G8 Cannot Afford to Ignore Emerging Economies." *Agence France Presse*, 4 June.

Jiang Zemin (2002). "Full Text of Jiang Zemin's Report at 16th Party Congress." <www.china.org.cn/english/features/49007.htm> (May 2008).

Kaplinsky, Raphael and Dirk Messner (2008). "The Impact of Asian Drivers on the Developing World." *World Development* 36(2): 197–209.

Kurlantzick, Joshua (2007). *Charm Offensive: How China's Soft Power is Transforming the World*. New Haven: Yale University Press.

Le Tian (2007). "China, India Agree to Work More Closely." *China Daily*, 8 June. <www.chinadaily.com.cn/china/2007-06/08/content_889715.htm> (May 2008).

Majumder, Sanjoy (2007). "India, China under Pressure at G8." *BBC News*, 6 June. <news.bbc.co.uk/2/hi/south_asia/6725453.stm> (May 2008).

Ministry of Foreign Affairs of the People's Republic of China (2005). "Hu Jintao Holds Talks with the Leaders of India, Brazil, South Africa and Mexico." 7 July, Beijing. <chinaembassy.org.nz/eng/topics/hzxcfelseng/t203480.htm> (May 2008).

Ministry of Foreign Affairs of the People's Republic of China (2008). "Countries and Regions." <www.fmprc.gov.cn/eng/gjhdq/> (May 2008).

Mittelman, James H. (2006). "Globalization and Development: Learning from Debates in China." *Globalizations* 3(3): 377–391.

Pang Zhongying (2006a). "Lengjing duichi '8 + N' guoji guanxi." ["Soberly Approach to '8+N' International Relations."] *Qiaowang [Outlook]* (3): 63.

Pang Zhongying (2006b). "Zhongguo zai guoji tixi de diwei yu zuoyong." ["China's Status and Role in the International System."] *Xiandai guoji gunxi [Modern International Relations]* 4: 17–22.

Payne, Anthony (2008). "The G8 in a Changing Global Economic Order." *International Affairs* 84(3): 519–533.

Shaw, Timothy M., Andrew F. Cooper, and Agata Antkiewicz (2007). "Global and/or Regional Development at the Start of the 21st Century: China, India and (South) Africa." *Third World Quarterly* 28(7): 1255–1270.

Spencer, Richard and Peter Foster (2007). "China and India Reject Climate Change Deal." *Telegraph*, 9 June. <www.telegraph.co.uk/news/worldnews/1554055/China-and-India-reject-climate-change-deal.html> (May 2008).

Subacchi, Paola (2008). "New Power Centres and New Power Brokers: Are They Shaping a New Economic Order?" *International Affairs* 84(3): 485–498.

Wang Jisi (2005). "China's Search for Stability with America." *Foreign Affairs* 84(5): 39–48. <www.foreignaffairs.org/20050901faessay84504/wang-jisi/china-s-search-for-stability-with-america.html> (May 2008).

Wang Yizhou, ed. (2003). *Construction without Contradiction: Multiple Perspectives on the Relationship between China and International Organizations*. Beijing: China Development Publishing House.

Wang Zaibang (2004). "The Implications of China's Revival for European and Global Governance." Presentation at the conference on "EU-China?: Ever Closer Integration?" 9 December. Brussels: European Institute for Asian Studies. <www.eias.org/conferences/euchina091204/zaibang.pdf> (May 2008).

Wang Zaibang (2006). "Principal Contradictions and Changes." *Contemporary International Relations*. <www.cicir.ac.cn/en/publication/cir_article_detail.php?lngID=480> (May 2008).

Wilson, Dominic and Roopa Purushothaman (2003). "Dreaming with BRICs: The Path to 2050." Global Economics Paper No. 99, October. New York: Goldman Sachs. <www2.goldmansachs.com/ideas/brics/book/99-dreaming.pdf> (May 2008).

Yu Yongding (2004). "Jueqi de Zhongguo yu Qiquojituan, Ershiguojituan." ["Rising China and the G7/G20."] *Guoji Jingji Pinglun [International Economic Review]* (5): 9–12.

Yu Yongding (2005a). "China's Evolving Global View." In *Reforming from the Top: A Leaders' 20 Summit*, edited by J. English, R. Thakur, and A.F. Cooper, 187–200. Tokyo: United Nations University Press.

Yu Yongding (2005b). "The G20 and China: A Chinese Perspective." *China and World Economy* 13(1): 3–14. <old.iwep.org.cn/wec/pdf/05-1-yuyd.pdf> (May 2008).

Zhang Jianjiang (2006). "Baguojituan: Xinlaizhe dui Zhongguo de Qishi." ["G8: How the Newcomers Enlightened China."] *Nanfeng Chuang [Southern Wind Window]* (14): 15–17.

Zheng Bijian (2005). "China's 'Peaceful Rise' to Great Power Status." *Foreign Affairs* 84(5): 18–24. <www.foreignaffairs.org/20050901faessay84502/zheng-bijian/china-s-peaceful-rise-to-great-power-status.html> (May 2008).

5

India and the G8
Reaching Out or Out of Reach?

Abdul Nafey

One of the dominant characteristics of the discourse on contemporary Indian foreign policy is a consistency in the vision for an open and inclusive world order, with a close nexus between globalization, multilateralism, and domestic economic transformation. This is how India's foreign minister Yashwant Sinha put it in 2003:

> If globalisation is the trend, then multilateralism is its life-sustaining mechanism, for no process will survive without a genuine spirit of multilateralism underlined by the belief that global problems require global solutions globally arrived at (cited in Baruah 2003).

The reformist imperative is tempered strongly by the idea of autonomy in foreign policy. Sonia Gandhi (2007), chair of the ruling United Progressive Alliance (UPA), for instance, made the plea in the context of Sino-Indian bilateral relations during her visit to China in October 2007: "Both China and India seek an open and inclusive world order based on the principles of 'Panchsheel'"—principles that had significantly led to the ideas of non-alignment and autonomy in Indian foreign policy.

Inclusive economic growth at home and an inclusive order abroad are the twin objectives of Indian foreign policy; and to achieve them—and there is no ambiguity about it—India must build its "strategic autonomy of choice" (Mukherjee 2007a). The eventual goal is to "regain" India's position as a "major global economy"—a position that it had enjoyed for centuries before the rise of colonialism. Although in part a response to the structural transformations in the world order, "much of the new thinking," according to

115

external affairs minister Pranab Mukherjee (2007b), "is driven by choices we have made due to our changing domestic situation." Two inferences are important. First, being a revisionist power, India has its own list of issues that require attention by the international community. Second, there is nothing transitory about these issues. The relatively long democratic culture established in the domestic arena has lent considerable consistency and consensus to these foreign policy goals.

A major task in the foreign policy domain is to sustain the current economic transformation, albeit within the pluralist, democratic context of India. As India is being transformed, the global situation is also changing, with a focus on the need for urgent structural change in the institutions of international governance. India looks at the evolving global geo-political and economic situation as a series of "widening concentric circles" (Menon 2007b). An extension of non-alignment in the national interest is a recalibration of an older concept in Indian foreign policy going back at least to Rajiv Gandhi. The consistent element has been an articulation of "specific objectives of security, global growth designs benign for India and relations with the developing world."[1]

Indian foreign policy also seeks a "democratic and prosperous periphery" in South Asia, a way forward to reintegrate India with its "extended neighbourhood" through various regional economic groupings; and the extension of its search for a "common and indivisible prosperity" through institutional mechanisms such as the East Asia Summit and the Sino-Indian-Russian trilateral dialogue (Mukherjee 2007a; see also Center for Security and International Studies 2007). The India–Brazil–South Africa (IBSA) Dialogue Forum is another effective instrument (Lai 2006). India is also becoming more engaged with the Shanghai Cooperation Organisation (SCO). For the first time since its independence, India encounters no "international constraints" on its engagements with the major powers (Dua 2008). Rather, progress in relations with one opens the doors for improvement in relations with all others.

The scale and intensity of economic interdependence and connectivity have reached levels where all major powers are politically engaging each other, and this situation works to the perceptible advantage of India. Today, India is attempting to build a strategic partnerships with as many as eleven countries and the European Union.[2] And as stated earlier, none of these strategic partnerships come at the expense of relations with others. On the contrary the deepening of one strategic partnership catalyzes growth in relations with other major powers. What it all entails is India's ability to use the advantage of its domestic economic transformation to engage and leverage relations and institutions. Certainly this approach demands maximum flexibility and creativity on the part of India's political and diplomatic leadership. An assessment of the direction of international system, however, gives rise to the optimism that "India is particularly well placed in this new era as its relationships with other major power centres could allow it to reach an optimal position" (Mukherjee 2007b).

As for the issues demanding attention of Indian foreign policy, a prime concern relates to a matter of values. From India's viewpoint, "imperatives of globalization, interdependence and connectivity" are defining the nature and intensity of global challenges (Mukherjee 2007a). Other salient challenges, not necessarily in the order of importance, are the challenges of cross-border and transnational terrorism; proliferation of weapons of mass destruction (WMD); maritime security, especially from Malacca Straits to the Persian Gulf; energy and food security; environmental protection and disaster management. It would be naive to expect the international system to deal with such complex challenges "without democratizing international decision-making" (Mukherjee 2007a). It is because the current global order is not delivering what is required "that we are compelled to seek ad hoc solutions like 'coalition of the willing' to contemporary security problems" (Menon 2007b). Only "multilateral solutions" arrived by means of broad participation within and through the United Nations system would address these new challenges and threats. In seeking and enabling global political and economic order, India therefore seeks "to strengthen multilateral institutions and mechanisms, particularly the United Nations" (Menon 2007b).

There is an unmistakable acceleration in the redistribution of power in the international order. The rise of China and India, in particular, has made old analytical paradigms—developed versus developing, North versus South—somewhat anachronistic. When it comes to the democratization of the international system, the foremost and the immediate starting point for the reform process must be the UN Security Council (UNSC): it is here that power lies, and it is one institution that is singularly out of step with the existing international power realities.[3] Another institution requiring substantive reform is the International Monetary Fund (IMF)—beyond the recent "vote and voice" quota adjustment—for its policies affect most the developing economies undergoing structural adjustment. In a similar vein, since development is the primary need of developing countries, these same countries must get adequate representation in the World Bank.

This discussion raises two key questions. Does India have an exaggerated view of its place and importance in the international system? And is power really being redistributed in the international order? Pranab Mukherjee (2007c), India's foreign minister, has cautioned that India's view of its own position in the world is not due to some "irrational exuberance." Rather this assessment is based on two important developments: India has begun the trajectory of sustained high economic growth rates, and India's relations with all the major powers are improving simultaneously. From a more conceptual perspective, foreign secretary Shiv Shankar Menon (2007a) has invited India's strategic community to ponder a realist appraisal of Indian foreign policy. Does India see itself as a major power? The old theory of balance of power has been replaced with the concept of balance of interests.

Shyam Saran (2007), the prime minister's special envoy, articulated this perspective in a speech to a Japanese audience in 2007: "We have all the reasons for emerging as, I would not say as a super power, but we believe that we can certainly be among the first ranking nations of the world if we make the right decisions today." India's capabilities—economic and technological, political and diplomatic, and military—are great and growing. Reinforcing this appraisal, Mukherjee (2007c) asserted: "Today's India is not a bystander to the actions of other powers. The choices India makes today have the potential to change outcomes on issues ranging from global environment to multiple balances."

A caveat needs to be added here. India perceives itself to be a developing economy, and it will continue to nurture its activism in the "traditional constituencies in the developing world" (Mukherjee 2007c). India has pursued global ambitions, not simply on military capacities and economic might but also on the moral authority as a champion of the world's poor and dispossessed. It has continued to lend strong diplomatic support for global regimes that redistribute the world's resources on the basis of equity. Much of India's diplomatic language continues to be that of the advocate of the interests of the developing countries (for example, the G20 developing countries in the World Trade Organization [WTO]) with strong echoes of self-sufficiency and anti-imperialism.

Significantly, Indian leaders begin to see their country in a natural bridging role between the Western world and developing countries. As noted above, India could exercise substantial influence on a wide range of global challenges. As C. Raja Mohan (2006, 4) suggested, "India is now emerging as the swing state in the global balance of power. In the coming years, it will have an opportunity to shape outcomes on the most critical issues of the twenty-first century."

This bridging role is in many ways the typical position of an intermediate power where the condition of interdependency is not only at its strongest but at its very most advantageous. India finds itself on both sides of a whole range of issues, as with intellectual property rights—where it is both a supplier and consumer. This condition must be differentiated from earlier stages of development: "In the past, issues like food, aid or even investment had been used to pressurise us on national security. Our growing strengths now allow us to address what risks there may be in greater engagement" (Mukherjee 2007b). In other words, under present circumstances India can pick and choose issues to champion and impress upon the international community its choices. It is not just the scope and substance that stand transformed; Indian foreign policy is also changing in attitudes and style. India is using its domestic economic transformation to leverage maximum flexibility and creativity in the international environment. It is increasingly integrating knowledge-based initiatives, science and technology, and business in its goals. Besides, given the nature of new global challenges, deployment of soft power assets and involvement of civil society are becoming as important as the hard power to win the peace ("A Famous Victory and a Tough Sequel" "A Famous Victory and a Tough Sequel: The U.S. Must Apply Softer Arts to Match Its Hard Power" 2003).

India, Emerging Economies, and Globalization

Varieties of global economic surveys, including the often-cited one by Goldman Sachs on Brazil, Russia, India, and China—the BRICs—have concluded with near unanimity that emerging markets are the new engines of global economic growth (Wilson and Purushothaman 2003). The emerging economies must therefore own up to their new responsibilities. There is also the need to write new rules and establish new mechanisms and institutions. In other words, the global economic and financial system must evolve new formats for deliberation and decision, and must also broaden the scope of its discussion. Seemingly non-economic issues, ranging from climate change to epidemics, have assumed global economic salience, necessitating more than ever the inclusion of emerging economies in the global economic and financial architecture.

How and where does India figure into the evolving global economic and financial architecture in terms of its weight, responsibility, and participation?

In the specific context of India, its economic and cultural resurgence is being likened "to a return to normality" in the global exchange of products and ideas (Saran 2007). It is also argued that the rise of India and China in particular marks a structural shift in the global economy toward Asia. India's economic transformation is restoring it to the trade and cultural crossroads of Asia; what therefore is happening is the "resumption of history in Asia" (Saran 2007).

A series of frequently heard arguments follows.

The first argument relates to demography. India's population is more than 1.1 billion, including some 550 million who are under 25 years of age. India's labour force is growing faster than the population. Analyses refer to India's "demographic dividend" (Johnson 2006). Indian universities produce more than 2 million undergraduates each year; their growing skills and know-how are converting this young labour force into an asset. The middle class of more than 300 million is steadily growing, and its consumption pattern is attracting foreign investors. There is no denying that there are serious problems, such as those of income and regional disparities, with some 300 million poor who live on less than a dollar a day, as well as technology and productivity lags in the agricultural sector and poor infrastructure; none of these however, is insurmountable.

Second, India's comparative advantage in knowledge-driven economic activities is recognized. A sort of knowledge revolution is underway; and the success of the information technology (IT) revolution is about to be replicated in new areas such as biotechnology and medicine.

The third argument is that the emerging economies of the BRICs— or BRICSAM, if South Africa and Mexico are included—are on the path of sustained high growth. The BRICs account for almost 40 percent of the world's gross domestic product (GDP) in terms of purchasing power parity (PPP). They have grown annually more than 7 percent on average since 2002. India has, in fact, registered an average growth rate of 8.5 percent in the same period and hopes to register double-digit growth rates. It is now the fourth largest economy in the world in PPP terms. Importantly, India's high economic growth rate is driven by domestic consumption and investment.

Fourth, emerging economies are integrating themselves into the global market for goods and services. The combined emerging markets' share of exports of goods and services doubled between the early 1990s and 2006, reaching roughly 30 percent. India's integration with the world market has been particularly more impressive: its share in exports of goods and services tripled between the early 1990s and 2006, to close at 1.5 percent. Notably, it is the rising exports of IT and IT-enabled services that have generated the momentum.

Trends in demography, capital accumulation, and productivity and the rising share in the global trade all indicate that the BRIC economies are on the path of sustained high growth. Investors from these countries are carving out a niche, including in the industrialized economies. Initial public offerings (IPOs) from the BRIC countries accounted for 39 percent of the volume raised globally in 2007. Goldman Sachs projected the BRICs to grow to be more than half the size of the six largest industrialised economies by 2025, and perhaps to overtake them by 2050 (Wilson and Purushothaman 2003). By then, India would be the third largest economy after China and the United States. Of course, there is nothing inevitable about these projections. Nevertheless, the shift that is taking place calls for an immediate, meaningful rebalancing of the global economic and financial architecture.

A fifth argument, particular to the case of India, is the synchronization of its economic growth with its rising influence in culture and science. With some 900 films produced in 2005, Bollywood has become a brand name in the world of entertainment. India boasts of some 40 million internet users; moreover, it is the Indian technicians who have established themselves in the world of information technology. The acquisition of Jaguar by Tata of India not only indicates where power is shifting but also demonstrates the soft power of India.[4] Being at the crossroads of trade and culture for most of its history, Indian culture is itself highly adaptable. As India seeks investments from abroad, others are discovering that Indian investors and professionals are equally adept at working in diverse cultural and economic settings. A multicultural democratic India is set to benefit, more than all others, from its "diversity dividend" in a globalized world economy. As for its scientific prowess, India is home to a number of cutting-edge technologies, ranging from its indigenous nuclear program to space research.

The rise of India, of all the B(R)ICSAM countries, cannot be downplayed. It constitutes a development of systemic proportions. Indeed, because of these structural dynamics, global economic and financial governance has been changing both in format and in substance for the past ten years or so. The motivating force is the integration of emerging markets; for instance, as part of their outreach process, the G7 finance ministers routinely invite their counterparts from the emerging economies to their meetings. Comprising all the systemically important economies, G20 finance ministers and central bank governors focus on macroeconomic coordination and have given important signals to global market participants with a degree of effectiveness and legitimacy since the group's inception in 1999. Extending the outreach process to the summit level of the G8—involving Brazil, India, China, South Africa, and Mexico, referred to in this context as the Outreach Five (O5)—that began in 2005 is a step further in establishing broader coordination and consensus in matters of global governance. From this perspective, the initiation of Heiligendamm Process (HP), involving a two-year, issue-specific dialogue with the O5, is one more step in the direction of reforming the international economic and financial architecture. Equally noteworthy, the broadening of the format is changing the substance of global economic governance. Many invaluable principles of transparency, good practice, and dialogue have been translated, for instance, into the standardization of information and many common practices in macroeconomic and financial matters.

Yet the transformative power of India's economic rise should not be over-exaggerated as a driver for institutional change at the apex of the international system. India's desire for participation in the context of meetings of the extended G8—as for membership of the UNSC—is driven more by its political or diplomatic objectives than by its view that this would serve its economic interest. However, as economic issues are discussed at these meetings and the communiqués contain the views of the group regarding economic issues, India wishes to participate so that its economic interests are understood by others and reflected in the groups' statements. India's economic interests are, of course, shaped by the recent development of its economy. The share of exports of good and services in GDP has tripled from 7 percent to 21 percent between 1990 and 2005, a result clearly of the reforms initiated in 1991. So the government has an interest in further liberalization. Also, India's growth is becoming more dependent on the world economic situation. The current turmoil has affected the stock market in India and so might affect investment. But, more importantly, the pace of industrial growth seems to be slowing. India has, thus, a strong interest in a well-functioning world economy. However, as the livelihood of 60 to 70 percent of India's population depends on agriculture it cannot undertake policy measures that would jeopardize their economic interests. Already the government is perceived as being more urban oriented, and an election is scheduled for 2009. So the interests of a large part of the population must be balanced against export interests. Also, the rural market is gaining greater importance to industrial producers so that the interests of agriculture and industry may be intertwined.

One aspect of the changes in India's economic interests not yet fully appreciated is capital flow. Until now the discussion has focused on why India was not attracting as much capital as China. Inflows have been increasing and are becoming significant. Also Indian companies have been investing abroad, and mainly in developed countries as they seek access to technology, markets, or brand names. So India has a very strong interest that the markets of developed countries remain open to investments and takeovers by Indian companies (such investments involve private companies and so this is not an issue about sovereign wealth funds). Furthermore, India has run a large current account deficit, which has been increasing with the rising price of oil. In this light, India has a vested interest in properly functioning world financial markets.

India's Diplomacy at the G8 Summit

How does India look at the G8 in terms of its participation as one of the O5 or B(R)ICSAM countries, in terms of the format and content of the dialogue, and in terms of the expansion of the G8, including its possible membership? India's approach to the issue of its own inclusion—making it a G9, or by including China making it a G10, or a G13 with the present O5 partners—is one of studied indifference. India is certainly in no hurry; and if offered a seat at the high table, it would likely make the G8 wait until it succeeds first in democratizing the UN.

As a founding member of the UN even before the country gained independence in 1947, India has always supported the organization as the sole legitimate body to secure international peace. A dominant aspiration is to join the UNSC as a permanent member. According to widely shared opinion in the country, India should have received a permanent seat along with veto power already at the founding in 1945. The basic arguments mobilized by India in its ongoing bid reveal a mix of structural and functional arguments. Representation by population remains a built-in component. But this traditional claim has been joined by new claims based on India's 21st-century status, because of its high rate of economic growth together with other features, most notably its access to the nuclear club.

The official position also consistently links the UNSC's lack of representativeness with the grave deficiencies of the global system and underlines the cross-cutting nature of the crisis of global governance (Sen 2006). According to the government's view, admission of India into the UNSC would be a crucial step to remedy the dysfunctional structures of the UN system.

New members would, it is claimed, take steps toward reform in the interest of all member states, also by modifying and restricting the execution of veto power. India's special attachment to the UNSC also shows in the fact that it is one of the few member states that has been elected six times to this body.

Under such circumstances the Indian government has left the debate about the need for reform of the G8's format and functioning to others. It offered no official response in the run-up to the 2007 Heiligendamm Summit, even when, a week or so before the summit, German chancellor Angela Merkel told the German parliament that "she did not want to create a G13" ("G8 to Expand Relationship with Emerging Nations" 2007).

At the same time, however, government officials have not commented openly when G8 leaders subsequently endorsed an enlargement model that privileged India's standing. This was true when French president Nicolas Sarkozy, visiting New Delhi in January 2008, backed the proposal of India's entry into G8 "to tackle the challenges of the 21st century" (Special Correspondent 2007). He said, "We can solve problems of the world by reorganising the G8." Indeed, on this occasion, Sarkozy went so far as to describe the practice of consulting O5 as an "injustice to the 2.5 billion inhabitants of these nations" and asked "Why this third grade treatment to them?" A week earlier, British prime minister Gordon Brown had made a similar plea: "major threshold nations" should be invited into the G8 in view of the "new realities." India should have a "prominent role" in an expanded G8: "There is no future for any big economic bloc which does not include India" ("UK Favours UNSC Seat for India, Entry into G8" 2008). It was true when Angel Gurría, the secretary general of the Organisation for Economic Co-operation and Development (OECD), made a similar plea: Global economic issues require urgent coordinated action. Therefore, the "G8 should become G13 as soon as we can and … they should all work together. The G8 cannot solve any problem without five and the five cannot solve problems without the eight, so why wait?" (cited in Waki 2008).

Indian diplomacy remains, first and foremost, focused on securing a seat on the UNSC. Almost every head of state and government visiting India states his or her country's support to India's claim. Sarkozy and Brown did the same during their visits. With the same serious intent, Indian leaders visiting global capitals or meeting in various forums take up the issue of UNSC expansion, including India's inclusion as a veto-wielding permanent member. In sum, the first priority remains the democratization of the UN.[5]

This priority is supported by the major newspaper articles detailing India's position on the G8. A strong view expressed in the media is that

India should not overplay its hand with respect to the G8. In the words of one commentator, "the crisis of G8's credibility is not India's or China's headache but that of its current member states. If the advanced industrial countries of the G8, especially the U.S., fail to collectively realize the folly of leaving out emerging economies, the loss is theirs, not of India or China" (Chaulia 2008).

In more subtle language, Amit Baruah (2008) suggests that India should adopt a hedging strategy toward the G8. India's main game should continue to be to gain entry to the UNSC as a permanent member. However, it should not reject outright the possibility of joining an expanded G8 whether on the basis of compensation or as a catalyst for the reform of the UN: "It remains to be seen whether leaders like Sarkozy and Brown will put their shoulder to the wheel in pushing India's case at the Security Council. Reforming the G8 is an entirely different proposition."

In either case, the policy dictum should be one of wait and watch. Given its foreign policy forays and priorities, especially under the UPA government, India is not in a hurry to signal its intentions. Besides, it is likely that India, if and when invited, would take along the tag of being a developing economy on the path of sustained high growth. In other words, India would strive to effect some changes in the work and agenda of the G8. Current foreign policy thinking posits India to be at the crossroads of Asian trade and culture, and the Asian geo-strategic architecture will see more of India's attention in the immediate future. India's presence in the G8, in whatever form and manner, will mark a change in the essentially trans-Atlantic character of the group. India is convinced that the centre of global economic gravity is shifting toward Asia. Although as finance minister Palaniappan Chidambaram has said, it will not happen quite as early as some as predicted. Indeed, Kishore Mahbubani and George Yeo Yong-Boon of Singapore have pronounced the shift already in favour of Asia, or, at the least, away from the United States.[6]

India could benefit from several factors by joining the G8. The G8 represents the power base of democratic, open market economies, and of all the prospective candidates, India has better credentials as an example of a successful and stable market democracy. A G9 with India would also help bring multilateralism back in international relations. India recognizes the UN's many failures to react effectively to international crisis situations. A G9 would require the U.S. to recommit itself to multilateralism, both within and outside the UN system. With the issues of trade, aid, health, and climate change gaining increasing importance on the G8 agenda since the 2005

Gleneagles Summit, India's inclusion would help a G9 strengthen multilateralism as well as secure American commitment. As an example, it was India that convinced the U.S. at Heiligendamm to agree to future negotiations on climate change under the UN Framework Convention on Climate Change (UNFCCC).

How does India look at the Heiligendamm Process? In place of membership expansion, the G8 offered the O5 this two-year, issue-specific, structured dialogue aimed at enhancing freedom of investment and investment conditions including corporate social responsibility, promoting and protecting innovation in national policies, defining common responsibilities for development and sharing knowledge for improving energy efficiency, and facilitating technological cooperation with the aim of reducing greenhouse gas emissions. Merkel (2008) hailed HP as a crucial mechanism for international cooperation—a process of permanent contact, established for the first time, between the industrialised countries and the major emerging market economies. The Indian media has described the HP in general terms as a sort of window dressing, and certainly not a precursor to institutionalizing the O5 or B(R)ICSAM. Of importance to India are also questions about the framework within which the ministerial-level dialogue will take place or about how the HP secretariat will operate. India is not keen to have the dialogue at the OECD.

India's experiences at Heiligendamm contrast with those it had at the 2006 St. Petersburg Summit. Indian diplomacy was skillful at St. Petersburg, building upon its "natural alliance" with the U.S. on the one hand and, on the other hand, successfully engaging China and Russia in the first ever trilateral summit in support of a "multipolar world" (Saran 2006).[7] A key development was the manner in which India effected a change by successfully adding the issue of cross-border terrorism to the G8 agenda. The St. Petersburg Summit was taking place just days after the serial bomb blasts in Mumbai suburban trains and terrorist attacks in the capital of Jammu and Kashmir. It was said that India steered and supplemented the G8 statement warning all those who organize, sponsor, and incite terrorism (see G8 and Outreach Partners 2006). Foreign secretary Shyam Saran had described it as a "major diplomatic gain for India" (Qisa'i 2006). Certainly there were three real gains for India from the statement: an unprecedented international solidarity with India's struggle against terror, a collective warning that Pakistan must watch out, and the assertion that terrorism in the region affects all countries and is a threat to international peace and security—an expression that carried the potential of a discussion and action at the UNSC. Prime

Minister Manmohan Singh (2006) expressed "satisfaction" at the outcome of the G8-O5 session, saying that it "embodied the spirit of international cooperation" and the documents adopted by G8 reflected "a willingness to work in partnership with developing countries."

By way of contrast, India found the spirit of cooperation and partnership missing at Heiligendamm. There were a series of disappointments that put a negative edge on its attitude concerning the 2007 summit. The G8 had issued the joint statement before any formal consultation with O5 had taken place. Singh (2007) brought this up with the G8 leaders and then later told the media:

> We were not active participants in the G8 processes, in fact G8 communiqué was issued even before our meeting and we did make the point that in future, if similar meetings have to take place, then we should get a chance to discuss issues of our concerns before the G8 meeting.

Indian media stressed the extreme seriousness with which the prime minister noted the future of O5 participation:

> I hope that next year's meeting, *if we are invited*, will be in a form in which we have a chance to interact with the G8 nations before they interact amongst themselves (Singh 2007, emphasis added).

His observations did not evoke any positive response from the G8 leaders. Rather, Indian officials accompanying the prime minister felt that G8 leaders were "patronising" toward the O5 (Bidwai 2007). It was once again the Indian prime minister who chose to correct the misperception:

> And I said we have come here not as petitioners but as partners in an equitable, just and fair management of the global comity of nations which we accept as the reality in the globalised world (Singh 2007).

India had anticipated that, in light of the G8 agenda, it would be pressured to agree to capping its greenhouse gas emissions. It was ready to resist and, if necessary, even hide behind the stated position of the U.S. to avoid any attempt at imposing quantified responsibility on emissions. However, what probably irked India most was the G8 statement on nuclear non-proliferation. It was discernibly more restrictive in terms of access to the nuclear fuel and technology, even for the signatories to the Non-Proliferation Treaty (NPT). It clearly spoke of "alternative strategies to reduce the proliferation risks associated with the transfer of enrichment and reprocessing goods and technologies" if the Nuclear Suppliers Group (NSG) failed to agree to tighter rules by next year (G8 2007).

There was more to India's disappointment. The Heiligendamm statement repeated *ad verbatim* the statement from the summit at St. Petersburg. It stated:

> We note the commitments India has made, and encourage India to take further steps towards integration into the mainstream of strengthening the non-proliferation regime so as to facilitate a more forthcoming approach towards nuclear cooperation to address its energy requirements, in a manner that enhances and reinforces the global non-proliferation regime (G8 2006; 2007).

The statement perceptibly belittled the series of domestic and foreign policy initiatives India has taken in recent years to strengthen global non-proliferation regime. Among Indian officials, there were two views on this. One view was that the round-about formulation reflected the lack of clear consensus among G8 members on civilian nuclear cooperation with India. The other view was that the G8 still looked at India as a target and not as partner in the global non-proliferation efforts. Germany and Japan were reportedly ambivalent on the issue of nuclear trade with India. What was most disconcerting from the Indian viewpoint was the clear U.S. push for tighter nuclear trade rules at the NSG at a time when the Indian government had announced its intention to negotiate with the group after working out an India-specific safeguard agreement with the International Atomic Energy Agency (IAEA).

The Heiligendamm Summit will most likely be known not so much for offering a structured dialogue but for the new dialectic that emerged among the O5. In keeping with the tradition started at the 2005 Gleneagles Summit and carried on through St. Petersburg, it was President Felipe Calderón of Mexico who invited the heads of O5 for a meeting in Berlin "to share perspectives and find convergences about the topics" that were to be discussed at the outreach session of the G8, as well as "to exchange views on various significant international issues" (Prime Minister's Office (India) 2007). The O5 statement welcomed the opportunity for collaboration with the G8 on the four subjects that had been identified in the joint G8-O5 statement. However, the O5 also insisted that all these issues must be addressed "from a multilateral, regional and bilateral perspective, taking into consideration the interests and capacities of the different states." Just as noteworthy was the O5's reaffirmation of the need for the active participation of developing countries in strategies to tackle global issues. The leaders asserted that they themselves can make a decisive contribution "to increase the participation of developing countries in this process."

Without disagreeing with the G8 or G8-O5 agendas, the five identified their own separate agenda. The topics that stood out as those of top concern to developing countries are global governance, international trade, biofuels, migration, climate change, and South–South cooperation. In matters of global governance, the O5 reiterated their demand for democratic governance, which required "priority" given to the reform of the UNSC and greater participation of developing countries in Bretton Woods institutions. On international trade, the five demanded the elimination of agricultural subsidies and trade-distorting practices by the developed countries. They also noted that international migration, as an aspect of globalization, must be seen positively in relation to the development of both the sending and receiving countries.

The five also signalled that their dialogue, on the margin of G8 summits, constituted a new form of South–South cooperation, which has become more feasible with the growing strength of developing countries. Indeed, the five reportedly engaged in some joint thinking on their future participation in the Outreach Dialogue. There was a broad unanimity that G8 has limited utility for the developing world. In this context, Brazil proposed a separate full-fledged summit of the five. Brazilian president Luis Inácio Lula da Silva proposed regular summit-level meetings so that O5 meetings no longer remain incidental to the meetings of the G8. All the five welcomed the proposal but deferred a formal decision on the shape of their future summit-level interaction. Nevertheless, they all agreed to hold regular consultations in the future on issues of common interest and to coordinate their positions.

To consolidate their separate dialogue, the foreign ministers of the O5 met at the margin of UN General Assembly (UNGA) session in September 2007. As *The Hindu* clarified, "the idea is not stop engaging with the G8 but to explore the full range of issues that the G5 can work on itself" (Varadarajan 2007a).

In principle, the idea of a grouping of the five high-growth emerging economies looked highly valuable. Admittedly, the system-shaping capability of the five remains limited, and they are known to take divergent positions on international issues ranging from UN reform to migration. However, their capabilities are growing. Besides, there is much that is already happening among the five. China was India's largest trading partner in 2007. The O5 may account for only 11 percent of the gross world product when measured in real exchange terms, but as a group they represent 42 percent of the world population. In absolute GDP terms, India accounts for about 2 percent of the global economy and is much smaller than the smallest of the G8 economy, but it is a market of more than 300 million middleclass consumers.

For all this, the O5 is neither a rival to the G8, organizing emerging and other developing economies, nor is it an alternative to the expansion of the G8. It is essentially a vehicle to leverage the format and agenda of the G8. As Shivshankar Menon put it, "this is slow, steady progress. We find value in this and we intend to do this in future" (Madhavan 2006). Playing on the word "outreach," he quipped, "It is out for them, not for us."

All five O5 countries contend with some distinct economic and strategic circumstances. "We come from the same interest—primacy to development—and we need to have a balance," explained Menon about what unites the O5 and distances them from the G8 (Madhavan 2006). The group's concerns are the stalled WTO trade negotiations, inclusive development, migration, terrorism, and reform of international institutions—subjects that did not arouse the interest of G8. What added heft to the O5 initiative was the disarray that was evident in the ranks of the G8 on issues of climate change and U.S.-Russian exchanges on the missile defence system. As Manmohan Singh (2007) told the Indian media, climate change "was essentially a dialogue among G8 countries with sharp differences between U.S. and EU [European Union] and they have been aiming to paper over those differences." Yet the G8 was trying to impose a glass ceiling on the O5. Singh admitted that "of course there are demands on countries like China, India and Brazil to accept obligations to reduce gas emission" and "we said that we have not come here to discuss targets or accept internationally enforced targets on us."

The final outcome of the summit—two vague, non-binding promises of more aid to Africa and a reduction in the greenhouse gas emissions—could hardly be described as success. Rather the compromised and short-term nature of the commitment raised the issue of the credibility of the future summits itself. There was some scepticism about India's participation as an outreach partner. One Indian official quipped: "I am trying to figure out why are we here? What do you gain out of it? India is not going to catch up even with China in the coming years and we are nowhere near the U.S." (Bhatt 2007).

The entire process of consulting with the O5 has also raised questions about ethics and propriety. As quoted earlier, Sarkozy described the process of consultation as third-grade treatment. In the assessment of *The Hindu* the outreach process is a "meaningless and demeaning ritual" that the O5 are being made to go through, while there are other respectable and useful forums such as the IBSA Dialogue Forum, the trilateral dialogue, and the BRICs (Varadarajan 2007b). The engagement of this last grouping is highlighted by the meeting in May 2008 in Ekaterinburg, Russia, attended by Indian foreign minister Pranab Mukherjee.

India remains keen to engage the G8, whatever the format and the level, if for no other reason than to leverage it for its domestic economic transformation. It would reach out to the G8 but bring along its own agenda. This dynamic can be seen most distinctively in the productive manner by which India has tried to engage in the area of energy. In policy terms, this is one of the country's priority issues along with trade and investment and also water. It is also an area where there are deep internal agreements in India. The practical test will be whether the O5 or B(R)ICSAM process addresses this type of agenda constructively.

As an emerging power, India is not walking out on the G8. But it is also using the G8 as part of an elaborate balancing act. Engagement with the G8 is not exclusive. India is attracted to other groupings and bilateral relations, and it fully appreciates its ascending rank in the evolving global order. The fundamental lesson of the HP for India is that it has accentuated the fact that the international system is truly in a state of flux, and that no single grouping of countries—even if they are the most powerful ones in economic terms—can presume to have the solutions to the world's problems (Varadarajan 2007a).

Notes

1 Yoginder Alagh, personal communication, April 2008.
2 For more on India's work on securing strategic partnerships see Blair, Singh, and Barroso (2005), Kapila (2004), United States State Department (2004), and Japan (2006).
3 For a discussion on the democratization of the UN see Mbeki (1999). On the debate over UN reform, see Luck (2005).
4 See Goldstein (2007) for further information on the growing strength of multinational corporations from emerging economies.
5 See Parthasarathy (2006) for greater discussion on India's attempts to reform the UN.
6 See Mahbubani (2004) and Waki and Ferreria-Marques (2008).
7 For more on the relationship between India and the U.S. see Cohen (2005).

References

"A Famous Victory and a Tough Sequel: The U.S. Must Apply Softer Arts to Match Its Hard Power." (2003). *Financial Times*, 10 April, 12.

Baruah, Amit (2003). "Push for Multipolar World Need Not Be Confrontationist." *The Hindu*, 19 October.

Baruah, Amit (2008). "Behind India's 'Entry' into G13." *Hindustan Times*, 3 February.

Bhatt, Sheela (2007). "Notes from the Sidelines in Heiligendamm." *Rediff*, 13 June. <www.rediff.com/news/2007/jun/13pmg.htm> (May 2008).

Bidwai, Praful (2007). "Development: G8, G5, or G4? A Tough Choice for India." *Inter Press Service*, 23 June. <ipsnews.net/news.asp?idnews=38289> (May 2008).

Blair, Tony, Manmohan Singh, and José Manuel Barroso (2005). "Press Conference at Launch of India-EU Strategic Partnerships." 7 September, London. <www.number-10.gov.uk/output/Page8145.asp> (May 2008).

Center for Security and International Studies (2007). "Sino-Indian-Russian Cooperation: India's Door into the UNSC?" 19 February, Bucharest. <www.csis.ro/articles/asia_pacific_19.html> (May 2008).

Chaulia, Sreeram (2008). "India, China Hold G8 Options." *Asia Times*, 29 April.

Cohen, Stephen P. (2005). "India: America's New Ally?" 18 July, Washington DC. Brookings Institution. <www.brookings.edu/opinions/2005/0718india_cohen.aspx> (May 2008).

Dua, H.K. (2008). "Breaking from the Past: India and U.S. Opt for a New Relationship." *Tribune*, 6 March. Chandigarh. <www.tribuneindia.com/2006/20060306/edit.htm#4> (May 2008).

G8 (2006). "Statement on Non-Proliferation." 16 July, St. Petersburg. <www.g8.utoronto.ca/summit/2006stpetersburg/nonprolif.html>

G8 (2007). "Heiligendamm Statement on Non-Proliferation." 8 June, Heiligendamm. <www.g8.utoronto.ca/summit/2007heiligendamm/g8-2007-nonprolif.html> (May 2008).

G8 and Outreach Partners (2006). "Statement by the G8, the Leaders of Brazil, China, India, Mexico, South Africa, Chairman of the Council of the Heads of State of the CIS, Chairman of the African Union, and the Heads of the International Organizations." 17 July, St Petersburg. <www.g8.utoronto.ca/summit/2006stpetersburg/outreach.html> (May 2008).

"G8 to Expand Relationship with Emerging Nations." (2007). *Deutsche Welle*, 8 June. <www.dw-world.de/dw/article/0,2144,2579939,00.html> (May 2008).

Gandhi, Sonia (2007). "India and China: A Harmony of Civilizations." Address at the Tsinghua University, 27 October, Beijing. <www.indianembassy.org.cn/press/20071029_1.htm> (May 2008).

Goldstein, Andrea (2007). *Multinational Companies from Emerging Economies*. London: Palgrave Macmillan.

Japan (2006). "Joint Statement towards Japan-India Strategic and Global Partner-ship." 15 December, Tokyo. <www.kantei.go.jp/foreign/abespeech/2006/12/15joint .pdf> (May 2008).

Johnson, Jo (2006). "Engaging India: Demographic Dividend or Disaster?" *Financial Times*, 15 November. <www.ft.com/cms/s/0/cd516aa8-749a-11db-bc76 -0000779e2340.html> (May 2008).

Kapila, Subhash (2004). "Russia Rekindles Strategic Partnership with India." Paper No. 1180. South Asia Analysis Group. <www.southasiaanalysis.org/papers12/ paper1180.html> (May 2008).

Lai, Kaia (2006). "India–Brazil–South Africa: The Southern Trade Powerhouse Makes its Debut." 15 March, Washington DC. Council on Hemispheric Affairs. <www .coha.org/2006/03/india-brazil-south-africa-the-southern-trade-powerhouse -makes-its-debut/> (May 2008).

Luck, Edward (2005). "The UN Security Council: Reform or Enlarge?" Paper pre-pared for the conference on The UN: Adapting to the 21st Century, 3–5 April. Waterloo ON. <www.sipa.columbia.edu/cio/cio/projects/LuckCIGI.pdf> (May 2008).

Madhavan, Narayanan (2006). "O5 Mulls Forming a Group of Their Own." *Hindustan Times*, 4 November.

Mahbubani, Kishore (2004). "When Asia Emerges, How Will the World Change?" *AsiaViews*, 12 April. <www.mahbubani.net/articles/asiaviews-12042004-pf.html> (May 2008).

Mbeki, Thabo (1999). "Sepeech at the 54th Session of the United Nations General Assembly." 20 September, New York. <www.southafrica-newyork.net/consulate/ genassembly.htm> (May 2008).

Menon, Shiv Shankar (2007a). "The Challenges Ahead for India's Foreign Policy." Speech at the Observer Research Foundation, 10 April, New Delhi. <meaindia.nic.in/cgi-bin/db2www/meaxpsite/coverpage.d2w/coverpg?sec =ss&filename=speech/2007/04/11ss01.htm> (May 2008).

Menon, Shiv Shankar (2007b). "India and International Security." Speech at the International Institute of Strategic Studies, 3 May, London. <www.indianembassy .org/newsite/press_release/2007/May/7.asp> (May 2008).

Merkel, Angela (2008). "Speech at the EU/LAC Buiness Summit in Lima." 15 May. <www.bundesregierung.de/nn_6566/Content/EN/Reden/2008/05/2008-05-15 -rede-merkel-wirtschaftsgipfel-lima.htmlS> (May 2008).

Mohan, C. Raja (2006). "India and the Balance of Power." *Foreign Affairs* 85(4): 17–32. <www.foreignaffairs.org/20060701faessay85402/c-raja-mohan/india-and-the -balance-of-power.html> (May 2008).

Mukherjee, Pranab (2007a). "India's Foreign Policy and the Future of India-U.S. Relations." Council for Foreign Relations, 1 October, New York. <www .meaindia.nic.in/speech/2007/10/03ss01.htm> (May 2008).

Mukherjee, Pranab (2007b). "India's Foreign Policy Priorities." Distinguished Public Lecture at the S. Rajaratnam School of International Studies, 20 June, Singapore. <www.meaindia.nic.in/speech/2007/06/20ss02.htm> (May 2008).

Mukherjee, Pranab (2007c). "India and the Global Balance of Power." 16 January, New Delhi. <www.meaindia.nic.in/speech/2007/01/16ss02.htm> (May 2008).

Parthasarathy, G. (2006). "Saga of India's Bid for UN Secretary-General's Post." *Business Line*, 11 August, 10.

Prime Minister's Office (India) (2007). "Meeting of Heads of State and/or Brazil, China, India, Mexico, and South Africa." 7 June, Berlin. <pmindia.nic.in/visits/content.asp?id=154> (May 2008).

Qisa'i, Ahmad (2006). "India, Washington, and the Middle East Crisis." *AgoraVox*, 26 July. <www.agoravox.com/article.php3?id_article=5008> (May 2008).

Saran, Shyam (2006). "Press Briefing by the Foreign Secretary at St. Petersburg after the G8 Summit and the Outreach Meeting." 17 July, New Delhi.

Saran, Shyam (2007). "Transcript of Address at the Japan Institute of International Affairs." 15 January, Tokyo. <www.meaindia.nic.in/speech/2007/01/15ss01.htm> (May 2008).

Sen, Nirupam (2006). *Remarks at the Joint Debate in the General Assembly on Agenda Item 9 and Agenda Item 111*. New York: United Nations. <www.un.int/india/2006/ind1310.pdf> (May 2008).

Singh, Manmohan (2006). "PM's Statement on Arrival from G8 Summit at St. Petersburg." 18 July, New Delhi. <pmindia.nic.in/visits/content.asp?id=105> (May 2008).

Singh, Manmohan (2007). "PM's On-Board Interaction with Media on Flight from Berlin to New Delhi." 9 June, New Delhi. <pmindia.nic.in/visits/content.asp?id=157> (May 2008).

Special Correspondent (2007). "Sarkozy Backs India's Entry into G8." *The Hindu*, 26 January. <www.thehindu.com/2008/01/26/stories/2008012657041500.htm> (May 2008).

"UK Favours UNSC Seat for India, Entry into G8." (2008). *Financial Express*, 20 January. <www.financialexpress.com/news/UK-favours-UNSC-seat-for-India-entry-into-G8/263570/> (May 2008).

United States State Department (2004). "United States–India Joint Statement on Next Steps in Strategic Partnership." 17 September, Washington DC. <www.state.gov/r/pa/prs/ps/2004/36290.htm> (May 2008).

Varadarajan, Siddharth (2007a). "Brazil Proposes G5 Summit." *The Hindu*, 11 June, 1. <www.thehindu.com/2007/06/11/stories/2007061115070100.htm> (May 2008).

Varadarajan, Siddharth (2007b). "Forget the G8, It's Time for a Brics Summit." *The Hindu*, 4 June. <www.thehindu.com/2007/06/04/stories/2007060402641100.htm> (May 2008).

Waki, Natsuko (2008). "DAVOS-G8 Should Become G13 as Soon as Possible—OECD's Gurría." *Reuters*, 25 January. <in.reuters.com/article/asiaCompanyAndMarkets/idINL2564177520080125> (May 2008).

Waki, Natsuko and Clara Ferreira-Marques (2008). "Wealth Funds Bristle at Rich Country Wariness." *Reuters*, 24 January.

Wilson, Dominic and Roopa Purushothaman (2003). "Dreaming with BRICs: The Path to 2050." Global Economics Paper No. 99, October. New York: Goldman Sachs. <www2.goldmansachs.com/ideas/brics/book/99-dreaming.pdf> (May 2008).

6

Brazil and the G8 Heiligendamm Process

Denise Gregory and Paulo Roberto de Almeida[1]

A new economic geography has taken shape, with many more players whose aspirations to play a stronger role in the global economic decision-making process need to be addressed. The rules of the game and the team of international institutions put in place after the Second World War appear inadequate to cope with today's situation and future issues. The world at that time encompassed no more than five dozen countries, compared to today's 192 members of the United Nations. It is clear that those more recently established states would like the present governance arrangements and decision-making processes to reflect this new world.

The Heiligendamm Process, which began at the 2007 G8 summit hosted by Germany, recognized that the major emerging countries should become key partners in shaping global governance.[2] Brazil, China, India, Mexico, and South Africa were invited to participate in the summit, due to their economic size and growth rates, their relevance for regional politics and security stability, and their role in managing social and environmental problems with global impact. As stated by the World Bank (2007, 30), "one of the biggest challenges will be shaping a new global architecture that can take into account the increasing diversity of countries and interests and allow for peaceful resolution of emerging global tensions," as, for example, increasing competition for scarce resources, availability and access to strategic commodities such as energy, and additional strains on the environment.

In this era of globalization, emerging powers have come to depend less on the North and more on each other. This phenomenon therefore explains the explosion of South–South flows of trade and investment. A larger, indeed increasing share of global trade is conducted among developing countries, and many new agreements for liberalizing trade are being negotiated between them.

This chapter examines the deep economic, social, and political trans- formations that Brazil has been going through, and its strategic and tacti- cal position in relation to the Heiligendamm Process. It touches on many questions, starting with whether this South American "giant" wants to be part of an enlarged club, whose rules have already been set by its older mem- bers. Or would it prefer to pursue options outside the G8, including cham- pioning the traditional solidarity with the developing world or its favourite South American regional associations? How ready is Brazil to commit fully to the international set of governance norms and values that were defined by the big powers? Does it see itself participating and sharing in the respon- sibility for global and regional schemes for peace and stability, in parallel with G8—in other words, does it see itself maintaining the status quo? Or alternatively, does Brazil seek to test its leadership independently and has thus decided to present itself as a source of a new legitimacy, contributing to what many call multipolarity? How does Brazil manage its various current undertakings, including the India–Brazil–South Africa (IBSA) Dialogue Forum, which has recently extended to include joint military exercises.[3]

Another undertaking is the restructuring and strengthening of South American integration, first through the enlargement of Mercosur to include Venezuela (and possibly also Bolivia), then by way of the South American Community of Nations (Comunidade Sul-Americana de Nações [CASA]), which has now been superseded by the Union of South American Nations (Unasur).[4] Furthermore, the new political grouping of Brazil, Russia, India, and China (BRIC), first conceptualized in a study paper by Goldman Sachs, is now converting itself into a diplomatic reality.[5] Other regional initiatives, such as the summits bringing together the leaders of South American and Arab countries on the one hand, and the African countries on the other, constitute structured means of expanding and strengthening the dialogue and economic ties among them. Should all those endeavours be seen as a part of Brazil's double attempt to change the world power axis and establish a new trade geography, as its leaders have repeatedly stated? Has Brazil the eco- nomic and political clout and the diplomatic leverage to handle all those issues within the possibilities of its existing resources and the capabilities of its professional diplomacy? How is the exercise of the Outreach Five— Brazil, China, India, Mexico, and South Africa, whose leaders have been invited to each G8 summit since the 2005 Gleneagles Summit—seen by Brazilian current political and diplomatic leadership?

This chapter addresses these issues by examining how Brazil is dealing with regional and international questions. It will focus on how Brazil is strengthening its relations with the G8, as well as on how Brazil is pursuing its own approach to the international agenda, both with regard to its allies in the Outreach Five and with regard to its bilateral dialogues with G8 members. First, it deals with the structural variables that influence Brazil's economic and diplomatic integration into the world economy and politics, specifically the economic leverage and diplomatic weight that support its willingness to play a greater role. Then, it analyzes Brazil's position *vis-à-vis* the international economy, and its status in the world, by highlighting its strengths and weaknesses compared with other relevant emerging countries.

The chapter then goes on to examine Brazil's current activities in practical diplomacy, that is, its efforts to acquire a new world leadership role—by presenting its candidacy for a permanent seat on the United Nations Security Council (UNSC)—and to establish its leadership credentials in South America. In this regard, some unique characteristics of Brazil's foreign policy and diplomacy, which are heavily influenced by its domestic party politics since the 2002 election of Luis Inácio Lula da Silva, are discussed.

Finally, the chapter deals with the Brazilian position toward the Heiligendamm Process, taking into account the common agenda with the other Outreach countries. This is a two-track approach, as Lula's diplomacy departs, in many respects, from the traditional worldview of the career diplomats in Itamaraty (Brazil's foreign ministry) as well as from the views of those outside official diplomatic channels—opinion makers, entrepreneurs, scholars, and other members of the foreign policy community.[6] These "outsiders" may have differing views on how Brazil could and should tackle the issues of economic interdependence. Some favour, for instance, an approach similar to the Organisation for Economic Co-operation and Development (OECD) in engaging Brazil more forcefully with the Heiligendamm Process. According to Rubens Barbosa (2005, translation by authors), "Lula's foreign policy somehow relegates relations with the developed world. Adhesion to OECD—which should deserve the same priority given to Brazil's campaign to gain a permanent seat in the UNSC—would repair this misperception." This discussion could be presented as an analytical view of current conceptual framework for Brazil's global action, by taking into account both the ideological mindset of its leadership and alternative visions that exist in the society.

Brazil on the International Stage

Brazil is often considered as an emerging power at the global level, having been seen as one of the major countries in the evolution of the world economy, as one of the BRICs. Together with Mexico, South Africa, India, and China, it has been invited to join the G8 countries in the Heiligendamm Process, which is still an incipient dialogue but could lead to a new group, perhaps a G13, to discuss issues regarding world governance and global economic decision making. Brazil is also recognized as an important player at the regional level, since its political leverage and economic strength are, of course, greater in the South American context.

The BRIC countries—which are actively engaged in the formalization of the group—have in common the continental proportion of the territories, the dynamism of their economies (especially China), high income and demographic concentration, and a high degree of informality in the sales and service sectors. These countries seek a strategic position in order to intensify their integration into the world economy and politics. Their shared agenda includes membership in the World Trade Organization (WTO)—with the exception of Russia, which is not yet part of it—and opposition to barriers to developing country exports. It also includes support for greater global equity and redistributive justice, i.e., defending special mechanisms to deal with the global trade regime inequalities and with their developmental needs. Additionally, there is an intensification of strategic alliances among these countries in trade, direct investment, and technology, as well as coordinated multilateral negotiations on energy and environmental issues, such as the adoption of defensive positions in climate change discussions.

Based on statistics from the last ten years, it is not difficult to acknowledge that Russia, India, and China—the "RICs"—have a much more dynamic economic scenario than Brazil does, in terms of economic growth, domestic transformations in infrastructure and information technology, and in technological and capital flows. In the recent past, the South American geographic giant has shown reduced capacity for savings and investments, due to an oversized state and government expenditures in line with OECD levels, with a per capita gross domestic product (GDP) five or six times smaller but well above (10 to 12 points) the average savings and investment rates of other emerging countries. Moreover, Brazil has historically presented a low coefficient of external opening (foreign trade ratio to GDP), and its economic and political leaderships are less prone to dismantle its protectionist policies. In this sense, and notwithstanding being the tenth major world economy—a rank due partly to the relative overvaluation of its currency—

Brazil has only around 1 percent of world exports, holding the 25th position as an exporter and importer. Of course, its sheer size and vast natural and economic resources give Brazil an importance on the world stage.

Despite being the only one of those countries not in possession of nuclear weapons or extensive and well-equipped armed forces, Brazil is capable of exercising a substantial degree of leadership in some of the issues on the multilateral agenda. Indeed, Brazil's leadership capabilities are more in the realm of economics—such as multilateral trade negotiations (although less in financial or technological issues)—than on peace or security issues, where Brazil has less leverage to act on its own. Brazil prefers to join UN initiatives in peacekeeping operations, rather than in peacemaking, as shown in the case of its command of the United Nations Stabilization Mission in Haiti (MINUSTAH) launched in 2004.

At the end of the Cold War, as the world order was being transformed by the demise of socialism and the affirmation of a sole superpower, Brazil struggled with its highly unstable, in fact erratic, economic policies of the 1980s. It still had to overcome the burden of external debt and an impervious inflationary process. The macroeconomic stabilization plan—*Plano Real*—started by Fernando Henrique Cardoso when he was finance minister (1993–94) was a success in a very long series of failed attempts at curbing inflation and reducing the public finance chaos.

In spite of the financial crises that affected Brazil in the late 1990s and early 2000s, which led to the three successive agreements with the International Monetary Fund (IMF) in 1998, 2001, and 2002, the stabilization plan was consolidated during Cardoso's two presidential terms (1995–98 and 1999–2002). As a consequence, Brazil was able to take a more assertive role in both the international and regional agendas and assume an increasing leverage in special topics of global impact, such as renewable energy sources.

The Brazilian industrialization process, since the second half of the 20th century, constituted one of the most successful examples of the import substitution model: a state-led industrial policy with strong import controls. During the 1960s and '70s the model incorporated the export component: the promotion and diversification of exports. As a proof of its efficacy, exports jumped from US$1.6 billion in 1964 to around US$33 billion in 1988.

In the early 1990s domestic fiscal constraints associated with external constraints—the creation of Mercosur and WTO, which imposed new rules and commitments—led the way to economic opening and trade liberalization.

The Cardoso years brought complex regulatory and institutional changes, which made a significant impact on Brazil's domestic macroeconomic reality, as well as on relevant elements in the realm of foreign policy. The country opened up to trade and investments and experienced one of the most ambitious privatization plans in the world, attracting huge amounts of foreign direct investment (FDI).

Brazil occupies a position that is singular within the contemporary system of international relations. It is certainly a "country-continent" that, in exploratory analyses, can be classified in the category of "monster countries," as George Kennan once referred to the other giants such as the U.S., Russia, and China, or even an "anchor country," as German political sociology prefers to call them (*Ankerländer*).[7] This type of political characterization is certainly ambiguous, since the primary dimension of the population data and the physical size of the territory do not always correspond to proportional importance in international relations or in the global economy, as is the case of China during a specific period of the 20th century or the case of Russia at the end of that century.

Among these major players, who are emerging or are already known as big powers, Brazil is presumably destined to play a prominent role in the changing scenarios of global governance. Based on trends to date, the role will be probably on the side of the economy rather than on the strategic military side. As a large producer of commodities and the first worldwide producer of a long list of raw, mostly agricultural materials, Brazil is blessed with substantial biodiversity and immense reserves of natural resources. In its first three or four centuries as a state, Brazil, quite efficiently, offered up to the world basically dessert products: sugar, coffee, cocoa, and a few others.

A wide range of other goods—grains, meat, orange juice, minerals—currently complements the list of raw materials, in addition to manufactured goods of low technological intensity (textiles, shoes, some appliances). Brazil's foreign trade is strongly diversified, both in terms of products and markets. In 2007, basic products exports were responsible for 32.1 percent of total Brazilian exports, while manufactured products represented 52.3 percent and semi-manufactured products represented 13.6 percent (Ministério do Desenvolvimento [MDIC] 2008). Today, Brazil is still a competitive commodities supplier—and it will certainly remain one, with more value-added foodstuffs and raw materials, but it is also on the front line of state-of-the-art technology, such as Embraer civil aircraft. In the future, and for the first time in its economic history, Brazil will become a relevant supplier of renewable energy products, from sugarcane ethanol to biofuels in general, not only in terms of the product itself, but also equally in its technological and scientific dimensions. The country will probably be able to put its imprint on something globally important: the energy matrix emerging from scarce oil resources. The process is still in the distant future, but it offers the opportunity, not only for Brazil, to define a new strategic industry with significant geopolitical dimensions. Brazilian expertise and technology in sugarcane plantation, the transformation of sugarcane into ethanol, and the associated farms and plants that can be used for many kinds of biofuels can, if properly managed, be transferred to lagging developing countries, such as those in Africa, starting by lusophone Angola and Mozambique, which have plenty of arable soil. This implies a mini-revolution in production trends and trade and investment flows into the developing world.

During the first and second industrial revolutions, Brazil was penalized for an absence of abundant sources of energy. Lack of coal and oil, together with the population's low level of education, hampered its entry into the modern industrial economy. Today, fully industrialized but still dragging the heavy baggage of a lagging educational system and with low technological production standards (despite a notable rise in academic and scientific output), Brazil is perhaps preparing to take on a more prominent role in several areas of the globalization process.

Brazil's economic growth has lagged behind other emerging economies. Growth rates have been constrained by a high public debt, excessive taxation, and insufficient investment, which in turn, has been limited by Brazil's high interest rates, extremely complex tax system, weak regulatory framework, and lack of a competitive labor force. The low growth rates experienced over the last two decades may, however, persist for the predictable future. Brazil's high fiscal burden, compared to other emerging countries, largely explains that: public current expenditures correspond to approximately 38 percent of GDP, similar to the OECD's average, compared to an average of only 28 percent for emerging countries and an even lower rate for the most dynamic of them (17 percent and 18 percent for China and Chile, respectively). In fact, total disbursement exceeds 41 percent of GDP, taking into account interest on the national public debt, which roughly corresponds to a similar ratio of the GDP (to service its debt the Brazilian government dedicates an equivalent of approximately 6 percent of GDP, partially covered by a budgetary primary surplus of about half of that ratio).

Early in 2007, the Brazilian government launched the Growth Acceleration Program, with the objective of achieving a growth rate of 5 percent per year from 2008 onward, by means of increased public and private investment in energy, logistics, housing, and water sanitation, totalling US$235 billion in four years. After the first year, the program has shown very modest results.

As stated previously, of the four BRIC countries, Brazil has been the least dynamic for the last few years. Nevertheless, maintaining a fairly modest average annual growth rate of 3.5 percent GDP up to 2050 would be enough to place Brazil into a new G6 of the world economy by then. Furthermore, among the BRICs, Brazil has the best market structures and entrepreneurial traditions. They result from a capitalist model developed in a relatively orthodox manner throughout the 20th century, in comparison with the diverse socialist experiments in the other three countries. Large Brazilian economic groups—mainly private, but including Petrobras, the state oil company—are quickly internationalizing their activities and direct investments, gaining footholds in the region and elsewhere. This trend is expected to increase in the foreseeable future, not only through direct Brazilian investment, but also by means of acquisitions.

A notable fact is that in 2006, Brazilian firms invested US$27 billion abroad, making Brazil, for the first time, a net exporter of capital. That movement gained some importance in the 1990s, and has been concentrated in South America, especially Argentina, with some incursions in North America.[8]

According to one of the big rating agencies, Brazil has just reached its investment grade; the primary fiscal surplus has remained above 4 percent of GDP; and reserves stand at around US$200 billion. In 2007, FDI almost doubled: US$37.4 billion against US$18.8 billion in 2006 (99 percent higher). The former peak was reached in 1994, when Brazil attracted US$32.8 billion due to privatization programs. That figure went down to US$10.1 billion in 2003.

Since 2002, Brazil has been experiencing an export boom, pushed by the growth of world economy, the huge and unprecedented world demand for commodities, especially from China and India, and the effects of that demand on world prices. Brazilian exports have grown almost 17 percent on average annually since 2000, while world exports grew at 11 percent. From a deficit of US$24.2 billion in 2000, the Brazilian current account jumped to US$40 billion surplus in 2007, a historical record.[9]

The balance of payments is in a remarkable condition, with current account surpluses sustained from 2003 to 2007 and exchange reserves amounting to the total foreign debt. Brazil thus has economic foundations that make the country less vulnerable to global financial instabilities and economic downturns in business cycles. An American recession would have a less severe impact on Brazil, due to its diversified trade partnerships and the mixed composition of its exporting list.

If Brazil succeeds in establishing a new social pact that reduces the weight of excessive taxation and regulation, the country would certainly enter into a virtuous circle of sustainable growth (although, probably, at more modest rates than other emerging countries), thus preserving macroeconomic stability. The previous pact, created by the federal constitution, had overburdened public expenditures. Brazil is still going to maintain, for one or two generations, an unequal profile in its income distribution, with a higher Gini coefficient if compared to world average, but it tends to decrease, albeit slowly, on the basis of macroeconomic stability, educational investments, and governmental transfers (among them the Bolsa-Família program of cash transfers to alleviate poverty).

Prospective scenarios drawn up by U.S. National Intelligence Council (2004), a centre for strategic thinking linked to Central Intelligence Agency (CIA), show a less optimistic trend both for Brazil and for Latin America:

> Brazil will likely have failed to deliver on its promised leadership in South America, due as much to the skepticism of its neighbours as to its frequently overwhelming emphasis on its own interests. It will, nevertheless, continue to be the dominant voice on the continent and a key market for its Mercosur partners. Brazil will still not have won a permanent seat on the Security Council, but it will continue to consider itself a global player. Although Brazil's economic improvements are not likely to be spectacular, the size of its economy, along with its lively democracy, will continue to have a stabilizing effect on the entire region. Trade arrangements with Europe, the USA, and large developing economies, mainly China and India, will help to keep its exports growing steadily enough to offset its overall lack of economic dynamism. Even after twenty years, efforts to pass vital reforms to Brazilian institutions will still be underway. Though the situation is bound to improve somewhat, the so-called "Brazil cost," itself a governance issue, will continue to thwart efforts to modernize the economy thoroughly. Brazil's complex and burdensome taxation system, fiscal wars between its states, and the limits of its internal transportation infrastructure, will persist. Taking advantage of Asia's hunger and improved ties with Europe, Brazil will endeavor to offset its structural limitations through its robust agribusiness sector. Brazil's sizeable debt and vulnerability to inflation will also remain matters of concern.

Notwithstanding this sobering projection, Brazil seems to have learned from the precedent of a permissive inflationary stance, and also seems to have overcome its financial external vulnerability. In fact, the emergence of Brazil as a major regional and global player depends heavily on the continuity of economic domestic reforms and adjustment to new policies.

Brazilian Ventures Into the Global Scenario and Into Regional Leadership

As Maria Regina Soares de Lima (2005) writes,

> The active participation in multilateral arenas has been a constant in Brazil's foreign policy since the end of the 19th century. As the sole country of South America having participated in the World War I, as a belligerent nation, Brazil ensured its presence at the 1919 Peace Conference and at the League of Nations, where it obtained a permanent seat in 1926. It was a founding member of the United Nations, one of the 23 original contracting parties of the 1947 General Agreement on Tariffs and Trade (GATT) and took an active part in the 56 countries conference that established the ill-born International Trade Organization (ITO), at Havana, in 1948. In the 1960s and the '70s, the political activism on the scope of the Third World coalition focused on economic questions at the United Nations Conference on Trade and Development (UNCTAD) and the GATT [translated by authors].

Since the mid 1980s, South American regional integration has been the most important subject of Brazilian diplomacy. Brazil's recent foreign policy measures included, at the beginning of the 1990s, abandoning a military nuclear program, moving toward non-proliferation and alleviating excessive protectionism in trade and industrial policies. The country came closer to the economic philosophy of OECD countries. Cardoso's "presidential diplomacy" aimed to consolidate Mercosur and ensure a larger Brazilian presence in the international scene: he confirmed Brazil's total de-nuclearization by adhering to the 1968 Non-Proliferation Treaty (NPT), a treaty that for three decades was considered by diplomats and military officials as iniquitous and discriminatory. Since his tenure as foreign minister (1992–93) and during his two mandates as president, Cardoso promoted a series of diplomatic initiatives in South America: the proposal, in 1993, of "the Amazonian Initiative, with the objective of increasing economic cooperation with countries of the Amazonian region, such as Venezuela, Bolivia and Peru" (Sennes and Barbosa 2005, 211); the mediation of Peru–Ecuador conflict (1995 and 1998); and the establishment of the Initiative for Integration of Regional Infrastructure in South America (IIRSA), an important instrument for improving infrastructure and increasing intra-regional trade.[10]

During the 1990s, under Cardoso, Brazilian diplomacy also underwent a cautious but relevant conceptual change, replacing adherence to the Latin America geographic dimension by the South America concept. This was proposed repeatedly, with attempts to enter into associations or sign trade liberalization agreements between Mercosur and all of its South American neighbours. In reaction to the American-backed project of a Free Trade Agreement of the Americas (FTAA), Brazil responded in 1994 by proposing a South American Free Trade Area (SAFTA). Although, at that time it aroused little enthusiasm in the region, Brazilian diplomats continued to show skepticism toward the FTAA and pushed toward a free trade zone between Mercosur and the Andean community, concluded only in 2004.

Mercosur's origins were purely bilateral, although conceived as the basis of a possible process of regional integration. In 1986, Brazil and Argentina started a program of integration and economic cooperation, based on sectoral protocols, followed by an integration treaty in 1988. It intended to create a full common market in ten years' time. After a decision taken in July 1990 by both countries to bring forward the planned common market to 1995, negotiations were enlarged at the request of neighbours; the treaty creating the Southern Common Market, or Mercosur, was signed in Asunción in 1991, joining Paraguay and Uruguay to the two big South American countries. The methodology for achieving a common market was greatly modified: with a view to completing a full customs union by 31 December 1994, a self-running process of free trade was established, instead of a gradual and sectoral approach for dismantling reciprocal trade barriers. Chile and Bolivia associated themselves with Mercosur in 1996, Peru joined them in 2003, and Venezuela asked to be admitted as a full member of Mercosur in 2006 (but ratification is pending in Paraguay and Brazil).

More significant changes in Brazil's foreign economic and political position, and in some aspects of its foreign policies, happened under Lula. His diplomacy has brought a new emphasis, preferential alliances, and a key change in discourse, and in the way external relations are handled. He has continued to support political multilateralism, which is traditional in Brazilian diplomacy (but now with an evident anti-hegemonic leaning, i.e., against American unilateralism), but has also brought a sharp focus on South–South diplomacy and a strong desire to see Mercosur reinforced and broadened to be the basis for political integration and a unified economic space in South America. As Lima (2005) states, "Brazil sees its capacity to mediate conflicts as its main contribution for the international stability … The recognition of its international projection derives from its diplomatic ability, rather than the recourse to the use of power" [translated by authors]. Lula has helped to diffuse potential crises in Venezuela, Ecuador, and Bolivia, and Brazil is commanding MINUSTAH in Haiti.

The downgrading of trade negotiations with the U.S. within the ranking of priorities was the first change initiated by the Lula government to the policies inherited from Cardoso. The FTAA was perceived as a project pushed by the U.S. and one that potentially threatened the unity of Mercosur. FTAA negotiations came to a standstill in 2004 and were totally abandoned in 2005. For all practical purposes, the FTAA is now dead (although not yet formally buried by an official decision), and this situation can be attributed not only to the opposition of some governments in South America—such as those of Argentina, Brazil, and Venezuela—but also to the unwillingness of the U.S. Congress to reduce sectoral protectionism, mainly in labour-intensive industries and in agriculture, and to scrap subsidies and trade-distorting subventions in agriculture.

Brazil's new foreign policy priorities have been made reasonably explicit on several occasions, starting from Lula's (2003) inaugural statement in January 2003, when he stated that the "greatest priority" of his government would be "the building of a politically-stable, prosperous and united South America, founded upon ideals of democracy and social justice. To this end, decisive action is required to revitalize Mercosur that has been so weakened by the crises afflicting each of its member states, and by narrow and sometimes self-serving standpoints in relation to integration." In the inaugural speech for his second mandate, on 1 January 2007, Lula (2007) reaffirmed Brazil's clear choice of multilateralism, the excellent political, economic, and trade relations maintained with the great world powers, while at the same time confirming that the ties with the southern world are a priority, especially with Africa, which he described as "one of the cradles of Brazilian civilization." The "surrounding South America" was newly emphasized as the "centrepiece" of his foreign policy, when he said that Brazil associates its political, economic, and social destiny to the continent, to Mercosur, and to CASA.[11]

Another main theme of Lula's new diplomacy is the very intense campaign for a permanent seat on the UNSC, which is probably the pet project of the current administration, and the choice of some privileged partners as strategic allies—namely South Africa, India, and China, with the possible inclusion of Russia, on some topics. Another is Brazil's return to a South–South activism and the reaffirmed integrationist vocation in South America. More recently, Lula has been actively engaged in the Russian project of converting the virtual BRIC group into a G4 group—a new formal mechanism of political coordination more amenable to certain diplomatic positions and different from, and perhaps opposed to, old postures of the G7. Brazil's relationship with China is also a case in point, as Brazilian leaders expected a lot coming from the biggest Asian country, including not only support for the UNSC candidacy but also huge Chinese investment flows to beleaguered Brazilian infrastructure. Nevertheless, the only tangible result up to now (as with other Latin American countries) has been a reversal in the bilateral trade surplus and an overflow of inexpensive Chinese manufactured goods competing with the domestic industry.

There has been much criticism in Brazil of the government's failure to conclude trade agreements with the more advanced economies such as the U.S., despite the fact that it is Brazil's most important individual trading partner, particularly for manufactured goods, and is responsible for approximately 17 percent of total Brazilian overall trade. Mercosur has concluded few preferential trade agreements, limited both in scope or coverage and in tariff cuts. The Mercosur-India agreement covers only 450 products and the agreement with the Southern Africa Customs Union (SACU) encompasses 958 products, but trade creation tends to be limited. In December 2007, Mercosur concluded an agreement with Israel. Also, there have been a few concrete results of the prioritized expansion of trade ties with countries in Africa, Asia, and Middle East. As Pedro da Motta Veiga (2005, 17–18) states, "the multiplication of South–South agreements becomes a political objective in itself, leading to a complete loss of focus and priorities in the negotiating agenda when analyzed from the point of view of [Brazil's] trade and investment interests."

The rhetoric about Brazilian leadership in South America changed somewhat during Lula's first mandate from being a more explicit approach toward a more subtle one, modulated according to the neighbours' reactions; but the intention was clear at the start and was affirmed even if in an indirect manner. Lula spoke many times about a "diplomacy of generosity," which implied Brazil assuming some of the costs of an integration project in the region. The president recommended that domestic importers should prefer neighbouring countries, even at relatively disadvantageous prices, to balance the flux of commerce—which clearly favours Brazil, due to the competitiveness of its industrial exporters, its size, and its industrial might on the continent—and thus contribute to common prosperity in the region. Mexico, in this context, is seen more as a competitor in regional markets, than a welcomed partner or a fellow Latin American, compounded by the fact that its commitments within the North American Free Trade Agreement (NAFTA) seem to lower the value of previous regional agreements in the framework of the Latin American Integration Association (Associação Latino-Americana de Integração [ALADI]).

Diplomatic activism in South America, preferably with an expanded Mercosur as the basis for diverse regional initiatives, may have paradoxically resulted in adverse reactions to an expansion of Brazil's influence. In Mercosur, for example, worries about Brazil's "excessive weight" may have likely influenced the decision of the smaller countries to support the political entry of Venezuela into the integration scheme of the Southern Cone. In fact, Venezuela's admission into Mercosur, as well as the acceptance of Bolivia—irrespective of the latter's incapacity to incorporate the whole set of new obligations in terms of trade policy, starting with Mercosur's common external tariff—could do more harm, instead of strengthening the fragile customs union.

Also, Brazil's proposal for CASA aroused mixed reactions among neighbouring countries, which resisted the Brazilian offer, made at the April 2007 meeting in Rio de Janeiro, to establish a technical secretariat in that city. Venezuelan president Hugo Chavez proposed its replacement by Unasur, and pushed for the secretariat to be established in Quito, apparently considered a more favourable location, under the presidency of Rafael Correa.

Such Brazilian diplomatic activism has been present since the very first day of the new administration, when Celso Amorim, Lula's minister of foreign relations, took advantage of the presence of his colleagues from India and South Africa, in Brasilia for the inauguration, to propose the creation of the G3 or IBSA. This initiative is one of most cherished by the current administration, and Itamaraty has invested a lot of resources—diplomatic, financial, technical cooperation—in a variety of areas (cultural, educational, technological, productive, and many others), which include summit-level meetings and the tentative coordination of political objectives of the three countries in relevant issues of the international agenda. IBSA is directed not only at coordinating multilateral issues such as peace and security, trade, and development, but also at strengthening bilateral ties in many other fields of common interest of the three countries. A critical note can be raised at this initiative: besides their similar condition as developing countries, Brazil, India, and South Africa do not share much in common in terms of social problems or educational patterns, to say nothing about political structures and economic systems, despite a political willingness to extend trilateral cooperation in educational, social, and other typical domestic issues. Also, shared views in the diplomatic domain could perhaps conceal many other differences regarding each one's positions in the international agenda.

The same activism has shown up in the inception of G20 developing countries, a coalition created at the 2003 WTO ministerial meeting in

Cancún, Mexico, with a view to promoting the interests of developing countries in agricultural negotiations.[12] It has been considered an essential instrument for reaching the goals of changing the world's power relationships and establishing a new international trade geography. Although the G20 developing countries is more consensual in its "offensive agenda" (the dismantling of protectionism and subsidies in rich countries) than in its "defensive agenda" (the retention of protectionism in industrial and farm policies in some countries, and the retention of agricultural subsidies in China and India), it has become a real protagonist in multilateral trade negotiations, and was perceived in Brazilian society as capable of generating significant results. The group is led by India and Brazil, with China assuming a more timid posture. The critical issue, however, is how to reconcile the interests of the more capitalist, open, and mercantile agricultural systems, such as those of Brazil and Argentina, with those of China and India, which are based on small, low-productivity family holdings that cannot compete on a world scale like the former.[13]

Comparable efforts have been made to transform the BRIC concept into a real diplomatic action. Several informal consultations have been held at foreign ministers level.[14] In May 2008, Russia hosted the first formal meeting of the BRIC foreign ministers, which is intended to repeat annually on the margins of the UN General Assembly. Its purpose is to institutionalize the dialogue and cooperation in the areas of trade, energy, environment, and development. This move would clearly be in Brazil's interests, as Russia, China, and India have a real share of world power due to their nuclear status and greater relevance in the global economy. Current Brazilian diplomacy, guided by the same political motivations that inspired equivalent initiatives at South–South level, sees those three countries as indispensable allies in opposing the unilateralism of great powers, that is, the United States, first and foremost.

Brazil's foreign policy priorities, under Lula, have been pursued through traditional diplomacy (Itamaraty's activism, reputed for the excellence of its diplomatic staff) and through especially active presidential diplomacy, to which it is possible to add the so-called party diplomacy of Lula's Workers' Party (Partido dos Trabalhadores [PT]). It consists of privileged links and alliances between the progressive and leftist movements, such as the socialist and Marxist parties—mainly in Latin America, where they are organized in the Sao Paulo Forum—as well as the so-called social movements, whose political agenda and focus are close to those of the World Social Forum.[15] The current priorities are the push for South American integration, the so-called South–South diplomacy, and the strategic alliances with some of the large non-hegemonic players. Moreover, the head of the president's foreign advisory staff is the former secretary for international relations of the PT.

The actual results are somewhat confusing, as Brazilian foreign policy can be marked by a double standard, one strand emerging from official diplomacy, the other being a political demand of PT.[16] Traditionally, Brazilian diplomacy was an Itamaraty monopoly. Under Lula, there are multiple players or political agents that participate in the formulation and implementation of current Brazilian foreign policy and can be found at different levels. Because sometimes they appear to be uncoordinated or engage in different kinds of discourses, they create the impression of a fragmented decision-making process. The explanation for this new feature of Brazilian diplomacy can be found in the multilayered character of decision-making that inserts novel actors into a previously more homogeneous procedure.

Thus foreign policy priorities are the result of many inputs, some not totally compatible, others openly contradictory. One example is the pursuit of active policies in the industrial sector, which supports the proclaimed objective of preserving "policy spaces" for national development strategies in "total sovereignty"; by contrast, another example is the acknowledged priority given to common policies in Mercosur. Brazil resists a greater opening in the multilateral trade negotiations, while, at the same time, it pushes for progress in the regional integration process, which demands diminished national sovereignty in macroeconomic as well as industrial policies.

As seen above, this hybrid character of Brazilian diplomacy, more than in any other area of executive governmental activity, combines two world visions: one grounded in the traditional priorities of the establishment and the other grounded in the views of the PT. For instance, economic policy continues to be ruled by the conservative standards of the previous administration, to the great discomfort of the party's militants. It is in the domain of foreign policy, especially regarding South America and the South–South orientation, that the choices of the Lula government are most similar to the political orientation of the PT.

Brazil's Views on the Heiligendamm Process

As explained above, the Brazilian government under Lula intends to build up an alternative system, composed of non-hegemonic vectors of power, rather than reinforcing old schemes such as the G8. Nevertheless, Brazil has not refused any invitation to participate in the annual G8 summits, although it has expressed its desire to come for the "main course," not just for the "dessert" (that is, that its involvement is reflected in more than just one or two paragraphs in the final communiqué). At the same time, Brazil intends to become one of the world's leading political powers, as evidenced by its campaign to gain a permanent seat on the UNSC.

Cardoso never attended any of the G7/8 meetings, despite having occasional contact during the financial turmoil of the late 1990s. As happened with some other leaders of important emerging democracies, he was never formally invited to any of the G7 meetings, which had begun to involve post-Soviet Russia. Nevertheless, he kept very close contact with various social-democratic G7 leaders, especially U.S. president Bill Clinton and British prime minister Tony Blair. These relationships led to an informal partnership between Cardoso and Clinton, who seemed to have a true personal empathy for him. Clinton was inclined to see Brazil assume a greater role in regional conflicts, such as Colombia's fight against the narco-guerillas of the FARC. That kind of involvement met with some reluctance by Cardoso, who was aware of the limitations on Brazil's ability to project its power abroad. Mindful of the objections that would be brought up by Argentina, he also did not insist on Brazil's candidacy for a permanent UNSC seat. Cardoso had always considered Argentinian relations with Brazil within Mercosur to be so strategic that they could not be endangered by some exhibition of Brazilian willingness to play alone in the great powers' game.

Lula came to power in 2003 aiming to gain more international space and engage Brazil widely at the same time, in multilateral negotiations and on the regional front. His objectives have been not only to gain international prestige for Brazil, but also to put diplomacy at the service of national development. This instrumentalization of Brazilian diplomacy is not new. Historically, this political vision, which regards the functionality of diplomacy as linked to the developmental process of the country, has long been a feature of Itamaraty's diplomatic policies designed, and has been described, by more than one author, as a "diplomacy of development" (see, for example, Ricupero 1989).

What may be new in Lula's government is that this same ideology in foreign policy is also present in a national project—with some conceptual linkages to the governmental planning of the military regime of the 1970s. According to Lula, this strategy requires a sovereign national integration into the world economy and a change in the world power relationships, together with other peripheral nations. Official statements regarding the reinforcement of multilateralism (as opposed to what may be the unilateralism of the hegemonic power) and a change in world trade system exemplified it. These changing trade relationships show the clear desire of the current administration for a union of developing countries to enable them to negotiate, in better political conditions, better exchanges between North and South, which are today seen as unequal, notably with regard to agricultural protectionism and subsidies.

In a broader sense, what the diplomatic authorities and Brazilian leaders proposed to regional partners and other developing countries outside the region was a southern coalition that would change the global power relationships (sometimes referred as the axis of world politics). Other proposals concerned the capacity of southern countries to establish a new world trade geography, based much more on South–South exchanges than on the supposed dependence on unequal trade with the North.

Countries that Brazil courted could have realized that, in fact, Brazil has been motivated by, on one hand, obtaining a permanent seat on the UNSC and, on the other, imprinting Brazilian economic interests on South America. These two national objectives are presented as the expression of a new multilateral order that takes all players' interests into consideration. However, the results have thus far been modest and frustrating, despite the large diplomatic (and financial) investments made in South America, Africa, and other regions.

This Brazilian option seems to depart from the ideal route that G7/8 members conceived for new candidates to join their restricted club. In fact, to gain access to the G8, Brazil should be working toward joining another restricted club, the Paris-based OECD, which seems to constitute a sort of "entry ticket" into a G8-plus. Brazil is not a stranger to OECD: it has been an observer on many of its committees, enjoys the status of full member in the Steel Committee, and has participated in many of its activities and seminars. Notwithstanding its adequate credentials to join OECD—compared to other BRIC countries—due to fulfillment of market democracy requirements, the current administration shows reluctance in Brazil's adhesion to this clubby organization, for both practical and ideological reasons.

The Brazilian government's unwillingness to join the OECD arises mainly from conceptual views, or political ideas located at the very heart of Brazil's new diplomacy. As seen above, this foreign policy draws on various political elements from party diplomacy (formulated, needless to say, while PT was still an oppositional party, which it was for 23 years). These ideas, as stated in the PT program, include solidarity among developing countries, and toward national liberation movements, the reform of economic capitalist institutions (supposedly dominated by the great powers), the essential identity of the South (of course against hegemonic countries), and so on. Those assumptions are not necessarily consensual within the Brazilian foreign policy community or even among some target partner countries (namely India, South Africa, or, in another manner, China or Russia). They emanate from the PT rather than from Itamaraty, which exhibits traditional ideas and concepts. Those ideas are a hindrance for a more realistic approach by Brazil's G8 diplomacy.

With regard to the possibility of Brazil becoming a member of the OECD,

> on the one hand, the economic sectors, but also the Ministries of Development and Finance, defend this option as part of a strategy of showing the country's definitive disposition in accepting new international economic regulations. On the other hand, the external sector, supported by bureaucracy segments, sees this option as a precipitated adhesion to the "club of the rich," which would cause damage to Brazil's alliances with countries such as South Africa, China and India [or, in a broad sense, South–South relations] (Sennes and Barbosa 2005, 225–226).

From a practical standpoint, Brazil's current leadership does not intend to renounce the country's present status as a developing country, as a full OECD membership could imply (with its consequences in terms of trade preferences and other differential treatment for developing countries). On balance, Brazilian leaders assume that the difference between the intended objectives of gaining admittance to the OECD and the actual gains derived from this new status could be negative for Brazil. The point of departure is a conception that supposes a fixed "peripheral" status for Brazil and a permanent or continuing status as a developing country, which cannot be overcome by the normal path of growth and development along the lines of other developed nations. Instead of relying on *de facto* economic interdependence among all countries—developed or developing alike—Brazil's leadership assumes, on ideological grounds, that the country needs its own agenda of sovereign integration into the world economy, with the consequent redefinition of the international political and economic order. Lima (2005, 30) writes that

> the eventual incorporation of Brazil, India, and South Africa to the G8, or the UNSC, although representing an amplified presence and voice of the countries of the South, may generate problems in their respective regions, and is not necessarily seen by the others as an improvement of

their political representation in those forums, but as a co-optation of the most developed among them. On the other hand, the incorporation of only one or two of them would undermine the bargaining power of the G3 vis-à-vis the industrialized countries [translated by the authors].

The Brazilian agenda of transforming the world "from the bottom" does not seem to attain measurable gains—either diplomatic or economic—even in the most successful test cases of the new diplomacy, namely the IBSA Dialogue Forum and the intended special relationship with China. Perhaps the new BRIC Dialogue will give new strength to the Brazilian world vision. None of the Brazilian candidacies to head international organizations (such as the WTO, the IADB, the World Intellectual Property Organization [WIPO]) received extensive support among its privileged partners—that is, developing countries—or among its own neighbors in South America. This is probably due to Brazil's modest weight in the relevant flow of goods, services, technology, and capital, as well as in the provision of technical assistance and cooperation in a world scale, in relation to its more vocal and quite visible role in some of the main world forums. In due course, based on the modest results achieved so far, the practical implementation of regional diplomacy and the South–South orientation—reaffirmed at the beginning of Lula's second term—shows a greater degree of pragmatism, compared to his first term.

In conclusion, Brazilian leadership, and also its traditional establishment—members of the industrial elite, high-ranking military, and diplomats—are eager to see Brazil incorporated into the inner core of the global governance, even though there is no clear strategy for achieving this objective, besides the old demand to be accepted as a permanent member of the UNSC and to be recognized, by neighbors and big countries alike, as the *de facto* leader in South America. PT's leaders and the president himself continue to show ideological restrictions to overcoming Brazil's status as a developing country and to jump decisively to a "graduate" status. Perhaps a new Brazilian government, from 2011 onward, can take a more active role in integrating the country into the world economy and be more receptive to working together with advanced countries, on the basis of a typical G8 agenda, instead of seeking, as it does today, leadership of the southern, developing world and pushing for a traditional approach to development (that is, the redistribution of world wealth, the transfer of technology, international justice, and so on).

For now, Brazil's leaders prefer the country to be seen as a responsible developing country, capable of engaging in a serious dialogue with G8 leaders, rather than to be perceived by other developing partners as adhering to a rich club agenda. In fact, to share some of the new responsibilities implied in such adherence, and indeed required by it, Brazil ought to have much more implicit and explicit powers than it currently enjoys, in terms of both economic relevance and military preparedness. Although Brazil is making a great effort at technical cooperation with other developing countries—mainly in Africa and in South America—its capacity to deliver financial aid or security abroad is limited. Brazil's "diplomatic GDP" is somewhat greater than its real GDP or its strategic capacity to raise the stakes, thanks to the high quality of its professional foreign service.

Based on its current pattern of economic stability, its traditional capitalist modes of production, a moderate appeal for the reform of international institutions and the restructuring of the world political order, a solid recognition of the virtues of international law and the "force of reason" (instead of the "reason of the force"), and its multilateral activism in almost all of the existing intergovernmental bodies, Brazil seems ready to move up the scale of international responsibilities and new endeavours. The question is: does Brazil want to accept the rules of the game, as set by a small group—the G8—that dominates most of the international agenda?

Brazil, of course, does not refuse to engage in a dialogue with current G8 members, from which it demands equal treatment and an unrestricted agenda for discussions. The point is that Brazil continues to press for a typical developing country agenda—not different, perhaps, from many of the issues also raised by India, but without its regional or nuclear weight—and continues to see the world as divided into these two groups of developed and developing countries. Today's leaders tend to choose the language of old-fashioned third world solidarity, while at the same time engaging in serious negotiations with other world leaders on relevant issues on the international agenda.

It may seem that changing this ambiguous course is the least difficult move in practical terms, considering the current advanced level of Brazil's industrialization and its technical superiority in terms of a highly successful tropical agriculture. However, such a paradigm shift in diplomatic ideology toward a "less developing" Brazil would represent a Copernican revolution in traditional beliefs and practices. The concrete fear—in a world divided according to old North–South lines—is to lose political ground with other developing countries, beginning with the undeclared claim to achieve regional leadership in South America.

For the Brazilian current leadership, joining the G8 club would mean recognizing that there will be no change in the world power axis simply because Brazil adheres to the existing one, thus amounting to a reversal in efforts to establish a new trade system. In fact, the members of the real Brazilian society and economy—those of modern entrepreneurs and urban elites, and even of most farmers, who produce the bulk of Brazil's trade surplus— are probably ready to pursue a new path to political alliances and economic interdependence with the global economy, if they have not already begun to. Political leadership is lagging behind on this new agenda, which explains its hesitation to undertake the complex set of structural reforms that could lead Brazil further into this brave new world of globalization. A "mental revolution" is needed in the Brazilian political structure, and the debate is still open.

Notes

1 The views reflected here are those of the authors and not of the Centro Brasileiro de Relações Internacionais or the Brazilian government.
2 The Heiligendamm Process was announced in the declaration on "Growth and Responsibility in the World Economy" released at the annual summit of the G8 (2007a) leading industrialized countriesin June 2007. The road map of this process is described in the joint declaration of the G8 presidency and Brazil, China, India, Mexico, and South Africa, which includes issues relating to investment conditions; the promotion of innovation and the protection of intellectual property rights; counteracting climate change, promoting energy efficiency and technology cooperation; and development policy, particularly in Africa (G8 2007b).
3 The IBSA Dialogue Forum is a trilateral initiative to strengthen South–South cooperation, promote themes of mutual interest in the international agenda, and increase trade and investment opportunities among the three respective countries with the purpose of alleviating poverty. The conversations began at the 2003 G8 Evian Summit and was formalized in the Brasilia Declaration in June 2003 (IBSA 2003). The first IBSA ministerial meeting took place in Brasilia, Brazil, in September 2006, and the second in Tshwane, South Africa, in October 2007. The original areas of cooperation were agriculture, climate change, culture, defence, education, energy, health, information society, science and technology, social development, trade and investment, tourism, and transport.
4 CASA is a Brazilian initiative launched in Peru in December 2004, as a basis for integrating the existing trade schemes—namely Mercosur and the Andean Community—and including in them other South American countries (Chile, Guyana, and Suriname). It also acts as technical coordinator for infrastructure or physical integration programs. After two ministerial meetings and a summit, member countries decided to replace CASA with Unasur. The treaty to establish Unasur was signed on May 23, 2008, in Brasilia, with the secretariat being located in Quito, Ecuador.
5 The proposal of an economic group comprising the four largest emerging countries was originally suggested in a study by Goldman Sachs economists Dominic Wilson

and Roopa Purushothaman (2003) in an exploratory paper on the evolution of the world economy up to 2005.Since then other studies, specially "Brics and Beyond" (Goldman Sachs Economic Group 2007), have enlarged and completed this perspective.

6 For the definition of foreign policy community, see Souza (2002).

7 George Kennan has referred to "monster countries" in several articles as well as books; see, for example, Kennan (1993). *Ankerländer* is almost official doctrine in the German foreign office.

8 Additionally, Brazil is the second largest market in the world for mobile telephones, executive jets, and helicopters. Brazilians constitute almost half of Latin American internet users.

9 There has been an impressive increase in trade between Brazil and the RICs: from US$488 million in 2000 to US$967 million in 2007, in the case of India; from US$529 million to US$1757 million with South Africa; and from US$1,560 million to US$10,748 million with China (MDIC 2008). Nevertheless, the ongoing crisis, unleashed by the subprime crash in the U.S. and the overvalued Brazilian currency, is slowing down this positive trend.

10 IIRSA was established at the first South American Summit in 2000 to map infrastructure projects in the region and facilitate investment in infrastructure, energy, and transport in the 12 South America countries, to be financed by Inter-American Development Bank (IADB), the Andean Development Corporation (Corporación Andina de Fomento [CAF]), the Brazilian Development Bank (Banco Nacional de Desenvolvimento Econômico e Social [BNDES]), and the private sector.

11 Brazil's aspiration for regional leadership is not accepted by Argentina, for matters of principle, and has recently raised some strain, due, in one side, to intense competition for comparable position by Venezuelan president Hugo Chavez, and, on the other side, to bargaining demands by small neighbouring countries. Indeed, Lula himself has expressed his inclination for a diplomacy of generosity toward South American and African countries, taking into account the relatively more advanced industrial basis in Brazil.

12 The G20—not to be confused with the G20 finance ministers and central bank governors—includes 23 members with a balanced geographic representation: five countries from Africa (Egypt, Nigeria, South Africa, Tanzania, and Zimbabwe), six from Asia (China, India, Indonesia, Pakistan, Philippines, and Thailand), and 12 from Latin America (Argentina, Bolivia, Brazil, Chile, Cuba, Ecuador, Guatemala, Mexico, Paraguay, Peru, Uruguay, and Venezuela). It has been constituted as a recognized interlocutor in the agricultural negotiations and represents almost 60 percent of the world population and 26 percent of the world's agricultural exports.

13 The Brazilian agribusiness sector underwent a significant modernization process in the 1990s, increasing its competitiveness both in productivity and in export capacity. The sector was able to draw on solid technical research, which was translated into demands to eliminate trade-distorting subsidies in international negotiations, as well as in WTO's dispute settlement panels.

14 The idea of constituting a strategic alliance of the BRICs was already expressed in Lula's government program. The first informal meetings came as a result of a

Brazilian initiative, although the idea of a formal group was first raised by the Russian foreign minister.

15 The World Social Forum (WSF) is an open meeting where social movements, networks, non-governmental organizations (NGOs), and other civil society organizations—opposed to neo-liberalism and globalization—debate ideas, formulate proposals, and exchange experiences. The first meeting was held in Porto Alegre, Brazil, in 2001. The WSF takes place annually at the same time as the World Economic Forum held in Davos, Switzerland, to increase mass protest and try to overshadow the latter's media coverage.

16 That ambivalence has resulted in some difficult choices, for instance, when the Colombian government tried to gain the political support of Brazilian government in order to label the guerrilla movement of the Revolutionary Armed Forces of Columbia (Fuerzas Armadas Revolucionarias de Colombia [FARC]) a terrorist group and faced obvious Brazilian hesitation.

References

Barbosa, Rubens (2005). "O Brasil e a OCDE." ["Brazil and the OECD."] 27 December. e-agora. www.e-agora.org.br/conteudo.php?id=3138_0_3_40_C20 (May 2008).

G8 (2007). "Growth and Responsibility in the World Economy." 7 June, Heiligendamm. www.g8.utoronto.ca/summit/2007heiligendamm/g8-2007-economy.html (May 2008).

G8 and Outreach Partners (2007). "Joint Statement by the German G8 Presidency and the Heads of State and/or Government of Brazil, China, India, Mexico, and South Africa on the Occasion of the G8 Summit in Heiligendamm." 8 June, Heiligendamm. www.g8.utoronto.ca/summit/2007heiligendamm/g8-2007-joint .html (May 2008).

Goldman Sachs Economic Group (2007). "BRICs and Beyond." www2.goldman sachs.com/ideas/brics/book/BRIC-Full.pdf (May 2008).

IBSA (2003). "Brasilia Declaration." 6 June, Brasilia. www.ibsa-trilateral.org/ brasil_declaration.htm (May 2008).

Kennan, George (1993). *Around the Cragged Hill: A Personal and Political Philosophy.* New York: W.W. Norton.

Lima, Maria Regina Soares de (2005). "A política externa brasileira e os desafios da cooperação Sul-Sul." ["Brazil's Foreign Policy and the Challenges of South–South Cooperation."] *Revista Brasileira de Política Internacional* 48(1): 24–59.

Lula da Silva, Luia Inácio (2003). "A New Course for Brazil." Address to the Congress by the President of the Federative Republic of Brazil on the Occasion of his Inauguration. 1 January, Brasilia. www.mre.gov.br/ingles/politica_externa/ discursos/discurso_detalhe3.asp?ID_DISCURSO=2068 (May 2008).

Lula da Silva, Luia Inácio (2007). "Discurso de posse do Presidente da República na Cerimônia de Compromisso Constitucional perante o Congresso Nacional." 1 January, Brasilia. www.mre.gov.br/portugues/politica_externa/discursos/discurso _detalhe3.asp?ID_DISCURSO=3010 (May 2008).

Ministério do Desenvolvimento, Indústria e Comércio Exterior, (2008). "Balança Comercial Brasileira." ["Brazilian Trade Balance."] BCE004A. www.mdic.gov.br/ arquivos/dwnl_1201180282.doc (May 2008).

Motta Veiga, Pedro da (2005). *Brazil's Trade Policy: Moving Away from Old Paradigms.* Draft 1. Washington DC: Brookings Institution Press. <www.brookings .edu./papers/2008/05_brazil_trade_veiga.aspx?rssid=latinamerica> (May 2008).

National Intelligence Council (2004). *Mapping the Global Future.* Report of the National Intelligence Council's 2020 Project. Washington DC.

Ricupero, Rubens (1989). "A Diplomacia do Desenvolvimento." In Três Ensaios de Diplomacia Brasileira, edited by J.H. Pereira de Araújo, M. Azambuja, and R. Ricupero, 193–209. Brasilia: MRE.

Sennes, Ricardo and Alexandre de Freitas Barbosa (2005). "Brazil's Multiple Forms of External Engagement: Foreign Policy Dilemmas." In Reforming from the Top: A Leaders' 20 Summit, edited by J. English, R. Thakur, and A.F. Cooper, 201–229. Tokyo: United Nations University.

Souza, Amaury de (2002). *A Agenda Internacional do Brasil: Um etudo sobre a comunidade brasileira da política externa.* Rio de Janeiro: Centro Brasileiro de Relações Internacionais. www.cebri.org.br/pdf/101_PDF.pdf (May 2008).

Wilson, Dominic and Roopa Purushothaman (2003). "Dreaming with BRICs: The Path to 2050." Global Economics Paper No. 99, October. New York: Goldman Sachs. www2.goldmansachs.com/ideas/brics/book/99-dreaming.pdf (May 2008).

World Bank (2007). *Global Economic Prospects 2007: Managing the Next Wave of Globalization.* Washington DC: World Bank go.worldbank.org/6PT7IQPSP2 (May 2008).

7

South Africa
Global Reformism, Global Apartheid,
and the Heiligendamm Process

Brendan Vickers

The presence of our eminent representatives at Heiligendamm must communicate the message, once again, that Africa's leaders are determined to use their bold and imaginative thinking to take the historic actions that will shape the future of our Continent in favour of the millions of African men and women who are proud to say—I am an African! —*Thabo Mbeki*

The HDP process is an opportunity to demonstrate our ability to work together. However, it is still too early to say how far the Process will go with its limited agenda and mandate. —*Jacob Zuma*

After decades of apartheid-induced international isolation, South Africa's transition to a multiracial democratic order in 1994 opened a heady and historical new chapter in the country's foreign policy. Resonating with the ethical claims and moral authority of the domestic and global anti-apartheid struggles, the new government—led by the country's first black president, Nelson Mandela, and the African National Congress (ANC)—articulated a set of highly idealistic foreign policy principles and normative precepts. South Africa's newfound "good international citizenship" translated into explicit commitments to promote and uphold human rights, democracy, and international law, placed Africa and the Southern African region at the centre of foreign policy deliberations, and mandated the new government to participate constructively in multilateral institutions to equitably transform North–South relations. Although it would be fair to argue that pragmatism trumped much of this early messianic enthusiasm, the embedded idealism in these lofty commitments has remained the quintessential normative touchstone of South Africa's global activism from the Mandela presidency (1994–99) through the Mbeki years.

The advent of the administration of Thabo Mbeki in 1999—with foreign policy decisions increasingly centralized in the presidency—refined South Africa's foreign policy. The lesson of the often inchoate Mandela era was that South Africa's international relations had to be better calibrated with the country's domestic capabilities, as well as its domestic policies and priorities as a developing country (Alden and le Pere 2003).

This consolidation exercise was twofold. First, South Africa's foreign policy was reinvigorated by Mbeki's articulation of the "African renaissance" vision and its later neo-liberal policy imprint, the New Partnership for Africa's Development (NEPAD). Second, Mbeki's avowed commitment to a "Better Africa in a Better World" saw the emergence of an ambitious agenda for the reform and democratization of the processes and institutions of global political, economic, security, and social governance. In this regard, Mbeki—acting as a self-styled spokesperson for Africa and the broader South—pressed the case for a more equitable, democratic, and people-centred world order. The strategic contours of this paradigm were presented to South Africa's National Assembly on 13 June 2000:

> At the centre of all the engagements ... is the critical question of our time, of how humanity should respond to the irreversible process of globalisation while addressing the fundamental challenges that face the bulk of humanity. These include poverty, underdevelopment, the growing North–South gap, racism and xenophobia, gender discrimination, ill health, violent conflicts and the threat to the environment ... This engagement must necessarily address among things the restructuring of the UN [United Nations], including the Security Council, a review of the functioning of such bodies as the IMF [International Monetary Fund] and the World Bank, the determination of agenda and the manner of operation of the WTO [World Trade Organization] and an assessment of the role of the G7. Central to these processes must be the objective of reversing the marginalisation of Africa and the rest of the South (Mbeki 2000).

Critics of this reformist approach to global governance are doubtful that it will change the world for the better, in the absence of more transformative policy impulses (e.g., Bond 2001, 2004; Nel et al. 2001). They make a fair, if perhaps poignant case. Nonetheless, the ambition, reach, and scope of this global agenda have seen Mbeki and senior state officials actively engaging the G8 countries on Africa's pressing developmental challenges.

Since his first invitation to Tokyo, on the sidelines of the G8's Okinawa Summit in July 2000, Mbeki has pressed Africa's case for enhanced debt cancellation; sustained capital inflows and foreign direct investment (FDI); increased official development assistance (ODA); ongoing deleterious northern trade protectionism; poverty, underdevelopment, and income divergence; and the need for technology transfer to overcome what Mbeki calls the global digital divide. Since 2007, this engagement has taken a salutary turn with the launching of the Heiligendamm Process (HP) of enhanced engagement with the Outreach Five (O5) countries, initiated under Germany's watch as the G8 president.

This chapter explores South Africa's enhanced engagement with the G8 under the HP. The chapter is divided into six sections. Section one explores South Africa's structural location in the world economy as well as the socioeconomic challenges that confront the country today. Section two discusses South Africa's regional, multilateral, and normative power as the basis for its possible inclusion into a new group of 13 (G13). This includes an analysis of South Africa's African agenda—this wording is important—and Mbeki's engagement with the G8, alongside his high peers from the continent. Section three explores South Africa's foreign policy priorities, particularly its North–South diplomacy in order to better appreciate the importance of the HP to South Africa. Section four investigates the ideas, interests and institutions that underpin South Africa's enhanced G8 engagement and participation in the four HP working groups. Section five critically considers the political arguments for South Africa joining a possible G13 under the HP. The chapter concludes by determining whether there is potential scope for the O5 to craft a common vision for global governance reform.

South Africa: From the "Rainbow Nation" to "Two Economies"

South Africa's Economic and Social Structure

South Africa was once identified as ranking among the world's "Big Ten" emerging markets (Garten 1997). However, compared to its partners in the HP, South Africa is marginal in global economic terms.[1] With a gross domestic product (GDP) in terms of purchasing power parity (PPP) worth US\$467 billion in 2007—the 25th largest in the world—there is little objective economic (or even demographic) rationale for the country's inclusion into the O5, let alone an expanded G13. But it is striking that for Africa as a whole, South Africa accounts for over a third of sub-Saharan African GDP. In other words, South Africa is Africa's continental colossus and its regional economic powerhouse—a *de facto*, but reluctant hegemon.

On the other hand, South Africa shares many of the socioeconomic pathologies that afflict Brazil, India, China, and Mexico. South Africa is a middle-income developing country with a medium human development ranking that is well below the other O5 partners, barring India (United Nations Development Programme 2007). This reflects the vast social and economic challenges that confront the young democracy, compounded by chronic capacity weaknesses within the state.

Although not ranked among the emerging world's "new titans," South Africa does hold considerable economic potential: since 2003, the economy has grown by an average of 5 percent per annum, GDP per person has increased by more than 20 percent since 2000, and investment as a share of GDP has risen from approximately 15 percent to 21 percent (with a target of 25 percent by 2014), as the government addresses some of the country's key infrastructural bottlenecks (Manuel 2008).[2] South Africa's economy is overwhelmingly oriented toward services (up to 70 percent of GDP), flanked by an efficient agricultural sector and a capital-intensive "minerals-energy complex" (Fine and Rustomjee 1996). The latter has benefited from bullish commodity prices, particularly the global demand for base metals. A relatively diversified manufacturing sector contributes roughly 18.5 percent to GDP. However, the latter is struggling to further develop, diversify, and compete against Asia's competitive advantages, a position compounded by domestic structural and policy constraints.

Notwithstanding these strong global integrationist impulses, a number of disconcerting trends blight the promise of the post-apartheid social dividend. These include high levels of income inequality (between a rich white minority and an affluent emerging black middle class, and an impoverished black majority), unemployment rates that are among the highest globally, rapid urbanization amid sprawling informal settlements, the highest incidence of HIV/AIDS in the world, with an estimated 5.3 million people infected, a dearth of skilled human resources, and corruption, crime, and domestic violence. Despite boasting the most generous social welfare policy in Africa, many South African citizens still live in conditions of grinding poverty.

South Africa's Economic Policies

As intimated above, the central challenge facing the new ANC-led government that took office in April 1994 was essentially to build a modern, vibrant, and outward-oriented economy that is internationally competitive, while simultaneously addressing the massive backlogs in access to social and economic services. The government initially adopted the Reconstruction and Development Programme in 1994, characterized by social-democratic redistributive impulses to meet basic needs. However, following the country's first post-apartheid financial crisis in 1996, the government launched headlong into the conservative Growth, Employment, and Redistribution (GEAR) macroeconomic strategy. GEAR espoused the virtues of the market, with a premium on export-led growth, fiscal discipline, investor confidence, and macroeconomic stability.

By 2000, GEAR's fiscal austerity had achieved little—besides stabilizing the economy after apartheid's spending excesses. The dearth of palpable socioeconomic dividends led the government to emphasize the need for a more activist "democratic developmental state" to facilitate economic growth and development, and to address the particular challenges of South Africa's "two parallel economies." According to Mbeki:

> The First Economy is modern, produces the bulk of our country's wealth, and is integrated within the global economy. The Second Economy (or the Marginalised Economy) is characterised by underdevelopment, contributes little to the GDP, contains a big percentage of our population, incorporates the poorest of our rural and urban poor, is structurally disconnected from both the First and the global economy, and is incapable of self-generated growth and development (Mbeki 2003).

As a nascent developmental state, the South African government must focus on two policy imperatives: the first is to improve the medium- to long-term cost structure of the economy by harnessing regulation, competition, and public investment strategies; the second is to ensure that the private and public sectors agree on long-term strategies for a selected set of industrial and services sectors, and work together to achieve them (Hirsch 2006). Advised by a team of international economists linked to Harvard University, in 2006, the government accordingly adopted a new growth strategy, the Accelerated and Shared Growth Initiative for South Africa (ASGISA). By identifying and targeting the six "binding constraints" that inhibit the economy's growth potential, ASGISA aims to catapult economic growth to 6 percent and halve the unemployment rate to 15 percent by 2014.[3] In order to address the challenges faced by the real economy, ASGISA has been complemented by a new industrial policy framework and action plan, which seeks to identify and emulate some of the best practices from East Asia's public interventionism.

South Africa's Regional, Multilateral, and Normative Power

In the post-apartheid period, South Africa has attracted various suggestive epithets, from "emerging middle power" and "pivotal state" to "regional hegemon." The G8's rationale for including South Africa in its fold—and arguably even a future G13—therefore rests on two logical levels: regional and global. Put otherwise, South Africa has been double courted by the G8, first as a member of the Africa constituency that has enjoyed privileged access to the G8 since 2000; and second as a member of the O5 emerging powers.

South Africa's African Agenda and the G8

Africa constitutes the central focus for the conduct of South Africa's foreign policy. The country is the most industrialized, diversified, and sophisticated economy in the continent. South Africa's GDP is 40 times larger than the average sub-Saharan economy. Moreover, it represents 25 percent of the total African economy, and constitutes one third of the economy of sub-Saharan Africa and almost two thirds of the GDP of the Southern African Development Community (SADC) (Grobbelaar 2007, 13). Not only does South Africa maintain a substantial trade surplus with most of the SADC and the rest of Africa, but by 2000, South Africa had become the largest single foreign investor in the rest of Africa. South African firms have established interests in mining, banking, retail, telecommunications, arms, and insurance (Grobbelaar and Besada 2007).

Understandably, post-apartheid South Africa has been expected to play the role of regional engine of growth and development. However, this role conceptualization fails to adequately recognize the tenuous political legitimacy that accompanies South Africa's perceived continental hegemony. The latter is compounded by perceptions of the country's protectionist trade and xenophobic immigration policies, and the aggressive market expansion by South African capital into Africa, which often displaces or crowds out local entrepreneurs. This situation has led some analysts to depict South African firms as "new exploiters" or "hegemons," while others argue that these firms are the "market developers" and "market leaders" that increase competition and trade in under-developed markets (see Adebajo 2007; Hudson 2007).

The South African government is acutely aware of these perceptions: "One cannot hope to make sense of the foreign policy predispositions of South Africa's policymakers without appreciating just how sensitive they are to views of the country being an African hegemonic state or bully" (Landsberg and Monyae 2006, 141). For this reason, the government has consistently stressed that it harbours no hegemonic ambitions in the continent. Its commitment to overhauling the continental institutional architecture—particularly the transition from the Organization of African Unity (OAU) to the new African Union (AU) and restructuring the SADC—to ensure their greater efficiency has been sincere. In pursuit of peace, security, and stability in the continent, South Africa has mediated in a number of continental conflicts, notably the Democratic Republic of Congo (DRC), Burundi, the Comoros, Côte d'Ivoire, Sudan, and Zimbabwe.[4] Moreover, under Mbeki's watch, South Africa has deployed more than 3,000 peace-keepers in African conflict situations, which has increased its credibility as a major geostrategic player in Africa (Adebajo et al. 2007). In addition, South Africa has many elements of soft power that it can more effectively harness to promote its interests and win friends in Africa:

> South Africa can use *Channel Africa*, which transmits to 33 African countries, to expose Africans further to South Africa and to improve the knowledge of South Africans about the rest of the continent. South African mobile giants, MTN and Vodacom, could connect the entire continent with their mobile phone network; while South African technology and capital could help build the roads, railways, and ports that Africa badly needs for its industrial take-off. South Africa already generates, by some estimates, half of sub-Saharan Africa's electricity needs and is investing in a trans-Africa electricity grid. South African Airways (SAA) is the most reliable aircraft carrier on the continent (Adebajo et al. 2007, 24).

From a regional perspective, the G8 countries recognize—but simultaneously foist upon South Africa—this continental leadership role and resulting responsibilities, as Africa's most advanced economy. Since the Okinawa Summit in 2000 through to the Hokkaido Toyako Summit in 2008, Mbeki, supported by colleagues drawn from the continent's more reformist camp, has leveraged his presence at the G8's annual summits to push for greater assistance for Africa, particularly through financial, technical, and other support for NEPAD. Notwithstanding widespread continental critique of this paradigm, NEPAD still constitutes the focal point for South Africa's ongoing engagement with Africa's development partners, notably the G8. In addition, the G8 Africa Action Plan, adopted at the 2002 Kananaskis Summit in Canada, remains the principal template for G8 support to Africa. Although additional commitments were subsequently made at the G8 summits in Evian (France) in 2003 and Sea Island (United States) in 2004, it was during 2005 at Gleneagles (United Kingdom) that the G8's support for Africa reached its highpoint. Two key developments stand out. The first was the establishment of the Commission for Africa (CfA), which released its final report in March 2005. The 17-member commission—with participation by South African finance minister Trevor Manuel—was constituted by British prime minister Tony Blair to define the challenges facing Africa and to provide fresh and clear recommendations on how to support the changes needed to reduce poverty. The second key event was the Gleneagles Summit itself, hosted by Blair in his fortuitous capacity as president of both the G8 and European Union. With Britain's Africa policy increasingly centralized in Downing Street, the Gleneagles commitments were understandably ambitious. Since these have become benchmarks for the G8's commitments to Africa, it is worth recalling that the summit agreed to, *inter alia*:

- double aid to Africa by 2010 and give an extra US$50 billion a year globally;
- cancel the debts owed by some of the world's poorest countries to the IMF, the World Bank, and the African Development Bank (AfDB); which will be worth more than US$50 billion when fully implemented, and 90 percent will go to Africa;
- write off US$18 billion of Nigeria's debt, the biggest ever single debt deal for an African country;
- get as close as possible to universal access to AIDS treatments by 2010; and
- help the AU to set up a standby force as part of the 2004 G8 commitment to train 75,000 troops for peacekeeping by 2010.

Africa's growth and sustainable development again featured prominently on the agendas of the 2007 Heiligendamm and 2008 Hokkaido summits, despite concerns from the Africa Progress Panel that the G8 were backsliding in their aid commitments.[5] In summary, South Africa appears to have become the G8's point of reference—arguably even their "point person"—on the African agenda, notably NEPAD.

South Africa's Global Governance Agenda

Just as important for the G8 is South Africa's soft power as an international norm entrepreneur and global reformer. Joseph Nye (1990) seminally defined soft power as co-optive power that involves intangible power resources such as culture, ideology, and institutions—essentially the normative attraction of good ideas. South Africa's soft power stems from a variety of vectors: its peacefully negotiated transition away from apartheid authoritarianism to

racial reconciliation; the unilateral dismantling of its nuclear weapons program; the towering personality and international stature of its former pris-
oner-to-president, Nelson Mandela, and the progressive global statesmanship
of his successor; and the country's adoption of one of the world's most liberal constitutions. In foreign policy making, these soft power resources find
salutary resonance with a deep-rooted internationalist commitment among
the ruling party, the ANC (Nel 1999). For instance, South African politicians
have enthusiastically touted the lessons and experiences of South Africa's
negotiated "rainbow nation" model for conflict resolution in Northern Ire-
land, East Timor, Israel and Palestine, Burundi, Rwanda, Iraq, and the DRC.
Put otherwise by a former director general of the Department of Foreign
Affairs: "South Africa has experienced time and again how countries, organisations and people have looked to us to provide leadership, new ideas and
breakthroughs in dead-locked situations" (Selebi 1999, 209).

South Africa's principled commitments to strengthening multilateralism, creating equitable global governance, and building partnerships for
progressive global change capture the normative essence and strategic rationale for the country's special relationship with the G8. As Deon Geldenhuys
(2006, 93) writes:

> Since its democratic rebirth, South Africa has been more than an exemplary
> upholder of major codes of good state conduct; it has also assigned itself the
> task of actively promoting such standards abroad, and has become a promi-
> nent norm formulator in multilateral forums, especially in Africa. By so
> doing, it has lived up to the standards of "good international citizenship."

In this role as an international norm entrepreneur, Pretoria's multilateral engagement aims to address the more pernicious effects of globalization
(particularly its atomizing and marginalizing tendencies for Africa) by being
a leading advocate for greater influence and participation by developing
countries in shaping a new paradigm for global governance. In this regard,
the democratization and reform of the multilateral institutions of governance is cardinal, with the objective of reversing the marginalization of
Africa and the rest of the South, and increasing their capacity to play a more
meaningful role in international affairs. This principled position has characterized South Africa's engagement with the G8 too.

South Africa has widely been portrayed as a middle power facilitator
with a strong reformist agenda, with an ability to build common ground
between the North and the South. South Africa believes that its two-
economies socioeconomic structure makes it well placed, structurally and

Table 7-1

South Africa's Multilateral and Regional Leadership Positions

Level	Leadership Positions, Alliances, and Initiatives
United Nations	United Nations Conference on Trade and Development (1996–2000) G77 and China (2006) United Nations Security Council (2006–2008) Four Nations Initiative on United Nations Governance and Management
World Trade Organization	Friend of the Chair (2001) Chair, Committee on Trade and Development (2004–2006) Africa Group, G20 developing countries, NAMA-11
International financial institutions	Chair, Development Committee G20 finance ministers and central bank governors (2007)
North-South	Commonwealth (1999)
South-South	Non-Aligned Movement (1999) Asian-African Sub-Regional Organizations Conference (2004) Heads of State Summit for the India–Brazil–South Africa Dialogue Forum (2007)
Africa	Southern African Development Community (1996, 2008) African Union (2002) Pan-African Parliament, host
Other	Progressive Governance Summit (2006)

Note: NAMA = non-agricultural market access.

normatively, to assist in equitably transforming North–South relations, through the G8 and elsewhere:

> The position in which South Africa finds itself is that it has features both of the developed and the developing world. It is truly at the point of intersection between both worlds—an industrialised state of the South which can communicate with the North on equal terms. Conversely, we can interpret the concerns and fears of the developed world (Nzo 1995).

Moreover, it may be argued that since South Africa's reformist approach to global governance is essentially technical and does not challenge the underlying structural power of the current hegemonic order, the G8 sees no problem with Pretoria's brand of global activism (Nel et al. 2001).

South Africa's approach to multilateralism is premised upon the need to deepen and strengthen the rules-based system (particularly the UN), which limits the possibility of unilateral actions by the major powers. Since 1994, this commitment to multilateralism has been diffuse, rather than discrete (see Table 7-1). In other words, Pretoria has engaged in niche building over a wide range of issues in the domain of security (disarmament, non-proliferation, small arms and mercenaries), human rights (women and children's rights, and the creation of the UN's Human Rights Council), international law (negotiating the Treaty of Rome to establish a permanent International Criminal Court), the "new" multilateralism (Kimberley and Ottawa processes on conflict diamonds and landmines), and the socioeconomic and the global commons agenda (sustainable development, fairer global trade rules, and enhanced debt relief). In 2006, South Africa was elected to the UN's Security Council (UNSC) as a two-year non-permanent member, dedicating its term to advancing the African agenda. However, given the high expectations placed on South Africa, Pretoria's voting behaviour and opposition to the West's insistence on placing Myanmar, Zimbabwe, and global warming on the UNSC's agenda has not proven uncontroversial (van Nieuwkerk 2007).

South African Foreign Policy: North, South, and International Partnerships

The government's International Relations, Peace, and Security cluster of departments has consistently prioritized the need to strengthen North-South cooperation further. In its medium-term strategic planning, the Department of Foreign Affairs now also elevates improved North–South cooperation to a priority in its own right. Two tactical vectors underpin this objective: first, strengthening relations with the G8 and European Union to advance the African agenda; and second, consolidating the country's enhanced engagement with the Organisation for Economic Co-operation and Development (OECD). South Africa's involvement with the OECD has deepened over the last few years, partly as a result of the OECD's broader engagement with Africa (see OECD 2003), but also because of the OECD's courting of the emerging powers. South Africa has adopted an incremental approach to possible OECD membership, participating in 15 committees. South Africa has also joined the OECD's Development Centre, which serves as an interface between its members and emerging and developing economies.

The obverse side to this strategy is the need to consolidate South–South relations in order to shape a common vision for global governance reform, to identify and share best practices for sustainable socioeconomic development, and to diversify South Africa's trading relations. The latter took shape through the adoption, in 1996, of a trade strategy premised on the metaphor of a butterfly. This conceived of Africa as the continental body of the butterfly, opening up its trading wings to the dynamic growth poles of Asia in the East (especially China and India) and Latin America in the West, while consolidating economic relations with the country's traditional, but economically sluggish Northern partners.

While trade with China, India, and Mercosur has rapidly grown (preferential tariff agreements are being negotiated with all three to enhance trade potential), the EU remains South Africa's most important trading partner and largest source of FDI. In 2006, total trade stood at R287 billion, underpinned by South Africa's first post-apartheid free trade agreement. The EU has also identified South Africa as one of its "strategic partners," alongside some of the other HP countries (Olivier 2006). The United States is the country's second most important trading partner. South African exports to the U.S. rose from R11 billion in 1998 to R41 billion in 2006. This represents a sizeable increase of 270 percent.

The political counterpart to this enhanced South–South engagement found fruition with Thabo Mbeki's idea, floated in 1998 when he was deputy president, of a countervailing "G8 of the South" (or G-South) to hold the North to account for policies that rode roughshod over southern interests. The formation of the India–Brazil–South Africa (IBSA) Dialogue Forum in 2003—quintessentially a South African brainchild—has arguably formed the initial incubator for such a tactical southern axis. In future, IBSA may extend its membership to encompass the remaining O5 partners, China and Mexico.

What is potent is that policy makers in Pretoria place a strong premium on building pragmatic partnerships to transform historical North–South relations of asymmetry. This provides the context for understanding and appreciating South Africa's enhanced engagement with the G8, as a middle power of the South:

> Leveraging its domestic experiment of a negotiated settlement, South Africa sees itself as a champion of building partnerships between South and South and North and South. Under the broad banner of "bridge-building," the models of partnership-building and alliance constructor are role conceptions that the Mbeki government, in particular, has emphasised (Landsberg and Monyae 2006, 138).

South Africa and the Heiligendamm Process:
Ideas, Interests, and Institutions

From the above observations, it would appear that the reform of the G8 under the HP—whether it is constituted into a G13 condominium or simply institutionalizes structured thematic dialogue—fits comfortably with the normative logic of South Africa's foreign policy calculations. French president Nicolas Sarkozy (2008), on a state visit to South Africa in February 2008, endorsed South Africa's candidature for full membership of the G13:

> South Africa is for us a partner in globalization. We have a common approach. And to put it bluntly, it is profoundly abnormal for the G8 not to give an equal place to the G5. We can't claim to be dealing with major world affairs unless we give an equal place to the G5, and so to South Africa.

However, the G13 is still a contested idea and no formal proposal has yet been made to South Africa. Although there is no unison among the O5 partners on the formalization of the HP into a G13, South Africa would not join the ranks of such a new club, simply to shore up its legitimacy. On the one hand, a G13 may be more legitimate, but it will still be quite exclusive and perpetuate a two- or three-tiered world. On the other hand, the G8 leaders are misguided if they believe that the easy inclusion of South Africa into their fold effectively resolves the "Africa" question. As was earlier noted, South Africa's continental leadership, its African identity and its NEPAD vision for socioeconomic renewal have not been uncontested. As Adekeye Adebajo (2007, 42) writes: "Paradoxically, South Africa is both the most pan-African and least pan-African country in Africa." Moreover, the departure from office of Mbeki's closest African allies—presidents Joaquim Chissano of Mozambique and Olusegun Obasanjo of Nigeria—coupled with unabashed critique from Senegalese president Abdoulye Wade, have arguably presaged a perceived waning in NEPAD's continental prominence. Ultimately, it is for Africa and not the G8 to decide who should represent the continent's citizens. There are, moreover, quintessential differences between the continent's anglophone and francophone constituencies.

These conundrums of representation and legitimacy are not confined to South Africa only, but arguably also apply to Brazil and India (see Alden and Vieira 2005):

> While each country, individually and collectively (within IBSA) has a foreign policy aimed at altering the North–South terms of global governance to redress the imbalance of power between developed and developing countries, each country in turn has been targeted as a pivotal 'anchor' state actor

by the G8 powers. The fact that this tends to place them in the invidious position of being perceived by the G8 as de facto leaders of the South (in spite of the South's economic and developmental pluralism), generates contentious issues of "legitimacy" in terms of how their leadership is viewed by other state actors in their respective regions (Kornegay 2007, 2).

It must also be recalled that the broad "universalism" of the Mandela era has now been replaced by Mbeki's stronger sense of purpose, vision, and direction for South Africa. South Africa would therefore find it prudent to first identify what it expects from a G13 and then evaluate the opportunity costs of this elitist engagement *vis-à-vis* the country's other priorities as standard bearer and norm entrepreneur within the global South.

Nonetheless, the HP raises interesting structure-agency questions about the place, role, interests, and identity of the post-apartheid polity in the world today. On the one hand, South Africa's involvement in the HP suggests that the country, notwithstanding its limited institutional capacity and resources, is prepared to take on additional responsibilities for managing the challenges posed by global governance and the more pernicious externalities of growing global interdependence (with Africa often a net loser).

However, it would be equally naive not to recognize the enhanced status and prestige that accompany South Africa's G8 engagement. G8 association also holds positive benefits for the country's "marketing power," particularly in a globalizing world economy where Afro-pessimism remains rife (van der Westhuizen 2006). Put otherwise, in the global contest for scarce international capital, South Africa cannot afford to be "just another country"—hence the premium it places on forging strategic global partnerships and its bidding to host major international conferences, advanced science and technology platforms (e.g., the Square Kilometer Array radio telescope) and hallmark sports events (e.g., 2010 FIFA Soccer World Cup). Unsurprisingly, South African business has been quick to welcome the country's possible inclusion in a G13 fold:

> This invitation is testament to the stability and vibrancy of our democracy, as well as the great progress that our economy has made since 1994. But more significantly, it expresses international confidence about the economic and political future of South Africa as she matures and grows (Motsepe 2007).

On the other hand, compared to the other systemically important O5 countries, South Africa is marginal in global economic terms and holds little sway, structural and relational, over global markets. Nonetheless, galvanized by the symbolism and moral capital derived from its post-apartheid dividend, the South African government has sought to position the country as a global reformer, norm entrepreneur, and a force for good. In this regard, it is significant—and testimony to his international credentials, reputation, and standing in the world—that Mbeki has accepted invitations to every one of the G8 summits since Japan's hosting of the Okinawa Summit in 2000. In doing so, he has personalized much of this extended contact with his G8 peers, who perceive him to be a reliable, trustworthy, and like-minded partner. His profile in these meetings over the past eight years arguably confers upon him the status of doyen of the O5 corps, which informally gives South Africa added authority among these countries. However, the idiosyncrasies of this engagement raise questions about the future role of South Africa in the G8 process, particularly as Mbeki's second term as president draws to a close in 2009.

Hopefully, there may be some continuity post-Mbeki. Jacob Zuma—elected president of the ANC in 2007—has also endorsed and supported the HP. Zuma has hailed the outreach process as a "significant development" in the history of G8-O5 relations. However, he has noted the limited terms of the HP's mandate and time, and emphasized the need for genuine ownership of the process by all 13 partners if it is to evolve meaningfully:

> It is an important dialogue process that should help us demonstrate our ability to work together on global issues of mutual interest in a more focused and sustained way. Success in these processes can only result from an honest dialogue based on mutuality of interest in the subject matter, respect, partnership and, most importantly, equality (Zuma 2008).

Zuma's perspectives on the HP are not unimportant. As Garth le Pere and Anthoni van Nieuwkerk (2004, 131) observe: "The influence of the ANC in foreign policy-making cannot be underestimated." This stems from the dual membership role of senior politicians that serve in the government's national executive as well as the party's National Executive Committee and National Working Committee. This relationship is particularly important at the strategic-political agenda-setting phase of policy formulation.

South Africa and the Domestic Politics of the Heiligendamm Process

With regard to debates over G8 reform, it is also useful to reflect on the broader alignment of South African political and social forces. Here the imperative for speedy global governance reform finds equal resonance in the declaratory statements of the ANC, its tripartite alliance partners— namely the Congress of South African Trade Unions (COSATU) and the South African Communist Party (SACP)—as well as domestic civil society actors, many of which are plugged into global advocacy and social justice networks (Van Rooy 2004). Together with a vibrant civil society, these actors have regularly participated in rich debates about the direction of the country's foreign policy. However, given the centralizing proclivities of the Mbeki administration, the extent to which policy making is "democratized" remains debatable (Nel and van der Westhuizen 2004).

There has, for instance, been no robust public debate on the strategic purpose and rationale of South Africa's outreach activities with the G8, or the content of the government's message to these meetings. To the attentive public, South Africa's annual participation in G8 outreach meetings is, arguably, already an institutionalized feature of the country's multilateral diplomacy. To the extent that there is public engagement—or accountability—regarding the G8, this is confined to effete parliamentary oversight and Mbeki's past attempts to popularize these meetings through his "Letter from the President" published by the ANC's online journal, *ANC Today*.

It is nonetheless important that policy makers in Pretoria better appreciate and harness civil society's critiques of the G8. In this regard, civil society has routinely rounded that the G8 lacks normative legitimacy and efficiency, and has palpably failed to live up to its lofty promises to assist with Africa's development. These actors, particularly those with ecumenical and social justice mandates, have drafted scorecards that rank and measure the G8's implementation of the Gleneagles commitments.

This critique of the G8 should not stand in isolation from broader normative debates about the need to fashion a more cooperative, equitable, just, and sustainable pattern of world order. In this regard, the G8's idiosyncrasies and shortcomings are symptomatic of the democratic deficits and dim performance of the post–Second World War global institutional architecture, particularly the World Bank, the IMF, and the WTO. Civil society perspectives—especially those "from below"—argue that these institutions, and the G8 could be included here, all embody state-based multilateralism, with little emancipatory potential for the poor:

> This lack of a firm social base means that such institutions, and indeed the multilateralist project as currently established, remain institutions where elites gather and talk. Invariably, problems affecting the elites are tabled for

discussion, and concerns of the ordinary citizen are rarely put forward. As such, the notion that dissatisfied elites within a multilateral organization will somehow coalesce to change the normative order—an order that serves to reify their own position—is viewed with skepticism (Nel et al. 2001, 45).

At a different level, this critique of top-down international relations finds resonance with the trendy, non-governmental activism and campaigns that accompanied the G8's Gleneagles Summit in 2005. The latter included the Live 8 concert, the Make Poverty History campaign, and the Johannesburg-based Global Call to Action Against Poverty. As Patrick Bond, Dennis Brutus, and Virginia Setshedi (Bond et al. 2005, 1) contend: "We worry that these projects, like many NGO activities in Africa, unintentionally legitimise the institutions, processes, and personalities through which neoliberalism and imperialism do their damage. A better approach would be to endorse, strengthen, and link the myriad of Africa's bottom-up anti-racist, feminist, and ecological struggles, especially those focusing on economic justice."

Employing a structural analysis of international relations, the ANC and its alliance partners cast the capitalist G8 nations as agents of global imperialism and subordination. The G8 are critiqued for perpetuating a global system of gross inequality, extreme underdevelopment, and social desperation for millions of working and poor people across the world. Recognizing the pressing need for Africa to push for a more equitable global deal, in 2005 the ANC's National General Council adopted a specific resolution supporting the continental leadership's special engagement with the G8, and called upon the G8 and other developed countries to cancel all debts owed by African countries (ANC 2005).

COSATU has been more forthright in its critique of the G8 countries and their policies. Prior to the Heiligendamm Summit in 2007, the trade union federation issued a bold statement that unabashedly condemned the G8: "In essence, the G8 is only interested in affirming their agenda of transforming the world into a haven for neo-liberal greed and corporate parasitism" (COSATU 2007). The South African government is not insensitive to these charges levelled against its northern partners. For this reason, the underlying rationale of Pretoria's reformist multilateralism is twofold: to secure the best possible deal for South Africa within the current world economy, while simultaneously persuading its leftist critics, particularly in COSATU and the SACP, that it has not sold out in the ongoing struggle to build a more just and democratic world order (Lee et al. 2006). Critics of this approach have accordingly characterized Mbeki's global reforms as "talk left, walk right" (Bond 2004).

South Africa's Sherpa Process and Institutional Arrangements

The South African government and the ANC as the ruling party since 1994 both appear to be strongly committed to the HP (compared to the earlier concept of the leaders' 20, or L20). This is certainly reflected by the high office and levels of competence invested in G8 outreach. The locus for HP engagement is situated in the presidency. Advocate Mojanku Gumbi— Mbeki's astute legal advisor and arguably the most influential female figure in the presidency—has been appointed as the responsible sherpa to manage South Africa's outreach activities. Given her strong negotiation skills and wide legal experience, Gumbi has increasingly taken on the foreign affairs brief, including peacemaking initiatives in Africa. Her prominence within Mbeki's inner circle—including the likes of the minister in the presidency Essop Pahad, finance minister Trevor Manuel, and the government's chief policy strategist, Joel Netshitenzhe—leads one analyst to opine that she is among the top five most powerful people in the country (Calland 2007).

In this role as sherpa, Gumbi relies heavily on the support of the Department of Foreign Affairs. The deputy director-general for multilateral affairs, George Nene—a seasoned diplomat who once represented South Africa in Geneva and Nigeria—accordingly acts as her deputy, the sous-sherpa. Patrick Krappie, an experienced trade hand who is now tasked with the department's G8 and OECD briefs, is another instrumental figure in South Africa's HP engagement. Krappie participates in all four HP working groups and directly reports to Gumbi. This allows the South African sherpa to develop a horizontal view and understanding of all the discussions and outcomes, which are often cross-cutting in nature.

Senior officials, mostly at the level of deputy director general (nominated by their superiors), actively participate in the four HP working groups. The Department of Minerals and Energy attends to energy; the Department of Science and Technology to innovation; the Department of Trade and Industry to investment; and the National Treasury to development, which has a specific focus on Africa. It is thus appropriate that South Africa has been mandated to co-chair the latter working group (with France), which has met twice: in February 2008 in Paris and June 2008 in Cape Town.

Within South Africa, this development brief is located with the National Treasury, politically supervised by one of the world's longest-serving finance ministers. Trevor Manuel brings an important contribution to this debate: not only was he a member of Britain's CfA (effectively lending continuity to the HP) but he also earned international respect for chairing the IMF and World Bank's Development Committee. Manuel was also invited to join the

Spence Commission on Growth and Development, which released its final report in 2008. The National Treasury (represented at HP engagements by Ismail Momoniat, the deputy director general for international finance and economics) has accordingly tabled an agenda that addresses some of the continent's most pressing socioeconomic and developmental challenges, *inter alia* poor infrastructure, capacity and institution building, aid effectiveness, the Millennium Development Goals (MDGs), and policies to catalyze stronger economic growth (e.g., commodity beneficiation). In addition, this working group provides a strategic platform to challenge the G8 on the numerous tariff and non-tariff barriers that inhibit Africa's export potential to northern markets.

South African Perspectives on the Heiligendamm Process and Agenda

It would be fair to say that South Africa is among the keener participants in the HP. The country's role in this process has been cast as very constructive and influential, particularly behind the scenes. South Africa—as the only African partner in this process (and contentiously the only representative of the "black world")—has a special role to play, as a dual bridge between the G8 and O5 as well as between the more developed and lesser developed constituencies within the O5. In this regard, South African officials have worked hard to ensure better coordination and caucusing among the O5 partners prior to the meetings of the HP's Political Steering Committee and the four working groups. Mojanku Gumbi has also pressed her O5 colleagues to demonstrate greater political commitment to the HP, in order to see the process through to its conclusion in 2009. The concern has been raised, for instance, that South Africa and Mexico are the only O5 partners that send senior officials to working group meetings. By contrast, the more cautious among the O5 deploy junior representation.

South Africa has also welcomed the partnerships encompassed in the four thematic working groups. The HP is accordingly viewed as a process of high-level dialogue and consultation, and not an agenda-based negotiation. The four working groups should aim to promote mutual understanding and provide a "laboratory" for the G8 and O5 to discuss common concerns. Since each working group determines its own work program and parameters, there is no danger of a preconceived outcome to the dialogue.

However, it is possible to discern some misgivings about the HP. Reservations have, for instance, been raised about the role of the Heiligendamm Dialogue Process Support Unit, housed in the OECD. Initial speculation that the OECD would seek to stage manage and own the HP have been vindicated by experience. Concerns have been expressed that the Support Unit, backed by the vast resources of the OECD, essentially drafts the annotated agendas and speaking notes for the four working groups and their co-chairs. This process effectively isolates the concerns of the O5, while raising onto the agenda those of the G8 and the OECD.

Moreover, South Africa is still in the early stages of its engagement with the OECD and has yet to develop a full understanding of the organization and its functioning. Some officials therefore believe that the United Nations Conference on Trade and Development (UNCTAD) may be better placed to support the HP, since this organization better understands and represents the interests of the O5 and the broader developing world. In recent years, UNCTAD—conventionally wary of upsetting the IMF and World Bank—has led a frontal critique of economic orthodoxy. Its outputs now routinely emphasize economic development, often invoking as exemplary the types of policies pursued by the East Asian countries, especially those that promote industry and technological upgrading (see UNCTAD 2006; 2007).

A second concern relates to the thematic focus of the working groups. The wording and implications of the four themes are not insignificant: a case in point is energy efficiency. None of the HP partners discounts the perils posed by global climate change and acknowledge the need for mitigation and adaptation strategies. Even South Africa has one of the highest levels of carbon dioxide (CO_2) emissions per capita in the world. However, since European companies are building their competitiveness and capacity as first movers in advanced green technology, there are concerns that the HP is pursuing a market-seeking agenda:

> In the international climate change regime, the North sees its role in developing the technology and "transferring" it to the South. Most European countries have developed or are in the process of developing their competitiveness in cleaner, environmentally sound technology and energy efficiency. On the demand side, housing insulation, building codes and energy-efficient appliances are now available. On the supply side, technology available for CO_2-free power generation, such as nuclear, wind power and hydro energy, as well as carbon capture and storage technologies have been developed (Pressend 2008).

There are also concerns about the potential loss of policy space entailed by investment freedom. By contrast, the focus on Africa is welcomed. The emphasis on determining joint responsibilities for Africa is a double-whammy for the continent: it suggests that the emerging powers will now also assume some responsibilities for Africa's future development. In addition, the G8's responsibilities toward the continent are now broadly diffused and better integrated with the O5. However, there is a danger that this premium on Africa could displace the legitimate developmental concerns of the other O5 countries.

South Africa and the G13: Insider or Outsider?

The foregoing discussion of South Africa's experience and engagement with the G8 essentially sets the stage for two critical questions. Should South Africa, the closest approximation to an African economic tiger, join a future G13 condominium? And is there sufficient common vision among the O5 partners to engage the G8 collectively?

Two generalized schools of thought appear to be discernible. The first perspective argues that it is in South Africa's best interests—and the African continent more broadly—to graduate the G8 into a G13. This would create a platform for more equal conversation on salient issues on the global agenda, and provide a strategic platform for South Africa to promote Africa-specific issues. The latter would include the reform of the Bretton Woods institutions; poverty reduction, and linked to this the MDGs; trade, aid, and debt relief; technology transfer; FDI to the continent; and the pernicious impact of HIV/AIDS on Africa's growth potential. Since the majority of Africa's citizens constitute the bulk of the world's "bottom billion," there is need for more focused engagement (Collier 2007).

ANC president Jacob Zuma (2008) therefore argues that the current HP is a limited form of engagement: "The reality is that, emerging powers are continuing to engage with the G8 through the usual post-Summit Outreach Sessions, whilst we remain convinced that the current format places artificial limits to a potentially powerful and real partnership amongst our countries." In addition, regional perspectives on complex global challenges—and the potential to partner with pivotal regional powers to address these—would certainly heighten the G8's efficacy in the world. To quote Zuma (2008) again: "The necessary question to ask is whether the G8 has the inclination and capacity to deal with the threats as experienced and perceived by the developing world." G13 deal making between the G8 and O5 would have to be based on a full partnership and mutual respect, including power sharing over agenda setting, effective consultation, and full participation in summits.

By contrast, the obverse perspective holds that it would be improper and impolitic for South Africa to formally join an expanded G8. G13 membership, it is argued, would compromise and undermine South Africa's political credibility and legitimacy as a strong proponent of South–South cooperation and solidarity. Put otherwise, some developing countries—chiefly African—may perceive South Africa's actions as a political betrayal of the South agenda. Related concerns over South Africa's possible co-optation by the North have been raised *vis-à-vis* the country's gradual accession to OECD membership.

In summary, South Africa's potential membership of an alluring G8-OECD institutional nexus is fraught with hard political choices and challenges—but opportunities, too. As was earlier noted, a recurring motif in South Africa's post-apartheid foreign relations is a not unfamiliar tension between pragmatic politics and principles (see Smith and Light 2001). This is reflective of South Africa's multiple identities and foreign policy role conceptions in the world (see Landsberg and Monyae 2006).

Conclusion: The Outreach Five and Heiligendamm Process—Toward a Common Vision?

South Africa's bilateral relations with the O5 countries are broadly positive. China and India are special cases, given their rising global prominence and growing commercial footprint on "Africa's silk road" (Boardman 2007). In 2008, South Africa and China celebrate a decade of formal diplomatic relations, to be marked by the signing of the ambitious new Partnership for Growth and Development.[6] Bilateral trade volumes between the two countries have grown spectacularly, from US$14 million in 1991 to more than US$2 billion by 2002 (le Pere and Shelton 2007). More significantly, in 2007 China's biggest lender, the Industrial and Commercial Bank of China, bought 20 percent of South Africa's Standard Bank for R36.67 billion (US$5.6 billion), the biggest foreign investment yet in Africa. Given South Africa's highly developed and sophisticated financial sector, this deal is likely to involve reverse technology transfer from South Africa to the mainland. A number of South African companies have already established a formidable commercial presence in China.

Commercial relations between India and South Africa—once home to Mahatma Gandhi between 1893 and 1915—are also growing, with potential opportunities for future business synergies. Furthermore, not only is South Africa home to the largest Indian population, or diaspora, born outside India, but also

> India and South Africa are natural partners. They share a rich history, maintain close cultural and political ties, face similar challenges both

domestically and internationally, and often adopt similar approaches to meeting them. These are unusually strong foundations upon which to build (Alves 2007, 104).

The parameters of a shared vision for global governance reform are discernible from the O5's joint position papers and statements prepared for the St. Petersburg Summit in 2006, the Heiligendamm Summit in 2007, and the Hokkaido Summit in 2008. The 2006 paper shared the Kremlin's concerns with energy security, education, infectious diseases, and international trade—but also emphasized mobilizing financial resources for development. The latter has been a regular refrain in Pretoria's diplomacy. South Africa's hand was further visible too: "The international community should continue to cooperate with the African countries in their quest for peace, development and social justice. A true partnership must be established bearing in mind the views and needs of African countries and people" (Mbeki 2006). At Heiligendamm, the O5 again outlined their shared concerns about global governance, international trade, international migration, and climate change. As in 2006, they endorsed strengthened South–South cooperation, but noted that it was complementary to and not a substitute for North–South cooperation. While the O5 may share elements of a common vision for systemic global reform, they do not share the requisite strategies, tactics, and plans of action to pursue these reforms. For example, the O5 partners have yet to find common cause on nuclear non-proliferation, Trade-Related Aspects of Intellectual Property Rights (TRIPS), and non-tariff barriers in the WTO. South Africa has also not yet staked its claim to a permanent seat at a reformed UNSC.[7]

Importantly, South Africa and the O5 countries have also forged alternative partnerships for pursuing global and continental change beyond the HP. Globally, it is worth recalling that the O5 all constitute the core membership of the G20 developing countries in the WTO, which is pressing the case for fairer global agricultural trade. In the non-agricultural market access (NAMA) negotiations, Brazil and India, with informal support from China, have also joined the ranks of the NAMA-11, coordinated by South Africa, which promotes tariff "policy space" for developing countries.[8] The latter suggests that the bulk of the O5 governments are challenging conventional economic orthodoxies. The idea of the Beijing Consensus—the strategic appropriation of state and market forces for development—is suggestive of this thinking (see Ramo 2004).

The bulk of the O5 countries have sought to develop special partnerships with Africa, in the spirit of the New Asian-African Strategic Partnership

(NAASP), as well as their own national development priorities and designs. China and India have both forged continental deals, respectively through the Forums on China-African Cooperation (FOCAC)—held in 2000, 2003, and 2006—and the first ever summit of the India-Africa Forum, held in Delhi in 2008. Brazil has recently also shown an interest in Africa's biofuels potential. As Chris Landsberg (2007, 197) notes: "At the heart of President Mbeki's African agenda is a search for a new relationship between Africa and the outside world, a shift from a relationship of 'patronage' towards one of partnership." This applies not only to Africa's historical relationship with the G8, but also to "new" South–South axes. In this regard, Mbeki has raised some reservations about the nature of China's growing imprint in Africa, and warned that Africa must guard against falling into a colonial relationship with the mainland.

Measured against this rich complex of diplomatic initiatives, IBSA arguably presents the closest approximation of common vision for systemic global governance reform among key O5 countries:

> The fact that the IBSA countries have so much in common, politically, economically and socially, lays a strong foundation for them to speak with greater levels of unanimity and a common voice on key global matters. IBSA's real strategic importance lies, therefore, in its ability to come up with well-thought through, co-ordinated, common, shared and collective stances and outlooks on key global, regional, and national questions (Landsberg 2006, 5).

While it is important to not over-romanticize South–South cooperation among very heterogeneous partners, there is latent potential in IBSA that has not yet been fully harnessed. Although their economies differ significantly in size, scope, and composition, all three are acknowledged to be leading, like-minded middle powers of the developing world, and respected examples of vibrant and progressive democracies. As a collective, IBSA represents 1.2 billion people, a US$1.2 trillion domestic market, and foreign trade worth US$300 billion, which gives it considerable voice on matters global.[9]

Since its launch in June 2003 (following the G8's Evian Summit), the three participating governments have held annual meetings of their foreign affairs and economic ministers rotating to the different capitals, backed up and followed by other less visible technical planning meetings (see Keet 2006). The first IBSA summit of heads of state was held in Brasília in 2006, followed by Pretoria in 2007. In other words, IBSA departs from pure clubbing to entailing the development, among the three countries, of a structure of trilateral cooperation in an expanding number of sectoral working groups accompanied by efforts at both private sector and civil society interaction (Kornegay 2007, 2). The three countries have also developed principled positions around the challenges of global hegemony, unilateralism and multilateralism, development, and global peace and security, particularly the human security–development nexus. The future challenge is to translate IBSA's declaratory statements and common positions into concrete strategies, tactics, and plans of action. In summary, IBSA's perspectives and impact on the international system will depend on four variables: IBSA's ability to focus on clear and possible areas of cooperation, the consolidation of its common strategy of balancing, the institutionalization of IBSA, and its enlargement in order to generate more weight in global bargains (Flemes 2007).

To conclude, it is evident that South Africa's foreign policy is normatively underpinned by a commitment to fighting inequality, poverty, and under-development—or what Thabo Mbeki has termed "global apartheid" between rich and poor. Read together with its perceived continental leadership in Africa and prominence in global multilateralism, South Africa makes for an ideal partner in the G8's eyes. However, while the government may be keen to play a more constructive role in global reformism, debates, and rule making, its foreign policy ambitions may ultimately be thwarted by the interplay of three factors: costs, capacity, and global constraints. Furthermore there are three other imponderables: the end of the Mbeki era in 2009, the twilight of NEPAD as its original progenitors pass from the political scene, and the tenuous legitimacy that attends South Africa's continental leadership, which must ultimately become the wellspring for its enhanced global status and activism.

Notes

1   South Africa does not feature in Goldman Sachs's projections of the world's next big economies by 2030–50, namely Brazil, Russia, India, and China—the BRICs—and the Next Eleven (N11). The latter includes two African countries, Egypt and Nigeria.
2   South Africa's expected economic growth for 2008 has been downgraded to 3 percent to 4 percent.
3   These binding constraints are the volatility and level of the currency; the cost, efficiency, and capacity of the national infrastructure and logistics system; the shortages of skilled human capital; the competitive environment and high cost structure of the economy; the onerous regulatory environment, particularly for small and medium-sized enterprises; and the state's institutional capacity.
4   South Africa also chaired the AU's Post-Conflict Reconstruction and Development Committee dealing with Sudan.

5 The Africa Progress Panel was set up to monitor implementation of the Gleneagles commitments. Prior to the 2008 Toyako Hokkaido Summit, a report by the panel suggested that under current spending plans, G8 aid to Africa will fall US$40 billion short of the Gleneagles pledge (Ooko 2008).

6 The Pretoria Declaration, signed in April 2000 by presidents Thabo Mbeki and Jiang Zemin, laid the foundation for a strategic Sino-South African partnership, with a strong commitment to advancing a new global order. This partnership is grounded on China's five principles of Sino-African relations: friendship, equality and sovereignty, common development and mutual benefit, consultation on international issues, and cooperation in advancing a new international political and economic order.

7 South Africa has supported the AU position, known as the Ezulwini Consensus, which holds that Africa should insist on two veto-wielding permanent and five non-permanent seats in a reformed UNSC. These representatives from Africa would be selected by the AU.

8 NAMA refers to tariffs on industrial goods, mining, forestry, fisheries, and other natural resources.

9 A grand IBSA trilateral free trade agreement is also mooted. Its aim would be to enhance the aggregate trilateral trade flows between Mercosur and the Southern African Customs Union (SACU), between Mercosur and India, and between the SACU and India from US$4 billion to US$10 billion in the short term in an attempt to develop trade convergence between the three partners.

References

Adebajo, Adekeye (2007). "South Africa in Africa: Messiah or Mercantilist." *South African Journal of International Affairs* 14(1).

Adebajo, Adekeye, Adebayo Adedeji, and Chris Landsberg, eds. (2007). *South Africa in Africa: The Post-Apartheid Era.* Scottsville: University of KwaZulu-Natal Press.

African National Congress (2005). "Consolidated Report on Sectoral Strategies." ANC National General Council, 29 June–3 July, Johannesburg. <www.anc.org.za/show.php?doc=ancdocs/ngcouncils/2005/consolidated_report.html> (May 2008).

Alden, Chris and Garth le Pere (2003). "South Africa's Post-Apartheid Foreign Policy: From Reconciliation to Revival?" Adelphi Paper No. 362. London: International Institute for Security Studies.

Alden, Chris and Marco Antonio Vieira (2005). "The New Diplomacy of the South: South Africa, Brazil, India, and Trilateralism." *Third World Quarterly* 26(7): 1077–1095.

Alves, P. (2007). "India and South Africa: Shifting Priorities?" *South African Journal of International Affairs* 14(2).

Boardman, Harry G. (2007). *Africa's Silk Road: China and India's New Economic Frontier.* Washington DC: World Bank.

Bond, Patrick (2001). *Against Global Apartheid: South Africa Meets the World Bank, IMF, and International Finance.* Cape Town: University of Cape Town Press.

Bond, Patrick (2004). *Talk Left, Walk Right: South Africa's Frustrated Global Reforms.* Scottsville: University of KwaZulu-Natal Press.

Bond, Patrick, Dennis Brutus, and Virginia Setshedi (2005). "Mainstream NGOs in Africa: Time to Rethink Alliances?" *Global Dialogue* 10(2).

Calland, Richard (2007). *Anatomy of South Africa: Who Holds the Power?* Cape Town: Zebra Press.

Collier, Paul (2007). *The Bottom Billion: Why the Poorest Countries Are Failing and What Can be Done About it.* Oxford: Oxford University Press.

Congress of South African Trade Unions (2007). "COSATU Statement on G8 Summit in Germany." 8 June. <www.cosatu.org.za/press/2007/jun/press16.htm> (May 2008).

Fine, Ben and Zavareh Rustomjee (1996). *South Africa's Political Economy: From Minerals-Energy Complex to Industrialisation?* London: Hurst.

Flemes, Daniel (2007). "Emerging Middle Powers' Soft Balancing Strategy: State and Perspectives of the IBSA Dialogue Forum." Working Paper No. 57. Hamburg: German Institute of Global and Area Studies. <www.giga-hamburg.de/dl/download.php?d=/content/publikationen/pdf/wp57_flemes.pdf> (May 2008).

Garten, Jeffrey E. (1997). *The Big Ten: The Big Emerging Markets and How They Will Change Our Lives.* New York: Basic Books.

Geldenhuys, Deon (2006). "South Africa's Role as International Norm Entrepreneur." In *In Full Flight: South African Foreign Policy after Apartheid,* edited by W. Carlsnaes and P. Nel. Johannesburg: Institute for Global Dialogue.

Grobbelaar, Neuma (2007). "South African Corporate Engagement with Africa: Experiences, Lessons, and Policy Recommendations." In *Unlocking Africa's Potential: The Role of Corporate South Africa in Strengthening Africa's Private Sector,* edited by N. Grobbelaar and H. Besada. Johannesburg: South African Institute of International Affairs.

Grobbelaar, Neuma and Hany Besada, eds. (2007). *Unlocking Africa's Potential: The Role of Corporate South Africa in Strengthening Africa's Private Sector.* Johannesburg: South African Institute of International Affairs.

Hirsch, Alan (2006). *Season of Hope: Economic Reform under Mandela and Mbeki.* Scottsville: University of KwaZulu-Natal Press.

Hudson, Judi (2007). "South Africa's Economic Expansion into Africa: Neo-colonialism or Development?" In *South Africa in Africa: The Post-Apartheid Era,* edited by A. Adebajo, A. Adedeji, and C. Landsberg. Scottsville: University of KwaZulu-Natal Press.

Keet, Dot (2006). "South–South Strategic Challenges to the Global Economic System and Power Regime." IGD Occasional Paper No. 53. Johannesburg: Institute for Global Dialogue. <www.igd.org/za : Publications : Occasional Papers> (May 2008).

Kornegay, Francis (2007). "IBSA: The Foreign Policies of India, Brazil, and South Africa." Discussion paper prepared for seminar on "Emerging Powers in a Changing World Order," Centre for Policy Studies, 7 August. Johannesburg.

Landsberg, Chris (2006). "IBSA's Political Origins, Significance, and Challenges." *Synopsis* 8(2): 4–7.

Landsberg, Chris and David Monyae (2006). "South Africa's Foreign Policy: Carving a Global Niche." *South African Journal of International Affairs* 13(2): 131–145.

Landsberg, Chris (2007). "South Africa and the Making of the African Union and NEPAD: Mbeki's "Progressive African Agenda"." In *South Africa in Africa: The Post-Apartheid Era*, edited by A. Adebajo, A. Adedeji, and C. Landsberg. Scottsville: University of KwaZulu-Natal Press.

le Pere, Garth and Anthoni Van Nieuwkerk (2004). "Who Made and Makes Foreign Policy?" In *Apartheid Past, Renaissance Future: South Africa's Foreign Policy 1994–2004*, edited by E. Sidiropoulos. Johannesburg: South African Institute of International Affairs.

le Pere, Garth and Garth Shelton (2007). *China, Africa, and South Africa: South–South Co-operation in a Global Era*. Johannesburg: Institute for Global Dialogue.

Lee, Donna, Ian Taylor, and Paul D. Williams, eds. (2006). *The New Multilateralism in South African Diplomacy*. Houndmills: Palgrave Macmillan.

Manuel, Trevor (2008). "Budget Speech 2008 by the Minister of Finance." 20 February, Cape Town. South African Government Information. <www.info.gov.za/speeches/2008/08022016151001.htm> (May 2008).

Mbeki, Thabo (2000). "Speech on the Occasion of the Consideration of the Budget Vote of the Presidency." 13 June, National Assembly, Pretoria. <www.dfa.gov.za/docs/speeches/2000/mbek0613.htm> (May 2008).

Mbeki, Thabo (2003). "Address to the National Council of Provinces." 11 November, Pretoria. Department of Foreign Affairs. <www.anc.org.za/ancdocs/history/mbeki/2003/tm1111.html> (May 2008).

Mbeki, Thabo (2006). "The G8—Time for Concrete and Properly Assessed Results!" *ANC Today*, 21–27 July.

Motsepe, Patrice (2007). "Address by the President of BUSA at the 12th NEDLAC Summit, Emperor's Palace." 1 September. Johannesburg. <www.busa.org.za/docs/NEDLAC%20Address%20by%20Mr%20Patrice%20Motsepe.doc> (May 2008).

Nel, Philip (1999). "The Foreign Policy Beliefs of South Africans: A First Cut." *Journal of Contemporary African Studies* 17(1): 123–146.

Nel, Philip, Ian Taylor, and Janis van der Westhuizen, eds. (2001). *South Africa's Multilateral Diplomacy and Global Change: The Limits of Reformism*. Aldershot: Ashgate.

Nel, Philip and Janis van der Westhuizen, eds. (2004). *Democratizing Foreign Policy? Lessons from South Africa*. New York: Lexington Books.

Nye, Joseph S. (1990). "The Changing Nature of World Power." *Political Science Quarterly* 105(2): 177–192.

Nzo, Alfred (1995). *Speech by the Minister of Foreign Affairs before the Portfolio Committee on Foreign Affairs.* 14 March. Pretoria.

Olivier, G. (2006). "The European Union and South Africa: Towards a Strategic Partnership." *South African Journal of International Affairs* 13(2).

Ooko, Daniel (2008). "Africa urges G8 leaders not to backtrack on promises to Africa." *China View.* 5 July. <http://news.xinhuanet.com/english/2008-07/05/content_8496219.htm>.

Organisation for Economic Co-operation and Development (2003). *Actions for a Positive Investment Environment in Africa to Promote Development: OECD-NEPAD Statement.* Paris. <www.oecd.org/dataoecd/2/37/20686317.pdf> (May 2008).

Pressend, Michelle (2008). "Its Business as Usual as Climate Trade Trumps Climate Change." South African Civil Society Information Service. <www.sacsis.org.za/site/news/detail.asp?iData=88&iCat=1434&iChannel=1&nChannel=News> (May 2008).

Ramo, Joshua Cooper (2004). *The Beijing Consensus.* London: Foreign Policy Centre.

Sarkozy, Nicolas (2008). "Speech by M. Nicolas Sarkozy, President of the Republic, to the Parliament of the Republic of South Africa." 28 February, Pretoria. <www.ambafrance-uk.org/President-Sarkozy-s-speech-to-the.html> (May 2008).

Selebi, Jackie (1999). "South African Foreign Policy: Setting New Goals and Strategies." *South African Journal of International Affairs* 6(2): 201–216.

Smith, Karen E. and Margot Light, eds. (2001). *Ethics and Foreign Policy.* Cambridge: Cambridge University Press.

United Nations Conference on Trade and Development (2006). *Trade and Development Report 2006: Global Partnership and National Policies for Development.* New York and Geneva.

United Nations Conference on Trade and Development (2007). *Trade and Development Report 2006: Regional Cooperation for Development.* New York and Geneva.

United Nations Development Programme (2007). *Human Development Report 2007/2008. Fighting Climate Change: Human Solidarity in a Divided World.* New York: Palgrave Macmillan <hdr.undp.org/en/reports/global/hdr2007-2008/> (May 2008).

van der Westhuizen, Janis (2006). "Pretoria and the Global Conference Circuit: Hot Air, or Hot Stuff?" In *In Full Flight: South African Foreign Policy after Apartheid,* edited by W. Carlsnaes and P. Nel. Johannesburg: Institute for Global Dialogue.

van Nieuwkerk, Anthoni (2007). "A Critique of South Africa's Role on the UN Security Council." *South African Journal of International Affairs* 14(1): 61–77.

Van Rooy, Alison (2004). *Global Legitimacy Game.* Houndmills: Palgrave.

Zuma, Jacob (2008). "Address by ANC President Jacob Zuma at the 7th FES-SWP North-South Dialogue hosted by the Friedrich Ebert Stiftung." 21 April, Berlin. <www.anc.org.za/ancdocs/history/zuma/2008/jz0421.html> (May 2008).

8

A Break with the Past or a Natural Progression?
Mexico and the Heiligendamm Process

Duncan Wood

Mexico's arrival on the world stage as an emerging power has been long predicted and much postponed. For many years the country has been identified as a potential great power due to its considerable population, extensive natural resources, geographic proximity to the United States, and its ongoing industrialization. But that arrival has been delayed over the years by a combination of poor economic management, corruption, financial crisis, political instability, and the complications of a prolonged transition to full democracy.

Mexico's identity in the international economic and political system has changed dramatically over the years as well. From active participant in the new multilateral system in the post-war world, to strong proponent of isolationism, and import substitution industrialization (ISI), to G77 participant, to convert to the General Agreement on Tariffs and Trade (GATT), and then the World Trade Organization (WTO) as well as the Organisation for Economic Co-operation and Development (OECD), to partially committed member of the G20 finance ministers and central bank governors, Mexico has been a rather difficult country to label in terms of its place in the society of states. Mexico continues to struggle with its identity as a country firmly located in North America's economic region, but desiring a cultural and political affinity with Latin America. At times Mexico has seen itself as a bridge between the two regions, but Latin America itself has been reluctant to accept Mexico in that role.

The possibility of closer collaboration between Mexico as a member of the Outreach Five (O5, usually referred to as the Group of Five or G5 in

Mexico)—or, from the perspective of this book, B(R)ICSAM (Brazil, India, China, South Africa, and Mexico)—and the G8 provides many tantalizing prospects both for the country and for the world's leading economic powers. Nonetheless, that collaboration as one of the five new powers can be questioned, both from the point of view of the G8 (why do we need Mexico) and from Mexico itself (why do we need the G8). The purpose of this chapter is to bring together the arguments for and against Mexico as a member of the O5 from both points of view. The argument put forward here is that, while it makes sense for the G8 to welcome Mexican participation, and while participation will not incur any significant costs for Mexico, the value added for Mexico will probably be minimal in the short to medium term. Nonetheless, the prestige or reputational argument and the potential for long-term recognition as a major power will likely propel this and future governments towards increased collaboration and membership of a Group of 13 (G13).

Mexico's Place in the World: An Active Participant *"hasta un cierto punto"*

Mexico has a long tradition of getting involved in world affairs through its fine history of multilateralism and its involvement in international organizations. But at the same time Mexico has maintained a certain distance from the society of states through its ongoing commitment to respecting state sovereignty and non-interference in the internal affairs of other states. In this sense, Mexico has maintained a special place in world affairs over the past 65 years: involved but not too much.

From the outset of the post–World War II period, Mexico has engaged in a foreign policy of restrained multilateralism by joining international organizations, but at the same time limiting its interference in the internal affairs of other states by placing a premium on the concept of state sovereignty. Mexico has been active in terms of both international and regional initiatives, recognizing the increasing demands of interdependence without sacrificing its dominion over internal political affairs. The strictures of the Carranza doctrine, prohibiting interference by the Mexican state in the internal affairs of other countries, have become as scripture. The doctrine has acquired a status of sacred cow that is only marginally surpassed by the constitutional commitment to keeping oil production in state-controlled hands.

Mexico also managed to remain neutral through the Cold War, keeping its distance from the bilateral conflict though its foreign policy, while at the same time keeping strict control on communist activity within its border and becoming a reliable trading partner with the United States, particularly in the context of supplying oil, both during times of conflict and when demand is on the rise and oil nationalism has been a threat.

This complex relationship with the international society of states, however, should not distract from the very strong tradition of multilateralism in Mexican foreign policy. In an earlier period, before the winds of political change had begun to shake the dominance of the ruling Partido Revolucionario Institucional (PRI) in Mexico, leading lights in the foreign ministry (or Cancillería) had spoken of the firm belief of both Mexico and the PRI in the principles of multilateralism. Victor Flores Olea (1987) argued that not only did Mexico benefit from multilateral participation in terms of international cooperation for peace and development, but it also provided a counterweight to the bipolar system then predominating, and in particular to the overwhelming influence of the country's northern neighbour, writing that Mexico "used the multilateral system as a counterbalance to the policy of spheres of influence."

Indeed, a Mexican ambassador and one-time Mexican undersecretary of foreign affairs for the United Nations, Africa, and the Middle East once wrote of the *"vocación multilateral"* of Mexican foreign policy (Moreno Toscano 2000, 143). Based in clause X of article 89 of the constitution, Mexican foreign policy seeks to combine the principles of international law with the responsibilities of membership in the global community.[1] Mexico's participation in multilateral forums has always been a key ingredient in its foreign policy mix and, as Carmen Moreno Toscano points out with reference to the administration of Ernesto Zedillo, has been driven by five guiding principles:

1. to promote the national interest and to face new challenges and opportunities in a changing world;
2. to promote economic and social development among all countries;
3. to promote common actions and approaches to global problems (such as drug trafficking and transnational organized crime);
4. to contribute to the strengthening of peace and international security, while preserving respect for state sovereignty and the legal equality of states; and
5. to contribute to the definition of new objective and new multilateral mechanisms and to the renewal of the decision-making structures and organs in the multilateral system to adapt them to modern times and to establish better balance and responsibility sharing among states.

During Zedillo's period, this last point referred to the democratization of the UN and the formation of the G20 in the wake of the crises that rocked the global financial system in the 1990s.

In more recent times, Mexico has become an active player in multilateral forums for a variety of reasons. Former foreign minister Luis Ernesto Derbez Bautista (2004) has written of the need to face the challenges of the changing global scene through multilateral mechanisms, at both the regional and international levels, naming the defence of multilateralism and international norms as one of the six priorities of the Cancillería under his leadership. As discussed later in this chapter, Derbez believed that Mexico should focus on political leadership in Latin America, the failure of which helped Mexico get to the position it is in today.

The administration of Vicente Fox in general, assumed a wholehearted commitment to multilateralism. This commitment reflected a belief that multilateral institutions and cooperation could be used not only to advance Mexican interests *vis-à-vis* other states, but also help reform internally. José Luis Bernal Rodríguez (2001) has argued that, of the five priorities of the Fox government, two were related to multilateral cooperation, at the regional and global levels. In these priorities he expressly links the goals of foreign policy and the issues of human rights, democratization, and economic competitiveness, both internationally and domestically. As he points out toward the end of his article, Mexico's international cooperation should become a fundamental support of the efforts toward achieving economic growth and social development.

Yet, once again, the idea of increasing Mexico's international freedom of action comes to the fore in the discussion of multilateralism, particularly at the regional level in the Americas. At the global level, there is an emphasis on Mexican leadership in forums, the need to revitalize keystone organizations such as the United Nations, and on the possibilities of employing Mexico's capacity to influence. The element of prestige is stressed by Bernal Rodríguez in his defence of Fox's foreign policy, and this, of course, cannot be ignored in any analysis of Mexican multilateralism.

Particularly after the events of September 11, as the bilateral relationship with the U.S. soured and the prospects for meaningful migration reform faded, Mexico turned increasingly to multilateral forums, seeking partners (such as Canada) that both understood the problems of dealing with the U.S. and that also believed in the advantages of effective multilateral institutions. Mexico has long argued for reform of the UN and has become an important and influential member of the "Friends of the United Nations."

Perhaps the most important aspect of the new era of Mexican multilateralism stems from the country's newfound confidence in its international role. As Castañeda (2001) has argued, the "new Mexican international activism" was driven both by the end of the Cold War and the exigencies and opportunities of globalization, but also by changes that had taken place within Mexican politics and society. Castañeda also (2001, 52, translated by author) points out, "factors such as the legitimacy of a government, the diplomatic tradition, or the weight of a national culture give the foreign policies of certain states international power. Clearly, the Mexico of today is one of these countries." Emphasizing Mexico's soft power, Castañeda goes on to say that "the central axis of the Fox government's foreign policy is to give Mexico an active role on the world scene." The idea that internal reform and change affected the nation's foreign policy has been put forward at the end of Carlos Salinas's presidency by Jorge Alberto Lozoya (1994, translated by author), who argued that "the reform of the Mexican state opened up new conditions in the structure of politics" that gave non-state actors influence and a voice in foreign policy. Although Lozoya was probably exaggerating his case, by the time of the Fox government the Mexican state's legitimacy was at hitherto unrivalled heights.

Under Fox, Mexico's foreign policy faced a number of challenges. The problems of the bilateral relationship with the U.S. were paramount after September 11, particularly because the promise of immigration reform soon faded. However, in the area of multilateralism, too, Mexico's role in the world was increasingly questioned. Although Mexico promoted itself for a permanent seat on the UN Security Council (UNSC), analysts both national and foreign argued that the constitution's strictures on sending troops overseas meant that Mexico would never be able to participate in UN peacekeeping missions and therefore lacked credibility, whereas Brazil, for example, was already active in Haiti. On a regional level, Mexico's aspirations to act as a bridge between North and South America were received with strong reservations by the other states on the continent. Brazil, in particular, looked at this foreign policy goal of the Fox administration as another sign of the government's inability to grasp political and economic realities in the Americas. The much-vaunted Plan Puebla-Panama, an economic development and infrastructure plan for Central America, was soon exposed as more declaratory rather than operational, and Mexican credibility in the region received a further blow due to repeated political controversies with both Cuba and Venezuela.

By the end of 2006, and the arrival of a new government under Felipe Calderón, Mexico's fine multilateralist tradition was looking a little worn around the edges. But at the level of the G8, Mexico continued to receive plaudits for its ongoing political reform and its steady rather than spectacular economic ascent.

The Rise of Mexico's Economy and Its Importance to the World

Despite Mexico's frequent foreign policy miscalculations, Bernal Rodríguez (2001) points out that Mexico's opportunities in the international system have been changed by the emergence of the country as a key player in the international economy. Mexico's prominent position in international trade, and its impressive record in attracting international foreign direct investment (FDI), has increased Mexico's stature and made it a force with which to be reckoned. This economic growth has, of course, been driven by the positive side of Mexico's economic affairs—the growth in trade and FDI, the progressive liberalization of the economy, increasing financial and economic stability, and rising income levels. Still, Mexico has, paradoxically, also benefited at the international level from its weaknesses. The Latin American debt crisis was a key turning point in Mexican economic history, both in terms of pushing through vital reforms in economic policy and economic thinking, and just as importantly in emphasizing Mexico's central place in the world's financial system. With the 1994 peso crisis, this centrality was made ever clearer, as the world's major powers, pushed and directed by the U.S., first created an enormous US$50 billion rescue package, and then later invited Mexico to participate in the G20 grouping of finance ministers from the world's major financial systems in both developed and developing states.

This invitation to participate in the process of designing international financial architecture reform is informative as it served several purposes. As Tony Porter and Duncan Wood (2002) have argued, the participation of influential developing countries such as Mexico increased the two-way information flow in financial issues, helped to provide an early-warning system for emerging country problems, and increased the legitimacy of the G7 and the process of international financial reform.

The success of the G20 almost immediately led to calls from national leaders such as former Canadian prime minister Paul Martin to incorporate the major emerging economies into a new system of global governance based on the "G8 Plus" idea. Propelled by the seeming failure of the UN to deal with the international dispute over the invasion of Iraq, new, more flexible mechanisms were sought that would be both effective and increase the legitimacy of the central organs of global governance. The countries to be included varied from discussion to discussion, but Mexico always seemed to hold its place alongside China, Brazil, and India. A large part of the perception of Mexico's importance has come from its economic and political transition over the past two decades. It has also come though from the notion that there is still so much to achieve in Mexico and, that if the true potential of the country can be unleashed, the world would benefit.

Mexico's economic growth over the past 20 to 30 years may not be that impressive, particularly when compared to Asian economies and especially China. But everybody recognizes the enormous potential of Mexico, given its geographical location lodged between the United States and Central America, its significant population, its manufacturing and tourism sectors and its impressive natural resources. By 2006, the country's gross domestic product (GDP), measured according to purchasing power parity (PPP), was US$1.269 trillion, giving Mexico a ranking of eleventh place in the world. Ahead of Mexico, the only developing countries on the list are Brazil, Russia, India, and China, and it lies ahead of Canada, South Korea, Indonesia, and Turkey. On the down side, Mexico has thus far failed to convert this potential into real economic power or a significant improvement in living standards for the vast majority of its population. The problems of fiscal, structural, and energy reform in Mexico at the beginning of the 21st century have become widely known around the world.

This mixed economic record, however, does not seem to be an obstacle for Mexico's prestige. On the contrary, the fact that Mexico seems to be mired in a period of slow growth and that the reasons for that are well known, combined with the hope that successive governments are committed to making the necessary reforms, has led economists, financial institutions, and, indeed, the leaders of G8 states to predict Mexico's full arrival as a global economic force later in this century. Although this is not seen as nearly so certain as the rise of China, India, or even Brazil, a number of influential actors have gone so far as to predict Mexico's place at the top of the global economic rankings by the middle of the century.

According to a survey in *The Economist*, by 2040 Mexico is predicted to have grown to the point where it is the fifth largest economy in the world, almost one fifth the size of the United States and, astonishingly, more than two thirds as big as Japan, and bigger than the economies of Germany, Britain, and France ("Emerging At Last" 2006, chart 4). A related study by Goldman Sachs saw Mexico in sixth place by 2050, just behind Brazil in the rankings (O'Neill et al. 2005, 8). The prestige that stemmed from these predictions was seized upon by both presidents Fox and Calderón, and consistently used as a point of reference in speeches to foreign investors and economic groups.

These predictions received very different reviews. Mexican analysts, familiar with the problems of economic reform in its many guises and the political obstacles in the way of meaningful reform, found it hard to believe that the country would be able to overcome these challenges in the medium term to make possible such impressive growth relative to other states by mid-century. Nonetheless, such cautionary views did not diminish international optimism about Mexico, particularly when reform-minded president Calderón took office in highly contested circumstances in 2006. The generally held perception is that Mexico will have to face its demons sooner or later, and that the full potential of the country will then be unleashed.

So what is the likely position of Mexico by 2040 or 2050? So much is uncertain, although things do look a touch brighter than they did back in the political roller-coaster years of 2005–06. The beginnings of fiscal reform, essential to giving the state the resources it needs to invest in infrastructure, social programs, education, and health care for the good of the majority of Mexican citizens have been a promising start. The commitment to invest in infrastructure, with the creation of a national fund totalling more than US$25 billion, should help to ease some of the country's transportation problems ("Anuncia Calderón Fondo Nacional de Infraestructura" 2008). The prospects for meaningful energy sector reform, and the possibility of allowing Petróleos Mexicanos (PEMEX) to work more freely with the private sector, although highly uncertain at the time of writing, would help to solve Mexico's pending energy challenges, particularly in the area of oil production.

Nonetheless, both the short- and long-term challenges remain daunting. First, various political obstacles need to be overcome, particularly those involving the left and far left of the spectrum. Second, the coming into effect of the agricultural provisions in the North American Free Trade Agreement (NAFTA) is hitting a large section of Mexico's small farmers by removing tariffs on a wide range of food products. Third, the recession in the U.S. will hit Mexico hard, although high oil prices will shield both the government and the balance of payments to some degree. Fourth, rising competition from Asia for Mexico's market share in the U.S. will hit a number of sectors, particularly manufacturing. In the long term, Mexico needs to deal with declining oil production, a changing demographic profile as the population ages, and stresses and strains on the pensions and social security systems. In short, the economic future is far from certain.

The Perceptions of Mexicans: Of Mexico, the G8 and the Outreach Five

This chapter has already commented on the somewhat divergent attitudes of Mexico both toward the international system and of the national identity. In the past, Mexico has vacillated between full participation and a desire to keep foreign intervention in national affairs to a minimum. Mexico is uncertain whether it is a North American or a Latin American country, a developing state or an emerging member of the developed world. From the G77 to the OECD to the G20 finance to G20 developing countries focused on trade, Mexico seems caught between two worlds, something that is apparent the moment on arrival in the country. That identity crisis (perhaps a slight exaggeration) is not helped by the ongoing political change through which the country is passing. The democratization process and its concomitant political struggles between left and right mean that foreign policy is necessarily a battleground for Mexican attitudes.

These attitudes have, until very recently, been somewhat of a mystery. Politicians assume that the public in general was not very interested in foreign policy and that it should therefore be driven by questions of prestige and anti-*yanquismo*. Beginning in 2004, however, two exhaustive national polls on Mexican attitudes to foreign policy have been conducted by the Centro de Investigación y Docencia Económica (Center for Teaching and Research in Economics [CIDE]) and the Consejo Mexicano de Asuntos Internacionales (Mexican Council on Foreign Relations [COMEXI]). The most recent of these, conducted in the election year of 2006, gives us a lot of evidence about the way in which Mexican attitudes are evolving (CIDE-COMEXI 2006). On questions of identity, for example, despite what opinion leaders might say, Mexicans still believe that they are Latin American rather than North American or "citizens of the world," by a margin of 62 percent to 29 percent (CIDE-COMEXI 2006, table 1.6). At the same time, Mexicans "have become more open to the outside world," as their attitudes toward foreigners have softened, presumably through increased familiarity with the outside world due to travel and improved communications (CIDE-COMEXI 2006).

What, then, do Mexicans want from their foreign policy? First, they do in fact want an active role in world affairs. Nationally, 56 percent of Mexicans believe it is better for the future of the country to play an active role in world affairs rather than stay out or do neither of the above. This suggests significant potential support for Mexico's participation in the Heiligendamm Process (HP), and reinforces the government's current position. It is interesting to contrast this slight majority in favour at the national level with overwhelming support (96 percent) from opinion leaders in the country. These are, of course, the people who are more closely consulted in the foreign policy process and the group whose opinion matters the most to the Calderón government at present.

An important supplementary question in the report concerned Mexico's participation in resolving "the world's grave problems" (CIDE-COMEXI 2006, 26). Whereas only 29 percent of Mexicans believed in participation *carte blanche*, a further 52 percent believed that Mexico should do so if those problems directly affect the country (CIDE-COMEXI 2006, table 2.2). Two points are worth making here: first, that the 29 percent reflects the fear that Mexico could become involved in an Iraq- or Afghanistan-like problem and, second, that this means that governments that can show Mexican contributions to the resolution of global problems that directly affect Mexico would receive more than 80 percent public approval.

In terms of Mexico and multilateralism, the poll is informative about the HP in one very obvious way. The organizing entities did not see the G8 as important enough a part of Mexican consciousness about foreign affairs to include it in the questionnaire. Whereas Mexicans were asked about, and showed a generally very positive attitude toward the UN, the WTO, the European Union, the Organization of American States (OAS), and even multinational corporations (MNCs) and international non-governmental organizations (NGOs), the G8 is conspicuous by its absence. When the summit itself took place in the summer of 2007, the dominant attitude was one of bewilderment, and news outlets felt obliged to explain to their (confused and rather uninterested) publics just exactly what the G8 is and why they might be interested in working more closely with Mexico. That the G8 is a club for the rich and powerful states has been an easy concept for the public to absorb; what it has to do with Mexico is an entirely different matter. It will be interesting to see whether the next poll includes a treatment of the G8 and the outreach process.

There are, however, some clues about the potential attitudes of Mexicans toward the outreach process by looking at their feelings regarding the other countries of the O5. Although South Africa was not included in the poll (Africa remains a very distant place in every sense for Mexicans), China (in fifth place), Brazil (in tenth), and India (in twelfth) all received strongly positive responses from the Mexican public. The prospects of working with these states would not seem strange to Mexicans, particularly if it meant placing Mexico firmly in the club of the elite emerging powers.

Calderón and Heiligendamm

In the first 18 months of the Calderón administration, the aforementioned principles of increasing international prestige, improving Mexico's influence in the world and helping with the domestic political and economic agendas can all be discerned in the government's emerging foreign policy. Apart from Heiligendamm, Mexico has been active in bilateral relations with the U.S., securing assistance from its northern neighbour in the fight against drug trafficking, and has been active in international forums as a promoter of inward FDI into Mexico. Indeed, Mexico has succeeded in overcoming the doubts concerning Calderón's election victory in 2006.

But the outreach process presents the Calderón government with a number of very interesting prospects for both short- and long-term foreign policy achievements, which will be outlined below. As such, Mexico has seized the opportunity to engage thoroughly in an intense dialogue with its O5 or B(R)ICSAM partners, having a perceptible influence on the statements coming out of the group.

Why is the Calderón government so interested in the HP? In 2007, just before the summit, the G8 Research Group at Oxford University put forward a number of reasons why, focusing on the questions of trade, security, and climate change (Myatt et al. 2007, 15–17). There is a broader range of issues why the outreach process matters to the Calderón administration, beginning first with the recent history of Mexico's foreign policy.

As mentioned earlier, at various moments in its history Mexico has tried to play a leadership role for the developing world, particular with reference to Latin America. The beginning of the Fox era saw just such an attempt, albeit unsuccessful. As Fox took power in 2000, he offered to act as a bridge between the U.S. and the rest of the continent. The offer was immediately rejected by the Brazilian government, arguing that Brazil did not need any intermediary with the United States. This apparent brush-off was followed by the high, ultimately unfulfilled expectations associated with the Plan Puebla–Panama. When it became clear that Mexico was not going to put any substantial funds behind the initiative, it quickly faded from the front pages of the press and the policy agenda in Central America. Mexican leadership in its region, and its reputation as a leading developing state, emerged significantly eroded from the debacle. In this context the outreach process presents an entirely new departure for Mexico, moving away from its pretensions in the region to a broader and more global role. Although the Calderón government continues to talk about the need to engage Latin America and has even resurrected the Plan Puebla–Panama, it is clearly time to move on to bigger and hopefully better goals. For sure, Mexico succeeded in gaining mention of the initiative in the communiqué that emerged from the HP, as an example of South–South cooperation.

Already, the administration has used the outreach process to enhance contact and negotiation prospects with its fellow O5 members. It is hoped that this will not only contribute to a healing of the relationship with Brazil, but also build a strong relationship with both India and China as they emerge as global economic powers. The relationship with China, in particular, is a complex one, with Mexico having negotiated tough terms concerning China's entry into the WTO, and facing stiff competition from Chinese exports to the U.S. market. In the past year or so the mindset in the Mexican business and economic policy communities has begun to shift away from viewing China as a threat, and toward an examination of the opportunities that Chinese growth provides. This way of thinking can only help with the long-term diversification of Mexico's export destinations and the prospects for new sources of, and destinations, for FDI. Towards this end, Calderón held bilateral talks with the heads of government of India, China, and Brazil during the summit (Arunda 2007).

In addition to strengthening its bilateral ties with the O5 states, Mexico clearly hopes to expand its influence and prestige on the global stage through participation in the group. In a press conference announcing Calderón's participation in the Heiligendamm talks, foreign affairs undersecretary María de Lourdes Arunda Bezaury (2007) emphasized over and over again that a major goal of this participation was to gain greater influence for Mexico in global affairs:

> To promote a better insertion of Mexico on the global stage … we seek to strengthen Mexico's presence in these spaces for dialogue and cooperation that will allow Mexico to have a greater influence in the definition of the international agenda and promote the issues that are of interest to her, as well as strengthening links with key actors on he global stage … In this way a greater capacity to influence the definition of the main issues on the international agenda will be built. (translated by author)

This is not just, however, a short-term goal. In the longer term, the Calderón government is holding to a long-established policy of participation in the process of redefinition of the institutions of global governance. Through South–South cooperation, the prestige of consultation at the G8 summit year on year, and the possibilities of meaningful reform of the UN, Mexico hopes to gain a privileged place in the process of global governance and institutional change. As John Kirton (2007) has pointed out, by 2009 when the G8 Summit will be hosted by Italy, the HP will have come to an end and the group will issue its final report. At this time the thorny issue of UN reform may be central to the G8 plus O5 process, and Mexico will not want to be left on the sidelines of such negotiations.

Timothy Myatt et al. (2007) have noted that a primary priority for Mexico may be to maintain the participation of Mexico in the O5. They argue that Mexico needs to justify its presence more than the other members due to the many problems it faces internally and because in recent years it has slipped in terms of relative economic size. As Thomas Fues (2007) writes, the argument is made that compared to the other members, in terms of O5 membership,

> Mexico's claims are less obvious. Presumably US interests come into play here: the USA wishes to provide its neighbor with a leading position in the global hierarchy. Having said that, by virtue of its OECD and NAFTA membership Mexico is suitable for a bridging role between North and South and in addition has strategic significance as a major oil exporter.

However, each of the presumptions Fues makes for Mexico's inclusion is flawed. First, it has been the UK and Germany, rather than the U.S., that have been the major promoters of Mexican participation. Second, as noted above, Mexico's bridging role has consistently failed to impress. Third, Mexico's oil reserves, while considerable, may be irrelevant unless the necessary energy reforms are undertaken this year to allow for PEMEX to acquire the capacity to access them. Nonetheless, despite all of these reasons why Mexico is a potentially weak member of the O5, the country has quickly established itself as a driving force.

To counter any doubts there may be, the Calderón administration seized the initiative with the other members. First, on 7 June 2007 it organized a meeting with the O5 countries to "share perspectives and find convergence around the themes" that would be discussed with the G8 leaders at the Heiligendamm Summit two days later. Second, Mexico put itself forward as the first host of O5 meetings, with a gathering of O5 undersecretaries of foreign affairs in Michoacán, Morelia, in August 2007, and then, at a meeting of foreign ministers in New York in September, Mexico was named as the coordinator of O5 work and as interlocutor with the G8 during the following year (Secretaría de Relaciones Exteriores 2007). This early success in setting the agenda of the O5 was seen as crucial by the Calderón government in maximizing the utility of participation.

The efforts of the Mexican ministry of foreign affairs to drive the G5 process and the HP forward stem not only from the coincidence between overall foreign policy goals and the attractions of the HP, but also from a quite personal, individual-level effort put in by Lourdes Aranda and her team. Aranda's belief in the process can be sensed in her numerous public statements on HP, her enthusiastic embrace of the coordinating role for the G5 in its first year, and her palpable disappointment when the 2008 G8 Summit agenda left little room for the HP. Having shown herself to be unwaveringly positive about HP until this point, Aranda was critical of the G8 for defining the agenda and for failing to allow for an "equal and enduring partnership" in the first year of the process (Williamson 2008). Nonetheless, Aranda's continuing determination that the G5 is an important new actor in the global dialogue was seen in her belief that the group "could play a stabilizing role" in the international food crisis.

The O5 Agenda and the Calderón Government

In the joint statement of the G8 and the O5 (2007) at the end of the Heiligendamm Summit, the issues to be dealt with by the HP were identified as:

- cross-border investment;
- research and innovation;
- climate change;
- energy; and,
- development, particularly in Africa.

With the exception of the final point, all of these issues have figured prominently on the Calderón administration's agenda. Of particular importance here for the foreign and domestic agendas are the linked issues of climate change and energy. The Calderón government achieved considerable foreign policy success in 2007 through its commitment to such issues in the Bali meeting on the United Nations Framework Convention on Climate Change (UNFCCC) in December 2007. At the end of that meeting, Mexico was ranked fourth, out of all countries, in terms of its commitment to climate issues on Germanwatch's (2007, 4) Climate Change Performance Index (Madrigal 2007). Not only did this give Mexico considerable prestige due to its placement above most European countries (only Sweden, Germany, and Iceland scored higher), but it was touted as an example for China, India and Brazil by Pankaj Bhatia, director of the Greenhouse Gas Protocol Initiative of the World Resources Institute, a sustainability think tank. Mexico thus has another opportunity to lead in the O5, and to show its good global citizenship in a surprising new way.

With reference to energy, the Calderón administration will be interested in pursuing cooperation in this area, primarily due to domestic political conflicts over the future of the sector in Mexico. The country is going through an increasingly worrying time as proven oil reserves diminish and PEMEX lacks the technology to be able to discover new reserves in the deep waters of the Gulf of Mexico. Although high oil prices have given both PEMEX and the government (through tax and royalties) a bumper dividend since 2006, the very real possibility exists that Mexico may have to begin importing oil before 2016 unless drastic changes are made in the legislation surrounding hydrocarbons. The focus of the G8 plus O5 agenda on energy is seen as a useful complement to the efforts of the Calderón government to secure meaningful energy reform at home. Nonetheless the focus of the energy agenda through the HP does not only coincide with Calderón's goals over oil. In the areas of energy efficiency and energy saving and also in renewable energy sources, there is considerable synergy with the government's programs and priorities.

It was, however, in the longer joint declaration of the O5 countries that Mexico's foreign policy priorities emerge more clearly. In terms of development, the fight against terrorism (where Mexico has an emerging and increasingly worrying problem), democratization, global governance, world trade, climate change, and South–South cooperation, Mexico's influence was indistinguishable from those of its fellow O5 states. However, in the middle of the statement, beginning at point 16 and extending through point 19, there appears a series of declarations and demands concerning migration, Mexico's foreign policy priority *par excellence* (G8 and Outreach Partners 2007). That migration should receive more attention in the joint declaration than trade, climate change, or South–South cooperation, and roughly the same amount as development, is truly remarkable and demonstrates the success of the Calderón team in influencing the agenda.

Given Mexico's difficulties in securing a loosening or even preventing a tightening of immigration legislation in the U.S., this is a clear attempt to gain O5 support for efforts to pressure the U.S. on the issue. With over half a million Mexicans emigrating to the United States every year (most of them undocumented migrants) and with Mexico receiving between US$20 billion and US$24 billion in remittances from the diaspora there annually (a source of foreign currency surpassed only by oil revenues), migration is one issue that the Calderón government needs to promote. Although progress with the U.S. is stalled, the success of getting migration onto the agenda of the O5 offers the administration an opportunity to placate domestic pressure groups.

Mexico as a Bridge

An evaluation of the potential for Mexico to act as a bridge between the G8 and the O5, B(R)ICSAM, or, as the G5, requires also an examination of the shift that has occurred over recent decades in Mexico's place in the world. In line with the country's ascent as an economic power and the progressive changes that have taken place in both domestic economic policy and foreign political and economic relations, since the 1980s it has come to redefine its position and its peer group in the international system. The shift from member of the G77 to an OECD state, from UNCTAD supporter to active GATT and WTO participant, and from ISI proponent to free trade crusader shows how dramatically Mexico has changed both its role in the system of states, and its peer group from the mass of developing countries to the leading economies of the world.

The clearest example of this is, of course, NAFTA. Mexico's clear economic priorities in the region, its shift toward free trade and its overwhelming and ever-growing dependence on the U.S. have been heightened by membership in NAFTA and have brought criticism from other Latin American countries that Mexico has become a further entrenched in the U.S. orbit. Yet Mexico has remained in touch with Latin neighbours, not only in the rhetorical pronouncements mentioned above, but also through active membership and a leading role in the Rio Group of Latin American and Caribbean countries. And Mexico has certainly maintained an independent, autonomous foreign policy, a reality highlighted by its relations with Cuba (notwithstanding the recent awkwardness found in this relationship), opposition to the U.S.-led invasion of Iraq, and its participation in the Ottawa process on landmines.

But Mexico's status as a proponent of the South and of southern unity is increasingly problematic. Despite its strong interests in Central America, and the growing importance of emerging markets around the world for Mexican MNCs such as Bimbo, CEMEX, and Telmex, Mexico has done little in recent decades to prove itself to the wider constellation of least developed countries (LDCs), or to offer them tangible reasons to build a strong bilateral relationship. Belatedly, Mexico is beginning to discover Africa and the Middle East, and Asia has been an area of growing importance over the past few years, but these efforts remain overshadowed by its foreign policy main game.

What does this, then, tell us about Mexican aspirations to act as a bridge between the other G5 states and the G8 itself? As the only OECD member among the G5, Mexico has come to view itself as a natural facilitator for a productive dialogue between the two sides and indeed Mexico has been an early leader in coordinating G5 activities and statements. Thus far Mexico's prior lack of credibility as an LDC leader seems to matter little and this can be explained by two main points.

First, the other G5 states are not, of course, just any LDC states. They are the most dynamic, powerful, and important emerging powers from the global South. Mexico's inability to engage other LDCs does not weigh heavily on the decision makers in Beijing, New Delhi, Johannesburg, or Brasilía. What matters more is Mexico's ability to marshal its diplomatic resources, to bring to the table its experience of dealing with the U.S. and other OECD states, and its impressive multilateral history.

Second, and this point should not be ignored, the facts that Ángel Gurría, a former Mexican foreign minister and finance minister, has become secretary general of the OECD and that organization has thrown its weight behind the HP give extra credibility to the Mexicans. Although the OECD technical support may be limited, its enthusiasm cannot be doubted, and the simple fact is that some form of secretariat is absolutely necessary to facilitate cooperation between the G5 states.

Last, it is worth pointing out that the bridging role suits Mexico in the sense that it may provide at least a temporary way out of the dilemma the country faces in terms of its identity. By bridging the gap between G5 and G8, Mexico is at last able to find a way to engage both worlds in which its interests lie. By resolving the Mexican dilemma, the G5 process has endeared itself to both members of the diplomatic corps (who embody the institutional memory for such issues) and decision makers in the Calderón government.

Concluding Thoughts

Mexico's position as one of the five most important emerging powers in the world remains uncertain. In terms of economic size, Mexico may be classed as a middle power in economic terms, with the potential to become one of the largest economies in the world by mid century, but it faces enormous obstacles before it can achieve that potential. Its international identity is constrained at least in part due to its refusal to engage in any kind of military action outside its borders, even with UN approval.

But today Mexico is emerging as a new force to be reckoned with on the international stage. With the democratic transition now consolidated, with predictions of impressive long-term economic growth and with economic reforms on the table (even if not yet approved), Mexico has gained prestige in the forums and circles of global governance. Mexico's movement toward a permanent seat at the table, although this may not happen in the near future at the UN, should be seen as a logical progression and entirely consistent with the traditions of Mexican foreign policy. This time around Mexico does not have to choose between the developed and developing worlds. Instead, Mexico joins the elite of the developing world as they engage more fully with the G8. In doing so, Mexico can speak as a representative of the South, while at the same time advancing its own interests and policy goals by dealing with the North.

Mexico's skillful diplomacy in the O5 or B(R)ICSAM has already brought results. The inclusion of migration issues as a priority for the group, reflects Mexican leadership, and the work agenda in general is consistent with a number of Mexican foreign and domestic policy priorities. Over the next year and a half, the challenge will be to expand the agenda, to establish clear goals within the grouping of emerging powers, and to take full advantage of the socialization opportunities that the HP offers.

Note

1   Moreno Toscano (2000) points to several key principles: *"La autodeterminación de los pueblos, la no intervención, la solución pacifica de las controversias, la proscripción de la amenaza o el uso de la fuerza, la igualdad jurídica de los Estados, la cooperación internacional para el desarrollo y la lucha por la paz y la seguridad internacionales"* ["The state's self-determination, non-intervention, peaceful resolution of conflicts, the prescription of the threat or the use of force, equality among states, international cooperation for development, and the pursuit of international peace and security"] (translated by the author).

References

"Anuncia Calderón Fondo Nacional de Infraestructura." (2008). ["Calderón Announces National Infrastructure Fund."]. *El Financiero*, 6 February.

Arunda Bezaury, María de Lourdes (2007). "Conferencia de Prensa de la Subsecretaria de Relaciones Exteriores con motivo de la Gira de Trabajo por Europa que realizará el Presidente Calderón." ["Press Conference of the Under Secretary of Foreign Affairs on the Occasion of President Calderón's European Tour "] 30 May, Miércoles. <www.presidencia.gob.mx/buscador/index.php?contenido=30371> (May 2008).

Bernal Rodríguez, José Luis (2001). "Politica exterior y promocion economica internacional: hacia una nueva diplomacia economica." ["Foreign Policy and International Economic Promotion: Toward a New Economic Diplomacy."] *Revista Mexicana de Politica Exterior* 62/63 (June): 7–27.

Castañeda, Jorge G. (2001). "El nuevo activismo international mexicano." ["The New Mexican International Activism."] *Revista Mexicana de Politica Exterior* 64 (October): 43–53.

Centro de Investigación y Docencia Económicas and Consejo Mexicano de Asuntos Internacionales (2006). *Mexico and the World 2006: Public Opinion and Foreign Policy in Mexico.* Mexico City. <mexicoyelmundo.cide.edu/repmexeng.htm> (May 2008).

Derbez Bautista, Luis Ernesto (2004). "Mexico ante un escenario mundial en transformacion." ["Mexico in the World's Transformation."] *Revista Mexicana de Politica Exterior* 70 (October/February): 13–25.

"Emerging At Last." (2006). *Economist*, 16 September.

Flores Olea, Victor (1987). "Defensa y promocion del multilateralismo." ["Defence and Promotion of Multilateralism."] *Revista Mexicana de Politica Exterior* 16 (July-September): 9–10.

Fues, Thomas (2007). "Global Governance Beyond the G8: Reform Prospects for the Summit Architecture." *International Politik und Gesellschaft* (2): 11–24. <www.fes.de/ipg/arc_07_set/set_02_07e.htm> (May 2008).

G8 and Outreach Partners (2007). "Joint Statement by the German G8 Presidency and the Heads of State and/or Government of Brazil, China, India, Mexico, and South Africa on the Occasion of the G8 Summit in Heiligendamm." 8 June, Heiligendamm. <www.g8.utoronto.ca/summit/2007heiligendamm/g8-2007-joint.html> (May 2008).

Germanwatch (2007). *Climate Change Performance Index 2008.* Bonn. <www.germanwatch.org/klima/ccpi2008.pdf> (May 2008).

Kirton, John J. (2007). "G8: An Economic Forum of the Enlarged Western Alliance? The Record from Rambouillet 1975 through Heiligendamm 2007 to Canada 2010." Paper prepared for the North American European Summer Academy of Centre International de Formation Européenn and the Zentrum für Wissenschaft und Weiterbildung Schloss Hofen, 24 July. Lochau, Austria. <www.g8.utoronto .ca/scholar/kirton2007/kirton-schlosshofen-070724.pdf> (May 2008).

Lozoya, Jorge Alberto (1994). "Mexico y la cooperación international." ["Mexico and International Cooperation."] *Revista Mexicana de Politica Exterior* 44 (Fall): 131–140.

Madrigal, Alexis (2007). "Bali Meeting Ends; Mexico Emerges as Leader on Climate Change." *Wired*, 14 December. <www.wired.com/science/planetearth/news/2007/12/mexico_climate> (May 2008).

Moreno Toscano, Carmen (2000). "La vocacion multilateral de la politica exterior mexicana." ["The Multilateral Vocation of Mexico's Foreign Policy."] *Revista Mexicana de Politica Exterior* 61 (October): 143–160.

Myatt, Timothy, Carlos Sayao, Diarmuid Torney, *et al.* (2007). '*Outreach 5' Country Objectives Report: 2007 Heiligendamm Summit.* 7 June. G8 Research Group—Oxford. <www.g8.utoronto.ca/oxford/g8rg-ox-objectives2007.pdf> (May 2008).

O'Neill, Jim, Dominic Wilson, Roopa Purushothaman, *et al.* (2005). "How Solid Are the BRICs?" Global Economics Paper No. 134, 1 December. New Delhi: Goldman Sachs. <www2.goldmansachs.com/hkchina/insight/research/pdf/BRICs_3_12-1-05.pdf> (May 2008).

Porter, Tony and Duncan Wood (2002). "Reform without Representation? The International and Transnational Dialogue on the Global Financial Architecture." In *Debating the Global Financial Architecture*, edited by L.E. Armijo. New York: State University of New York Press.

Secretaría de Relaciones Exteriores (2007). "Se Reúnion Los Cancilleres del Crupo de los Cinco en Nueva York." ["Meeting of the Group of Five Foreign Ministers in New York."] 27 September, New York. <www.sre.gob.mx/csocial/contenido/comunicados/2007/sep/cp_253.html> (May 2008).

Williamson, Hugh (2008). "Rich Nations Stall Dialogue with "G5" Powers." *Financial Times*, 2 July. <www.ft.com/cms/s/0/d9724a12-4858-11dd-a851-000077b07658.html?nclick_check=1> (August 2008).

9

ASEAN and the G8
Potentially Productive Partners or Two Ships Passing in the Night?

Paul Bowles

Would the Association of South East Asian Nations (ASEAN) fit in an expanded G8? The question is simple but the answer is complex. Furthermore, the question is not often asked. In the discussion of whether the G8 should expand to include, in some form, the Outreach Five (O5) as a way of increasing the legitimacy of the former, the focus of the O5 is firmly on the "emerging economies" of the 21st century, a formulation that typically excludes ASEAN and its member states. And yet, ten years ago, before the Asian financial crisis began in 1997, this would not have been conceivable. Ten years ago, Malaysia, Indonesia, and Thailand were all considered "miracle" economies in the terminology of the World Bank (1993). Any discussion of expanding the G8 then would undoubtedly have had some role for them. And South Korea would have figured prominently too. And perhaps even Argentina, whose adoption of a currency board in 1994 appeared to herald a new era of growth and stability. But it was not to be: the Asian financial crisis led to a new assessment of the Malaysian, Thai, Indonesian, and South Korean political economies. The language of miracles, underpinned by seemingly productive deliberation councils, was quickly replaced by that of crony capitalism. Then Argentina imploded in 2001. A new set of emerging economies has since been identified by Dominic Wilson and Roopa Purushothaman (2003).

This introductory historical point has two salutary lessons. First, the identification of which countries outside of the G8 are doing well can be short lived (Chile was a favourite for some in the 1970s, to give another example) and is primarily determined by economic factors (such as growth and size of gross domestic product [GDP]). International political and institutional structures, however, tend to have greater longevity (witness, for example, membership in the Permanent Five [P5] members of the United Nations Security Council [UNSC]) and so linking the often ephemeral indicators of economic success with the more enduring implications of institutional change is a problematic exercise. Partly, for this reason, Andrew F. Cooper (2007, 3) has suggested moving beyond economic indicators to also consider "diplomatic weight focusing less on structure and more on behaviour or agency," as more enduring measures of which countries might be suitable candidates for an expanded G8. On this basis, he proposes that as a group, Brazil, Russia, India, China, South Africa, and Mexico—the B(R)ICSAM countries—constitutes such countries, a formulation could include ASEAN even though ASEAN is not conventionally included under this rubric.

Second, it poses problems for those countries outside of the G8 that are courted in one phase but marginalized in another: how are their international ambitions to be realized? What forums can they use to maintain or advance their interests? When they have slipped down (or off) the G8 interest ladder, what strategies are left open to them? In many ways, these are the questions that ASEAN now faces.

Bringing these two points together raises two related but reversed questions. The first is whether what Cooper (2007, 4) has called the G8's "crisis of legitimacy and efficiency" would be partly solved if it were expanded to include ASEAN or a representative from it. Or, to put the question more bluntly, what is the value of ASEAN for the G8? The reverse question can also be asked, namely, what is the value of the G8 for ASEAN?

These are the two central questions that this chapter addresses. Answers to these two questions will determine whether the G8 and ASEAN are likely to be productive partners, whether they have divergent interests that are more likely to lead to parallel rather than converging forms of cooperation, or whether both institutions are destined to continue to be exposed to problems of effectiveness. My argument can be summarized as follows. Economically, ASEAN remains important but its "diplomatic prowess" is open to question. On one reading, ASEAN is an ineffective organization and, as such, is unlikely to be of significant interest to a G8 seeking to enhance its own effectiveness. This interpretation of ASEAN is not the only one available, and a case has been made for its diplomatic importance. However, if this interpretation is accepted, then it is much more likely that ASEAN will use its resources for the building of a regional community and the promotion of inter-regional dialogues rather than in an expanded G8. Hanging over ASEAN is the spectre of China and how and whether ASEAN is able to respond to the rise of China's economic and diplomatic power will be crucial to determining whether it is able to remain at the centre of regional initiatives or whether it will be further marginalized and suffer the same crisis of legitimacy and effectiveness that the G8 currently does.

ASEAN: Who Is in An Acronym?

This question is necessary because ASEAN appears in many formulations with the focus of discussion ranging from the ASEAN+4, ASEAN+5, ASEAN+6, ASEAN+10 to consideration only of the largest and putative leader of the group, Indonesia. ASEAN consists of ten countries: Brunei Darussalam, Cambodia, Indonesia, Laos, Malaysia, Myanmar, the Philippines, Singapore, Thailand, and Vietnam. However, based on economic size, population, and level of per capita income, attention is often focused on a so-called ASEAN+4 (Indonesia, Malaysia, the Philippines, and Thailand). Other formulations expand this to ASEAN+5 by including Singapore on the grounds that the latter, while only a city-state, has an economy larger than that of the Philippines and comparable to that of Malaysia. For other purposes, it is the ASEAN+6 (that is, the ASEAN+5 plus Brunei) that are identified, these being the members of ASEAN before the recent expansion to include the four new recruits—Cambodia, Laos, Myanmar, and Vietnam, collectively known as CLMV—all of which are at lower levels of economic development (although Vietnam's growth has placed it in some kind of transition state between the ASEAN+6 and Cambodia, Laos, and Myanmar). The organization itself consists of all ten members and has its own secretary general and secretariat. Nevertheless, in analyses of including ASEAN in other arenas it is not necessarily the holder of the secretary general's position that is viewed as the appropriate representative of ASEAN. For example, Cooper (2007, 2) argues that Indonesia, as a "member of the ASEAN-4," be included in an expanded G8 (see also Cooper et al. 2006, 3). He further continues that "on the basis of diplomatic logic Indonesia would appear to be the best country to add to the B(R)ICSAM group. In part this is because of an international standing built up over the years as a member of the Non-Aligned Movement [NAM], not only because it hosted the path-breaking Bandung conference but also because of the 50th anniversary of the institution) as well as the G77. But these credentials have been reinforced by its status as a country with a large Islamic majority and an emergent democratic culture (with its democratic values extended onto the international arena through its support for the new ASEAN charter)" (Cooper 2007, 9). Indonesia's credentials are also enhanced by its membership of the G20 finance ministers and central bank governors.

The question of the mechanics of ASEAN's inclusion in an expanded G8 is therefore subject to some imprecision. In some formulations, it is ASEAN's diplomatic importance that warrants its inclusion; in others, the economic importance of its major members; while in others, it is Indonesia's case for inclusion that is strengthened by its membership of ASEAN. These complexities are clear from the involvement of ASEAN states in the ministerials and meetings associated with the 2008 G8 Hokkaido Toyako Summit. For example, the meeting of the G8 development ministers (G8 Development Ministers 2008), in April 2008, included as outreach partners Indonesia, Malaysia, and the ASEAN secretariat. The finance ministers' meeting was attended by Thailand while Indonesia attended, as one of eight outreach countries, the climate change meetings at the conclusion of the Hokkaido Summit.[1] Japan's invitation to Indonesia to the latter meeting arose not only from Indonesia's significance as an actor in the potential solutions to climate change but also from its status as an ASEAN state, a developing country, and a "close friend" of Japan. For Japan, as the host, Indonesia's participation as an Asian country and a member of ASEAN could be viewed as desirable within the context of the regional dynamics of Asia; that is, it offers Japan an opportunity to exercise its own diplomacy in the region. Whether other G8 countries would have the same incentives to invite Indonesia to future summits, or whether its Islamic status would offer similar appeal, remains doubtful. Indonesia's profile at the Hokkaido Summit, therefore, probably has as much to do with the host country's interests as it does with Indonesia's position in the world.

The dynamics of how ASEAN might be included, therefore, are complex. There is not room here to enter into the finer points of this debate. This discussion uses a broader brush but, acknowledging these nuances, where appropriate, disaggregates ASEAN economic performance by country and sub-group and also pays particular attention to the region's "'real' political economy of development" (Cooper et al. 2006, 20).

What Does ASEAN Offer the G8?

Economically, ASEAN still remains important in global economic terms even if its dynamism of the 1990s (up to 1997) is now only a distant historical

memory and if ASEAN has been eclipsed in the 2000s by the economic powerhouses that are 21st-century China and India.

The combined GDP of the ASEAN+5 economies (Indonesia, Malaysia,
the Philippines, Singapore, and Thailand) is close to US$1 trillion, a figure
that puts it on par with that of Brazil and India, ahead of Mexico, and close
to four times larger than that of South Africa as indicated in Table 9-1.

In terms of this measure of economic size or economic leverage, therefore, ASEAN can make a case for its importance. Of course, there are other
metrics that could be used, such as purchasing parity power (PPP) measures,
but these do not change this conclusion (see Cooper et al. 2006). Furthermore, ASEAN growth rates have rebounded from the crisis years of the late
1990s (see Table 9-2) and inflows of foreign direct investment (FDI) have now
returned to pre-crisis levels (see Table 9-3), indicating a return of international investor confidence in the region. The aggregate economic indicators
thus show the region regaining some of its former significance.

Added to this, ASEAN plays a significant role in world trade as shown
in Table 9-4. The high trade-to-GDP ratio in some ASEAN countries means
that the association's share of world trade is larger than its share of world
income. In fact, the ASEAN+10 share of world merchandise trade is comparable to that of China, as Table 9-4 illustrates, and, furthermore, exceeds
that of Japan and the United Kingdom.

Table 9-1
Total Gross Domestic Product of ASEAN+5
and Selected Other Countries, 2006

Country	Total Gross Domestic Product (Current US$ billions)
Indonesia	364
Malaysia	148
Philippines	117
Singapore	132
Thailand	206
Total ASEAN+5	969
Brazil	1068
China	2668
India	906
Mexico	839
South Africa	255

Source: World Bank (2007).

Table 9-2

Annual Average Gross Domestic Product Growth Rates, Selected ASEAN Countries and ASEAN+10, 1997–2005 (percent)

	1997	1998	1999	2000	2001	2002	2003	2004	2005
Indonesia	4.7	−13.1	0.8	4.9	3.8	4.3	4.8	5.1	5.6
Malaysia	7.3	−7.4	6.1	8.9	0.3	4.4	5.5	7.2	5.2
Philippines	5.2	−0.6	3.4	4.4	4.5	4.4	3.7	6.2	5.0
Singapore	8.3	−1.4	7.2	10.0	−2.3	4.0	2.9	8.7	6.9
Thailand	−1.4	−10.5	4.4	4.8	2.2	5.3	7.1	6.3	4.5
ASEAN+10	4.2	−7.2	3.6	5.9	3.4	4.8	5.4	6.1	5.6

Source: ASEAN Secretariat (2006, 38–39).

Table 9-3

Annual Foreign Direct Investment Flows, ASEAN+5 and ASEAN+10, 1997–2005 (US$ million)

	1997	1998	1999	2000	2001	2002	2003	2004	2005
ASEAN+5	29,676	19,181	24,555	21,013	17,005	13,176	14,696	23,440	35,293
ASEAN+10	34,099	22,405	27,375	23,413	19,197	15,773	19,664	25,661	38,083

Source: ASEAN Secretariat (2006, 160).

Table 9-4

Shares of World Merchandise Exports and Imports, ASEAN+10 and Selected Countries, 2005 (percent)

	Share of World Merchandise Exports	Share of World Merchandise Imports
ASEAN 10	6.45	5.65
China	7.53	6.30
Brazil	1.17	0.74
Mexico	2.11	2.21
Russia	2.42	1.19
South Africa	0.51	0.64

Source: Calculated from World Trade Organization (2007, 11).

These aggregate figures mask continuing problems, however. On the economic side, for example, registered unemployment (itself a misleading indicator in the context of most ASEAN economies) exceeds 10 percent in both Indonesia and the Philippines (ASEAN Secretariat 2006, 22). The percentage of the population living below the national poverty line is 11.2 percent in Thailand (2004), 16.0 percent in Indonesia (2005), and 30 percent in the Philippines (2003) (284). Added to these economic problems are political issues. Thailand has slid back into military rule and secession movements remain active in the Philippines. ASEAN's putative leader, Indonesia, with the largest economy and population in the group, continues to be politically fragile. The post-Soeharto period has been viewed favourably by some as marking a significant move in the direction of democratic institutions and a more transparent capitalism reflecting the triumph of neo-liberal governance principles over the structures of crony capitalism. According to Vedi Hadiz (2007), however, Indonesia continues to display the logic of predatory capitalism of the Soeharto period and continues to structurally resemble the previous era but with new state-business alliances operating at the local instead of national level. Hadiz (89) argues that

> a new phase in Indonesia may have begun since the fall of Soeharto in which local constellations of power are able to forge alliances with national and international business interests, relatively free from the shackles of Jakarta. However, this is likely to do little for the cause of market-facilitating transparency and accountability at the local level, but may yet contribute to the proliferation and entrenchment of new local networks of predatory power. New local politico-economic business alliances can be further cemented as the cost of running successful campaigns for local office skyrockets, especially in the context of newly devised popular elections for district heads and the like.

Given this, it is perhaps not surprising to find that in Transparency International's 2007 Corruption Perceptions Index, Indonesia ranked 143rd out of 178 countries (Transparency International 2007). The economic recovery from the Asian financial crisis notwithstanding, many individual ASEAN states exhibit considerable economic and political weakness, including the largest country, Indonesia. This is definitely a case where the economic statistics mask more fundamental problems at the level of the real political economy.

Then there is Myanmar. The failure of ASEAN, as a regional grouping, to provide any kind of restraint on the actions of the Myanmar junta during the bloody repression in 2007, much less provide pressures or a framework for a gradual regime opening or change, has brought into sharp focus whether, despite its economic size, ASEAN as a group and as an organization has anything to offer. In short—to repeat the question posed by Sarah Eaton and Richard Stubbs (2006)—is ASEAN powerful? This question is important for understanding not only the dynamics of the region but also whether the organization is worth courting by extra-regional bodies such as the G8. If there is a process of G8 expansion, assessing ASEAN's power as an organization, or its diplomatic leverage, is critical to understanding whether it would (and should) be included in such as expansion.

Eaton and Stubbs (2006) provide a valuable guide to answering whether the question of whether ASEAN is powerful. As they illustrate, the answer depends upon how the concept of power is analyzed. To summarize their argument, they argue that neo-realist approaches view ASEAN as an empty vessel, lacking authority and devoid of influence. For neo-realists, the failure of ASEAN to provide an effective response to the 2007 crisis in Myanmar illustrates well the limitations of the organization. And in this, it follows the failure to provide a collective response to the economic crisis of 1997. The much vaunted "ASEAN way" turns out to be an excuse for inactivity based on an anachronistic notion of sovereignty. As such, as Eaton and Stubbs argue (137–138), "the general picture that emerges from neo-realist critiques is of an ASEAN that is more concerned with process than problem solving, an ineffectual talk shop masquerading as a potent regional organization." This assessment is matched by critics from within the region as well. For example, prominent academic and activist Walden Bello (2007) describes ASEAN as "a fragile economic scaffolding with little substance."

Constructivists, however, provide a quite different reading of ASEAN's accomplishments and reach a more positive assessment of the organization's power. For them, ASEAN has been a success in maintaining peace between its members and its functional layers have been sufficiently influential as to require the attention of the great powers. Thus, the ASEAN Regional Forum, to use the most obvious example, has been joined by the U.S., Japan, and China and provides a framework for the discussion of regional security issues. Other examples could be given of the "disproportionate regional influence of ASEAN" such as "APEC [Asia-Pacific Economic Cooperation] and ASEAN Plus Three (APT) [ASEAN plus China, Japan, and Korea]. APEC meets every other year in an ASEAN country and, with its agenda driven each year by the host country, ASEAN members have had considerable leverage over the forum's development. As for the APT, ASEAN members initiated the regional grouping and each year the summit meeting takes place on ASEAN soil. ASEAN essentially sets the APT agenda" (Eaton and Stubbs 2006, 141). Although the APEC pattern of meeting in an ASEAN country every other year has now been broken (with the 2007 meeting in Australia being followed by Peru in 2008), nevertheless, for constructivists, ASEAN has proven itself successful in promoting in what Eaton and Stubbs refer to as "regional resilience" (146) and provides evidence of ASEAN's ability to act in a powerful way.

There are also signs that, as ASEAN passes the 40-year-old mark, it is seeking to reinvigorate itself. Its "mid-life" choices, as the literature likes to term ASEAN's current stage (see Acharya 2007; Cossa 2007), include the possibility of further enhancing its regional role. The ASEAN Summit in Singapore in November 2007 marked the signing of the ASEAN Charter, aimed at renewing the organization to meet the challenges of the coming century. Included among its provisions are the recognition of ASEAN as a legal entity, the respect for human rights, the principle of non-interference, and mechanisms for a more effective development and implementation of policies through organizational changes. This renewal of ASEAN is also intended to enhance what Ralph Cossa (2007) aptly refers to as ASEAN's "self-proclaimed 'driver's seat' role in East Asian community building."

To summarize, ASEAN is an economically important player on the global economic stage. Underlying this, however, are significant economic and political problems in many of the constituent countries, including in Indonesia. These problems temper the appeal of ASEAN in an expanded G8 as does the neo-realist critique of ASEAN as an ineffective talking shop lacking any real purpose or power. Not only is ASEAN ineffective, its critiques both inside and outside of ASEAN regard it as lacking legitimacy. Its continued silence on human rights abuses, most obviously but not restricted to Myanmar, and failure to support democracy in the region point to this. Civil society organizations in ASEAN participated in the process leading to the formulation of the ASEAN Charter but ultimately many found it disappointing and limited. While recognizing the "landmark" decision to include human rights in the Charter's preamble, the Solidarity for Asian Peoples' Advocacies Working Group on ASEAN (2007), nevertheless argued that

> the Charter is all about how Governments will interact with each other, but not about how they also should interact with the people. There are no clear spaces created or procedures established to institutionalize the role of citizens and civil society organizations in regional community-building. And where the Charter is able to protect sovereign interest of Governments, and enshrine confidence building through consensus, it lacks the necessary

details for the settlement of disputes, dealing with internal conflicts, and disciplining or sanctioning Members who are remiss in their obligations.[2]

The charter has therefore failed to secure legitimacy for ASEAN among many civil society organizations that have called for an alternative ASEAN People's Charter. On this reading, ASEAN has little to offer the G8 in terms of providing a potential partner to restore the G8's own legitimacy or effectiveness.

Constructivist interpretations, and the advent of the ASEAN Charter, in contrast, point to a more credible and effective organization, one whose inclusion in an expanded G8 would offer considerable benefits. However, according to the constructivist position, it does not automatically follow that it is necessarily in ASEAN's priorities or interests to pursue reform and expansion of the G8. It is more likely that ASEAN's influence will be used to pursue regional community building as explained further in the next section.

What Does the G8 Offer ASEAN?

To answer this question requires, in part, a consideration of ASEAN's objectives and identity. Of course, ASEAN's place in the world has been the subject of debate since its formation in 1967. In the early 1990s, ASEAN was faced with defining its purpose in the face of the fall of the Berlin Wall and a China that was "opening up" as well as the increasing interest in Asia by the U.S., which led to the eventual formation of APEC. How ASEAN could maintain its identity within a larger Asia-Pacific grouping led to vigorous debate about alternative conceptions of the region with Mahathir's East Asian Economic Caucus (EAEC) model contrasted with the larger APEC model (see Higgott and Stubbs 1995). In the end, the latter won out but not before ASEAN had been able to position itself as a central component of it.

Since 1997, however, APEC has declined in importance and the regional grouping of the most significance is ASEAN+3 (sometimes referred to as APT). This grouping, in which China, Japan, and South Korea have joined with ASEAN countries at Asian economic summits to discuss issues of mutual interest in many ways goes back to the vision of Mahathir's EAEC. There are still tensions over defining the region to be sure. For example, Amitav Acharya (2007) reports that "due to lobbying by Japanese and Singaporean leaders, Australia, India, and New Zealand were invited to participate in the East Asian Summit. But this does not settle the geographic scope of the East Asian Community, as China still wants the group to keep out non–East Asian nations, including the United States." According to Masahiro Kawai (2007, 20), China "regards ASEAN+3 as a natural grouping for East Asia's trade and investment cooperation" while "Japan regards the … ASEAN+6 as an appropriate grouping for East Asia's trade and investment." These disputes notwithstanding, the pendulum has swung decisively in favour of an East Asian–only regional community compared to the pre-1997 processes.

ASEAN+3 emerged in the post-1997 period to provide a collective defence for Asian economies against currency crises. The role of the International Monetary Fund (IMF) in the crisis has led to it being universally discredited in the region as a result of its (mis)handling of the crisis and its aftermath. The suspicion and discrediting of the IMF also extends to its major western funders that were viewed as attempting to capitalize at a time of Asia's weakness. The "politics of resentment," as Higgott (1998) aptly called it, was firmly entrenched.

Since then, the (larger East Asian) region has sought to establish its own mechanisms to prevent needing future recourse to the IMF. Official foreign exchange reserves have increased rapidly in the region, especially in China, but this trend has also been followed in ASEAN. The ASEAN+10's official foreign exchange reserves stood at close to US$400 billion in mid 2007, comparable to the European Union's US$480 billion total (based on data from the Asian Development Bank [ADB] 2007).

While a formal Asian monetary fund has not emerged as was proposed in the immediate aftermath of the Asian financial crisis, a *de facto* fund has emerged under the auspices of the ASEAN+3 framework. The emphasis has very much been on regional monetary cooperation with the pooling of reserves and central bank swap agreements and the development of an Asian bond fund the most prominent achievements (see Darayanta-Banda and Whalley 2007). This has also raised the question of whether further forms of monetary cooperation might emerge in the future including some form of Asian currency (see Chung and Eichengreen 2007). Even though the initial focus of the grouping has been on the rather narrow issue of financial stability, the size of the region's reserves has meant that its actions have considerable international importance. Once China's US$1.3 trillion and Japan's US$950 billion reserves are added to those of ASEAN, then the group's reserves dwarf those of the other major regions.

Together with this increased regional monetary cooperation, the region's economies have also become more closely linked economically over time. Intra-regional trade shares have risen.[3] Real GDP growth correlations

undertaken by Pradumna (2007) are reported by Kawai (2007, 6) as show-
ing that "correlations have been increasing, especially after the financial crisis, suggesting greater synchronization of business cycles among ASEAN+3 ...
On the other hand, correlations of business cycles of the ASEAN+3 group
as a whole with those of the U.S. and the EU countries, however, are falling
over time."

Thus, new regional institutional and economic interdependencies are
developing and the key point is that ASEAN is central to the new regional
architecture. ASEAN's own institutional development, including the ASEAN
Charter and the commitment, in 2003, to develop a more integrated "ASEAN
Economic Community" are evidence of its own internal development.[4] With
respect to the importance of this regionally, Kawai (Kawai 2007, 23) concludes that "given the political economy dynamics in East Asia, it is likely that
the 'ASEAN Economic Community' to be created by 2015 will be the hub of
East Asian economic cooperation. It is now understood that the core of East
Asian cooperation lies in ASEAN as the major 'driving force,' with ASEAN+3
as the 'main vehicle' for the realization of an eventual East Asian economic
community." Furthermore, he adds, "Japan and the PRC [People's Republic of China] seem happy having ASEAN assume a leadership role in East
Asian community building."

The emergence of ASEAN+3, with ASEAN as a leading player in it, is
one of the factors that, as seen above, constructivists point to in making
their case for the diplomatic importance of ASEAN. However, this body has
a regional focus and a developmental orientation. One of the prime reasons
for its emergence was precisely that existing international organizations,
especially the IMF, failed to take development objectives into account.
ASEAN's development objectives are clearly set out in its pronouncements
and development issues continue to play a central role in its discourse.
Within the ASEAN+3 framework, the importance of development issues
needs no further elaboration. China and South Korea, notwithstanding the
latter's graduation to the ranks of the Organisation for Economic Co-operation and Development (OECD), both espouse strong developmentalist
positions and Japan, its developed country status notwithstanding, has
retained its developmentalist orientation as was illustrated, for example, in
the behind the scenes wrangling that took place over the contents of the
World Bank's (in)famous "East Asian Miracle" project (see Wade 1996).

The ASEAN+3 framework provides ASEAN with an important regional
body through which to advance its development agenda and that also provides a vehicle for its international aspirations. The importance of the

ASEAN+3 countries economically partly explains the interest by other regions' institutions in it despite ASEAN+3's limited agenda and institutional development. The meetings of the Asia Europe Meeting (ASEM), with the EU, are the most important example of this and indicate the ways in which inter-regional dialogues are now taking place.

The question that must be asked, therefore, is whether expansion in an expanded G8 could offer ASEAN anything comparable to the importance and influence that it now achieves through membership in, and promotion of, ASEAN+3. The answer is no, and any membership of an expanded G8 would be of decidedly secondary importance to the emerging wider Asian grouping. There are several reasons for reaching this conclusion. First, the G7's democratic credentials may make for an uneasy relationship with an ASEAN containing non-democratic members; if there had been a G8-O5 meeting in late 2007, it is inconceivable that ASEAN would not have come under strong pressure from the G7 to intervene in Myanmar in some meaningful way—the G7's publics would have demanded this.[5] Thus, political dynamics make the relationship potentially much more difficult than it does with the "+3" members. Second, and perhaps more important, the G8 is tarnished by the same brush as the IMF, namely, that it remains wedded to neo-liberal ideology and rejects East Asian developmentalism. While the G7 has included development issues on its agenda as, for example, the New Partnership on Africa Development (NEPAD) illustrates, it is still premised on accompanying good governance and broadly neo-liberal policies. It is precisely these approaches and policies that were rejected by Asian countries in the wake of the Asian financial crisis and the spur for the creation of the ASEAN+3 framework in the first place.

The failure of the international financial institutions (IFIs), the World Trade Organization (WTO), and the G7 to permit greater policy space for developing countries has led not only to the formation of the ASEAN+3 but also to the proposal for a bank of the south, and other coalitions of developing countries such as the South African president Thabo Mbeki's proposal for a southern G8. These development concerns are likely to be minimized in a G8 forum, expanded or otherwise. Indeed, at G7 meetings in October 2007, concern was expressed over sovereign wealth funds and their lack of transparency. While China's recent decision to establish the China Investment Corporation, funded by a US$200 billion transfer from China's foreign exchange reserves, was undoubtedly a main target of the G7's concerns, sovereign wealth funds have also been an important part of Singapore's state-led development strategy. The tensions remain between a neo-liberal, rule-making G7 and a more developmentalist ASEAN and East Asia.

Thus, in light of how ASEAN best projects its interests at the international level, it is currently through the ASEAN+3 and its ability to engage in inter-regional dialogues such as that with the EU. Participation of ASEAN's secretary general or Indonesia's prime minister as ASEAN's representative in an expanded G8 offers much less in terms of both the broadness of participation and the influence over the agenda than ASEAN is able to achieve through its role in the wider East Asian regional formulation of ASEAN+3. It is this latter framework that has attracted most of ASEAN's energies in the recent past and this might be expected to be the direction for the future as well. If the constructivist interpretation of ASEAN's power is correct, therefore, it is a power that is more likely to be used in projecting ASEAN's interests through regional and then inter-regional dialogues, than through an expanded G8; ASEAN and the G8 are more likely to be ships that pass in the night.

Such a conclusion is premised on the view that, to quote Cossa (2007) again, ASEAN remains in the self-proclaimed driver's seat role in East Asian community building and that Japan and China are willing to continue to allow ASEAN to occupy that position. Given the dynamics of China's re-emergence it is worth considering a little further whether ASEAN will remain able to maintain its pole position. This, and its implications, are discussed in the next section.

ASEAN in the Shadow of China

While ASEAN has been able to retain its central regional role, and a voice in international economic governance debates, through the ASEAN+3 framework, it has nevertheless been challenged by the rise of China both economically and politically. With respect to the economic, like other developing countries, and perhaps even more keenly so given geographical location and export composition, ASEAN is faced with the challenge of how to respond to China's manufacturing export growth and competition for FDI. ASEAN has been faced with either seeking to take advantage of China's large economy and rapid growth by integrating with it or seeking to develop more independently of China. Through the China-ASEAN Free Trade Agreement, signed in 2002, ASEAN leaders have signalled their intention to follow the first option. But this path has risks. David Roland-Holst and John Weiss (2004) find that, at least in the short run, China and ASEAN are competitor economies. John Ravenhill (2006) agrees with this assessment as far as third-party markets go but argues that ASEAN benefits from increased exports of components to China through an increase in intra-industry trade.

Critics within ASEAN countries have doubted whether increased trade with China would necessarily be to the benefit of ASEAN. For example, Bello (2007, 186) argues that "an ASEAN-China FTA [free trade agreement] at this juncture can only lead to de-industrialization and an agricultural crisis in ASEAN." China can out-compete ASEAN in both labour-intensive manufactured goods and in high-tech goods. In the agriculture sector, China is argued to be "clearly super-competitive in a vast array of agricultural products" (183). This leaves ASEAN to export its natural resources in return. This raises the prospect of "re-peripheralisation," meaning that ASEAN economies will find themselves increasingly replicating colonial patterns of trade. In this respect, ASEAN is experiencing in intensified form, because of its geographical proximity, the same fears as other developing countries including other B(R)ICSAMs such as Brazil, Mexico, and South Africa. James M. Cypher (2007), for example, argues that the commodities boom since 2002, driven in large part by demand from China and India, has led a process of primarization in Latin America where primary commodity exports have risen as a share of total exports with the share of agricultural and manufacturing exports falling, replicating the resource booms of the 19th century. The current primarization process, which has been the result of shifts in South–South trade, has turned the terms of trade dramatically in favour of Latin American countries. The question Cypher raises is what will be done with the windfall gains in the forms of higher rents in the commodities sector—will be they be used for long-term development projects or squandered on short-term luxury consumption by the region's elites?

The re-emergence and economic dynamism of China, therefore, presents both opportunities and challenges for other developing countries. Due to their geographical proximity, the ASEAN countries feel these particularly acutely. On the one hand, supplying a growing market and integrating into regional and international production networks offers opportunities. On the hand, the competition for FDI and with Chinese goods, at both ends of the labour-intensity range provides challenges. China appears as a newly globalizing country that, despite its low level of per capita GDP, has established trade patterns more akin to developed country patterns (Rodrik 2006). The development aspirations of ASEAN and other industrializing developing countries have therefore been threatened by China's re-emergence.

It is not surprising, therefore, to find critics within ASEAN who argue that ASEAN itself faces marginalization if it fails to respond more effectively to the China challenge. Thus Bello argues that ASEAN should revert to its original vision and place greater emphasis on the ASEAN regional market for growth and should resurrect the regional developmentalist industrial policies which were tried in the 1980s. To this end, he concludes that "ASEAN as a project of regional integration has become necessary in order to avoid the steady marginalization of its member economies" (Bello 2007, 186). This route would involve ASEAN seeking a more independent form of development from China, although it would require a degree of institutional cooperation that is perhaps beyond ASEAN's current capacity. ASEAN's largest country, Indonesia, remains politically fragile and ASEAN members such as Malaysia, Singapore, and Thailand have actively pursued numerous bilateral trade agreements, including with the U.S. and Japan, indicating that ASEAN members do not always act in concert.[6]

But while ASEAN struggles to define its relationship with China, the latter has been diplomatically active in the region and sees itself as the regional power (see Van Ness 2004/05; Wu Guoguang 2007). All this points to the fact that while the nomenclature of ASEAN+3 may survive, the reality may be that it is ASEAN that is the add-on to an increasingly economically and politically powerful China; it might better be termed China Plus Ten. That is, China will be the regional hub and driver rather than ASEAN. In which case, ASEAN will lose much of the effectiveness that constructivists attribute to it, will lose legitimacy as an important regional organization by failing to maintain its influence in the face of a rising China adding to its existing failures of not responding to the political challenge of a repressive regime in Myanmar and the economic challenge of the Asian financial crisis. ASEAN's failure to respond to these external challenges, and to satisfy its own internal constituencies, is likely to lead to the increasing marginalization of the organization; in short, ASEAN will face its own crisis of legitimacy and effectiveness, a condition that will ironically unite it with the G8.

Conclusion

In any consideration of the reform of the international economic governance structure, therefore, a number of scenarios are possible for ASEAN and the G8. The first is that the G8 will expand to include participation in some form by ASEAN. Whether ASEAN is of sufficient diplomatic importance to warrant such attention from the G8 is questionable, as the neo-realist position illustrates. If the constructivist interpretation of ASEAN is accepted and ASEAN is viewed as a qualified success, then expanding the G8 to include ASEAN becomes a more attractive proposition for the G8, and they may become productive partners.

However, if the constructivist interpretation is accepted, then it is more likely that ASEAN would use its power and influence to pursue the wider regional ASEAN+3 framework and to use this for the projection of its interests onto the international level through inter-regional dialogues. ASEAN is currently the hub of East Asian integration initiatives and emerging regional architecture. It is unlikely that ASEAN would wish to divert its interests away from this project in order to become a part of a more active G8-O5 group, which offers it less in terms of influence and ability to realize its development objectives. More likely is that ASEAN and the G8 will be ships passing in the night. The viability of this scenario depends, though, upon ASEAN being able to maintain its influence in the face of a rising China, an outcome that is by no means certain; if it is unable to do so, ASEAN risks becoming the passenger rather the driver of the regional processes that are now underway.

Notes

1 When the G7 set up the Financial Stability Forum (FSF) in 1999, however, Singapore was the only ASEAN country accorded permanent membership. Indonesia, Malaysia, the Philippines, and Thailand have participated in regional meetings organized since 2002.
2 It should be noted that the charter also fell short of the recommendations made by ASEAN's own Eminent Persons' Group.
3 The share of intra-regional trade between the ASEAN+3 increased from 30.2 percent in 1985 to 38.3 percent in 2006 (Kawai 2007, 3).
4 On the ASEAN economic community see Lloyd (2005).
5 In shifting from the G8 to the G7 here, the problematic nature of Russian democracy is pushed to one side. More importantly, though, it is the G7 that sets the agenda and the G8 might itself be best described as the G7+O1 with Russia the "outsider."
6 See Masahiro Kawai and Ganeshan Wignaraja (2007) for details of bilateral free trade agreements.

References

Acharya, Amitav (2007). "ASEAN at 40: Mid-life Rejuvenation?" *Foreign Affairs*. <www.foreignaffairs.org/20070815faupdate86481/amitav-acharya/asean-at-40 -mid-life-rejuvenation.html> (May 2008).

ASEAN Secretariat (2006). "ASEAN Statistical Yearbook." Jakarta.

Asian Development Bank (2007). *Asian Development Outlook 2007 Update: Change Amid Growth.* <www.adb.org/Documents/Books/ADO/2007/Update/ad007 update.pdf> (May 2008).

Bello, Walden (2007). "A Roller Coaster Ride: A Perspective from Southeast Asia." In *Regional Perspectives on Globalization,* edited by P. Bowles, H. Veltmeyer, S. Cornelissen, et al., 169–188. Basingstoke: Palgrave Macmillan.

Chung, Duck-Koo and Barry J. Eichengreen (2007). "Exchange Rate Arrangements for Emerging East Asia." In *Toward an East Asian Exchange Rate Regime,* edited by D.-K. Chung and B.J. Eichengreen, 1–21. Washington DC: Brookings Institution Press.

Cooper, Andrew F., Agata Antkiewicz, and Timothy M. Shaw (2006). "Economic Size Trumps All Else? Lessons from BRICSAM." CIGI Working Paper No. 12. Waterloo ON: Centre for International Governance Innovation. <www.cigionline.org : Publications : Working Papers> (May 2008).

Cooper, Andrew F. (2007). "The Logic of the B(R)ICSAM Model for G8 Reform." CIGI Policy Brief No. 1. Waterloo ON: Centre for International Governance Innovation. <www.cigionline.org : Publications : Policy Briefs> (May 2008).

Cossa, Ralph A. (2007). "ASEAN at 40: Coming of Age or Mid-life Crisis?" PacNet Number 33, 4 September. Honolulu. <www.csis.org/media/csis/pubs/pac0733 .pdf> (May 2008).

Cypher, James M. (2007). "Back to the 19th Century? The Current Commodities Boom and the Primarization Process in Latin America." Mimeo.

Darayanta-Banda, OG and John Whalley (2007). "Regional Monetary Arrangements in ASEAN+3 as Insurance through Reserve Accumulation and Swaps." Working Paper No. 22, April. Waterloo ON: Centre for International Governance Innovation. <www.cigionline.org : publications : working papers> (May 2008).

Eaton, Sarah and Richard Stubbs (2006). "Is ASEAN Powerful? Neo-realist versus Constructivist Approaches to Power in Southeast Asia." *Pacific Review* 19(2): 135–155.

G8 Development Ministers (2008). "Chair's Summary." 6 April, Tokyo. <www.g8 .utoronto.ca/development/chair_summary_080406.html> (May 2008).

Hadiz, Vedi R. (2007). "Neoliberalism and Predatory Capitalism: A Perspective from Indonesia." In *National Perspectives on Globalization,* edited by P. Bowles, H. Veltmeyer, S. Cornelissen, et al., 78–92. Basingstoke: Palgrave Macmillan.

Higgott, Richard A. and Richard Stubbs (1995). "Competing Conceptions of Economic Regionalism: APEC versus EAEC in the Asia Pacific." *Review of International Political Economy* 2(3): 516–535.

Higgott, Richard A. (1998). "The International Politics of Resentment: Some Longer Term Implications of the Economic Crisis in East Asia." *New Political Economy* 3(3): 333–356.

Kawai, Masahiro (2007). "Evolving Economic Architecture in East Asia." Discussion Paper No. 84, 7 December. ADB Institute. <www.adbi.org/discussion-paper/ 2007/12/07/2423.evolving.economic.architecture.east.asia/shaping.the.new .economic.architecture.in.east.asia/> (May 2008).

Kawai, Masahiro and Ganeshan Wignaraja (2007). "ASEAN+3 or ASEAN+6: Which Way Forward?" Discussion Paper No. 77. Tokyo: Asian Development bank Institute. <www.adbi.org/discussion-paper/2007/09/13/2359.asean.3.asean.6/> (May 2008).

Lloyd, Peter J. (2005). "What Is a Single Market? An Application to the Case of ASEAN." *ASEAN Economic Bulletin* 22(3): 251–265.

Pradumna, B. Rana (2007). "Economic Integration in East Asia: Trends, Prospects, and a Possible Roadmap." Economic Growth Centre Working Paper Series No. 2007/01. Singapore: Nanyang Technological University.

Ravenhill, John (2006). "Is China an Economic Threat to South East Asia?" *Asian Survey* 46(5): 653–674.

Rodrik, Dani (2006). "What's So Special about China's Exports?" NBER Working Paper No. 11947. <www.nber.org/papers/w11947> (May 2008).

Roland-Holst, David and John Weiss (2004). "ASEAN and China: Export Rivals or Partners in Regional Growth?" *World Economy* 27(8): 1255–1274.

Solidarity for Asian Peoples' Advocacies Working Group on ASEAN (2007). "Analysis of the ASEAN Charter." 10 November. Focus on the Global South. <www.focusweb.org/analysis-of-the-asean-charter.html?Itemid=28> (May 2008).

Transparency International (2007). "Corruption Perceptions Index 2007." <www .transparency.org/policy_research/surveys_indices/cpi/2007> (May 2008).

Van Ness, Peter (2004/05). "China's Response to the Bush Doctrine." *World Policy Journal* 21(4): 38–47.

Wade, Robert (1996). "Japan, the World Bank, and the Art of Paradigm Maintenance: 'The East Asian Miracle' in Political Perspective." *New Left Review* 217 (May/June): 3–36.

Wilson, Dominic and Roopa Purushothaman (2003). "Dreaming with BRICs: The Path to 2050." Global Economics Paper No. 99, October. New York: Goldman Sachs. <www2.goldmansachs.com/ideas/brics/book/99-dreaming.pdf> (May 2008).

World Bank (2007). "World Development Indicators 2007." Washington DC. <go .worldbank.org/3JU2HA6oDo> (May 2008).

World Trade Organization (2007). *WTO World Trade Report 2007.* Geneva. <www.wto .org/english/res_e/booksp_e/anrep_e/world_trade_report07_e.pdf> (May 2008).

Wu Guoguang (2007). *China Turns to Multilateralism: Foreign Policy and Regional Security.* London: Routledge.

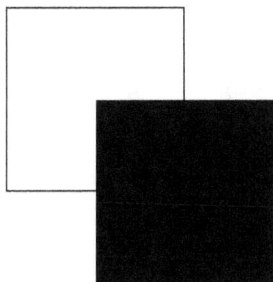

THE EVOLVING ARCHITECTURE OF CHANGE

Germany and the Heiligendamm Process

Thomas Fues and Julia Leininger

At the 2007 G8 summit in Germany, Chancellor Angela Merkel launched an innovative outreach effort toward a group of five rising nations from the global South. The Heiligendamm Process (HP) engages Brazil, China, India, Mexico, and South Africa in an informal "structured dialogue" for a duration of two years with a thematic focus on four key issues of global governance. This German initiative was guided by several objectives: First, the chancellor wanted to embrace emerging powers since she understood their indispensable role for global problem solving in areas such as climate change. Second, the initiative sought to consolidate Germany's influence in international affairs at a time when the political centre of gravity was moving from west to east. Third, German diplomacy strove for incremental summit reform since neither formal enlargement nor the status quo were viable options for Berlin.

While the HP promises a new quality of interaction between leading industrialized and a select group of developing countries, it is not free of risks and ambiguities for all participants. So far, the German initiative lacks collective ownership within the G8 and might deepen internal divisions. On the other side of the negotiating table, the Group of Five (G5) still has to arrive at a common understanding on substance and behaviour that would enable the group to counterbalance western predominance.[1] A fundamental impediment to meaningful progress in the HP is the difference in notions of legitimacy. With a focus on process, Germany and other G8 members see promoting dialogue and building trust as key objectives of the exercise (thus constituting input legitimacy) (Benterbusch and Seifert 2008, 4), whereas G5 countries are concerned mainly with tangible results, not only for themselves but also for the developing world in general (that is, output legitimacy). It remains to be seen what the German approach can deliver on such contradictory expectations within the short time span of only two years, and what consequences might come about if it ends in frustration and acrimony.

Against this backdrop, this chapter evaluates Germany's G8 policies and Merkel's motives for introducing the HP. It begins by analyzing the domestic environment as shaped by government officials, opposition parties, non-governmental organizations (NGOs), academia, and business. Next, it takes a close look at German objectives and expectations for the HP and the bureaucratic-institutional arrangements at the national level. The chapter then assesses the international context in relation to the European Union and the G8. Finally, it comes to some conclusions on the opportunities and limits of the HP and its possible impact on the expansion debate.

Germany and the G8

From both a realist and a behavioural viewpoint, Germany, the third largest economy worldwide, can be considered a middle power (Otte 2000).[2] Its role in the international system, however, cannot be adequately explained by the realist paradigm since, to this day, German foreign policy is influenced by the long stretch of limited sovereignty following World War II. Even two decades after unification, German instincts still tend to shy away from an assertive representation of self-interest, as noted by two realist scholars: "The unified Germany has not yet found its way out of the prescribed immaturity of the postwar period" (Hulsman and Techau 2007, 18, translation by authors).[3] It is therefore more from a behavioural perspective that Germany should be understood as middle or civilian power with an explicitly pacifist orientation after the catastrophic Nazi regime.[4] Since that tragedy, the country has consistently pursued cooperative multilateralism and liberal institutionalism as guiding principles of its external policies (Maull 1994; Hellmann et al. 2007).

The use of hard power resources in economic and military terms is constrained not only by German history but also by successive stages of European integration. German foreign policy is based on the undisputed domestic consensus that coordination and harmonization within the EU form the cornerstone of peace, prosperity, and global influence (Staak 2007, 85). German governments have, nevertheless, found it attractive to engage in certain forms of club governance outside the European framework, especially in situations where the country's economic resources put it at the apex of the global hierarchy. The most significant of these cases is the Group of Eight leading industrialized countries, which assumed even greater significance for German policy makers after the recent failure to gain permanent membership of the United Nations Security Council (UNSC). In light of the full spectrum of foreign policy options, Germany may soon need to sort out its strategic orientations. The more it invests in G8 reform and the HP, the more it will need to explain how this projection of national power can be reconciled with commitment to Europe and to universal institutions such as the UN.

Government Positions on Summit Reform

Traditionally, international affairs, which is considered an executive domain, draws little public attention in Germany. A key former advisor of Chancellor Helmut Kohl provides the following observation: "In Germany, people talk very little about international politics. We do not have a discussion culture in this policy field. We are not used to thinking globally" (Teltschik 2008, translation by authors). Not surprisingly, political elites usually do not see foreign policy as an attractive field for career advancement, thus leaving a political and intellectual void in a key area of policy formulation (Maull 2007, 83).

The importance of the G8 in German foreign policy has undergone noticeable changes over time (May 2007, 808). In the 1970s and at the beginning of the '80s, Helmut Schmidt—1975 one of the founding spirits of the then G6, as Canada only began participating in 1976—looked at informal summit arrangements as key instrument of international policy coordination among industrialized countries. Throughout his chancellorship, from 1982 to 1998, Kohl put more emphasis on bilateral ties with France and the U.S. than on the G8, except during the demise of the Soviet Union, as described by an eminent scholar, "Interest [in the G8] was very strong ... in the early 1990s after unification, in the phase when European relations and East–West relations within Europe were in flux. Then, the interest in and the commitment to that process decreased" (Maull 2004).

The renewed interest in the G8 by Kohl's successor, Gerhard Schröder, led to German support for an important institutional innovation. After the financial crises in Asia and Latin America at the end of the 1990s, Germany promoted the creation of a ministerial club of leading powers from North and South. The G20 finance ministers and central bank governors met for the first time 1999 in Berlin at the invitation of G7 finance ministers and today is generally credited with serving as a useful platform for dialogue and consensus building.[5]

It took the dual presidencies of the G8 and the EU in 2007 to draw the attention of Merkel and her government to the state of the summit architecture (Fues 2007). While she never seriously considered reform by enlargement (Hajnal 2007), early on Merkel (2007c; 2007b) recognized the need for a new quality of interaction with emerging powers in international policy areas such as climate change, trade, and property rights. This insight had been sharpened by her previous experience as environment minister when, in negotiating the outcome of the 1992 Earth Summit in Rio, she had realized how the protection of global commons depends on the collaboration of major developing economies.

The ostensible argument given by Merkel against formal G8 expansion rested on the assertion that a higher number of members would have a negative impact on effectiveness. While there was, of course, some basis to this claim, it did not deter the German government from investing enormous political resources in trying to gain a permanent seat in the UNSC. The formula promoted by the G4 (Brazil, India, Japan, Germany) jointly aspiring to such status would have meant an expansion of the principal UN organ from 15 to 25 countries.

The deeper reason for Merkel's objection to expanded membership may rather be found in her normative world view. The chancellor wanted to protect the G8 as like-minded community based on the western values of liberal democracy and market economics. In this context, the regrettable but irreversible inclusion of Russia (at German prodding, ironically) had already led to a substantial loss of credibility for the group, which would only be compounded by taking authoritarian China on board (Manz 2007, 36). The German opposition to enlargement had certainly been amplified by the lack of democratic progress in Russia, contrary to expectations, as noted by Hanns Maull (2004), "It was primarily Germany in the early 1990s that pushed for Russian membership. The idea in German diplomacy was that bringing in Russia would help support the transformation of Russia into a western, democratic, capitalist partner—an ally—or into a great important country one could co-operate with easily."

In the run-up to the summit, Merkel was able to silence initial dissent on G8 reform within her cabinet. At one point, Peer Steinbrück, the influential finance minister, had expressed sympathy for an inclusive leaders forum (L20) tailored after the G20. In November 2006, on the sidelines of the G20 ministerial in Australia, he surprised everybody by stating that the G8 would become superfluous in the medium term and should be replaced by a new body of select leaders from the North and South, "not next year, but in two or three years" (Falk 2006). With this reasoning, Steinbrück followed the position of his predecessor in office, Hans Eichel, who had also shown some leanings toward the L20 concept (Cooper 2007). He reiterated his position at a meeting of the finance ministers of the G7 plus G5 in February 2007, albeit in a more muted tone, "At this stage, there is no formalized process toward enlargement, but it is my political prophecy that things are moving in this direction" (Stahl and Kaufner 2007, translation by authors).

One further government actor that could have been expected to take an active interest in G8 reform was the Ministry for Economic Cooperation and Development (Bundesministerium für wirtschaftliche Zusammenarbeit und Entwicklung [BMZ] 2007b) since it propagates the ambitious framework of "international structural policies." As part of this agenda, the department wished to strengthen the voice and participation of developing countries in the global system. The development minister, Heidemarie Wieczorek-Zeul, however, focused on global governance innovations under the umbrella of the United Nations rather than the G8, "In the short term we can reach substantial progress on the reform and strengthening of ECOSOC [United Nations Economic and Social Council] … In the long term, ECOSOC should be upgraded into an effective 'Global Council' with a comprehensive mandate for coordination and harmonization in economic, social and environmental policies" (Wieczorek-Zeul 2005, translation by authors). Another indication that the ministry wanted to stay clear of the debate on G8 reform could be found in the 2007 meeting, to which it invited the G5 and African countries before the Heiligendamm Summit. The agenda did not include any reference to the future shape of the summit architecture (BMZ 2007a).

In understanding Merkel's resistance to far-reaching innovations, one must keep in mind the general German disinterest in the subject. The following analysis of more than a decade ago still holds true today: "Summit reform is a specialists' issue in Germany, about which few people think very deeply … There do not seem to have been any serious efforts within the SPD, or elsewhere (the Greens, the Bundestag), to develop coherent and systematic ideas about summit reform. The same is true of research centres and think tanks" (Maull 1994, 135). Hence, there is little domestic incentive for policy makers or political actors to move forward on G8 reform.

Besides internal factors, there is also an external impediment to German support for formal enlargement. Given possible summit constellations from a European perspective, good reasons can be found for a joint representation of member states from the European Union. With four seats (Britain, France, Italy, and Germany) plus the participation of the European Commission, the continent is obviously over-represented in the present set-up. A similar problem exists in the Bretton Woods institutions and the UNSC. Any enlargement without abolishing outdated European privileges would not be acceptable to the global South. In pushing for summit reform, Merkel could therefore run the risk of catapulting her country from one of the few remaining arenas where the projection of economic and soft power is possible without the straitjacket of European policy coordination.

Domestic Environment

Decision making on foreign policy, even in liberal democracies, used to be one of the most restricted public domains. Today, this principle no longer applies to G8 summits since they attract huge media attention and often lead to mass mobilization, not only in host countries. As expected, the 2007 Heiligendamm Summit became the focus of heated controversies in German society long before the heads of government and state assembled at the Baltic coast resort. Early criticism forced Merkel to abandon her original intent of concentrating on core issues of the global economy. Development in Africa was added to the G8 agenda to placate public concern over global poverty.

Parliament and Political Parties   A few years back, the German Bundestag established a commission of parliamentarians and independent scholars that was charged to formulate effective political responses to globalization. While the commission recognized the need for summit reform, it came up with only vague policy recommendations due to the lack of consensus (Deutscher Bundestag 2002). The final report recommends the establishment of a new global governance group with leaders from 24 countries that would be selected by a representative formula. The proposal emulates the executive boards of World Bank and International Monetary Fund (IMF), which consist of 24 members from all world regions (disregarding the asymmetrical distribution of voting rights). The parliamentary commission also recommended keeping the original G8 as an exclusive forum of policy coordination among industrialized countries.

The debate in parliament on the 2007 Heiligendamm Summit corroborated the divisions among political parties in Germany. While the Conservatives (CDU/CSU) and the Liberals (FDP) (Westerwelle 2007) denied the need for global reform, the Social Democrats (SPD) recognized institutional deficiencies in this regard (Staffelt 2007). The SPD wanted to remedy those by strengthening and democratizing the UN and, in a long-term perspective, advocated the creation of a new UN organ for economic, social, and environmental security analogous to the traditional UNSC. As to the summit architecture, the SPD saw the G8 complementary to the UN.[6]

Fundamental criticism of the G8 was voiced by the Left Party. It demanded the dissolution of the summit architecture and supports the UN as the only acceptable authority of global decision making, as indicated by a leading party official, "The G8 is not legitimized. It claims the status of world government. However, there is not a single resolution by the United Nations that would legitimize that … We want a democratically reformed UN which is in charge of world politics" (Gysi 2007, translation by authors). The Green Party did not go to the extreme of advocating the disbandment of the G8 but spoke out for the inclusion of emerging powers. It also insisted on the leading role of the UN in global affairs and wanted to explore the potential of the so-called L27 as a representative body of leaders under the UN's ECOSOC (Kuhn 2007).

Academia Opinions in German academia on the summit architecture are strongly polarized between those in favour of structural reform and those on principle opposed to any form of club governance. The G8 as it exists today does not find much scholarly support since the inclusion of emerging powers is recognized as an irreversible trend (Maihold 2005). Harald Müller (2008, 291; translation by authors) sees the main function of global policy coordination in containing conflicts among major powers, including the G5, "The adequate form that this can take is the concert: A continuous round of consultation among the G13, i.e., an extension of the G8."

A critical position toward the G8 is taken by scholars such as Elmar Altvater (2007) and Franz Nuscheler (2007) who denounce the group as an instrument of western dominance that cannot and should not be reformed. In a similar vein, the G20 finance is seen as serving the interests of the "hegemon club." The L20, the envisioned platform of leaders from North and South, has not found many takers in German academia or in the general public. As one of few exceptions, Andrew F. Cooper and Thomas Fues (2005) propose an institutionalized link of the L20 to the UN in order to safeguard the supreme authority of the world organization.

Political foundations play an important role in Germany in advising the particular party with which they are aligned as well as contributing to public debates. The Friedrich Ebert Foundation of the SPD has been especially productive in providing analytical contributions aimed at Germany's twin leadership of the EU and the G8 in 2007. The foundation commissioned about 30 studies to explore various dimensions of German objectives, roles, and strategies in international relations. Some of them had a particular country or regional focus (e.g., China, India, Latin America, and the Middle East) while others looked at global issues such as disarmament, health, and the global economy.

One of the reports focused on multilateral institutions and the global system. Its author argued for a reform of the summit architecture along the lines of the proposed L20:

> One good approach to improving the coordination of global politics would be to establish a new, permanent initiative and coordination mechanism. Not only the Security Council needs to be enlarged, the G8 does as well. Together with its European partners, Germany should review the proposals that have been tabled on this issue and then work for one of these options. Former Canadian Prime Minister Paul Martin, for instance, proposed the establishment of a group of 20 leading industrialized and emerging nations that would regularly meet at the level of the heads of state and government (the so-called L20) (Stetten 2007, 15).

In a synthesis of all the foundation reports, Jochen Steinhilber (2007, 55; translation by authors) referred to the L20 as a medium-term perspective coming only after the gradual integration of emerging powers into multilateral arrangements, "From the perspective of large emerging economies, deepened economic integration leads to a lock-in effect which forces them to become more involved in global policy coordination. This gradual involvement could, in the medium-term, open the door for new structural elements in international relations, such as the L20." In his assessment, the HP is a very restrained opening signal of the G8, which will not facilitate the quick and comprehensive integration of rising powers into the existing institutional system. His colleague, Thomas Manz (2007), was similarly skeptical about the German outreach since it could not bridge the legitimacy gap between exclusive membership (club governance) and self-mandated global responsibility.

With immediate relevance to the debate on European representation within the G8, the renowned political philosopher Jürgen Habermas (2007) specified two reasons why Europe as a whole rather than individual nation-states should play a stronger political role in the world: First, single European states can hardly exert influence unless they act jointly. Second, the institutionalization of "global domestic politics" will only come about when nation-states band together in regional groupings, with the exception of born global players such as the U.S., Russia, China, and India.

Hanns W. Maull (2004) of Trier University also supports the notion that G8 members from the region should strive for European rather than national objectives, "I wish that Germany would use the G8 more forcefully and more systematically. I also wish that Germany would perhaps consider the possibility of co-ordinating European Union positions in the G8 … The EU aspires to a common foreign security policy. It has done more than talk about co-ordinating positions in the UNSC, so why not the G8? That would be a way of taking the G8 more seriously or promoting it as an important part of global governance."

In its study of the IMF, an influential European think tank recommended a new mode of regional representation that could be similarly applied to the G8, "Against this background, the case for a single European or, more realistically, a euro-area seat at the IMF Board is strong … [A] unified representation would actually solve two problems. It would allow a better representation of emerging and developing countries and strengthen Europe's influence" (Ahearne et al. 2006, 7). Similarly, Martin Ortega (2007) of the EU's Institute of Security Studies suggests that EU groupings should be established in international institutions such as the UN and the IMF. This principle could also be followed in the G8 and any future modifications of the summit architecture.

The few statements so far on the HP from the academic community signal cautious support. Marco Overhaus (2007) from Trier University welcomes the initiative but considers it as not ambitious enough, "The Heiligendamm process to streamline the G8 agenda and transfer more of the dialogue with other countries into existing international institutions is a step in the right direction, but it is still a timid one." Katharina Gnath (2007) of the German Council on Foreign Relations underlines the necessity to institutionalize the integration of rising powers further. With a thematic focus on climate change, the German Advisory Council on Global Environmental Change ([WBGU] 2007, 15) calls for strategic cooperation between G8 and G5 through an innovation pact, "The Council proposes the launch of strategic decarbonization partnerships with those newly industrializing countries that are likely to play an important role in the future world's energy sector."

Civil Society and Private Business In general, German NGOs are highly critical of the G8 and invest little energy on its reform. The 2007 summit demonstrated the strong resonance for rejectionist positions in German civil society. Contrary to this, a wide range of mainstream NGOs accepted the invitation to engage in dialogue with all the G8 sherpas and, for the occasion, mobilized expert knowledge on a wide range of pertinent issues. According to the minutes of the meeting, which took place in April in Bonn, none of the NGO representatives raised the point of G8 enlargement or the HP. The debate rather stayed within the thematic confines of the official summit agenda (Civil G8 Dialogue 2007). The position paper of the German NGO G8 alliance also lacked any reference to structural reform (G8 NGO Platform 2007). Similarly, the Confederation of German Trade Unions (Deutscher Gewerkschaftsbund [DGB] 2007) did not address summit reform, although its representatives were heavily involved in the societal debate on the G8.

Critics from the extreme left have denounced the faith of NGOs in the good intentions of G8 governments and, instead, called for uncompromising resistance to ruling interests (Bundeskoordination Internationalismus [BUKO] 2007). The German branch of the international civil society network Attac (2007) considered the Heiligendamm Summit a complete failure and wanted to abolish the G8 altogether since the forum represented, in their eyes, an imperial form of global governance. On top of the legitimacy gap, the G8 had become superfluous in their view, since it cannot provide effective solutions for global problems. Rainer Falk and Barbara Unmüssig (2007, translation by authors), leading civil society voices, criticized the HP as fake due to its exclusive focus on issues relevant mainly to the G8, "This is neither dialogue nor efficient management of globalization." The German UN Association similarly insisted that the purpose of the HP must be to strengthen decision making in established multilateral forums (Deutsche Gesellschaft für die Vereinten Nationen [DGVN] 2007).

Jens Martens (2007, 306), a respected NGO analyst, was equally critical in his assessment, "Evidently, however, the agenda for the Heiligendamm Process only indirectly addresses pressing global issues such as climate change or financial-market stability. From the outset, this Process lacks what political scientists call 'output legitimacy'... But even if G8 plus O5 had dared to tackle the main challenges humankind is facing, large sections of the world's peoples would still be excluded." As an alternative approach, he favoured strengthening ECOSOC through the newly established Development Cooperation Forum. While this particular initiative represented an important step forward, it could not serve the fundamental objective of integrating emerging powers into the global governance system.

German corporations and their federations have not yet developed a definite position on G8 enlargement but will support outreach efforts, in particular the Heiligendamm Process (Bundesverband der Deutschen Industrie e.V. [BDI] 2007; Deutschen Industrie- und Handelskammertages [DIHK] 2007).

Media   German media often question the use of G8 summits in general. Josef Joffe (2007), influential editor of the prestigious weekly *Die Zeit*, lists three reasons why G8 summits should be abolished: The huge public attention they receive focuses on trivial issues (such as demonstrations) and not on global challenges; summits arouse the egos of participating leaders and stimulate an unproductive competition for the spotlight; and summits mean posturing without serious work on real-life problems. The costs of security measures for the summit in 2007 were also given as reason for a negative perception, "German commentators concur in their judgement that the benefits of the mega event in Heiligendamm do not justify the expenses. Twelve million euros for a fence that will be immediately knocked down afterward—and for what?" (Volkery 2007).

Another point of criticism refers to the exclusion of emerging powers: "In effect, the G8 is an anachronism. An entity, not yet touched by the frenzied change of the world" (Weiland 2007). Helmut Schmidt (2007), former chancellor and present publisher of *Die Zeit*, spoke out strongly for the inclusion of China, India, big oil and gas exporting countries such as Saudi Arabia and Nigeria, and other emerging powers such as Brazil and South Africa. Two renowned journalists, Harald Schumann and Christiane Grefe (2008, 385; translation by authors), provided a highly critical perspective on the HDP, "The attempt to include the leaders of nations with a population of billions by offering them a seat at the side table, rather created the impression of condescension." This sentiment was echoed by yet another media opinion, "The openness for dialogue quickly hits upon constraints. As soon as the liberalization of trade, e.g., opening of agricultural markets, is raised the G8 defend their one-sided interests which exacerbate poverty in the developing world. Emerging powers are not really given any rights in decision making" (Volkery 2007).

Germany and the Heiligendamm Process

Motives, Interests, and Objectives: Germany as Initiator

The HP, a German innovation, represents an incremental move to formalize the outreach process below the critical threshold of regular expansion for which no consensus among G8 members is in sight. The launch was formally announced to the public in a joint statement by the German presidency and the heads of government of Brazil, China, India, Mexico, and South Africa at the end of the summit (G8 and Outreach Partners 2007). Leading up to Heiligendamm, Berlin had organized ministerial sessions that brought together G8 and G5 officials in the areas of finance, development, and the environment. This can be seen as a deliberate effort to create a broader framework for future issue-focused interactions. Also, a series of talks that took place between the G8 and G5 sherpas were concluded in Heiligendamm (Benterbusch and Seifert 2008, 3). Berlin saw the HP as a limited, ad hoc step that does not aim at enlargement through the backdoor. In choosing the preferred group of five partners, Merkel decided to build on the British formula for the 2005 Gleneagles Summit. She had originally intended to carry the new modalities of dialogue into a wide range of multilateral bodies beyond the G8. However, there remains no evidence of a concerted effort of this kind.

The German government cannot commit future G8 hosts to a particular outreach strategy, as emphasized by the German sherpa, Bernd Pfaffenbach (2006, translation by authors), "The current presidency cannot prescribe to future presidencies whom they should invite ... Maybe it will make sense to invite a completely different group in two or three years." Berlin also fully understands that there is no automatism in having the substance of the HP dialogue incorporated into the proceedings of subsequent summits. German officials were, however, determined to persuade Japan and Italy—hosts of the 2008 and 2009 summits respectively—to recognize and respect the special relationship with the G5 and to create room in the official agenda for the interim (2008) and final (2009) reports.

What motivated Merkel and her government to get involved in incremental, but nevertheless significant, summit innovation? Germany was ready to invest considerable political and financial resources in a process of uncertain ending. At home and abroad, German diplomacy and Merkel personally would be judged by the HP outcome. The German initiative has been driven by a combination of leadership qualities and national interests of a middle power with civilian characteristics. Merkel clearly realized that the post–World War II order has come to an end. At the 2006 World Economic Forum, she acknowledged that a "creative imperative" would be necessary to cope with current global changes (Merkel 2006). At the 2007 World Economic Forum, Merkel (2007a, 2, 5) summed up her position as follows: "During the past 200 years we, and indeed Europe as a whole, became accustomed to taking a highly Eurocentric view of the world. Today we see that this simple view no longer applies ... Therefore my aim is for Germany's G8 Summit, in Heiligendamm in June, to place special emphasis on new forms of dialogue with the major emerging economies, i.e., Brazil, China, India, Mexico and South Africa." The depth of Merkel's commitment to systemic reforms can be gauged by her recent proposal for universal carbon equity. She pleaded for equal per capita emission rights on the basis of drastically reduced global volumes. National quotas would be set on the basis of population. According to press reports, Merkel adopted this idea from Indian prime minister Manmohan Singh, which would be an impressive example of mutual learning within the HP ("Angela Merkel: 'Vergesst Indien nicht'" 2007).

Given national interests, the HP has obviously been driven by the specific objectives of a civilian power that can only project (soft) power through coalition building and multilateral arrangements. German diplomacy understands the need for more inclusive structures that reflect the tectonic power shifts at the beginning of the 21st century (Kaplinsky and Messner 2008). The alternative to an open international system could only be a concert of great powers reminiscent of a constellation in Europe during the 19th century (Drezner 2007). Middle powers, such as Germany, would then be marginalized in global decision making. By introducing the HP, Germany can continue to play a balancing role within the G8 and increase its policy leverage in a global context.

A second motive of Germany in promoting the HP refers to its desired leadership role in the global debate on climate change. Using her double presidencies in 2007, Merkel campaigned heavily for a post-Kyoto agreement on carbon dioxide reductions. Granting emerging powers a privileged position vis-à-vis the G8 might help to generate their support for binding limits on greenhouse gases. The success of the climate talks in Bali in December 2007 demonstrates the growing openness of key players from the South to collective strategies and can be attributed, at least in part, to the HP and the preceding G8 outreach by the British (which was called the Gleneagles Dialogue on Climate Change, Clean Energy, and Sustainable Development).

In summary, the following main objectives of German diplomacy in the HP can be identified:

- to provide a forum for the exchange of perceptions and interests between existing and emerging powers on issues of global importance (short term);

- to consolidate Germany's influence on global agenda setting (medium term);
- to reform the global governance system (long term).

As already stated, G8 and summit reform are not prominent issues in German public debates. Nevertheless, the topic would re-emerge with the Hokkaido Toyako Summit in July 2008, where a mid-term review of the HP would be presented. At that point, G8 critics as well as opposition parties of the German Bundestag would certainly make a first assessment of the process. The 2009 summit would be even more important for Merkel, since the HP comes to an end just a few months before German national elections are scheduled.

Expectations of Heiligendamm Process Outcomes

The German government has high expectations of the HP to achieve effective results by 2009. However, in public those aspirations are toned down to protect against possible disappointment. German officials continuously emphasize that the HP constitutes something like "unknown territory" because nothing similar has been tried before. Just to get it started is generally considered a major success of German diplomacy. Expectations do not vary much among officials of different ministerial affiliation. This comes somewhat as a surprise considering the highly decentralized nature of the political system in Germany (Weller 2007). Although ministries have diverse thematic interests, there seems to be a high degree of convergence with regard to desired HP results. Officials stress the importance of process in the dialogue exercise rather than referring to specific policy outcomes. In interviews with German officials conducted by the authors, five main expectations emerged:

- the creation of trust and dependability among G8 and G5 countries;
- enhanced mutual understanding of motives and interests on critical global issues;
- more awareness of common responsibilities for global problems;
- the exploration of possible corridors of compromise for stalled negotiations in international organizations ("pathfinder" function); and
- increased legitimacy of the G8 by involving the G5.

Overall, one perception dominated among all German actors: they see the lack of trust and mutual understanding as the main limitation on effective cooperation between western and emerging powers. It is hoped that the informal atmosphere of HP working groups, through exchanges rather than negotiations, will facilitate rapprochement. However, it is also acknowledged that time may be too short since suspicions run high on both sides. As a first step, German officials are eager to learn more about the "real" interests of the G5 countries. They underline that such a learning process is better served by a focus on specific topics rather than dealing with comprehensive foreign policy agendas. German officials seem to detect a convergence of perceptions with the G5 in regard to universal risks and challenges, such as climate change. They also see a growing willingness among the emerging powers to accept common global responsibilities. HP discussions are expected to build on this and, eventually, to lead to appropriate political responses at national and multilateral levels. German officials, however, are aware that demanding too much too soon from G5 countries could be counterproductive. Dissent among G8 states on various issues, such as intellectual property rights (IPR) or the reduction of carbon dioxide emissions, further complicates consensus building.

Beyond the "internal dialogue" between the two country groupings and among their respective member states, in the perception of German officials, the HP could also provide a catalytic function for global politics in a broader sense. They see the possibility of a breakthrough for stalled negotiations, as in the Doha trade round. This argument is used to demonstrate how the HP could complement and support multilateral institutions, but is not free of self-serving interest. There is a danger that the HP could be perceived as a Trojan horse by the G5 through which western countries promote their agenda in global policy arenas. Such ambitions could undermine the whole process and create resentment within the G5.

With regard to concrete policy issues within the four working groups ("pillars") of the HP, there is no certainty about possible outcomes. Germany has shown a special interest with regard to development cooperation, particularly toward Africa. The recent engagement of China and other emerging providers has triggered a debate in the West whether this will undermine standards and procedures of the Development Assistance Committee (DAC) of the Organisation for Economic Co-operation and Development (Fues et al. 2006). The HP is expected to foster a dialogue on development assistance toward low-income developing countries.

A key expectation of Germany—as well other countries—is to raise the legitimacy of the G8 by involving G5 in a more systematic manner. This may work for a transition period of two years, after which the question of formal expansion will become more urgent than ever. While most G8 countries may feel comfortable in continuing with a structured dialogue, the G5 could insist on full-fledged inclusion. Thus, Germany's incrementalist approach may unwittingly have sparked off a dynamic that, at the end, leaves few options to the G8. Either its members agree to a fundamental overhaul of their club or they risk a major clash with the G5.

Germany's Bureaucratic Institutional Arrangements for the Heiligendamm Process

This section looks at the bureaucratic institutional provisions taken by the German government with regard to the HP. Also, the particularities of the German political system and its style of decision making are explained. While the foreign office assumes a coordinating role, the development ministry, the chancellery, the defence ministry and various other departments are engaged in shaping German relations with the outside world (Eberlei and Weller 2001). Consequently, a high number of government offices are also involved with the G8 in general and with the HP in particular. Since the G8 constitutes a leaders' body, all policies related to it are of top priority to the chancellor. Nevertheless, coordination of G8 policies does not happen through the chancellery but through the task force of the sherpa, who holds the office of state secretary at the Ministry of Economics and Technology (see Figure 10-1).[7] This exceptional institutional choice has influenced German G8 agenda setting and might explain its strong emphasis on world economic issues in the political G8 summits.

Other ministries are actively involved in the G8 when their specific issue areas are addressed, and each sherpa meeting of the annual G8 policy cycle is supported by these ministries. Whereas the finance ministry plays a special and relatively autonomous role in handling the G7 ministerials, the foreign office addresses security issues. Due to public interest in North–South relations, the Ministry of Economic Cooperation and Development assumed an outstanding role in recent German summits. At Cologne (1999) and Heiligendamm (2007), high priority was given to global development issues. In the past, Germany has, rightly, been criticized for its lack of coherence in foreign policies. But G8 policies constitute an exception since they are centrally coordinated by the sherpa task force. One example of such interministerial coordination, quite unusual in matters not related to the G8, concerns the initiative of the finance ministry—in close cooperation with the development ministry—toward African countries that led to the adoption of the action plan on "Good Financial Governance in Africa" (Bundesministerium der Finanzen 2008, 82).

Figure 10-1

Organizational Chart of German Provisions for G8 and the Heiligendamm Process

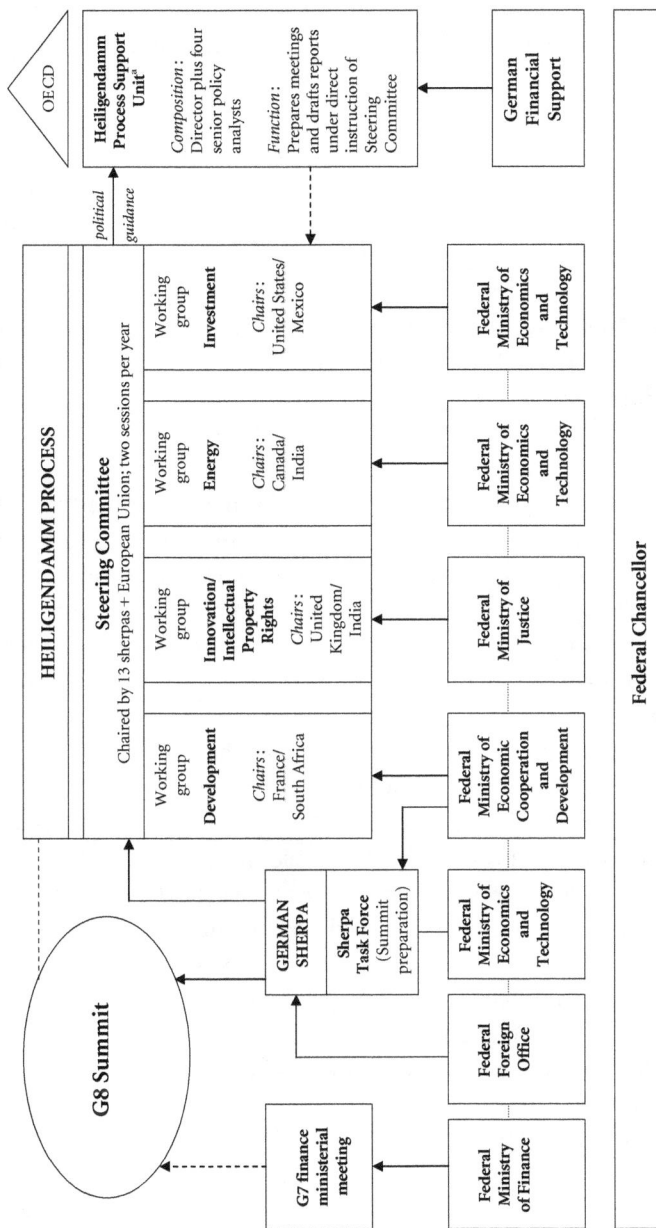

Note: [a] This platform is institutionalized in the office of the Secretary General of the Organisation for Economic Co-operation and Development and is headed by a German official.

Three different ministries are assigned to the four working groups of the HP (see Figure 10-1). The Ministry of Economics and Technology participates in the pillars on energy efficiency and investment; the development ministry represents Germany in the working group on development with special focus on Africa, while the justice ministry is in charge of German representation in the working group on innovation due to the high importance of IPR in this pillar. The involvement of the justice ministry is exceptional since IPR constitutes a topic normally addressed by the finance ministry. It may become more difficult to create policy coherence in this context, than compared to regular G8 processes, because ministries are autonomously discussing with G8 and G5 countries within their respective working groups in an informal setting. The sherpa task force thus faces a major challenge in coordinating the German positions for the HP steering committee.

Germany has provided substantial human and financial resources to institutionalize the HP. Most importantly, Germany promoted the creation of a support unit in Paris as an independent entity within the office of the OECD secretary general. Its main tasks consist of drafting reports and preparing the meetings of the working groups and the steering committee. The unit is staffed by four senior policy analysts and led by a director, who was a senior German official from the Ministry of Economics and Technology, who headed the sherpa task force before his appointment. Germany has been the sole significant financial supporter of the unit, with symbolic contributions coming from Japan and Italy.

Additional resources for the HP within the German bureaucracy have until now only been provided by the development ministry. Furthermore, there are plans to increase the size of the sherpa task force in the Ministry of Economics and Technology. In light of the higher coordination needs among ministries on the one hand and the requirements of numerous additional international meetings throughout the year on the other, the commitment of more human and financial resources seems inevitable if German support for the HP is to be maintained at a high level.

Political Dynamics: Germany's International Environment

The HP was agreed upon by all G8 members. However, after the Heiligendamm Summit, diverging positions among G8 members on the appropriate form of integrating the G5 became ever more pronounced. Despite its weight within the EU, Germany was not able to harmonize the positions of Britain, Italy, and France on the HP and the G8. In sharp criticism of the HP, French president Nicolas Sarkozy launched a campaign to offer formal membership to G5 states. On 22 November 2007 he stated: "I am sorry, but I think that it is misguided to invite a country such as China, a country such as India, a country such as Brazil, a country such as South Africa, or a country such as Mexico for merely participating at a breakfast on the third day [of the G8 summit]. We are highly interested in bringing them together at the negotiating table, to treat them as partners and to confront them with their responsibilities ... We are in the 21st century and here a G13 fits better" (Sarkozy 2007, translation by authors). This statement was underlined by an official letter that Sarkozy addressed to the leaders of all G8 countries in order to promote formal expansion by January 2008.

The British government has not taken an explicit position on membership of the G5. But it seems to support the idea of inviting only India to "formally" join the G8, as Prime Minister Gordon Brown announced during his visit to India in January 2008, "I support changes in the World Bank, IMF and G8 that reflect the rise of India in Asia" (10 Downing Street 2008). It is important to note, however, that Brown's predecessor, Tony Blair, had pushed for formal inclusion of the G5 shortly before the Russian-hosted St. Petersburg Summit in 2006. Although Russia has not taken a clear position in the current debate, it has promoted formal G8 enlargement before. In particular, Vladimir Putin called for India's formal inclusion into the summit architecture ("Putin to Back G8 Expansion to Include India" 2006) and also supported official membership for China and Brazil after the St. Petersburg Summit. Italy has not yet voiced an opinion on the issue; nor has Canada.

The U.S. and Japan are firmly opposed to formal enlargement, presumably because of their political rivalries with China. Whereas Japan and China have been competing for political supremacy in East Asia throughout the 20th century (Nabers 2006), the U.S. sees its status of global superpower endangered and is vitally concerned about China's rise (Yong Deng and Moore 2004). The polarized debate on formal G8 expansion has caused problems for the HP because Japan and the U.S. want to stall any dynamic that would lead to automatic membership after 2009. Consequently, the Japanese G8 presidency was not keen to integrate the HP officially into the agenda of the 2008 Hokkaido Summit. To balance the focus on the five Heiligendamm countries, Japan decided to also invite Australia, Indonesia, and South Korea. This move may not have delighted the G5 since it undercuts their privileged position.

While G8 members are discussing the status and form of inclusion of G5 members into their exclusive club, another major political issue remains untouched. The EU, formerly the European Community, has been part of the G8 meetings (then G7) since 1977 (Hajnal 2007, 3). It has by now become a full G8 member without the formal status. As a matter of fact, the G8 should be called G9, or even a hybrid G31. It is not clear to what extent the EU represents its member states, excluding France, Germany, Great Britain, and Italy, which are directly represented. There is no mechanism for coordinating European positions in the G8. Any talk about G8 expansion should include a reflection on the present role of the EU and how regional representation could be used for future membership models. In the long run, the sole participation of the EU rather than of individual European states may open the door for the inclusion of emerging powers and other regional groupings. Major European powers such as France, Germany, and Great Britain can be expected to resist this arrangement as they are not ready yet to give up national privileges and the Europe's Common Foreign and Security Policy is still in the making.

Opportunities and Limits of the Heiligendamm Process from a German Perspective

The HP comes at a critical juncture of global politics (Cooper and Jackson 2007). Emerging powers of the global South are challenging western predominance in the international order. Deepening political interaction with industrialized countries is only one of several options they can pursue. South–South cooperation and regional integration, for example through the East Asia Summit or through Mercosur, are gaining increasing attention. There may be only a small window of opportunity for inclusive reform of the summit architecture before emerging powers seize alternative opportunities. The Heiligendamm Process must, therefore, quickly deliver tangible benefits for the G5, and the developing world in general, if the G8 is to remain an attractive forum of dialogue and policy coordination in their eyes.

What are the prospects for success before the summit of 2009? A fundamental divergence between G8 and G5 exists in the different notions of legitimacy each side associates with the HP. While industrialized countries focus on input legitimacy in keeping the process open ended, the G5 members are mainly interested in output legitimacy, i.e., concrete results that would imply significant policy shifts of the G8 in areas such as trade or voting rights in international financial institutions.[8] At this stage, there is no indication how this growing gap could be bridged.

At the invitation of Mexico, G5 countries met the evening before the Heiligendamm Summit, on 7 June 2007 in Berlin, to formulate a joint position paper vis-à-vis the G8. In comparing that G5 paper with the joint declaration of the German G8 presidency and the G5, Mario Riestra (2007) has provided an in-depth analysis of the compromise reached by the two country groupings. The G5 paper emphasizes technology transfer and gives less attention to the protection of innovation while development ranks high in both documents. The investment and energy issues are strongly emphasized in the G8/G5 declaration but play a rather modest role in the G5 paper. Riestra also notes that climate change is treated as an extension of the energy topic at the insistence of the G5, which resists the western focus on binding emission targets. Three major issues of importance to the G5 are excluded altogether from the HP agenda, which was unilaterally set by the German G8 presidency: reform of global governance institutions, international trade, and migration. The inclusion of these topics could be beneficial for the dialogue, Riestra argues, because it would improve the sense of ownership by the G5 with regard to agenda setting.

Another critical issue is linked to the role of the OECD in the HP in hosting the support unit. Most G5 countries have been skeptical of this idea because they see the OECD as a "rich countries' club." While Brazil seems to consider OECD membership, China and India keep their distance. Mexico undoubtedly played a crucial role in convincing the G5 to accept the arrangement, given that it is not only a member of the OECD but that the organization's secretary general is Mexican. Since the HP support unit is kept separate from the regular OECD administration, the G5 may eventually develop trust in this solution.

The biggest mistake the G8 could make is taking for granted the G5 members' interest in continued interaction without reflecting on their specific perspectives and expectations. The HP can only bring about progress if it operates as a dialogue of equals where both sides are ready to search for new modalities in cooperative multilateralism. It is not yet clear if German diplomacy has fully understood the challenge this represents. Berlin appears interested in shepherding the emerging powers into the inner circle of power, committing them to the G8 agenda, and getting them to adopt rules and standards set by the OECD and other multilateral institutions under the influence of industrialized countries. This would be a tragic misperception, because the G5 countries hardly see themselves as needing outside assistance in order to understand global challenges and, considering their growing economic and political clout, do not depend on western largesse to be admitted to the centre of power. The G5 countries would also dispute the notion that the OECD and other multilateral institutions, where they are not represented, are legitimate sources of universal norm creation.

The HP has great potential for fostering political dialogue between the G8 and the G5 through trust building and cross-bargaining in an atmosphere of informality. This is especially important since the international debate is increasingly shaped by stereotypes that incite anxieties and aggravate the rivalry between old and emerging powers. Hence, one major advantage of the HP could be its potential to reduce destructive tensions in the global system and open up avenues of cooperative multilateralism with a clear focus on pressing global problems. The issue of summit reform will, however, need a new concerted effort after the HP comes to an end in 2009.

If Germany wants to consolidate its role in global agenda setting and actively foster global governance reform, the government would first need to expand its political and financial commitment to the HP in order to ensure its successful completion. Second, given the prevailing reservations toward globalization and emerging powers, especially China, the government should also campaign for global governance reform aimed at its domestic audience and not only in its international relations. In addition, Merkel should start to work for a common position of the EU on summit enlargement, to be prepared for the period after the HP terminates in 2009. Any model for inclusion should, however, recognize that the value of club governance lies in informal dialogue and consensus building, complementary to formal multilateral institutions. At the same time, the UN should be strengthened to serve as an effective platform for formal decision making for global problems.

Notes

1 Since the five HP countries reject the outreach label and refer to themselves as G5, this terminology, which is now officially used by the German government, is used in this chapter.
2 Since middle power is a relative term, this concept is contested in political science. From a realist perspective, international relations are organized hierarchically (great, middle, and small powers) according to the distribution of hard power resources. From a behavioural viewpoint, middle power refers to a specific role these states play in the international order, e.g., as consensus seeker and promoter of multilateral solutions to global problems—a role model that aptly describes Germany's foreign policy. In the academic discourse, German identity and behaviour in international relations are captured by the concept of civilian power rather than that of middle power in its realist sense. In the German language, the term "middle

power" (*Mittelmacht*) is scarcely used. This stems from the fact that it denotes a specific historical constellation, i.e., the military alliance during World War I between the German Empire, Austria-Hungary, the Ottoman Empire, and Bulgaria. In this text, references to Germany as a middle power are used in the behavioural sense.

3 All translations are by the authors unless otherwise indicated.

4 As Thomas Risse (2007, 58) argues, foreign policies of civilian powers are not necessarily pacifist.

5 However, empirical evidence seems to indicate that the industrialized countries have been more successful than member states from the global South in shaping the agenda and position papers of the G20 (Martinez-Diaz 2007).

6 Ulrich Klose (2008), an influential SPD foreign policy expert, advocated summit reform by including emerging powers.

7 Germany's situation is exceptional because in most G8 members the sherpas are placed in the foreign ministry or are directly assigned to the leader.

8 Although the HP itself might generate high input legitimacy among participants, it might be perceived as less legitimate from a global perspective, especially by those actors generally critical to exclusive club governance.

References

10 Downing Street (2008). "PM Calls for World Institutions Shake-Up." 21 January, London. <www.number10.gov.uk/output/Page14319.asp> (May 2008).

Ahearne, Alan, André Sapir, Jean Pisani-Ferry, et al. (2006). *Global Governance: An Agenda for Europe*. Bruegel Policy Brief 2006/07. Brussels: Bruegel.

Altvater, Elmar (2007). "Der Abbau globaler Ungleichheit findet nicht statt." In *G8 Macht Politik: Wie die Welt beherrscht wird*, edited by H. Melber and C. Wilß, 12–20. Frankfurt: Brandes and Apsel.

"Angela Merkel: 'Vergesst Indien nicht.'" (2007). *Rheinische Post*, 28 October. Düsseldorf. <www.rp-online.de/public/article/politik/deutschland/494565/Angela-Merkel-Vergesst-Indien-nicht.html> (May 2008).

Attac Germany (2007). "Gipfelproteste voller Erfolg für globalisierungskritische Bewegung: Tiefe Legitimationskrise der G8 offenkundig." Press release, Frankfurt. <www.attac.de/erfolge/detailansicht/datum/2007/06/06/gipfelproteste-voller-erfolg-fuer-globalisierungskritische-bewegung/?type=123&cHash=380d3eafcf> (May 2008).

Benterbusch, Ulrich and Juliane Seifert (2008). *The Heiligendamm Dialogue Process: Joining Forces to Meet the Challenges of the World Economy*. Dialogue on Globalization, Fact Sheet No. 3. Berlin: Friedrich Ebert Foundation. <library.fes.de/pdf-files/iez/global/05310.pdf> (May 2008).

Bundeskoordination Internationalismus (2007). "Glaubwürdigkeit von NGOs auf dem Prüfstand: Eine Replik der Bundeskoordination Internationalismus auf das 'NGO-G8 Positionspapier.'" Hamburg. <www.buko.info/publikationen/positionen/start_ngo_replik.html> (May 2008).

Bundesministerium der Finanzen (2008). *Bilanz der deutschen G8-Präsidentschaft.* Monatsbericht des BMF, January. Berlin. <www.bundesfinanzministerium.de/ nn_17844/DE/BMF__Startseite/Aktuelles/Monatsbericht__des__BMF/2008/01/0 00__mb__januar.html?__nnn=true> (May 2008).

Bundesministerium für wirtschaftliche Zusammenarbeit und Entwicklung (2007a). "Added Momentum for Heiligendamm." 27 March, Bonn. Bundesministerium für wirtschaftliche Zusammenarbeit und Entwicklung. <www.bmz.de/en/ eu_g8/Teaserseite_Aktuelles/AktuelleMeldungen/20070327_g8ministertreffen _110/index.html> (May 2008).

Bundesministerium für wirtschaftliche Zusammenarbeit und Entwicklung (2007b). *The G8: Players in a Global Development Partnership.* Bonn. <www.bmz.de/en/ service/infothek/fach/spezial/spezial150.pdf> (May 2008).

Bundesverband der Deutschen Industrie e.V. (2007). *BDI-Präsident Thumann zum G8-Gipfel: Positive Zeichen für die Weltwirtschaft.* Press release 57/2007. Berlin: Bundesverband der Deutschen Industrie. <www.bdi-online.de/8605.htm> (May 2008).

Civil G8 Dialogue (2007). *Round Table Discussion between NGO Representatives and G8 Sherpas at the Civil G8 Dialogue in Bonn.* Minutes. Bonn. <forum-ue.de/file admin/userupload/g8dialogue/civil_g8_dialogue_roundtable_minutes.pdf> (May 2008).

Cooper, Andrew F. and Thomas Fues (2005). "L20 and ECOSOC Reform: Complementary Building Blocks for Inclusive Global Governance and a More Effective UN." Briefing Paper No. 6/2005. Bonn: German Development Institute. <www .cigionline.org : Publications: Research Project Publications : Leaders' 20 (L20) Project> (May 2008).

Cooper, Andrew F. (2007). "The Logic of the B(R)ICSAM Model for G8 Reform." CIGI Policy Brief No. 1. Waterloo ON: Centre for International Governance Innovation. <www.cigionline.org : Publications : Policy Briefs> (May 2008).

Cooper, Andrew F. and Kelly Jackson (2007). "Regaining Legitimacy: The G8 and the 'Heiligendamm Process.'" *International Insights* 4(10). <www.igloo.org/ciia/ Library/ciialibr/intern~1/internat> (May 2008).

Deutsche Gesellschaft für die Vereinten Nationen e.V. (2007). *Heiligendamm—eine gemischte Bilanz für die Vereinten Nationen.* Berlin. <www.dgvn.de/news .html?&no_cache=1&tx_ttnews%5Btt_news%5D=61&tx_ttnews%5BbackPid %5D=225&cHash=ba23d7b527> (May 2008).

Deutschen Industrie- und Handelskammertages (2007). *Signal für eine liberale Weltwirtschaftsordnung 'wichtigstes Ergebnis.'* Berlin. <www.dihk.de/inhalt/ informationen/news/meldungen/meldung009818.html> (May 2008).

Deutscher Bundestag (2002). *Globalisierung der Weltwirtschaft, Schlussbericht der Enquete-Kommission.* Opladen: Leske und Budrich.

Deutscher Gewerkschaftsbund (2007). "Globale soziale Standards: Den Worten müssen Taten folgen, G8-Gipfel-Info." Berlin. <www.nord.dgb.de/article.php ?article=820> (May 2008).

Drezner, Daniel (2007). "The New New World Order." *Foreign Affairs* 86(2): 34–46.

Eberlei, Walter and Christoph Weller (2001). *Deutsche Akteure von Global Governance. Eine Bestandsaufnahme der auswärtigen Beziehungen der Bundesministerien.* INEF Report 51. Duisburg: Institut für Entwicklung und Frieden.

Falk, Rainer (2006). "Steinbrück: G8 mittelfristig überflüssig." Baustellen der Globalisierung. 2 December. <baustellen-der-globalisierung.blogspot.com/2006/12/steinbrck-g8-mittelfristig-berflssig.html> (May 2008).

Falk, Rainer and Barbara Unmüssig (2007). "Das war der G8-Blog des Informationsbriefs Weltwirtschaft & Entwicklung und der Heinrich-Böll-Stiftung." G8-Blog: der Weg nach Heiligendamm. 11 June. <g8-blog.blogspot.com/2007/06/das-war-der-g8-blog-des.html> (May 2008).

Fues, Thomas, Sven Grimm, and Denise Laufer (2006). "China's Africa Policy: Opportunity and Challenge for European Development Cooperation." Briefing Paper 4/2006. Bonn: German Development Institute. <www.die-gdi.de : Publikationen : Analysen und Stellungnahmen : English : 2006> (May 2008).

Fues, Thomas (2007). "Global Governance Beyond the G8: Reform Prospects for the Summit Architecture." *International Politik und Gesellschaft* (2): 11–24. <www.fes.de/ipg/arc_07_set/set_02_07e.htm> (May 2008).

G8 and Outreach Partners (2007). "Joint Statement by the German G8 Presidency and the Heads of State and/or Government of Brazil, China, India, Mexico, and South Africa on the Occasion of the G8 Summit in Heiligendamm." 8 June, Heiligendamm. <www.g8.utoronto.ca/summit/2007heiligendamm/g8-2007-joint.html> (May 2008).

G8 NGO Platform (2007). *Glaubwürdigkeit der Mächtigen auf dem Prüfstand: Konkret für Umwelt und Entwicklung handeln!* Position paper of German Nongovernmental Organizations on the Heiligendam G8 Summit. <forum-ue.de/fileadmin/userupload/g8dialogue/G8_NGO_Positionspapier.pdf> (May 2008).

German Advisory Council on Global Change (WBGU) (2007). "New Impetus for Climate Policy: Making the Most of Germany's Dual Presidency." Policy Paper 5. Berlin. <www.wbgu.de/wbgu_pp2007_engl.html> (May 2008).

Gnath, Katharina (2007). "Beyond Heiligendamm: The G8 and Its Dialogue with Emerging Countries." *Internationale Politik* 8(3): 36–39. <www.g8.utoronto.ca/scholar/IPGE_3_Gnath.pdf> (May 2008).

Gysi, Gregor (2007). "Rede zum G8-Weltwirtschaftsgipfel vom 6. bis 8. Juni 2007 in Heiligendam." 24 May. Berlin: Deutscher Bundestag.

Habermas, Jürgen (2007). "Europapolitik in der Sackgasse. Nicht die Bevölkerungen, die Regierungen sind der Hemmschu." Lecture at Willy Brandt Haus, in discussion with Frank-Walter Steinmeier (SPD), 29 November. Berlin. <www .kulturforen.de/servlet/PB/show/1734071/Vortragsfassung Habermas.pdf> (May 2008).

Hajnal, Peter I. (2007). "Summitry from G5 to L20: A Review of Reform Initiatives." CIGI Working Paper No. 20, March. Waterloo ON: Centre for International Governance Innovation. <www.cigionline.org : Publications : Policy Briefs>

Hellmann, Günther, Reinhard Wolf, and Sigmar Schmidt (2007). "Außenpolitik in historischer und systematischer Perspektive." In *Handbuch zur deutschen Außenpolitik*, edited by S. Schmidt, G. Hellmann, and R. Wolf, 15–48. Wiesbaden: VS Verlag.

Hulsman, John C. and Jan Techau (2007). "Zu hohe Erwartungen?" *Internationale Politik* 62(1): 16–25.

Joffe, Josef (2007). "Go Home, G8." *Die Zeit*, 5 June. <www.zeit.de/online/2007/23/ g8-abschaffen> (May 2008).

Kaplinsky, Raphael and Dirk Messner (2008). "The Impact of Asian Drivers on the Developing World." *World Development* 36(2): 197–209.

Klose, Ulrich (2008). "Beyond the Heiligendamm Process." Conference organized by the Stiftung Wissenschaft und Politik and the Friedrich Ebert Stiftung, 22 April. Berlin.

Kuhn, Fritz (2007). "Rede zum G8-Weltwirtschaftsgipfel vom 6. bis 8. Juni 2007 in Heiligendam." 24 May. Berlin: Deutscher Bundestag.

Maihold, Günther (2005). "Neue Führungsmächte des Südens als Partner deutscher Außenpolitik." In *Deutsche Außenpolitik nach Christoph Bertram*, 81–84. Berlin: Stiftung Wissenschaft und Politik.

Manz, Thomas (2007). "Allianzen und Gruppen im Global Governance-System— Multilateralismus zwischen partikularen Interessen und universellen Anforderungen." *Internationale Politik und Gesellschaft* (2): 25–45.

Martens, Jens (2007). "Controversy over 'Heiligendamm Process': The Wrong Forum." *Development + Cooperation* (July/August): 306. <May 2008> (www.inwent.org/ ez/articles/056684/index.en.shtml).

Martinez-Diaz, Leonardo (2007). "The G20 after Eight Years: How Effective a Vehicle for Developing-Country Influence?" Global Economy and Development Working Paper No. 12. Washington DC: Brookings Institution.

Maull, Hanns W. (1994). "Germany at the Summit." *International Spectator* 29(2): 113–139.

Maull, Hanns W. (2004). "Germany and the G7/G8." G8 Online, Lecture 10, Toronto. G8 Research Group. <www.g8.utoronto.ca/g8online/2004/english/lectures/ lecture010.html> (May 2008).

Maull, Hanns W. (2007). "Deutschland als Zivilmacht." In *Handbuch zur deutschen Außenpolitik*, edited by S. Schmidt, G. Hellmann, and R. Wolf, 73–84. Wiesbaden: VS Verlag.

May, Bernhard (2007). "G7/G8-Gruppe." In *Handbuch zur deutschen Außenpolitik*, edited by S. Schmidt, G. Hellmann, and R. Wolf, 802–814. Wiesbaden: VS Verlag.

Merkel, Angela (2006). "Rede von Bundeskanzlerin Angela Merkel auf dem Weltwirtschaftsforum." 25 January, Davos. Bundeskanzleramt.

Merkel, Angela (2007a). "Opening Address." World Economic Forum, 24 January, Davos. Bundeskanzleramt. <www.weforum.org/pdf/AM_2007/merkel.pdf> (May 2008).

Merkel, Angela (2007b). "Regierungserklärung zum Europäischen Rat am 21. und 22. Juni 2007." 24 May, Berlin. Press and Information Office of the Federal Government. <www.bundesregierung.de/nn_1502/Content/DE/Regierungserklaerung/2007/2007-06-14-regierungserklaerung-eu-gipfel.html> (May 2008).

Merkel, Angela (2007c). "We Aim to Give Globalization a Human Face." 24 May, Berlin. Press and Information Office of the Federal Government. <www.g-8.de/Content/EN/Artikel/2007/05/2007-05-24-merkel-regierungserklaerung-g8-heiligendamm__en.html> (May 2008).

Müller, Harald (2008). *Wie kann eine neue Weltordnung aussehen? Wege in eine nachhaltige Politik*. Frankfurt: Fischer.

Nabers, Dirk (2006). "China-Japan Antagonism as a Source for Structural Change in East Asia." Paper prepared for GIGA conference on "Regional Powers in Asia, Africa, Latin America, and the Middle East," 11–12 December. Hamburg.

Nuscheler, Franz (2007). "Global Governance durch G7/G8—Warum die 'Club-Hegemonie' der G8 ein Auslaufmodell ist." In *G8 Macht Politik: Wie die Welt beherrscht wird*, edited by H. Melber and C. Wilß, 58–64. Frankfurt: Brandes and Apsel.

Ortega, Martin (2007). "Building the Future: Europe's Contribution to Global Governance." Chaillot Paper No. 100, April. Paris: Institute for Security Studies.

Otte, Max (2000). *A Rising Middle Power? German Foreign Policy in Transformation, 1989–1999*. New York: St. Martin's Press.

Overhaus, Marco (2007). "Reform Requirements of the G8 and the Heiligendamm Summit." *Foreign Policy in Focus* (325). <www.deutsche-aussenpolitik.de/digest/op-ed_inhalt_40.php> (May 2008).

Pfaffenbach, Bernd (2006). "Interview." *Der Tagesspiegel*, 11 December. Berlin.

"Putin to Back G8 Expansion to Include India." (2006). *Times of India*, 16 July. <timesofindia.indiatimes.com/articleshow/1767615.cms> (May 2008).

Riestra, Mario (2007). "The Heiligendamm Process: A Breath of Fresh Air for the Discussion of Global Challenge." Unpublished. Bonn: German Development Institute.

Risse, Thomas (2007). "Deutsche Identität und Außenpolitik." In *Handbuch zur deutschen Außenpolitik*, edited by S. Schmidt, G. Hellmann, and R. Wolf, 49–61. Wiesbaden: VS Verlag.

Sarkozy, Nicolas (2007). *Discours du Président de la République lors de la réunion du Club franco-japonais.* 22 November. Paris: Elyssée. <www.elysee.fr/documents/index.php?mode=cview&press_id=706&cat_id=7&lang=fr> (May 2008).

Schmidt, Helmut (2007). "Ladet China und Indien ein!" *Die Zeit*, 7 June.

Schumann, Harald and Christine Grefe (2008). *Der globale Countdown.* Köln: Kiepenheuer & Witsch.

Staak, Michael (2007). "Deutschland als Wirtschaftsmacht." In *Handbuch zur deutschen Außenpolitik*, edited by S. Schmidt, G. Hellmann, and R. Wolf, 85–100. Wiesbaden: VS Verlag.

Staffelt, Ditmar (2007). "Rede zum G8-Weltwirtschaftsgipfel vom 6. bis 8. Juni 2007 in Heiligendam." 24 May. Berlin: Deutscher Bundestag.

Stahl, André and Thomas Kaufner (2007). "Deutscher G8-Vorsitz: Steinbrücks leiser Auftakt." 10 February. n-tv. <www.n-tv.de/764810.html> (May 2008).

Steinhilber, Jochen (2007). *Deutschland in den internationalen Beziehungen: Ziele, Instrumente, Perspektiven, Kompass 2020 Synthesebericht.* Berlin: Friedrich Ebert Stiftung.

Stetten, Jürgen (2007). *Multilateral Institutions: Building New Alliances, Solving Global Problems, Kompass 2020.* New York: Friedrich Ebert Foundation.

Teltschik, Horst (2008). "Es mangelt an strategischem Denken." *Süddeutsche Zeitung*, 8 February, 12. <www.sueddeutsche.de/deutschland/artikel/308/156892>

Volkery, Carsten (2007). "Warum der G-8-Gipfel besser ist als sein Ruf." *Spiegel*, 31 May. <www.spiegel.de/politik/ausland/0,1518,485777,00.html> (May 2008).

Weiland, Severin (2007). "Club der Weltelite will geschlossene Gesellschaft bleiben." *Spiegel*, 31 May, 8 June. <www.spiegel.de/politik/deutschland/0,1518,487498,00.html> (May 2008).

Weller, Christoph (2007). "Bundesministerien." In *Handbuch zur deutschen Außenpolitik*, edited by S. Schmidt, G. Hellmann, and R. Wolf, 210–233. Wiesbaden: VS Verlag.

Westerwelle, Guido (2007). "Rede zum G8-Weltwirtschaftsgipfel vom 6. bis 8. Juni 2007 in Heiligendam." 24 May. Berlin: Deutscher Bundestag.

Wieczorek-Zeul, Heidemarie (2005). "A Year of Opportunities: UN Reform and Development Finance." Presentation delivered at the Friedrich Ebert Foundation, Washington DC, 16 April. Bonn: Federal Ministry for Economic Cooperation and Development.

Yong Deng and Thomas G. Moore (2004). "China Views Globalization: Toward a New Great-Power Politics?" *Washington Quarterly* 27(3): 117–136.

11

Why Is the OECD Involved in the Heiligendamm Process?

Richard Woodward

Although it seldom receives public acclaim, the Organisation for Economic Co-operation and Development (OECD) and its predecessor, the Organisation for European Economic Co-operation (OEEC), have starred in many of the decisive junctures of post-war economic history. In the 1950s, the OEEC oversaw the reconstruction of the European trade and payments system and in the 1960s the OECD's Working Party Number 3 on Policies for the Promotion of Better International Payments Equilibrium (WP3) mitigated the strains in the international financial system. Over the next three decades the OECD assisted in managing the oil crises, dissolved obstacles to the completion of the Uruguay Round trade negotiations, finessed the transition of eastern Europe's economies, and was the genesis of the Millennium Development Goals (MDGs). In the new millennium, the OECD continues to research cutting-edge problems including aging societies, genetics, online security, sustainable development, corruption, and corporate governance (see Woodward 2008, ch. 5).

Predictably, surveys of global governance regularly pinpoint the OECD as a central figure in the management of the world's economic affairs. Nevertheless, scholarly treatments of the OECD's contribution to global governance are scarce (for an exception see Aubrey 1967), and most commentators appear content to reduce the organization to hackneyed catchphrases such as "the rich countries' club" (Camps 1975,10; Gilpin 2000, 184) or simplified descriptions such as "a think tank" ("OECD Fails to Put Its Own House in Order" 2002) or a "club of government economic analysts and forecasters" (Hutton 2002, 218). Even the OECD's self-portrait—"a unique forum where the governments of 30 market democracies work together to address the economic, social and governance challenges of globalization" (OECD 2005, 7)—is somewhat vague. A flurry of recent publications suggests the academic community have belatedly woken up to the OECD's importance (see Mahon and McBride 2008; Woodward 2008; Jakobi and Martens 2009), but it remains the least written about and least well understood of the major multilateral economic organizations (for a summary of the existing literature see Woodward 2007b). This and other recent work provide a detailed contemplation of what and how the OECD affects national economic policies and contributes to global governance in discrete policy areas (see, for example, Long 2000; Armingeon and Beyeler 2004; Sharman 2005). However, this chapter follows in the footsteps of Theodore Cohn (2002), Jörg Michael Dostal (2004), and Morten Ougaard (2004) to adjudicate where the OECD fits into the architecture of global governance. In particular, it is concerned with the evolution of the OECD's relationship with the G7/8 system, whether and to what extent it has contributed to the latter's emergence as an "effective centre of global governance" (Kirton 1999, 46), and the implications of the Heiligendamm Process (HP) for this relationship and the OECD's future role. The following section sketches a framework for understanding the OECD's role in global governance. Then the chapter turns to consider the increasingly close relationship that exists between the OECD and the G7/8, and details the OECD's role in supporting the HP. The final section examines why the OECD was chosen as a home for the Heiligendamm Process Support Unit and the implications this might have for both the initiative and the OECD's prospects in the years ahead.

The OECD and Global Governance

Article 1 of the Convention on the Organisation for Economic Co-operation and Development (1960) states the aims of the organization shall be:

> to promote policies designed:
>
> a) to achieve the highest sustainable economic growth and employment and a rising standard of living in Member countries, while maintaining financial stability, and thus to contribute to the development of the world economy;
>
> b) to contribute to sound economic expansion in Member as well as non-member countries in the process of economic development; and

c) to contribute to the expansion of world trade on a multilateral, non-dis-criminatory basis in accordance with international obligations.

In contrast to many other multilateral economic institutions, the OECD does not have recourse to legal or financial mechanisms to promote policies or persuade states to comply. Instead, it pursues its mission by institutionaliz-ing interstate cooperation. In this context, then, article 3 obliges signatories to:

a) keep each other informed and furnish the Organisation with the infor-mation necessary for the accomplishment of its tasks;

(b) consult together on a continuing basis, carry out studies and partici-pate in agreed projects; and

(c) co-operate closely and where appropriate take co-ordinated action. (OECD 1960)

As international relations scholars suggest, however, material and ideational barriers to international cooperation are legion. The conundrum therefore is what the OECD does to overcome these hurdles.

Martin Marcussen (2004) distinguishes among three dimensions of OECD governance: cognitive, normative, and legal. Ironically, the most remarked-upon dimension of OECD governance, the legal dimension, is arguably the least important. Legal governance refers to the authoritative instruments passed using the OECD Council's decision-making apparatus. With only 219 OECD acts in force as of March 2008, the OECD is not a copi-ous legislator, but its rules and guidelines infuse almost every facet of social and economic life (see Table 11-1). Moreover, some of these benchmarks have exerted considerable influence over the trajectory of global governance. For example, the Code of Liberalization of Current Invisible Operations and the Code of Liberalization of Capital Movements, both ratified in 1961, have helped underpin the removal of impediments to trade and finance (Henderson 1993). Likewise, the voluntary benchmarks established by the 1976 Declaration on International Investment and Multinational Enterprises and, more recently, the 1999 Principles on Corporate Governance (revised in 2004) are prominent standards in the field of international commerce. Indeed, the latter are amongst the Financial Stability Forum's (FSF's) 12 Key Standards for Sound Financial Systems and are the template for the corpo-rate governance element of the Reports on the Observance of Standards and Codes (ROSCs) set out by the World Bank and International Monetary Fund (IMF). Some more esoteric OECD guidelines, such as those dealing with the control of chemicals, have also achieved global acceptance or found

Table 11-1

Compendium of OECD Acts by Type and Subject, March 2008

	Decisions	Recommendations	Others	Total
Agriculture	4	3	0	7
Anti-corruption	1	3	3	7
Capital movements	1	0	0	1
Competition law and policy	0	10	0	10
Consumer policy	1	9	0	10
Corporate governance	0	1	1	2
Current invisibles operations	1	1	0	2
Development assistance	0	3	3	6
Education	0	2	1	3
Employment, labour, and social affairs	0	2	2	4
Energy	1	0	0	1
Environment	14	50	4	68
Financial markets	0	7	0	7
Fiscal affairs	0	16	1	17
Information, computer, and communications policy	0	7	4	11
Insurance	1	10	0	11
International investment and multinational enterprises	4	7	3	14
Nuclear energy	1	4	3	8
Public management	0	3	0	3
Scientific and technological policy	0	6	5	11
Shipbuilding and maritime transport	0	2	4	6
Steel	0	0	1	1
Tourism	1	2	0	3
Trade	0	4	2	6
Total	30	152	37	219

Source: Derived from OECD (2008).

their way into international agreements such as Guidelines for the Identification of Polychlorinated Biphenyls of the United Nations Environment Programme (UNEP) and the International Code of Conduct on the Distribution and Use of Pesticides of the Food and Agriculture Organization

(FAO) (Busch 2006, 8). However, only 30 OECD acts are in the form of decisions or conventions that are legally binding on their signatories. The remainder are non-binding, soft law recommendations, agreements, declarations, and arrangements. Moreover, article 6 of the OECD Convention allows members to abstain from council meetings where these decisions are agreed, absolving them of the need to comply.

The predominance of soft law and the paucity of sanctions available to the OECD mean that it relies on cognitive and normative governance to secure compliance. An important but less renowned attribute of international institutions is their ability to forge the system in which their members act, and to articulate a philosophy that sutures certain states together as imagined communities. Cognitive governance refers "to the OECD's capacity to engender and reproduce a sense of identity amongst its members by engineering and propagating a set of values perspectives, expectations, and discourses about their place and that of the organisation in the global polity" (Woodward 2008; c.f. Marcussen 2004). The OECD wilfully advertises itself as a club of like-minded countries (see, for example, OECD 2004b) whose common ideals define what it and its members are and, essentially, what they are not. The characterization of the OECD as the economic counterpart of the North Atlantic Treaty Organization (NATO) (OECD 2004a) is somewhat simplistic; nevertheless, at the time of the OECD's foundation these values were inextricably linked to the Cold War's ideological battleground. The OECD's incarnation as a society of nations based on democratic and capitalist principles stood in stark contrast to the authoritarian and centrally planned regimes of the communist bloc. Paradoxically, the collapse of communism in eastern Europe and the spread of capitalism throughout much of the world prompted an identity crisis at the OECD as it now needed a more "positive" character rather than being simply a bulwark against the communist bloc. In the 1990s, a number of new market democracies acceded to the OECD including Mexico (1994), the Czech Republic (1995), Hungary, South Korea, Poland (1996), and Slovakia (2000). Nevertheless a number of market democracies could not be accommodated or remained sceptical about the benefits of OECD membership. Consequently, although they remain central to the like-mindedness at the heart of the OECD, capitalism and democracy alone no longer identify OECD countries as a discrete community. Identifying and labelling the contemporary OECD community is more difficult, but it could be described as a community of states that are identified as (or wish to be identified as) "modern, liberal, efficient and market-friendly" (Porter and Webb 2008).

Normative governance is about the "development and diffusion of shared knowledge structures—ideas" (Marcussen 2004, 106) and norms through discussions at the OECD and the ongoing cycle of surveillance and peer review. Every year some 40,000 officials from national capitals come to the OECD to participate in its 240-strong labyrinth of committees and working groups (OECD 2005). By repeatedly bringing together interested high-ranking officials from national capitals, discussions at the OECD lead to the adoption of common languages, enable officials to identify shared concerns, and foster converging understandings of policy problems. The influence of the OECD secretariat is ultimately conditioned by the member-driven nature of the organization. Nevertheless, OECD committees and working groups rely heavily on the logistical, analytical, and statistical muscle of the secretariat, which has proven especially adept at defining and promulgating agreed principles and terminology for emergent policy problems. For instance, the principle that the "polluter pays" and the notion of "trade in services" are just two examples of conventional wisdom that began life at the OECD (see Long 2000; Cohn 2002). However, normative governance not only refers to the development and diffusion of shared ideas but also to the behaviour of the members. Martha Finnemore and Kathryn Sikkink (1998, 891) understand norms as "standard(s) of appropriate behaviour for actors with a given identity." In other words, if the foregoing argument that an OECD identity persists, there are certain standards of behaviour befitting OECD members. At the OECD, the expectation is that once an agreed policy position or prescription has been attained members will adjust their policies in accordance with the prevailing view. Failure to do so is "inappropriate" behaviour that will damage the reputation of the recalcitrant member and the officials representing them. The knowledge that the extent of their compliance will be measured via the OECD's peer review process creates strong moral imperatives for national officials to implement recommendations agreed with their peers (Pagani 2002).

Opinion is divided about the effectiveness of these "soft" mechanisms of governance at the national level. In their early work on transgovernmental relations Robert Keohane and Joseph Nye (1974, 45) surmised that these "regularized patterns of policy coordination can therefore create attitudes and relationships that will at least marginally change policy or affect its implementation." In his work on the OECD's Environment Directorate, Markku Lehtonen (2005) discovered that many governments felt compelled to respond publicly to the conclusions of the OECD's environmental performance reviews. Likewise, in 2006, the Belgian treasury deployed the secretariat's dissection of aging societies to overcome opposition to the reform of the country's welfare state (Kanter 2006). Personal amities developed through recurrent OECD meetings can help to prevent or defuse potentially explosive international situations. One of the first inquiries into the OECD suggested officials become implanted with "the habit of cooperation" routinely taking the positions of their counterparts abroad into account when formulating policies in their national capital (Palmer and Lambert 1968). Equally, private OECD meetings afford officials an opportunity to explain occasions where national policies depart from a promised position. This "informed divergence" (Slaughter 2004, 171–172) can prevent states from resorting to a public slanging match. Nonetheless, while recognizing the OECD may apply a "subtle discipline" (Bayne 2000, 48) over the course of global governance there are grounds to doubt the extent of the OECD's influence on policy worldwide (Armingeon and Beyeler 2004). Despite Bill Long's (2000, 124) claim that the OECD is "in the centre of international efforts to define environmental goals, strategies and programme priorities for governments," his book on the OECD's environmental work tenders few concrete examples of where this translated into concrete policy changes at the national level. Similarly, despite noting the promise of the OECD's environmental performance reviews, Lehtonen (2005) contends there are strict limits on their influence. National debates stoked by OECD interventions tend to be ephemeral and domestic policy changes were the exception rather than the rule. A similar picture emerges on the economic plain. Ougaard (1999, 16) suggests there is "no foundation in the empirical record examined here for claims that OECD peer reviews exert decisive influence on members' policies," particularly among more prominent members. Larger and more powerful states, with their lavish bureaucracies, are better equipped to repudiate OECD peer reviews. In addition, there is some evidence of powerful states trying to manipulate the peer review process directly. One draft report from the Economic and Development Review Committee so angered British prime minister Margaret Thatcher that she petitioned the secretary general to replace the director of the economic division (then a British citizen). The secretary general rebuffed the request but the tone of the document was diluted as a consequence (Guilmette 2007).

Elsewhere it has been suggested that the confluence of cognitive, legal, and normative aspects of OECD governance gives rise to a fourth dimension of OECD governance, which for want of a better term, can be labelled palliative governance (Woodward 2007b, 2007a). Palliative governance is a catch-all phrase that encompasses the sum of the many ways in which the

OECD greases the wheels of national and international policy making. Of particular salience to this chapter are the various "support services" the OECD supplies to other international institutions (Woodward 2004). The expertise and ingenuity of the OECD secretariat and the smaller, more homogeneous OECD membership leave it ideally placed to resolve impasses facing its counterpart international organisations. Cohn (1993), for example, documents how the OECD acted as a "prenegotiating forum," easing the path of multilateral trade talks from the 1960s to the 1990s (see also Blair 1993). By producing studies and reports, furnishing them with reliable statistics and new diagnostic tools, and allowing the OECD Trade Committee to be used as a venue for candid discussions between sporadic meetings of the General Agreement on Tariffs and Trade (GATT), the OECD helped states to conquer ostensibly irreconcilable conflicts such as those over agricultural subsidies during the Uruguay Round (Shelp 1986). The OECD has lent its acumen to the preparations and follow-up activities of a string of international conferences and institutions. The aforementioned polluter-pays principle was the bedrock of the 1972 declaration by the UN Conference on the Human Environment and the 1992 Rio Declaration on Development and the Environment. Later, the 1987 Vienna Convention for the Protection of the Ozone Layer, the 1989 Montreal Protocol, and the 1989 Basel Convention on the Control of Transboundary Movements of Hazardous Wastes and their Disposal drew heavily on research undertaken by the OECD. All this is neatly encapsulated by Nicholas Bayne (1987, 30), the UK's ambassador to the OECD from 1985 to 1988, who asserted that the OECD is the "Cinderella among international organizations ... it does not always go to the balls like its grander sister organizations, though it often runs up their dresses and sometimes clears up the mess after the party." No fewer than 72 international organizations currently hold observer status at the OECD and multilateral economic institutions are intimately involved in various OECD committees. Arguably, in the early 21st century, the OECD's most important relationships are now with the G7/8 family.

From Hell to Heiligendamm—The Changing Nature of OECD–G7/8 Relations

Since the G7/8 system materialized in the 1970s, relations with the OECD have evolved from mutual suspicion to mutual dependence. Ambiguities in the OECD Convention have long dogged the OECD. On the one hand, the convention confers clear responsibility upon the OECD to promote sustainable economic growth and development, maximize employment and living standards, and nurture the global trading regime. The pursuit of such blanket goals has necessitated the OECD's entanglement with a host of social and economic issues, and its adroit colonization of new policy domains has unquestionably contributed to its resilience and longevity. On the other hand, the convention allocates the OECD responsibilities in areas that overlap with other, often more powerful, agencies of governance capable of imitating or sequestrating its functions. Initially the OECD "functioned steadily" (Putnam and Bayne 1987, 25) in conjunction with bodies such as the IMF, World Bank, and the GATT. By the 1970s, however, these institutions were trespassing on the OECD's customary terrain, imperilling its place in the architecture of global governance. Alterations to the IMF's Articles of Agreement, after Bretton Woods' denouement curtailed the OECD's economic surveillance duties (Pauly 1992), while the World Bank usurped "much of the necessary research, coordination, setting of standards, goals etc." that the OECD's Development Assistance Committee undertook in the 1960s (Camps 1975, 29). The OECD continued to enjoy a healthy relationship with the GATT but it was overshadowed by the renaissance of European integration. The expansion of the European Economic Community and its penchant for free markets and democracy made it a serious regional and ideational competitor for the OECD. Against this background, the emergence of the G7 as a forum where leading OECD members could meet to discuss and make commitments on a variety of economic matters caused some consternation in Paris.

This led, in the initial stages, to an uneasy if peaceful coexistence between the OECD and G7. The G7 leaders' summit was scheduled so that the deliberations of the annual OECD ministerial council meeting could feed into it, and from 1977 to 1980 the OECD's Economic Policy Committee prepared the macroeconomic segment of the G7 agenda. This arrangement expired when the attitudes of the G7 states, particularly the United States and the United Kingdom, began to diverge from those prevailing in the OECD secretariat. Throughout the 1970s there were signs of the secretariat challenging key precepts of the Keynesian consensus (Marcussen 2001; Ougaard 2004). Nevertheless, U.S. president Ronald Reagan and British prime minister Margaret Thatcher perceived it as "too Keynesian" for the brave new world of monetarism they sought to advance (Putnam and Bayne 1987, 16) and the IMF assumed responsibility for preparations for the G7 summit. The band of ministerial groupings that emerged to relieve pressure on the crowded summit timetable further marginalized the OECD. The quadrilateral group of trade ministers (the quad) and the finance ministers and central bank governors (who began meeting annually in 1998 as the G20) were direct competitors for the OECD's Trade Committee and the vaunted WP3. Whereas in the 1960s and early 1970s, WP3 was a vital location for the discussion and management of balance of payments disequilibria (Russell 1973), in the 1980s headline deals such as the Plaza Accord (1985) and the Louvre Accord (1987) were negotiated by the finance ministers and central bank governors, relegating the WP3 to the periphery (Funabashi 1988; Krugman 1991).

Two related factors led to a rapprochement between the G7 and the OECD. First, after the OECD secretariat annulled its marriage with Keynesianism and eloped with a new monetarist mistress, its economic medicines became more palatable to the G7. Second, economic elites downgraded the importance of international cooperation in securing sustained non-inflationary growth and instead placed greater emphasis on countries pursuing the correct domestic policies, in other words encouraging states to "get the fundamentals right." The G7's sorties into macroeconomic policy coordination achieved some success but their concise and spasmodic political get-togethers were unqualified to wrestle with the complexities of the domestic policies on which they were increasingly fixated. In contrast, subjects such as trade, labour market policy, investment, competition policy, agriculture, migration, urban affairs, and energy had been studied by the OECD for up to a quarter of a century and successful G7 deliberations increasing came to rely on preparatory work by the OECD secretariat and prior discussions in OECD committees. Formal acknowledgement of this came in the communiqué of the 1990 G7 Summit in Houston, which "welcome[d] the major contributions of the Organisation for Economic Co-operation and Development (OECD) in identifying structural policy challenges and options" and "encourage[d] the OECD to strengthen its surveillance and review procedures, and to find ways of making its work operationally more effective" (G7 1990). Although it is a crude measure, communiqués released following G7 meetings confirm the trend (see Table 11-2). The 37 references to the work of the OECD in G7 communiqués in the third summit cycle (1989–95) exceeds the 26 references in the first two cycles (1975–81, 1982–88) together. There were also qualitative changes to OECD–G7/8 acquaintances. In the first two cycles allusions to the OECD were primarily reactive, endorsing existing OECD achievements or swearing to continue cooperating in the OECD. In contrast, in the third cycle, the G7/8 was more proactive acting as the impulse for fresh OECD projects

Table 11-2

References to the OECD in G7/8 Communiqués, 1997–2002

	1st cycle (1975–81)	2nd cycle (1982–88)	3rd cycle (1989–95)	4th cycle (1996–2002)
Reference to OECD work	0	0	6	62
Endorsement of OECD work	7	8	16	64
Endorse and ask for increased OECD effort	0	1	6	15
Urge OECD to act	0	0	7	23
Pledge to cooperate in OECD	5	5	2	20
Total	12	14	37	184

on six occasions and coaxing additional efforts from the organization on a further seven. The allure of structural issues perpetuated in the fourth (1996–2002) and fifth (2002–2009) cycles with the G7/8 catalyzing OECD work on aid untying, bribery, investment, aging, food safety, biotechnology, e-commerce, and online security. Citations of the OECD increased five-fold in G7 communiqués issued in the fourth cycle fuelling earlier speculation about the possibility of exploiting the organization as a permanent G7 secretariat (de Guttry 1994; Ikenberry 1993).

The tightening associations between the G7/8 and OECD are also reflected in institutional arrangements. Senior OECD officials liaise intermittently with the sherpas and sous sherpas to the summit meeting and for many years the lead sherpa has briefed the OECD Council about summit preparations. Since 1999, one of the OECD deputy secretary generals has coordinated the work between the G8 and OECD and, in 2007, the OECD secretary general was for the first time invited to participate in the summit.

Bonds between the OECD and G7 were fortified following the announcement at the Heiligendamm Summit in 2007 of "a new form of specific cooperation with major emerging economies … to discuss substantive topics in a comprehensive follow-up process with the aim of reaching tangible results in two years" and selected "the OECD to provide a platform for this new dialogue process" (G8 2007). The communiqué goes on to identify four areas for the dialogue:

- promoting and protecting innovation,
- enhancing freedom of investment through an open investment environment including strengthening corporate social responsibility principles,

- defining common responsibilities for development with special regard to Africa,
- sharing knowledge for improving energy efficiency and technology cooperation with the aim to contribute to reducing CO2 [carbon dioxide] emissions. (G8 2007)

In July 2007, OECD countries approved the creation of the Heiligendamm Dialogue Process Support Unit within the office of the secretary general. Headed by Ulrich Benterbusch, formerly Germany's sous sherpa to the G8, the unit has four policy analysts, one assigned to a working group concerned with an individual aspect of the Heiligendamm dialogue. The unit's function is to prepare the meetings of the working groups and to provide the research expertise to undergird these gatherings. It is too early to state categorically that the HP marks another qualitative shift in the OECD–G7/8 relationship. Nevertheless, it is novel because of the breadth of the issues the G8 simultaneously asked the OECD to investigate and extent of the resources being used to support the G8 system. Closer ties with the G8 seemed indispensable if the OECD was to prove its continued relevance.

Why the OECD?

Despite its burgeoning connections with the G8, at first glance the OECD seems a puzzling choice of institution. Of the Outreach Five (O5) countries only Mexico is a member of the OECD (the other countries are Brazil, China, India, and South Africa). If the HP is an attempt to bolster the G8's dwindling legitimacy by improving the representation of groups from the global South, it seems strange to conduct the process through the OECD, which has also been denounced for its lack of legitimacy as a global standard setter (Sanders 2002) and is widely, if inaccurately, perceived as the rich country's club. The choice of the OECD rests on five interrelated factors. First, the OECD is the only single international organization that encompassed all of the issues in the HP. As James Salzman (2000, 777) has argued, the OECD is a "restricted forum for virtually unrestricted topics" and its extensive cross-disciplinary research leaves it ideally placed to understand how different policy domains interact and synchronize. The second factor relates to the cognitive and normative aspects of OECD governance. Like the OECD, the G8 system relies overwhelmingly on soft mechanisms of governance to pressure governments into action. Deeper participation in a body such as the OECD could have important socialization effects for the O5 countries exposing them, and possibly making them more amenable, to the norms of behaviour in the OECD–G7/8 world. Third, and related, even before the conception of the HP, the OECD was already drawing the O5 members into its ambit. In addition to Mexico's membership, in the last two decades the OECD has evolved from an organization that talks about non-members to an institution that talks to them (Wolfe 2008). One recent development, heralded by the 2007 ministerial council meeting, is the "enhanced engagement programs" with Brazil, China, India, Indonesia, and South Africa (OECD 2007a). Programs are tailored to different countries but involve participation in OECD committees and the various peer review processes of the organization, most notably economic surveys, adherence to OECD instruments, absorption into the statistical reporting systems, and contributing to the economic sessions of OECD council meetings (OECD 2007a). Fourth, the OECD's reputation for palliative governance, especially providing a forum to pave the way for agreements and progress elsewhere, is vital. The privacy afforded by the OECD may lead to convergence in official positions or may even enable deals to be brokered within and between the OECD and the O5 countries that would not be possible in the glare of international publicity. Finally, the OECD has had a perennial struggle to define its role and most commentators, not least those within the OECD, concur that this has been exacerbated in the post–Cold War era by the plethora of competing mechanisms of global governance (OECD 1997; Julin 2003; Marcussen 2004; Woodward 2004). The most recent secretaries general have ruminated about consecrating the OECD's relationship with the G8 as a way of entrenching its position in the global governance architecture (see, for example, Johnston 2005). The HP is a logical step in this direction and its location in the OECD owes much to the personal entrepreneurship of Angel Gurría, the organization's current Mexican secretary general.

In terms of scope, it is difficult to conceive of an organization that could substitute for the OECD in the HP. How far the other purported benefits of the process develop is more uncertain. In the first instance, the attitudes of the various parties involved in the HP may limit the extent of socialization. The chapters on China (see Chapter 4) and Brazil (see Chapter 6) reveal serious misgivings amongst the O5 about the OECD, a predominantly northern institution, as the setting for the Heiligendamm dialogue. The main fears are that cozying up to the OECD might damage nascent South–South relations or that this choice reflects a devious attempt by northern states to indoctrinate leading non-OECD countries rather than engage in genuine dialogue. The statements emanating from prominent OECD members suggest these concerns are well founded. Writing in the

OECD Observer Matei Hoffman (2007), Germany's ambassador to the OECD, stated with regard to the HP that:

> we must drive home the message that market-oriented rules, together with a social concept of globalisation and a sustainable approach to resource management, are preconditions for global development and prosperity. It is in this context that we wish to come to an understanding with our partners on the core challenges facing the global economy.

Without the prospect of genuine dialogue, O5 countries may not send their top officials to these meetings, preferring instead to concentrate their resources elsewhere. The support unit's administrative detachment from the rest of the OECD may surmount this in time (see Chapter 10) but the project's two-year duration may be too abbreviated for this purpose. A second factor that may limit the socialization of non-OECD O5 countries is an absence of incentives. The successful socialization of the new members that joined in the 1990s rested on their desire to become OECD members. Some O5 countries, noticeably China (see Chapter 4) and India (see Chapter 5), are reticent to embrace OECD membership, rendering them less susceptible to persuasion and adoption of the organization's model or working practices.

A third factor is the ambiguity surrounding, and potential schisms between, the HP and the OECD's program of enhanced engagement. The enhanced engagement program predates the HP and differs in terms of timescale, scope, and teleology. Enhanced engagement is part of the OECD's broader enlargement and outreach strategy (see OECD 2004a). It is an open-ended program that involves selected non-members in virtually all of the OECD's policy-making and policy-reviewing activities and envisages the possibility of participant countries eventually joining the organization (OECD 2007b). In contrast, the HP has a specified lifespan, concentrates on four specific policy domains, and makes no mention of future membership. Theoretically, cross-contamination between the two processes could yield benefits with the links and lessons forged under one dialogue spilling over into the other. In practice, the picture is less straightforward. Whereas Mexico is already an OECD member and South Africa and Brazil are extensively implicated in its committees (see Table 11-3) and have shown some enthusiasm for eventual membership, China and India are cooler on the idea. For the former two countries, overlaps between the projects might be viewed favourably helping to maintain the momentum toward membership. Given their reservations about the OECD, the latter two will wish the tracks to remain parallel. The other complication is the incongruous posi-

Table 11-3
Membership and Observership in OECD Committees
of Selected Non-Members, March 2008

	Member	Observer	Total
Russian Federation	9	73	82
South Africa	16	40	56
Brazil	12	43	55
China	2	32	34
India	2	26	28
Indonesia	2	3	5
ASEAN	0	0	0

tion of Indonesia, a leading member of the Association of Southeast Asian Nations (ASEAN) and the only country partaking of the OECD's enhanced engagement package but not of the HP. While this factor lends weight to the argument that the two processes are and will be kept separate, it raises questions about why Indonesia was excluded from the HP, whether it feels slighted, and what bearing this will have on the dialogue.

Disquiet and fissures among OECD members could also hinder the socialization process. It is clear that there is little agreement among the G7/8 (the larger OECD members) about precisely how to engage with the O5 or what the ultimate outcome of any engagement should be (see chapters 4 and 10). If the OECD was picked because of its capacity to socialize non-members, the thornier problem of what the O5 countries are being socialized into appears unresolved. Moreover, although it builds on precedents and initiatives with non-members from previous G7/8 summits, the HP is an avowedly German initiative. The bulk of the financial support for HP has come from Berlin but, in order to be effective, it will likely require more than the symbolic financial contributions so far made by Japan and Italy. In the longer term, the support of middle-ranking G7/OECD powers is also questionable. As Thomas Fues and Julia Leininger make clear in Chapter 10, the HP reflects German attempts to steer a middle course that concurrently incorporates emerging powers into the architecture of global governance but maintains Germany's place at the top table. A successful HP could be a pyrrhic victory for Germany because, despite the reticence of China and India, it would make the accession of O5 countries to the OECD more likely, dissipating Germany's influence in the organization.

Although they approved the creation of the HP support unit, the 23 non-G8 OECD countries are also likely to have concerns about the impact of this development. Privately, many smaller OECD members complain that the growing ascendancy of the G7/8 has squeezed their influence in the organization and they are far from enamoured with the fresh cabal of large influential non-members and prospective new members. In particular, there is a sense that the OECD's obsession with reaching out to and cooperating with non-members is at the cost of cooperation among OECD members. The smaller members are weak in the sense that collectively they account for less than a quarter of the OECD's main budget and less than half of the OECD's committee chairs. Nevertheless, they could make the OECD's life awkward elsewhere. With the OECD working by consensus, something albeit slightly weakened by changes to its internal governance structure in 2006 (see OECD 2006), small countries can impede the organization's work. Furthermore, article 16 gives members an effective veto over new members of the organization. While this may not necessarily impact on the HP it may impede the organization's wider enlargement strategy.

Finally, whether the HP will bolster the OECD's place in the architecture of global governance is open to debate. There are serious obstacles to the OECD's emergence as a secretariat to the G8. With occasional exceptions, the G7/8 has consistently repudiated the notion of a permanent secretariat, not least because part of the rationale for the G8's creation was to conquer the bureaucratization of international diplomacy. Likewise, many OECD officials are concerned about the impact such a move would have on their operational independence and, as before, smaller states agonize about their marginalization within the organization (Kanter 2005). The Heiligendamm vignette reflects the wider contradictions besieging the OECD's enlargement and outreach strategy. The OECD aims to restore its legitimacy by seeking new alliances with powerful states and civil society voices lying beyond its existing membership. The problem is that adding these voices will coincidentally undermine its legitimacy of the various dimensions of OECD governance. Cognitive governance will be impaired by diluting or dramatically altering the OECD's identity. Normative and legal governance will be weakened by the addition of those with drastically different world views or who do not respond to softer mechanisms of governance. Finally, palliative governance might be harmed because having to take more viewpoints into account may render the OECD as cumbersome as some of the more inclusive international organizations. In other words, while a wider membership might confer legitimacy on

OECD directives, it makes it less likely that such compacts will be realized in the first place.

Conclusion

Since the mid-1980s the paths of the G7/8 and the OECD have steadily converged. Today, the G7/8 structure relies heavily on the research and analysis of the OECD while the OECD's associations with the G7/8 fortify its place in the international political system. This chapter has argued that the HP is the latest act in the G7/8–OECD saga. The choice of the OECD to house the HP support unit reflects the diversity of the subjects studied by the OECD, its ability to socialize states into its behavioural norms, its track record for pursuing informal dialogue in support of work in other organizations, its growing linkages with powerful non-member states, and the beneficial spinoffs to the OECD from closer ties with the G7/8 system. With the dialogue half way through its life cycle, it is too early to provide a definitive statement of its impact on the relationship between the OECD and the G7/8 system. Nevertheless, this chapter suggests that the remuneration from this process may not be as great as many presume. The various parties to the HP have expressed qualms about the choice of the OECD as a venue for the dialogue. The O5 countries are apprehensive that the choice of the OECD will lead to diatribe rather than dialogue, but smaller OECD countries fret about being marginalized within an institution that previously enabled them to project their power on the global stage. Whether O5 countries can be socialized into the G7/8–OECD model will depend as much on their motivation as that of the OECD. There is little appetite among certain O5 countries for OECD membership, the traditional carrot dangled in front of non-member states, and there are questions about how far the O5 will benefit from moving toward the organization's model. Additionally, the possibilities remain that the HP will prove incompatible with, or at least impair, the OECD's wider enlargement and outreach strategy. Finally, and again with the broader OECD picture in mind, one must query what impact this will have on the OECD. The idea being mooted in some quarters that the HP marks the first step toward the OECD becoming the G7/8 secretariat are far-fetched. Equally, the breadth and intensity of the issues involved could be the beginning of a new epoch in the OECD–G8 relationship. The HP brings into sharp relief one of the problem besetting the OECD since its inception, namely how to reconcile the exclusivity of its membership with the legitimacy of its actions. The OECD's present strategy may well enhance the legitimacy of its actions through welcoming new members and closer relationships with systemically important players but paradoxically the expanding membership and more eclectic set of non-member relations may prejudice its ability to reach the consensus upon which such actions depend.

References

Armingeon, Klaus and Michelle Beyeler (2004). *The OECD and European Welfare States.* Cheltenham: Edward Elgar.

Aubrey, F. (1967). *Atlantic Economic Cooperation: The Case of the OECD.* New York: Frederick A. Praeger.

Bayne, Nicholas (1987). "Making Sense of Western Economic Policies: The Role of the OECD." *World Today* 43(2): 27–30.

Bayne, Nicholas (2000). *Hanging In There: The G7 and G8 Summit in Maturity and Renewal.* Aldershot: Ashgate.

Blair, David J. (1993). *Trade Negotiations in the OECD: Structures, Institutions, and States.* London: Kegan Paul.

Busch, Per-Olaf (2006). "The OECD Environment Directorate: The Art of Persuasion and Its Limitations." Working Paper No. 20, October. Amsterdam: Global Governance Project.

Camps, Miriam (1975). *"First World" Relationships: The Role of the OECD.* Paris: Atlantic Institute for International Affairs.

Cohn, Theodore H. (1993). "The Changing Role of the United States in the Global Agricultural Trade Regime." In *World Agriculture and the GATT*, edited by W.P. Avery, 17–38. Boulder, CO: Lynne Rienner.

Cohn, Theodore H. (2002). *Governing Global Trade: International Institutions in Conflict and Convergence.* Aldershot: Ashgate.

de Guttry, Andrea (1994). "The Institutional Configuration of the G7 in the New International Scenario." *International Spectator* 29(2): 67–79. <www.g8.utoronto.ca/scholar/guttry1994> (May 2008).

Dostal, Jörg Michael (2004). "Campaigning on Expertise: How the OECD Framed EU Welfare and Labour Market Policies—and Why Success Could Trigger Failure." *Journal of European Public Policy* 11(3): 440–460.

Finnemore, Martha and Kathryn Sikkink (1998). "International Norm Dynamics and Political Change." *International Organization* 52(4): 887–917.

Funabashi, Yoichi (1988). *Managing the Dollar: From the Plaza to the Louvre.* Washington DC: Institute for International Economics.

G7 (1990). "Houston Economic Declaration." 11 July, Houston. <www.g8.utoronto.ca/summit/1990houston/declaration.html> (May 2008).

G8 (2007). "Growth and Responsibility in the World Economy." 7 June, Heiligendamm. <www.g8.utoronto.ca/summit/2007heiligendamm/g8-2007-economy.html> (May 2008).

Gilpin, Robert (2000). *The Challenge of Global Capitalism: The World Economy in the 21st Century*. Princeton: Princeton University Press.

Guilmette, Jean-H. (2007). *The Power of Peer Learning: Networks and Development Cooperation*. Ottawa: Academic Foundation/International Development Research Centre <www.idrc.ca/en/ev-110388-201-1-DO_TOPIC.html> (May 2008).

Henderson, David (1993). "The Role of the OECD in Liberalising Trade and Capital Flows." *World Economy* 19(1): 11–27.

Hoffmann, Matei (2007). "Building Global Partnerships." *OECD Observer*, May. <www.oecdobserver.org/news/fullstory.php/aid/2203/Building_global_partnerships.html> (May 2008).

Hutton, Will (2002). *The World We're In*. London: Little Brown.

Ikenberry, G. John (1993). "Salvaging the G7." *Foreign Affairs* 72 (Spring): 132–139.

Jakobi, A. and K. Martens (2009). *The OECD: International Incentives for National Policymaking*. Basingstoke: Palgrave. Forthcoming.

Johnston, Don (2005). "Look No Further for a Home for Global Bodies." *Financial Times*, 28 November, 13.

Julin, Jorma (2003). "The OECD: Securing the Future." *OECD Observer*, 48–51. <www.oecdobserver.org/news/fullstory.php/aid/1197/The_OECD:_Securing_the_future.html> (May 2008).

Kanter, James (2005). "Mexican Plans to Raise OECD's Low Profile." *International Herald Tribune*, 30 November.

Kanter, James (2006). "When a Club of Winners Loses Its Way." *International Herald Tribune*, 30 November.

Keohane, Robert O. and Joseph S. Nye (1974). "Transgovernmental Relations and International Organizations." *World Politics* 27(1): 39–61.

Kirton, John J. (1999). "Explaining G8 Effectiveness." In *The G8's Role in the New Millennium*, edited by M.R. Hodges, J.J. Kirton, and J.P. Daniels, 45–68. Aldershot: Ashgate.

Krugman, Paul (1991). *Has the Adjustment Process Worked?* Washington DC: Institute for International Economics.

Lehtonen, Markku (2005). "OECD Environmental Performance Review Programme: Accountability (f)or Learning." *Evaluation* 11(2): 169–188.

Long, Bill L. (2000). *International Environmental Issues and the OECD, 1950–2000*. Paris: Organisation for Economic Co-operation and Development.

Mahon, Rianne and Stephen McBride (2008). *The OECD and Global Governance*. Vancouver: University of British Columbia Press.

Marcussen, Martin (2001). "The OECD in Search of a Role: Playing the Idea Game." Paper presented to the ECPR, 6–11 April. Grenoble: European Consortium for Political Research.

Marcussen, Martin (2004). "OECD Governance through Soft Law." In *Soft Law in Governance and Regulation: An Interdisciplinary Analysis*, edited by U. Morth, 103–126. Cheltenham: Edward Elgar.

"OECD Fails to Put Its Own House in Order." (2002). *Financial Times*, 28 May, 9.

Organisation for Economic Co-operation and Development (1960). *Convention on the Organization for Economic Cooperation and Development*. Paris. <www.oecd .org/document/7/0,3343,en_2649_34483_1915847_1_1_1_1,00.html> (May 2008).

Organisation for Economic Co-operation and Development (1997). "The OECD: Challenges and Strategic Objectives 1997." Note by the Secretary General, C(97) 180. Paris.

Organisation for Economic Co-operation and Development (2004a). "A Strategy for Enlargement and Outreach." Report by the Chair of the Heads of Delegation Working Group on the Enlargement Strategy. Paris. <www.oecd.org/dataoecd/ 24/15/37434513.pdf> (May 2008).

Organisation for Economic Co-operation and Development (2004b). *Getting to Grips with Globalisation: The OECD in a Changing World*. Paris. <www.oecd.org/ dataoecd/43/23/31499355.pdf> (May 2008).

Organisation for Economic Co-operation and Development (2005). *Annual Report 2005*. Paris. <www.oecd.org/dataoecd/34/6/34711139.pdf> (May 2008).

Organisation for Economic Co-operation and Development (2006). "Resolution of the Council on a New Governance Structure for the Organisation." C(2006)78/ FINAL, 24 May. Paris. <www.olis.oecd.org/olis/2006doc.nsf/LinkTo/NT00000 FAE/$FILE/JT03209473.PDF> (May 2008).

Organisation for Economic Co-operation and Development (2007a). "OECD Council Resolution on Enlargement and Enhanced Engagement." Paris. <www.oecd .org/document/7/0,3343,en_2649_34487_38604487_1_1_1_1,00.html> (May 2008).

Organisation for Economic Co-operation and Development (2007b). "Innovation: Advancing the OECD Agenda for Growth and Equity." Chair's Summary of the OECD Council at Ministerial Level,w 15–16 May, Paris. <www.oecd.org/ document/22/0,3343,en_2649_201185_38604566_1_1_1_1,00.html> (May 2008).

Organisation for Economic Co-operation and Development (2008). *Instruments of the OECD by Subject*. Paris. <www.olis.oecd.org/horizontal/oecdacts.nsf/ subject?openview&count=1000> (May 2008).

Ougaard, Morten (1999). "The OECD in the Global Polity." Paper prepared for the research prroject "Globalisation, Statehood, and World Order," supported by the Danish Social Science Research Council. Coventry.

Ougaard, Morten (2004). *Political Globalization: State, Power, and Social Forces*. Basingstoke: Palgrave.

Pagani, Fabrizio (2002). *Peer Review: A Tool for Co-operation and Change*. Paris: Organisation for Economic Co-operation and Development <www.oecd.org/ LongAbstract/0,3425,en_2649_34483_1955278_119835_1_1_1,00.html> (May 2008).

Palmer, Michael and John Lambert, eds. (1968). *European Unity: A Survey of the European Institutions*. London: George Allen and Unwin.

Pauly, Louis W. (1992). "The Political Foundations of Multilateral Economic Surveillance." *International Journal* 47(2): 293–327.

Porter, Tony and Michael Webb (2008). "The Role of the OECD in the Orchestration of Global Knowledge Networks." In *The OECD and Transnational Governance*, edited by R. Mahon and S. McBride. Vancouver: University of British Columbia Press.

Putnam, Robert and Nicholas Bayne (1987). *Hanging Together: Co-operation and Conflict in the Seven-Power Summit*. 2nd ed. London: Sage Publications.

Russell, Robert W. (1973). "Transgovernmental Interaction in the International Monetary System, 1960–1972." *International Organization* 27(4): 431–464.

Salzman, James (2000). "Labor Rights, Globalization, and Institutions: The Role and Influence of the Organisation for Economic Co-operation and Development." *Michigan Journal of International Law* 21: 769–848.

Sanders, Ronald (2002). "The Fight Against Fiscal Colonialism: The OECD and Small Jurisdictions." *The Round Table* 365(1): 325–348.

Sharman, Jason (2005). *Havens in a Storm: The Struggle for Global Tax Regulation*. Ithaca: Cornell University Press.

Shelp, Ronald (1986). "Trade in Services." *Foreign Policy* (65): 64–83.

Slaughter, Anne-Marie (2004). *A New World Order*. Princeton: Princeton University Press.

Wolfe, Robert (2008). "From Reconstructing Europe to Constructing Globalization: The OECD in Historical Perspective." In *The OECD and Global Governance*, edited by R. Mahon and S. McBride. Vancouver: University of British Columbia Press.

Woodward, Richard (2004). "The Organisation for Economic Cooperation and Development." *New Political Economy* 9(1): 113–124.

Woodward, Richard (2007a). "The Organisation for Economic Cooperation and Development: Meeting the Challenges of the 21st Century?" In *Neo-Liberalism, State Power, and Global Governance*, edited by S. Lee and S. McBride, 231–244. Dordrecht: Springer.

Woodward, Richard (2007b). "Global Governance and the Organisation for Economic Co-operation and Development." In *Global Governance and Japan: The Institutional Architecture*, edited by G. Hook and H. Dobson, 59–75. Abingdon: Routledge.

Woodward, Richard (2008). *The Organisation for Economic Co-operation and Development*. London: Routledge.

12

Russia and the Evolution of the Heiligendamm Process

Victoria V. Panova

The G7, and later the G8, has gone through a plethora of ups and downs since it began in 1975. The very idea of the leaders of the most powerful industrially developed and rich countries meeting on their own to discuss whatever issues they deemed important looked suspicious to the rest of the world from the start, and was frequently seen as yet another conspiracy of the strongest to retain their power and not allow any others to join in on the "joy ride."

Over the next three decades, the initial concept of shared responsibility that developed into the Trilateral Commission and idea of like-minded leaders mending their own fences and building western solidarity in response to the various crises of the mid 1970s developed into a demand for a new form of global governance and the realization that in order to make progress they would have to adjust to present-day realities.

The first of such adjustments was the gradual inclusion of Russia into the club, where cooperation (or, rather, supervision at the beginning) started in the form of outreach sessions primarily with the Soviet Union, and then its successor, the Russian Federation.[1]

The last decade of the 20th century was very important in terms of western alliances and institutions remodelling themselves in order to adapt and gain the most out of the end of the Cold War and the demise of the socialist bloc and the Soviet Union. Thus, to keep important global issues on the agenda, along with the reconceptualization of the North Atlantic Treaty Organization (NATO), and to expand into the newly created "vacuums of power," the G7 also had to adapt to the situation, and thus sent dual messages to what remained of the West's former adversary, which had now become Russia.[2] The first message was rather nasty: "You lost, so now we will make the rules and you must accept—no more superpower status; no more toys in the form of security, spheres of influence or independent decisions, at least none without preliminary consultations." But thanks to lessons from history, namely from the experience with Germany after World War One, or any other big, temporarily weak state, there was another pacifying message—nobody wanted to tease the Russian bear too much, so now came "carrots" in the form of suggested (but gradual, so the bear would remember its place) membership into the elite G7 club, with support for joining other international institutions, receiving economic aid, and requesting credit lines from international financial institutions (IFIs)—all coming as worthy substitutes for the lost superpower status.

Nevertheless the purpose of this chapter is not to talk about the motives behind Russia's inclusion. After the initial period of turbulence and the "redistribution" of the former Soviet territories in the 1990s, attention within the G7/G8 shifted back to the global challenges. Here geopolitics finally got a clear view of the necessity of managing global economic development, taking into account grand shifts in economic and financial powers from the countries of the "Golden Billion" to the stronger stance of selected developing countries. If in the 1970s, the G7's response to the demands of New International Economic Order—as a way of strengthening bloc solidarity—was successful, at the dawn of the 21st century, a new challenge became clear.

In addition to the shift in the global distribution of wealth, the G7—accompanied by Russia, which, in the 1990s, was weak—overstrained its own capacities and did not have enough resources to deal with the rising problems of poverty, climate change, terrorism and drug trafficking.

Another issue of concern was that, notwithstanding its efforts in the 1990s, the G7 did not manage to incorporate the notion of humanitarian intervention into the framework of universally recognized international law, primarily due to opposition from much of the world community. This failure led to the need for a more comprehensive recognition of the right of developing countries to their own ways and perceptions of managing current problems (for example, limiting the ability of the United States to intervene with its Monroe doctrine in its "backyard," which led to worsened relations with a number of big Latin American countries—including Brazil, which had even worked out a military plan with the U.S. as a potential adversary).

This chapter discusses Russia's engagement in the possible reformulation of G8-centred global governance into the G8+ by means of the Heiligendamm

Process (HP), initiated at the 2008 Heiligendamm Summit. It first considers Russia as a G8 member, reviewing some of its actions, participation in, and contribution to G8 activities. Then the chapter argues that Russia has unique difficulties in the philosophical and geopolitical definitions of its place within the international structure, thus providing for a variety of visions on necessary actions and strategies for the Russian political establishment and civil society. Despite Russia's preferred western affiliation, its geo-economic and sociopolitical development at the beginning of the 21st century nevertheless predetermine several common features with the Outreach Five (O5) bloc of Brazil, China, India, Mexico, and South Africa. This commonality, along with the slow development of the HP, in turn allows for preferred bilateral relationships with the O5 countries, rather than a joint G8 position. So the third part of this chapter will briefly consider the current state of Russian bilateral relations with each of O5 countries. The chapter will end with a consideration of the structure of the HP and its first conceptual achievements, with further brief outline of its place within the G8.

From Within or From Outside

Being the latest to join the G8, and still retaining its specificity, Russia remains uncertain about where it belongs most—in the West and the G8, which seemed to be the obvious choice of the Russian elite in the 1990s, or within the community of emerging economies often referred to as the B(R)ICSAM—which includes Russia along with the O5 members. For example, with regard to energy, the Russian national oil company Gazprom belongs with the New Seven Sisters as opposed to the old ones.[3] It is very important first to specify Russia's present-day status and perceptions within the G8 before going further to identify Russian participation and outlook on the Heiligendamm process.

The answer to the question of how much Russia belongs to the G8 is double-sided. On one side, the 2002 Kananaskis Summit could be taken as the first year of recognizing Russia as a full-fledged member.[4] Russia was thus perceived as an equal partner at the highest leadership level, although debates over its eligibility for membership in the elite club continued within the political opposition of the G7 governments and in the media and intellectual circles, who enjoyed playing with the idea that Russia (along with other potential adversaries such as, most frequently, China or emerging developing countries as a whole) continued to be on the other side of the barricades. For these observers, Russia remained a potential major threat and had to be "excluded from the G8" and shown its true place on the world arena.[5]

Meanwhile, on the other side, at the leaders' level, with Vladimir Putin at the summits, Russia came to be an indispensable and constructive partner, who contributed a great deal to the issues raised and not seen as an obstacle to reaching joint decisions.[6]

The issue of the economy proves this point well enough. Russia still experiences certain economic difficulties and is not at the same level of per capita gross domestic product (GDP) as the rest of the G8 countries. It ranks 157th in the world in terms of life expectancy at birth, one of the key indicators of the well-being of a state, and has not surpassed the income threshold of US$15,000 per capita; it still has a very large gap between the richest and the poorest and high inflation rates; and it is still a largely hydrocarbon-dependent economy. Nevertheless, Russia has recovered as a major player in the world arena and participates fully in global G8 initiatives, which are discussed in more detail later on. Its GDP is now larger than that of Canada, France, and Italy, which makes it impossible to talk of Russia as an "economic pygmy" in the G8. Unemployment in Russia constitutes 5.9 percent, lower than that in France, Germany, and Italy and comparable to Canada.

In terms of political and ideological clout, Russia is unquestionably an energy superpower. It is one of the Permanent Five (P5) members of the UN Security Council (UNSC), thus party to an official nuclear club, and is one of the participants of the Six-Party Talks on North Korea's nuclear program, and it is engaged in negotiations with Iran.

Russian remains the language of communication in a large post-Soviet area (even within the Baltic states, now members of the European Union, an indigenous young population is learning Russian again), and the country is an attractive place for the labour force from the members of the Commonwealth of Independent States (CIS), particularly Ukraine and Moldova, and from Central Asia. Russia is also still one of the most consistent proponents of the supremacy of the international rule of law.

Nonetheless, Russia still stays out of some mechanisms within the G8, which remain the purview of the G7—namely, the finance ministers meetings. There have been only two cases of full participation so far, at two meetings in Moscow in 2006 when Russia held the G8 presidency. This exclusion, however, is politicized too much in the media. A similar situation applied to Italy and Canada until 1986 (that is, for a decade of their membership in the G7), when they finally participated in all G7 mechanisms, including that of the finance ministers. But to those seeking closer affiliation with the G7/8,

Table 12-1

Comparison of Group of Eight and Outreach Five Potential (2007)

Country	GDP (PPP) (billion international dollars)	GDP (PPP) per capita (thousand international dollars)	GDP (PPP) share of world total	Population July 2008 est. (size and rank)	Life expectancy at birth (rank)	Unemployment (% of total labour force)	Territory in sq km (rank)
Brazil	1,835.642 (9)	9,695.199 (78)	2.82	191,908,598 (5–2.9%)	72.51 (113)	9.8	8,511,965 (5)
Canada	1,265.838 (13)	38,435.394 (14)	1.96	33,212,696 (37–0.50%)	81.16 (7)	5.9	9,984,670 (2)
China	6,991.036 (2)	5,292.020 (128)	10.86	1,330,044,605 (1–19.91%)	73.18 (102)	4.0	9,596,960 (4)
France	2,046.899 (8)	33,187.764 (25)	3.18	64,057,790 (21–0.95%)	80.87 (8)	8.0	643,427 (42)
Germany	2,809.693 (5)	34,181.175 (23)	4.36	82,369,548 (14–1.2%)	79.10 (33)	9.1	357,021 (62)
India	2,988.867 (4)	2,659.214 (126)	4.60	1,147,995,898 (2–17%)	69.25 (142)	7.2	3,287,590 (7)
Italy	1,786.429 (10)	30,448.310 (27)	2.77	58,145,321 (23–0.87%)	80.07 (18)	6.7	301,230 (70)
Japan	4,289.809 (3)	33,576.764 (24)	6.63	127,288,419 (10–1.9%)	82.07 (3)	4.0	377,835 (61)
Mexico	1,346.009 (12)	12,774.597 (60)	2.08	109,955,400 (11–1.6%)	75.84 (71)	3.7	1,972,550 (15)
Russia	**2,087.815 (7)**	**14,692.377 (52)**	**3.19**	**140,702,094 (8–2.1%)**	**65.94 (157)**	**5.9**	**17,075,200 (1)**
South Africa	467.089 (25)	9,761.387 (76)	0.72	43,786,115 (28–0.65%)	42.37 (213)	24.2	1,219,912 (25)
United Kingdom	2,137.421 (6)	35,134.347 (22)	3.31	60,943,912 (22–0.91%)	78.85 (37)	5.4	244,820 (78)
United States	13,843.825 (1)	45,845.477 (8)	21.44	303,824,646 (3–4.5%)	78.14 (46)	4.6	9,826,630 (3)

Notes: GDP = gross domestic product; PPP = purchasing power parity.
Sources: Calculations are made on the basis of information provided by the International Monetary Fund, the World Bank, and the CIA Factbook.

this situation could serve poorly, especially if given special emphasis in the media, for it could be seen as a mere tendency of the old G7 to preserve its exclusivity and a way to keep the newer members "at the door," instead of fully inside.

All that said, Russia has become an indispensable G8 partner and participates fully in the G8 initiatives. One such initiative has been debt write-offs. According to different experts combined with figures released by Russia's Ministry of Finance, since 1995 Russia has absorbed debts up to US$75.5 billion (Zuziaev 2008).[7] Meanwhile since 2004, Russia has written off more than US$40 billion within the framework of the International Monetary Fund (IMF) and World Bank, and will write off a further US$1.3 billion of debts from African countries. However, there is great deal of discontent among the population regarding those policies, which many view as a "waste" of financial resources that could have been used instead for improving the quality of life of Russia's own citizens, many of whom live on the verge or even below the poverty line.

Another example of Russia's full participation on the world stage concerns climate change. The Kyoto protocol was able to enter into force when it was ratified by Russia—unlike other G8 members—in 2004.

Russia is fully involved in the G8's mediation of the conflicts in all parts of the world. Along with the U.S., the EU, and the UN, it is a member of the Quartet on the Middle East, whose work is reviewed by the G8, as with the Six-Party Talks. Another example of its constructive role is the way the G8 dealt with the Lebanon crisis at the St. Petersburg Summit in 2006. Due to active steps undertaken by the political directors during the summit, as G8 host, Russia managed to achieve consensus on the Russo-European wording in the final document on the necessity of proportionate use of force by Israel. Acknowledging that Hizbollah was "in violation of the Blue Line" and had reversed the "positive trends that began with the Syrian withdrawal in 2005, ... undermining the democratically elected government of Prime Minister Fuad Siniora," counter to U.S. initial reservations, the declaration on the Middle East stated that, "while exercising the right to defend itself," Israel should "be mindful of the strategic and humanitarian consequences of its actions" (G8 2006a). Thus, the G8 called "upon Israel to exercise utmost restraint, seeking to avoid casualties among innocent civilians and damage to civilian infrastructure and to refrain from acts that would destabilize the Lebanese government."

Nevertheless, it is impossible to tell that the G8 has exerted real influence over the situation. After the St. Petersburg Summit the war continued for over

Table 12-2
Debt Written Off by Russia to Major Debtors

Country	US$ billion
Iraq	12.0 (+ 0.9 to be restructured within 17 years)
Mongolia	11.4
Afghanistan	11.1
Syria	9.78 (out of 13 total)
Vietnam	9.4
Ethiopia	6 (4.8 in 2001 +1.2 in 2005)
Angola	5.0
Algeria	4.7
Mozambique	4.3
Nicaragua	3.0
Nigeria	1.3

Sources: Based on data from Ministry of Finance of the Russian Federation, Prime-TASS news, Global Affairs, Rossijskaya gazeta, Agency of Political News, Rossijskaya gazeta (7 August 2007, 26 January 2005), Agency of Political News (13 July 2006), Russia in Global Affairs (March–April 2008).

a month. The G8 could not repeat its success in dealing with Kosovo in 1999, when the resolution drafted by the foreign ministers in the run-up to the Cologne Summit was later adopted with almost no changes by the UNSC (1999).[8]

Coming Together with the Outreach Five

Thanks to its history and geography, Russia has always struggled with a philosophical as well as a political dilemma, trying to define where it actually belongs: whether it is a European state, is more like an Asian state, or occupies a special position as a bridge between two parts of the world.

Being a superpower during the Cold War frequently made Russia seem as an imperialistic state, and the majority of developing countries tried to distance themselves from both it and the U.S. (culminating in the creation of the Non-Aligned Movement [NAM]). Today, although sympathetic with the demands of the emerging developing countries, Russia does not fully belong among them nor does it share the needs they claim. Indeed, China is increasingly finding itself in a similar position (joined also by the rest of the B[R]ICSAM countries)—many developing countries can no longer identify with the tumultuous growing economic and political giant. Also among the Republicans in the American establishment, China is today often seen as the most significant potential adversary in the medium term.

Apart from geopolitics and the economy, what also puts Russia in some instances more into the B(R)ICSAM camp is its vibrant economic development.[9] It set record-high standards with volumes of capital inflows, reaching around US$80 billion in 2007.[10] Investment grew to about 20 percent in 2007 (over the past seven years, average investments inflows amounted to 11 percent). In 2007, total GDP reached approximately US$1,250 billion (according to Rosstat GDP growth in 2007 amounted to 8.1 percent compared to 2006[11]), and GDP per capita was US$11,000–12,000. Forecasted growth for the next three years was around 6.2 percent, while inflation was supposed to go down in 2008 to 6 percent, in 2009 to 5.5 percent, and in 2010 to 5 percent (Regnum 2007a), meanwhile judging from figures for this year, according to IMF forecasts it could well finish at 11.4%. Russia's external debt went down to US$46.5 billion, and gold reserves surpassed US$460 billion.

To make the Russian economy less vulnerable, steps were taken to make it depend less on the hydrocarbon sector. The new budget, adopted in 2007 for the three-year period of 2008–2010 (also an innovation), introduced the new concept of a non-oil-and-gas balance. The year 2007 was also a turning point in the dangerous trend of industrial growth at lower levels than GDP growth.

Recent trends in the world have shown that there is growing recognition of the role of the emerging economies, although the situation is not yet at the point of the absolute loss of power by the global North. Recent studies have led to downward revisions for GDP based on purchasing power parity (PPP) of the two largest emerging economies, namely China and India, with the former dropping from 15.8 percent to 10.9 percent, and the latter from 6.4 percent to 4.6 percent (according to the *IMF Survey* magazine). Nevertheless, both kept their second and fourth places in absolute figures respectively. Comparatively, the global GDP of the U.S. has been revised upward from 19.3 percent to 21.4 percent. The recent IMF reform is evidence of the recognition of emerging economies as the main drivers of the world development, as is, on a more general level, the G8's decision to engage in a dialogue with the most vibrant representatives of the global South.

Furthermore, the four BRIC countries are forecasted to be among the six largest economies of the world by 2050, which is likely if current trends prevail. In 2007, their share in global GDP had grown from 5 percent in 2000 to 15 percent; their combined gold reserves reached US$2.5 trillion, surpassing the cumulative share of the G7; and the BRIC countries' share of initial public offerings (IPOs) was 80 percent of all developing markets (Gref 2008).

Bilateral Relations between Russia and the Outreach Five Countries

Apart from, or maybe even despite, the G8 and O5 process, Russia actively engages with all of the O5 countries on a bilateral level, as well as through multilateral institutions.

Relations with China

Russia's relations with China are based on the Treaty of Friendship, Neighbourliness, and Cooperation, which was signed in 2001 in Moscow. They are sustained by regular meetings of the national leaders—mutual visits (for example, Hu Jintao, chair of the People's Republic of China [PRC], visited Russia in March 2007 and Russian president Dmitri Medvedev visited Beijing in May 2008) as well as bilateral contacts on the sidelines of the Asia-Pacific Economic Cooperation (APEC) forum (September 2007) and the Shanghai Cooperation Organisation (SCO) (most recently in November 2007). The SCO is important in its own right, for while it represents a specific mechanism of power sharing in the eastern part of Eurasia, it could also be regarded in the realm of security as a potential counterbalance to western-dominated NATO (although it was not created as such). To a certain extent, the SCO is an issue-specific organization that deals with international peace and security (mounting the large-scale Peace Mission 2007), the economy (creating the SCO Business Council and the Interbank Association), energy security (establishing the Energy Club), and humanitarian issues. However, it also provides for the overall ideological and political guidelines for further development of the region, and represents a stabilizing force and a potential model of cooperation for other international actors.

In terms of economic cooperation, in 2006 Russia occupied tenth place among China's trading partners (among the G8 and O5 countries, ahead of only the U.S., Japan, and Germany). China takes most interest in Russia's hydrocarbon resources, essential for its vibrant economic development. Thus during the first half of 2007 hydrocarbons accounted for 49.6 percent of Russia's exports to China, with 4.6 million tons of oil being delivered by Russia only by rail (with deliveries growing by 14.7 percent). China is greatly interested in cooperating further in the energy sphere, and was very unhappy when Japan expressed its wish to enter the Eastern Siberia–Pacific Ocean (VSTO) pipeline project, which in the end resulted in Russia's decision not to focus exclusively on China, but to allow for deliveries to more than one consumer, namely taking Japan onboard. The importance of such cooperation is confirmed by large-scale military exercises, such as with the Peace Mission 2005.

Russia also cooperates successfully with China on a multilateral level, while at the same counterbalancing the unilateral politics frequently adopted by the sole superpower of today and the at times aggressive stance of the western-oriented institutions such as NATO (the G7's "iron hand"). It does so by engaging in activities and mechanisms supported or sponsored by the leading developing countries—one of the best examples of which is SCO.

Relations with India

Russia and India signed the Treaty on Friendship and Cooperation in 1993, and in 2000, during Putin's visit to India, the two country's leaders signed the Declaration on Strategic Partnership, which began an annual exchange of official visits at the highest level. In January 2007, when Putin visited India, he signed a joint statement on cooperation on the peaceful use of atomic energy and also agreed to several projects in the metallurgy and oil and gas industries, among others; later, during Indian prime minister Manmohan Singh's visit to Russia in November, there was an agreement on the possible transformation of rupee debt into Russian investments in India, as well as agreements in the aviation industry and in the fight against drug trafficking. Bilateral trade between the two countries is expected to reach US$10 billion by 2010, with the assistance of Russian-Indian Forum on Trade and Investments, which held its first meeting in February 2007.

With regard to major joint projects of the two countries, Russia has made a considerable contribution to the construction of the Kudankulam nuclear power station, and the development of the Sakhalin-1 oil field has involved an agreement between India's ONGC Videsh Ltd. and Russia's Rosneft in 2001, with the first oil tanker arriving in India in December 2006. Another project is Gazprom's participation in exploration and development on the shelf of Bay of Bengal. There are also more energy projects with the Tehri and Koteshwar hydropower stations and the Korba power project. In the realm of antiterrorist activities, every two years since 2003 Russia and India have conducted Indra, joint military exercises.

Some experts find it more and more difficult to talk about India in terms of being a integrated member of the B(R)ICSAM, with the Singh government taking more pro-American stance and not willing to practise much solidarity with the rest of the group. India's independence in this regard began with the deal struck in 2005 on nuclear issues, which de facto included India in the exclusive nuclear club. This deal opened the door to lifting the American moratorium on the sale of nuclear fuel and reactor components to India, which led to 14 out of 22 Indian reactors being classified as civilian and subject to the international inspection regime—although India has still not signed on to the Nonproliferation Treaty (NPT) (Ullmann and Krasheninnikova 2006). However, this deal did not go smoothly—a blow to the Indian government came not from outside, but from within, when the communist contingent in parliament refused to vote on its ratification.

Relations with Brazil

Russia's relations with Latin America went through a difficult period in the 1990s, when, due to structural weaknesses, Russia had to withdraw completely from most regions of the world. However, Russia (or, previously, the Soviet Union) did not have a very close relationship with any country in Latin America, with the exception of Cuba.

Today, Brazil is a leading commercial partner of Russia in Latin America. Although the biggest portion of Brazilian imports is agricultural products, there is huge interest expressed in high technologies, primarily space development (such as the joint development of geostationary satellites for Brazil, Brazil's participation in the global navigating system GLONASS, and the commercial use of the Alcântara spaceport), and supplies of Russian MI-26 and MI-171A helicopters and Be-103 and Be-200 amphibious aircrafts (Ministry of Foreign Affairs of the Russian Federation 2007).

Another important issue is energy. Russian companies have supplied equipment for the Pôrto Góis and Corumbá-3 hydropower stations, Brazilians have contributed much in terms of production and use of ecologically clean fuels. Gazprom and Petrobras have begun a dialogue on the possible use of Russian know-how in developing recently discovered gas fields in Brazil. This could also mean joint entrance to additional, including through the use of Gazprom potential, especially if construction of a transcontinental gas pipeline through Venezuela, Brazil, Argentina begins.

Relations with Mexico

Of all the Outreach Five countries, Mexico seems to have the lowest level of relations developed with Russia, being to a great extent oriented politically and economically with the United States, and with exports of more than 85 percent to its northern neighbour. Also Mexico focuses mostly on its traditional partners in the U.S., western Europe, and Japan, and high import duties remain on a number of Russian goods (primarily steel). However, in 2005, the Russian Ministry of Industry and Energy and the Mexican Ministry of Energy signed the protocol of intentions.

Relations with South Africa

The start of the 21st century marked Russia's renewed interest in cooperation with the African continent, which, during the havoc of the 1990s, was almost completely abandoned by the country. South Africa, being one of the leaders of the continent, has today an intensive cooperation scheme with Russian Federation.[12] While leaders of the two countries have frequently met on the sidelines of the UN General Assembly and the G8 summits, the landmark for the bilateral relations was Putin's official visit to South Africa in September 2006, the first in history of a Russian leader to the country in sub-Saharan Africa. During this visit, the two states signed the Treaty on Friendship and Partnership between Russia and South Africa, which was accompanied by a range of intergovernmental agreements as well as large-scale agreements between large corporations of both countries.

One quarter (26.5 percent) of Russian exports to South Africa are fuel and energy goods. There are good prospects for bilateral cooperation in atomic energy, starting with the development and extraction of uranium for the construction of atomic power stations.[13] Cooperation is carried out within the framework of an intergovernmental commission co-chaired by Russia's minister of natural resources and South Africa's foreign minister. In early 2008, the South African government sent a request to Gazprom offering possible cooperation in energy.

The Heiligendamm Process

As already discussed, as the 20th century turned into the 21st century, there was still a marked need for the G8 to adjust its ways and strategies of global governance. As Andrew F. Cooper and Kelly Jackson (2007) underline, "the group's under-representation of the global South (via regional participation) erodes its ability to set priorities for the international community and detracts from its capacity to mobilize governments to broker solutions to pressing global problems."

Recognizing the need to involve the most important developing countries in the decision-making process (or, perhaps, in an attempt to get the

O5 countries to consent to the line elaborated by the "geriatric" developed countries), at the 2007 Heiligendamm Summit the German G8 president Angela Merkel suggested a new, structured, topic-driven dialogue with Brazil, China, India, Mexico, and South Africa. The decision to create the HP was stated in the G8 (2007) declaration on "Growth and Responsibility in the World Economy," which was later modified due to discontent among the O5 countries with non-consultative manner of both that document and the joint statement issued by the German presidency (G8 and Outreach Partners 2007). The HP rests on four main pillars: encouraging and protecting innovation; promoting freedom of investments by means of transparent investments regime, including encouragement of socially responsible corporate behaviour; energy, especially with regard to increasing energy efficiency and fostering technological cooperation in order to reduce carbon dioxide emissions; and improved cooperation and coordination in the field of sustainable development, particularly in Africa. The discussion below focuses Russia's role with regard to those four pillars.

Investments

The German presidency suggested that within the HP there should be a discussion of the institutional and legal mechanisms of investment regulations, the economic benefits from foreign investments, and the use of market mechanisms of technology transfers, and there should be an exchange of views with business leaders regarding corporate social responsibility. The Germans emphasized the liberalization of investment regimes, but the process is intended to provide equal opportunities and conditions for both national and foreign investors:

> Open and transparent procurement markets are an important precondition for cross-border investments. We invite all our partners, in particular the major emerging economies, to create a level playing field for national and foreign tenderers. This may include considerations to join the WTO's Government Procurement Agreement (G8 2007).

The O5 did not welcome this statement and in fact opposed discussions within the HP of the concept of "equal conditions" because there was no consensus on the matter among the participants. Their view was that it is vital that interests of the countries—recipients of those investments—should be taken into account, apart from protecting investors' interests. Another problem raised by the O5 is that developing countries themselves often run into limitations on investments on the western markets.

This is an extremely important question for Russia as well, because it has experienced similar problems—as the O5 point out—in its relations and negotiations with the rest of the G8 members. Western countries demand unrestricted participation in Russian industries, while the country retains state control over strategic sectors of its economy (particularly in the energy sector). At the same time western governments and supra-national structures such as the EU take measure to limit investments from the other countries, mostly scared by Russian, Chinese, and Arabic inflows of capital. Recent examples include the introduction of legal mechanisms such as the EU restricting investments of sovereign wealth funds and developing a "Voluntary Code of Conduct" for such funds worked, with similar limitations in the U.S. under the July 2007 *Foreign Investment and National Security Act.*

Earlier, in 2006, Russian and Chinese companies met with specific difficulties, particularly Gazprom was blocked from buying the UK's Centrica, or China's CNOOC (offering US$18,5 billion) had to withdrew from buying Unocal, leaving it to Chevron (which offered US$17.3 billion).

O5 countries took great interest in the issue of corporate social responsibility, pointing out that the discussion should be based on the work done by the UN, such as the Global Compact and the Norms on the Responsibilities of Transnational Corporations with Regard to Human Rights of August 2003, rather than the OECD Guidelines for Multinational Enterprises produced by the Organisation for Economic Co-operation and Development (OECD) (UN 2008; UN United Nations Commission on Human Rights 2003; OECD 2000).[14] However, it is to the OECD that the G8 turns to for elaboration of those principles:

> We commit ourselves to promote actively internationally agreed corporate social responsibility and labour standards (such as the OECD Guidelines for Multinational Enterprises and the ILO [International Labour Organization] Tripartite Declaration), high environmental standards and better governance through OECD Guidelines' National Contact Points. We call on private corporations and business organizations to adhere to the principles in the OECD Guidelines for Multinational Enterprises. We encourage the emerging economies as well as developing countries to associate themselves with the values and standards contained in these guidelines and we will invite major emerging economies to a High Level Dialogue on corporate social responsibility issues using the OECD as a platform (G8 2007).

Russia takes a position similar to that of the O5, especially as it is one of the most important players in the UN and is not a member of the OECD.[15]

Innovations

Germany offered to make its centrepiece discussions at the summit on the issues of efficient market incentives for promoting innovation and the use of patents and licensing as mechanisms for international technology transfer, along with discussion of joint actions by the G8 and O5 on protecting intellectual property rights (IPR) through the World Trade Organization (WTO) and the World Intellectual Property Organization (WIPO).

However, the O5 countries believe that market mechanisms are no panacea for the development of innovation processes, and the positions outlined in the G8 Heiligendamm documents on IPR inherently oppose their interests. They have serious reservations about the proposals to strengthen international standards for protecting IPR and have suggested shifting to the issues of strengthening institutional capacities, undertaking explanatory work, and training qualified personnel.

> A fully functioning intellectual property system is an essential factor for the sustainable development of the global economy through promoting innovation. We recognize the importance of streamlining and harmonizing the international patent system in order to improve the acquisition and protection of patent rights world-wide (G8 2007b).

The O5 maintain that discussions on IPR protection should be balanced by the commitments of the developed countries to transfer technologies and services to the developing countries at reasonable prices.

Russia is a part of G8 rather than the O5, so it cannot side explicitly with the latter group on all the issues, although its interests here clearly coincided to some extent with those of the emerging economies.

Energy Efficiency and Reduced Emissions

The statement issued by the German presidency suggested a focus on elaborating national programs to promote increased energy efficiency and technical cooperation in reducing carbon dioxide emissions with the introduction of innovative technologies and international standards in different sectors of economy (G8 2007). It emphasized minimum or zero energy consumption from external sources, clean coal technologies, and improved efficiency of coal power stations.

However, the O5 countries believe that energy security questions should be also included in the discussion. They supported the initiative proposed by China and formulated on the sidelines of the 2006 St. Petersburg Summit. The issue of energy efficiency could thus be complemented by the use of alternative and renewable sources of energy, such as wind, solar, geothermal, tidal, hydro energy, and biofuel.

This O5 suggestion has been supported by Russia, which in turn proposed that discussions of energy security be based on the provisions outlined in the St. Petersburg declaration on "Global Energy Security" (G8 2006b). As a result, the revised concept paper produced for the HP (2008) in January 2008 stated that "dialogue partners will include in their discussions relevant aspects of energy security as contained in the Summit Declaration of St. Petersburg as well as proposed by the G5, focusing inter alia on enhancing mutually beneficial cooperation on energy development and utilization as well as capacity building for using demand side management energy systems." Support for the working group is to be provided by the International Energy Agency (IEA), focusing on establishing a sustainable buildings network, enhancing energy efficiency in the field of power generation, and researching alternative sources of energy and renewable energy.

Sustainable Development

At the nucleus of the pillar on sustainable development are the Millennium Development Goals (MDGs), primarily with regard to increased efficiency of aid to Africa in order to advance its development and eradicate poverty. The G8 and all the O5, countries except Brazil, adhere to the "Paris Declaration on Aid Effectiveness," adopted in March 2005, also reiterated the undertaken commitments (OECD 2005). The O5 partners, committed to fulfilling MDGs, believe that it is vital to expand the list of topics for discussion to include new sources of financing development, debt write-offs, and unified policies for trade, investments, and financial systems.

The O5 also insist that the G8 confirm their pledged support for Africa, suggesting a repeat of post–World War Two reconstruction of Europe with massive financial inflows under the Marshall plan.

Overall, Russia does not oppose the suggestions of the O5 partners with regard to the HP and could in fact be characterized as neutral toward both the G8, to which it belongs (staying to a great extent ideologically unique and outside the mainstream of the western world), and the prospective emerging economies of the O5.

The Heiligendamm Process within the G8 Work Plan

Nevertheless it is clear that not all the original G8 powers are ready to accept the attempts of the O5 countries to maintain independent positions on certain HP issues. Thus, the U.S. has declared that HP should aim to extend time-tested G8 practices, rather than search for new common approaches. The rest of the G8 members are more discreet, preferring to concentrate on issues that are most likely to lead to consensus among all the participants, and thus the German presidency revised the HP concept paper to omit certain disputable points.[16]

There are not many options for the HP to develop significantly in its first year, especially since the 2008 Japanese presidency does not see this process as a very convenient one. Japan believes that further expansion would only hamper the consensus-reaching process, and thus has not considered the HP a priority during its hear as G8 host.

Russia remains a responsible actor on the international arena and supports the concept of the multipolarity (although it is often viewed as a contraposition to the existing unipolarity or, rather, unipolar pluralism).[17] As such, it regards the Heiligendamm Process as a positive phenomenon and a necessary step in order to ensure fair and equal participation of all major systemically significant parties in global governance and in overcoming the major threats and challenges facing the world today. To this end, the Russian sherpa Igor Shuvalov took part in the first meeting of HP steering committee in early 2008 and Russia has drawn up a preliminary list of representatives and experts from specialized ministries and the Ministry of Foreign Affairs for the working groups.

In 2000, in the run-up to the Okinawa Summit, there was speculation that China, on its own, might join the G8. Japan as host did invite China to participate, but China rejected the invitation, primarily not wanting to be associated with the rich and lose its leadership status with the rest of the developing world. At that time Russia was also asked about its attitude to possible enlargement, but it responded cautiously, for it did not yet have a full-fledged status within the G8 club.

In 2006, during the year of its own presidency, Russia also invited the O5 countries, in the process receiving a fair amount of criticism for "setting a precedent" by repeating the invitation to the same participants as had been invited the previous year.[18] It held regular consultations on all the developments and discussions within the G8 and among its O5 partners (on a level equal to G8 sherpas). The idea of expansion could become an interesting option for Russia in the current climate, for it would bring more like-minded countries to the negotiations table.

Conclusions

Several ideas arise as a summary of the previously discussed issues regarding the future cooperation between the G8 and O5 as well as the possible place for Russia in this regard.

For all the O5 countries it is rather a difficult choice of whether to engage in further integration with the G8 (in the event that there is a consensus on the matter within the G8 itself), and thus there are possible problems from such association with the rich club and the perception by the rest of the developing world as renegades of their just cause.

Nevertheless, apart from China, participation within the G8 plus O5, or even further, a G13 format, may turn out to be beneficial and in fact exciting for the same reasons, as the G8 is cherished by half of its original members: with UN reform staggering, the G8+ offers a unique opportunity to significantly increase the weight of those countries that do not hold permanent seat on the UNSC and allow them a say in shaping the global governance architecture. In this regard the G8+ is being seen more and more as the most important global governance mechanism, albeit complementary to the UN.

Russia supports in principle the German-initiated HP and agrees with the notion that present-day global challenges and threats cannot be dealt with narrowly by the G8 alone. At the same time, Russia does not actively push forward the rather slowly unveiling Heiligendamm cooperation process, instead going along with the natural developments as they arise.

Although Russia could benefit from a new, expanded G13 as a result of the HP, with like-minded countries coming on board, at the moment it is concentrating more on its bilateral relations with Brazil, China, India, South Africa, and, to a lesser extent, Mexico. Nevertheless it is impossible to claim that there is a complete concurrence of interests within the B(R)ICSAM as opposed to the G8.

To end with a little provocative idea, notwithstanding all the politically correct statements about collective shared responsibility and the impossibility of tackling world pressing issues without the involvement of the biggest emerging systemically significant economies, not all the original partners of the G8 deeply enjoy the idea. Thus, as inevitable as further institutionalization or remodelling of the G8 into the G13 may appear, there seems to be a clear idea that the old G7 will, eventually, have to find a way to invent a new mechanism of its own, so it could continue to benefit from closed consultations within only the familiar and trusted "family circle."

Notes

1 Outreach sessions with non-member countries did not occur only with the USSR. At the beginning the initiative for outreach did not come from the G7. Thus, in the run-up to the 1989 G7 Paris Summit, four leaders of the developing countries— Hosni Mubarak of Egypt, Rajiv Gandhi of India, Abdou Diouf of Senegal, and Carlos Andrés Pérez of Venezuela—met in Paris and issued a news release in the name of 15 major developing countries stating their wish to hold regular consultations with industrially developed countries at the summit level.

2 With the demise of the Warsaw Pact, there was also a "security vacuum," as stated by Hungarian prime minister József Antall, that needed to be filled in by the incoming presence of the United States and the expansion of NATO.

3 The New Seven Sisters consist of the following national oil companies: Saudi Aramco (Saudi Arabia), Gazprom (Russia), CNPC (China), NIOC (Iran), PDVSA (Venezuela), Petrobras (Brazil), and Petronas (Malaysia). Some analysts say these companies now have the upper hand over the traditional Seven Sisters, of which only four western international oil companies remain (Exxon Mobil, Chevron, Royal Dutch Shell, and BP, with only Exxon Mobil in undisputed first place in the world ranking) (Hoyos 2007).

4 The documents released at the Kananaskis Summit, for the first time in G7/8 history, set out a rotation list of hosting responsibilities of eight years in advance, carving out a place for Russian presidency in 2006—after the United Kingdom and before Germany, which demonstrated the special relationship between the that country and Russia at the time of chancellorship of Gerhard Schroeder.

5 The frontrunner of such adversarial talk is John McCain, the presidential candidate from the Republican Party for the 2008 U.S. election. In an article in the *Suddeutsche Zeitung* he declared once again that the West has to work out a united stand against Russia and make sure that the G8 resurges as a club of leading democratic market economies (McCain 2008). To this end, he said, it is vital to include India and Brazil and exclude Russia. McCain also proposed created a league of democracies, which could come into play whenever the UN fails.

6 Meanwhile, the European and American partners were more frequently divided, be it on the issue of climate change or the International Criminal Court, or military operations against Iraq.

7 However, Russia has no single system of classification and accounting for aid and debt write-offs.

8 Its success is arguable nowadays, since in early 2008 some of the authors of the resolution themselves easily violated its provisions in pushing for Kosovo independence and applying double standards to international relations and international law.

9 The recognition of the growing role of emerging economies can be seen in the reform of the IMF (2008) in April 2008, as a result of which quota shares for 54 countries increased by between 12 percent and 106 percent, with China's increasing by 50 percent, India by 40 percent, Brazil by 40 percent, and Mexico by 40 percent. The aggregate shift in quota shares for these 54 members is 4.9 percentage points. Meanwhile, the quota and voice shares for Russia (along with Canada, France, and the UK) shrank.

10 During the 1990s US$25 billion fled the country annually, while its GDP amounted to US$20 billion. (2007b).

11 Russia's GDP growth surpassed that of the major western powers by more than twice: in 2007, the growth of EU countries, the U.S., and Japan was no more than 3 percent.

12 Indeed some even suggest that a so-called collective leadership of three major African states, namely Egypt, Nigeria, and South Africa, could be constituted.

13 South Africa has 12 percent of world's proven uranium reserves. It also has 35,000 tons of thorium-232, being in the top seven countries with this important resource (overall world reserves constitute around 1.2 million tons, enough to generate 1,000 GW of electricity for 1,000 years) (see Yakovlev et al. 2007).

14 The OECD document was adopted on June 27, 2000, at the organization's annual ministerial in Paris and comprises all 30 OECD members as well as ten non-member countries (Argentina, Brazil, Chile, Egypt, Estonia, Israel, Latvia, Lithuania, Romania, and Slovenia), and constitutes a set of voluntary recommendations to multinational corporations in most areas of business ethics, including employment, human rights, environment, the struggle against bribery, consumer interests, and competition.

15 One of primary objectives of Russia joining the G7 in the early 1990s was the need to become fully integrated into the western-dominated world structure, meaning its major mechanisms and institutions. G7 support allowed for this to finally happen with a number of institutions such as the IMF, the Council of Europe, and the Paris Club and the London Club (although some conditions were not met by Russia, such as the abolition of capital punishment). But the declared support did not result in OECD membership (and Russia eventually dropped it from its agenda) and Russia is not yet a member of the World Trade Organization (WTO).

16 It was agreed that the HDP process would be chaired for the first half of 2008 by Germany, second half of the year by Japan, and in 2009, up to the G8 summit, by Italy.

17 For more on the concept of multipolarity see Bogaturov (1997; 2003).

18 Russia had originally planned to invite only the heads of the international organizations, but the idea evolved into outreach for both states and organizations.

References

Bogaturov, A.D., ed. (1997). *The Great Powers at the Pacific Ocean*. Moscow: Academic Educational Forum on International Relations.

Bogaturov, A.D., ed. (2003). *Systemic History of International Relations 1918–2003*. Moscow: Academic Educational Forum on International Relations.

Cooper, Andrew F. and Kelly Jackson (2007). "Regaining Legitimacy: The G8 and the 'Heiligendamm Process.'" *International Insights* 4(10). www.igloo.org/ciia/Library/ciialibr/intern~1/internat (May 2008).

G8 (2006a). "Middle East." 16 July, St. Petersburg. www.g8.utoronto.ca/summit/2006stpetersburg/mideast.html (May 2008).

G8 (2006b). "Global Energy Security." 16 July, St. Petersburg. www.g8.utoronto.ca/summit/2006stpetersburg/energy.html (May 2008).

G8 (2007). "Growth and Responsibility in the World Economy." 7 June, Heiligendamm. www.g8.utoronto.ca/summit/2007heiligendamm/g8-2007-economy.html (May 2008).

G8 and Outreach Partners (2007). "Joint Statement by the German G8 Presidency and the Heads of State and/or Government of Brazil, China, India, Mexico, and South Africa on the Occasion of the G8 Summit in Heiligendamm." 8 June, Heiligendamm. www.g8.utoronto.ca/summit/2007heiligendamm/g8-2007-joint.html (May 2008).

Gref, Herman (2008). "Gref: Brazilia, Rossiya, India i Kitai k 2050 godu voidut v shesterku vedushchikh ekonomik." ["Graf: Brazil, Russia, India, and China Will Enter the Six Leading Economies by 2050."] 25 January, Moscow. Gazeta. www.gazeta.ru/news/business/2008/01/25/n_1167494.shtml (May 2008).

Heiligendamm Dialogue Process (2008). *Concept Paper Regarding the Heiligendamm Process*. Paris.

Hoyos, Carola (2007). "The New Seven Sisters: Oil and Gas Giants Dwarf Western Rivals." *Financial Times*, 11 March. www.ft.com/cms/s/2/471ae1b8-d001-11db-94cb-000b5df10621.html (May 2008).

International Monetary Fund (2008). "Reform of IMF Quotas and Voice: Responding to Changes in the Global Economy." April, Washington DC. www.imf.org/external/np/exr/ib/2008/040108.htm (May 2008).

McCain, John (2008). "In alter Freundschaft." ["As Old Friends."]. *Suddeutsche Zeitung*, 7 February. www.inopressa.ru/sueddeutsche/2008/02/08/11:32:29/McCain (May 2008).

Ministry of Foreign Affairs of the Russian Federation (2007). "O seminare po voprosam cotrudinchestva gruppu BRIK—Braziliya, Rossiya, Indiya, Kitai, a takzhe Meksiki y IUAR." ["Seminar on Issues of Cooperation between Brazil, Russia, India, China and Also Mexico and South Africa."] 18 April, Moscow. www.ln.mid.ru/ns_publ.nsf/ca618d5746fee68cc32571f4002a5d7c/e40668b23e668531c32572c10029349a?OpenDocument (May 2008).

Organisation for Economic Co-operation and Development (2000). *The OECD Guidelines for Multinational Enterprises*. Paris: Organisation for Economic Co-operation and Development. www.oecd.org/dataoecd/56/36/1922428.pdf (May 2008).

Organisation for Economic Co-operation and Development (2005). *The Paris Declaration on Aid Effectiveness: Ownership, Harmonisation, Alignment, Results, and Mutual Accountability*. Paris. www.oecd.org/dataoecd/11/41/34428351.pdf (May 2008).

Regnum (2007a). "Prezident RF podpical pervyi v istorii strani trekhletnii biudzhet." ["Russian President Signs the First Three-Year Budget in the Country's History."] 27 July, Moscow. www.regnum.ru/news/862344.html (May 2008).

Regnum (2007b). "Glava komiteta Gosdumy po Ekonomiueskoi politike." ["Head of the Committee of the State Duma on Economic Policy."] 19 December, Moscow. www.regnum.ru/news/934586.html (May 2008).

Ullmann, H. and V. Krasheninnikova (2006). "USA and India: Strategic Partnerhsip or Temporary Rapprochement?" *Export of Weapons*, 21 December.

United Nations (2008). "Global Compact." www.unglobalcompact.org (May 2008).

United Nations Commission on Human Rights (2003). "Norms on the Responsibilities of Transnational Corporations and Other Business Enterprises with Regard to Human Rights." E/CN.4/Sub.2/2003/12/Rev.2. 26 August. www.unhchr.ch/huridocda/huridoca.nsf/(Symbol)/E.CN.4.Sub.2.2003.12.Rev.2.En (May 2008).

United Nations Security Council (1999). "Resolution 1244 (1999)." 10 June. daccess-ods.un.org/TMP/8565475.html.

Yakovlev, R.M., E.L. Petrov, M.N. Tikhonov, *et al.* (2007). "Reshenie problem yadernoi energetiki v strategii uran-torievogo toplivnogo tsikla." ["Solutions of Nuclear Energy Problems in the Strategy of the Uranium-Thorium Cycle."] 16 May, St. Petersburg. Proatom. www.proatom.ru/modules.php?name=News&file=article&sid=970 (May 2007).

Zuziaev, Alexander (2008). "Rossiya razdarivaet milliard' dollarov." ["Russia Is Giving Out Billions of Dollars."]. *Komsomolskya Pravda*, 20 February. www.kp.ru/daily/24052/103956 (May 2008).

13

The United States and Summit Reform in a Transformational Era

Colin I. Bradford, Jr.

The United States is at a critical turning point. The 2008 presidential contest and election represent a potential watershed in American politics and foreign policy. This chapter begins by exploring some of the elements defining both the watershed and the potential principles and practices for managing the transition to a new era in global politics. Summit reform is examined within the context of this transition to see what place it has for the U.S. in the mix of broader approaches to a new era and what potential it has for the U.S. as an instrument for transition. To better grasp the importance of summit reform in prospective American approaches to reshaping its role in the world, a survey was undertaken specifically for this book to determine what U.S. experts and officials think about summit reform in comparison to their counterparts from 15 other major countries. The results of this survey provide insights into the outlook for the Heiligendamm Process (HP) of outreach to non-G8 countries and into the degree of convergence of views within the international community on summit reform. The survey also reveals the specific points of divergence between the views of leading Americans and their peers from other G8 countries as well as those from emerging market countries that are potential new members of an expanded summit grouping. These results provide the basis for reflections on prospective pathways forward for summit reform, in both its country composition and mandate, for 2009 and beyond.

The United States as a Security Threat to Itself in a Polarizing World

The U.S. is undergoing a transformational shift in the foundations and nature of its foreign policy.

The world is increasingly splintered, fractured, and even polarized. Forty percent of the world lives on $2 a day or less while the world's wealthiest people have accelerating incomes and assets. Growing inequality blemishes the spread of globalization. Backlashes against globalization fuel anger, violence, and terrorism, generating a cultural divide between extremists and fundamentalists on one side and industrial country societies on the other (Akbar Ahmed 2007, 143). The U.S. has become what Joseph Joffe (2006) calls the "uberpower," the highest power in military, technological, economic, and cultural terms.

As a result, the U.S. is now "the other" for much of the world and is resented, resisted, and reproached by those confronting American power. The overarching threat to the United States is now the U.S. itself and how it is perceived in the world. Hyper-power generates new vulnerabilities for American security. How the U.S. is seen in the non-western world generates dissent, disturbance, violence, and terrorism, which in turn feed into security threats to the U.S. itself.

This is not just an issue of a decline in the image of the U.S., as found in the Pew Global Attitudes Project (2007), but a more profound shift. A survey by Harris Research for the *Financial Times* reported that "32 per cent of respondents in five European countries [France, Germany, Italy, the United Kingdom, and Spain] regard the US as a bigger threat than any other state," with "35 per cent of American 16- to 24-year-olds identifying it as the chief danger to stability" (Dombey and Pignal 2007). The view of others beyond the North Atlantic is sufficiently distrustful as to undermine confidence in the U.S. among Europeans and young Americans themselves. This is a new situation for the U.S. to be in, with major implications for its role in the world.

The challenge facing the U.S. is how to meet global challenges facing the rest of the world by contributing ideas, institutional innovations, policies, and resources toward improving the human condition. The U.S. has always been respected globally when it has contributed to the world beyond its immediate self-interest. In the end, such actions rebounded back to America's benefit.

The question facing the U.S. is how to hold this world together in a singular global community engaged in common enterprises and how to keep the world from falling into "us versus them" politics, regional blocs, and civ-ilizational divides.

Sustaining a global approach to global issues is threatened by those such as Hugo Chavez and Mahmoud Ahmadinejad who would drive the world into oppositional corners, by the uncertainty regarding the objectives of Russia in energy and China in military matters, and by the cultural divisions embodied in the "clash of civilization" mentality brought to the world by the growth of terrorism. It is also threatened by U.S. behaviour that has relied too heavily on hard power, competition, narrow alliances, driving self-interest, and over-assertiveness. The transition to a new global order needs to be based on a new set of values of respect and reciprocity, common interests and compromise, and cooperation and coordination.

Based on these values, the U.S. needs to blend realism with idealism, good intentions with shrewdness, and pragmatism with vision to keep the world working together rather than breaking apart, and it needs to transform its role from one of dominance to one of trusted global leadership in the process.

Pluralism and Linking Domestic Concerns to International Engagement

Two principles could help guide the U.S. through the foundational shifts currently underway. The first principle is that America is both a melting pot and the embodiment of pluralism: a country of immigrants has become a nation. But individual communities retain their identity. Muslim Americans are increasingly prominent in local and state governments as elected officials but Muslim Americans also have a strong sense of cultural identity and community among themselves. Multiple identities and roles are part of 21st-century life. Membership in the global community can be based on a similar fusion of belonging to an overarching global society and to a nation with state interests and identities to advance. Pluralism and unity have been foundational ideas for America since the beginning. Simplified ideologies that overwhelm difference and distinctiveness contribute to the polarization of world opinion and the alienation of "others" from the West. The notions of embracing difference, engaging others, and incorporating distinctive perspectives into brokered approaches to common problems are not only consistent with the *e pluribus unum* foundation of America but they also provide a fresh, new approach for U.S. foreign policy today.

Second, during the 20th century there was a division between U.S. foreign policy and U.S. domestic policy. American foreign policy was driven by an elite with internationalist experience and outlook but the internal links and resonance were weak. The 21st century is characterized by globalization, which means the inter-penetration of domestic domains into each other, breaking down the boundaries between states and between internal and external affairs. U.S. foreign policy now needs to synergize with domestic concerns, issues, and interests.

These principles of unity, which are derived from pluralism and the fusion of internal and external issues, can be translated into practices that can help America in transforming the world (from unilateralism to multilateralism, for example) by transforming its behaviour in the world. Instead of asserting American hegemony based on a liberal ideology of democracy and markets, the U.S. can embrace the pluralism of economic and political models as an organizing motif for global integration. China, Japan, Germany, and the UK each have different forms of capitalism. A good example is China. China's economic model is more directed but market forces are effervescent and irresistible now. China has been more successful in reducing extreme poverty than any other state in the world over the last 20 years. This experience needs to be brought to the global table as an example of forging capitalism with a human face, not to be replicated by others (no one else has 1.2 billion people) but to be studied and selectively drawn from for applications elsewhere. China's experience is an indispensable asset in a global approach to poverty reduction in a world in which 40 percent of the world's poor are in middle income countries, even though China is not a shining example of Anglo-American market capitalism.

China's economy and economic experience needs not to be marginalized but to be fully integrated into the global economy and global institutions. The World Bank and the International Monetary Fund (IMF) need China to be invested in their missions and to act as a leader with a stake in their success, not as a passive participant in institutions that China regards as western or trans-Atlantic. As it becomes more integrated in the global economy, China will stimulate more internal, consumption-driven growth to balance its export growth, and the contentious exchange rate issues between the U.S. and China will attenuate. In fact, a shift by the U.S. toward emphasizing internal-demand expansion over advocating market-driven exchange rate determination would demonstrate a new pluralism and pragmatism in economic ideas, and would ease tensions in the current debate on global imbalances.

A similar shift in America's internal-external dynamic would be facilitated by the U.S. beginning to deal with health and poverty, energy and environment, jobs and growth as seamless domestic and international issues. Forty million Americans without health insurance constitute a poverty issue in America. Global health threats loom as one of the highest priorities on the international security agenda, closely linked to the global poverty challenge. Achieving energy independence for America is a myth, and is unnecessary if the world is treated and managed as a global energy system. Solving U.S. energy security requirements needs a global approach, not an idea exclusively relegated to national autonomy. America's angst over losing domestic jobs abroad is directly linked to fears of globalization blinding Americans from seeing the gains from trade. Finding the right balance between trade and jobs, between internationalism and nationalism, faces all nations in a new way now, exemplifying the fusion of domestic and foreign policy concerns everywhere, including in the United States. Free trade and protectionism are too often presented as dichotomous choices in U.S. foreign policy. In fact, trade regimes constitute a wide spectrum along which countries, including the U.S., can position themselves in a differentiated fashion. A shift toward greater pluralism and pragmatism in U.S. trade policy would resonate internally and make more sense externally to countries with widely different views on trade.

So rather than returning to 19th-century foreign policy principles of balance of power or to 20th-century ideas of American hegemony, America needs to build new foundations for the future based on the linkage of pluralism and belonging and the fusion of domestic and foreign policy interests. Diversity is a higher value than "shared values," economic multipolarity is a greater source of security than balance of power, and cooperation based on shared interests is a better basis for global order than competition built on ideological commitments to democracy and markets. As Chinua Achebe (2000, 96) says, "diversity is the engine of the evolution of living things, including living civilizations."

From Principles to Practice: Four Shifts in the U.S. Approach

What specifically could be done to translate these principles to practice?

First, there is a need to address major global issues in a cooperative framework of mutual responsibility. Urgent global challenges will drive new behaviour more than new forms will. Form should follow function, not the other way around. Two global challenges are reinvigorating the major global effort to reduce extreme poverty along with improving global health and initiating a new effort to guide the future of global energy supplies consistent with constraining carbon emissions; confronting these challenges can forge new cooperative behaviour, institutions, and results.

The Second Global Conference on Financing for Development in Doha in December 2008 requires a major push to accelerate progress if the Millennium Development Goals (MDGs) are to be achieved by 2015. The MDGs embody a commitment by 185 nations to an agenda that integrates poverty, health, gender equality, education, environment, and cooperation into a multisectoral plan to galvanize greater public support for the domestic-international interface of these issues. But leaders must lead their publics and parliaments at Doha in December and beyond to mobilize resources and policies to reach the MDGs as the global effort for reducing global poverty. An expanded summit group would be an appropriate instrument to steward the MDG agenda to 2015.

The global energy market exists but there is no focal point for it. The Organization of the Petroleum Exporting Countries (OPEC) represents the oil producers and the International Energy Agency (IEA) at the Organisation for Economic Co-operation and Development (OECD) is seen as the "consuming countries' watchdog." The private sector and many ambitious states like the fact that there is no global guidance group for energy, even though it is now clear that the spill-over effects of investment decisions, technological innovations, and supply disruptions affect everyone's vital interests. There are major opportunities for cooperation and coordination to meet the burgeoning energy demands over the next 50 years as 3 billion more people will inhabit the planet.

Second, there is a need to embed the new powers into full membership in the global system and the global steering group. Responsibility is a function of role, not just attitude. Bringing major emerging market economies into fuller membership, greater leadership roles, and larger voting shares in the global institutional architecture gives them a stake in the system because they see it as their system as well, and not just the West's. The G8 mechanism is obsolete, 20th-century aberration parading in the 21st century as a global steering committee for a world in which G8 countries are a distinct minority in terms of people, culture, religion, and economic size. The 2007 G8 Summit in Heiligendamm, Germany, repeated the gestures of recent summits by inviting the heads of state of China, India, Brazil, South Africa, and Mexico (the Outreach Five [O5]) to a session on energy and climate change after the G8 had completed its own discussions and decisions and issued a communiqué on the issue. This is an outrageous practice. The G8 Plus Five is not the same as a G13/L13. Until the G8 is transformed into a G13 or some larger, more inclusive grouping, there will be no global steering committee with real legitimacy, and no one can expect the new powers to feel fully engaged in the international system. The West is not the rest. As long as the G8 pretentiously purports to decide for the globe, the "us versus them" divide prevails over a valid global governance mechanism.

Third, there is a need to remove ideology as the centrepiece of American involvement in the international arena. Democracy and the market economy are not the compelling ideals in the rest of the world that Americans think they are. Realism requires us to recognize that autocracy and authoritarian behaviour are elements of governing in some regions, even as pluralism grows. Holding progress on other issues hostage to force democratic ideals and market fundamentalism on countries with different practices blocks progress rather than facilitating it. Human rights, representativeness, and the encouragement of economic openness, initiative, and innovation are important drivers for social change. Confidence that people the world over want the fruits of greater freedom and opportunity is not an invitation to prescribe the path they should take to get them. The new idea of a concert or league of democracies would further divide the world rather than unite it. Some important countries that are vital to global progress will not join. Demonstrating openness to diversity of political and economic models will facilitate, not deter, policy dialogue and international engagement conducive to the development of greater democratic practice and market competition. Encouraging China, India, and Russia to participate more fully in the activities of the OECD (including the IEA), known as the club of industrial democracies, without insisting on full membership is an example of a highly effective way of sharing best practice, engaging in harmonizing policies, coordinating behaviour that affects each other, and integrating these critical countries into the global system without proselytizing.

Fourth, the withdrawal of U.S. prerogatives to enhance the participation of other countries in global leadership would motivate engagement and responsibility rather than constituting U.S. retreat, withdrawal, or loss of power. Soft power is more effective as a tool for engagement and cooperation than hard power, which is a better tool for competition and confrontation. As an example, if the U.S. and Europe could agree to abandon their tradition of appointing the president of the World Bank and the head of the IMF respectively, this would be evidence of trust in the capacity of leaders from other regions and countries to lead these institutions in the global interest. The crisis over Paul Wolfowitz's leadership of the World Bank in 2007 highlighted the bankruptcy of the practice of having the head of the institution be a political appointee of the U.S. president, much like a member of the U.S. cabinet. If Wolfowitz himself had been selected in an open competition of nominees from around the world and voted on by the entire board of executive directors as the merit-based candidate, he would have felt that he was there in behalf of the international community and not as a representative of the United States. A withdrawal of this prerogative by the United States in a "grand bargain" with the Europeans, wherein they withdraw their right to name the head of the IMF, would constitute a major step toward making the governance of these important institutions more multilateral, increasing their effectiveness, and enhancing the spirit of cooperation within them. This is just one example where a change in current practice could transform behaviour.

This brief overview of four practical actions that could constitute a new approach by the U.S. to defining its role in the world and in a new global order reveals that summit reform is a critical element of a larger strategy. Summit reform by itself is not a powerful enough step to have the transformative effect required to reshape the global order and the U.S. role in it. Rather, these systemic impacts require a broader approach within which summit reform could play a key role. Moreover, the degree to which summit reform can be transformative depends on whether a compositional shift toward greater inclusion of new powers is accompanied by a new mission for summits. In addition, the degree to which U.S. support for summit reform in a new administration is an effective transformative tool for U.S. foreign policy depends upon whether such reform is seen by leading figures in other countries as an important step. These are all questions raised and elucidated by the survey results.

Prospective Views on Summit Reform in the United States: Survey Results

In the context of U.S. views on the G8 enlargement process within and beyond the HP, it seemed less than enlightening to consult with the current administration on its members' attitudes toward summit reform since the election would be over around the time this book is published. Furthermore, it seemed more important to ascertain the degree to which there was consensus or discord in the international community on the issue of summit reform. Each country has its own calculations to make. Most of the current members of the G8 are extremely reluctant to support a formulation of an expanded summit that might diminish their stature and dilute their influence in this exclusive club. The four European countries in particular are reluctant to reduce their four seats to one. The O5 members seem like the most likely candidates for possible entry into an expanded G8 or into a new summit grouping. But none of them, not even China, wants to be "cherry picked" to enter alone, or even as one of two new entrants, for a variety of reasons. Both of these facts of life in the politics of summit reform make Republican presidential candidate John McCain's proposals to remove Russia and add Brazil and India infeasible.

The variety of interests and perspectives that come to play on summit reform are enormous and complex. Hence an unbroken progression from G8 to a G13, where the O5 members are asked to join as full members—as logical as it may seem since the five have been present at all the summits since the Gleneagles Summit in 2005—is not the inexorable next step. As a consequence of these complexities, it is not at all certain *ex ante* that there would be a convergence of opinion, much less a consensus, on summit reform among senior officials from major industrial and emerging market countries and experts knowledgeable about international reform. Indeed, it might well have been the case that a survey among these two groups of participants involved in the international debate on reform might well reveal the great diversity of opinion that exists in the international community, which itself would complicate the reform process.

The "Heiligendamm Process Questionnaire" consisting of 17 questions was sent to more than 150 officials and experts from G20 countries. The questions covered five main topics: the role of the G8, the recent evolution of the G8 into the G8 Plus Five, beyond the G8 Plus Five, summit mandate and mission, and the U.S. in a polarized world. Seventy-six people responded, 30 of whom were officials and 46 of whom were from think tanks, academic institutions, or research centres. Twenty-six Americans and 50 officials and experts from 15 other countries responded. Quite unexpectedly, the findings are extremely clear. On most important questions, the results are robust, in that the responses are by and large well over 65 percent or less than 25 percent, which means that even if there were a substantial margin of error, there is still a clear set of outcomes. The questions included in this questionnaire and the statistical results appear in the appendix at the end of this chapter. What follows here is a discussion of the main results in a policy context.

The Role of the G8

The positive news is that the G8 was widely viewed by both U.S. respondents and those from other major countries as serving a useful role as the pivotal club for its members and was perceived to be actually performing that role. But there was a widespread view (over 90 percent of both groups) that the G8 is not viewed by world public opinion as either effective as a mechanism for international cooperation or as legitimate in its country composition.

Furthermore, 94 percent of those from other major countries and 80 percent of Americans surveyed thought that the world needs a global steering mechanism. (Elsewhere in the survey, a global steering mechanism was defined as "taking on the broad, evolving agenda of global challenges and provide strategic guidance to the international institutions on how to address them.") But, despite this, 83 percent of those from other major countries and 87 percent of those from the U.S. thought the G8 is not actually performing that role. As a consequence, it seems that part of the perception regarding the lack of effectiveness and legitimacy of the G8 is determined by its over-reach in trying to be something it is not: a global steering mechanism instead a pivotal club of like-minded western countries. The sense of crisis in the functioning of the G8 is derived from the "unrepresentativeness" of the G8 membership undermining its legitimacy and is also due to the fact that it is unable to do what more than 90 percent of officials and experts from other major countries questioned thought the world needs, namely to perform the functions of a global steering mechanism, in part because the countries that need to be part of addressing global challenges are not there. Hence, the effectiveness and representativeness deficits of the G8 interact with each other to drive the drama of the G8 to a legitimacy crisis.

Therefore, the conclusion seems to be that the G8 is in crisis in terms of its larger global public role in the representativeness, effectiveness, and legitimacy of its country composition but that it should be maintained by its members as a pivotal club. In light of these results, G8 enlargement seems to be a less promising path forward than the alternative of creating a new summit group for dealing with global issues and providing a global steering mechanism. This has to be considered a significant conclusion, since most of the international debate on summit reform has been about G8 enlargement.

Recent Evolution of the G8 into a G8 Plus Five

Since the G8 summit in Gleneagles in 2005, the G8 summits have regularly included the O5 in part of the meeting. At the Heiligendamm Summit in 2007, German chancellor and host Angela Merkel in particular pushed for a secretariat to be established at the OECD in Paris to support work on four key issues by the G8 Plus Five to prepare the issues for possible discussion at leaders level. This Heiligendamm Process will come to a head with a report on the progress of this process at the G8 summit hosted in Italy in 2009.

This section surveyed the views of these officials and experts on this recent evolution of the G8. Between 91 percent and 100 percent of respondents from the U.S. and between 95 percent and 97 percent of those from other major countries see "the recent evolution of the G8" as important, positive, and necessary. Seventy-one percent of those from other major countries would "favor the permanent transformation of the G8 summit group into an L13 where all 13 countries would be full members of the group." And yet only 23 percent to 24 percent of all surveyed thought that "the recent evolution of the G8" into a G8 Plus Five is adequate.

Finally and importantly, 79 percent of U.S. respondents and 85 percent of those from the other major countries preferred "other changes in the leaders-level summit, beyond the 13." This is an unequivocal conclusion with importance for the future.

Beyond the G8 Plus Five

Despite this clear result in favour of changes beyond the 13, there is less clarity and consensus about what paths forward are most promising in terms of the specifics of the country composition of an expanded summit grouping. Forty-two percent of U.S. respondents selected "adding a permanent seat for an Islamic country to the L13" and 42 percent also chose "adding rotating seats (to the L13) to represent smaller, poorer countries." Curiously, only 30 percent and 18 percent of the respondents from other major countries picked these two options, respectively. The other results are:

- 38 percent of those from other major countries preferred "converting the G8 into an L20" whereas only 26 percent of U.S. respondents favoured doing so;
- 32 percent of U.S. respondents and 30 percent of those from other major countries chose "variable geometry," adding seats to the L13 depending on the issue under discussion; and
- 30 percent of respondents from other major countries preferred "limiting the size of the new leaders-level summit group to 16," whereas only 16 percent of U.S. respondents favoured doing so.

There was not much support for adding an Arab Middle Eastern country to the L13 (11 percent of U.S. respondents; 22 percent of other major countries), for adding a permanent seat for Nigeria (15 percent of U.S. respondents; 20 percent of other major countries), or for adding other countries (5 percent of U.S. respondents; 13 percent of other major countries).

Whereas 72 percent of U.S. respondents, but only 50 percent of other major countries, thought that "the EU members should consolidate their seats into one seat in the G8 summits," 4 percent of U.S. respondents and none of those from other major countries thought that "EU governments are likely to agree to this option in the near future, say by 2010."

In summary, these results indicate some support for varied options of expansion beyond the 13 such as using variable geometry, adding an Islamic country, and rotating seats for smaller, poorer countries. The stronger U.S. support for these options relative to the responses from other major countries is consistent with the relatively weaker support (52 percent versus 71 percent) by Americans in favouring "the permanent transformation of the G8 into an L13."

Summit Mandate and Mission

In answering whether they would "favor a stronger mandate and clearer mission for an expanded summit group," 78 percent of U.S. respondents and 81 percent of respondents from other major countries prioritized "[taking] on the broad, evolving agenda of global challenges and [providing] strategic guidance to the international institutions on how to address them" and 43 percent of U.S. respondents and 67 percent of those from other major countries selected "push for international institutional reform in the IMF, World Bank, UN [United Nations], and other international institutions." Forty-three percent of U.S. respondents and 33 percent of those from other major countries supported "[returning] to the original emphasis on international economic coordination issues." What is interesting here is the degree to which these three priorities relate to each other, given that there was a choice among six options.

None of the U.S. respondents and only 4 percent of respondents from other major countries felt that an expanded summit group should "limit the focus to geopolitical military security issues." Nine percent of U.S. respondents and 6 percent of those from other major countries favoured a single-issue focus, and 9 percent of U.S. respondents and 27 percent of those from other major countries preferred dealing primarily with current crises. There is great clarity in these responses regarding what an expanded summit grouping should not focus on.

In summary, there is great clarity (roughly 80 percent of both groups) about the primary summit mandate that there is a need to take on "the broad, evolving agenda of global challenges and provide strategic guidance to the international institutions on how to address them." This conclusion seems consistent with the overwhelming support by both groups (80 percent of U.S. respondents and 94 percent of those from other major countries) for the view that "the world needs a global steering mechanism" and, for the purposes of this analysis, defines that term.

The United States in a Polarized World

Sixty-seven percent of U.S. respondents and 85 percent of those from other major countries favoured "the next president of the U.S. announcing her/his support for the 2009 summit in Italy to be convened in an expanded group of permanent members."

On average, respondents from both the U.S. and the other major countries viewed reformed and expanded summits as "important" to the United States as "a vehicle for engaging the rest of the world" and as "important" as "a high-profile political step toward changing the perception of the U.S. in the world."

On average, those from other major countries viewed reformed and expanded summits as "possibly helpful" for "addressing global challenges," whereas the U.S. respondents viewed them as "important" for doing so.

These average responses mask the fact that the distribution of responses on all three of these questions regarding the US. role and response were highly skewed toward "possibly helpful" and above, with virtually none of the responses indicating these issues were "unimportant." Thus the "very unimportant" responses pulled the average toward the mean (3.5 = important), when in fact the distribution was more toward the upper end.

In summary, it is clear from these results that summit reform is perceived by both U.S. respondents and those from other major countries as a significant instrument for engaging the rest of the world, as an effective political step for American foreign policy in "changing the perception of the U.S. in the world," and as a way of "addressing global challenges." It is interesting to note the extremely high support (67 percent of U.S. respondents; 85 percent of those from other major countries) from those who would like the next U.S. president to suggest the 2009 Italian-hosted summit be convened in an expanded, permanent group. These results indicate that support for summit reform is viewed as important to the U.S. by Americans and even more strongly by respondents from other major countries.

Implications for the Future

The first thing to note about these results in terms of their usefulness in discerning pathways forward for summit reform is that they are clear. Indeed, one could argue that they are surprisingly clear. One would have thought there might have been a greater diversity of views among the *cognoscenti* in the international community who are not only knowledgeable but actively involved in these issues. Indeed, on the fundamental issues there is a consensus on major conclusions. That does not necessarily mean that the actual pathway forward will follow from the consensus on the conclusions in the survey, but it does mean that there is broad agreement that some reform is necessary and that there is a focused range of options that define the likely direction of change.

The second aspect of consequence for interpreting the significance of the results for the reform process itself, is the degree to which the different dimensions of the results are inter-related, as well as mutually reinforcing. The survey results on the G8 that perceive it to be primarily a "pivotal club" of like-minded states rather than a global steering mechanism helps illuminate the choice between G8 enlargement on the one hand and the creation of a new summit grouping on the other. Both options are open, and it is hard to predict which of the two pathways might be taken in practice. There is certainly momentum toward G8 enlargement, as the HP makes manifest. There is also a strong push for a new expanded summit grouping beyond 13, which is consistent with 80 percent support for prioritizing a global steering mechanism role for it and 80 percent/94 percent of respondents who think "the world needs a global steering mechanism." But if a new expanded summit were created and the G8 were retained, then one would anticipate that a separate G5 would also be brought into being, adding another new element to the politics of summitry.

Nonetheless, the fact that approximately 65 percent of all 76 respondents viewed "the G8 as a pivotal club" and roughly 60 percent thought that "the G8 is performing the role of pivotal club" means that the G8 has a viable and valued role for its members that might well continue in the future, even as—or perhaps especially as—a new, expanded summit grouping is formed to deal with global issues beyond the purview of the relatively narrow membership of the G8. The finding that 80 percent of U.S. respondents and 94 percent of respondents from other major countries felt the world needs a global steering mechanism, while only about 15 percent of all respondents thought the G8 is actually performing that role, highlights the degree of over-reach by which the G8 is undermining its legitimacy.

These results mesh with the fact that 80 percent of all respondents favoured the global steering mechanism role (to "take on the broad, evolving agenda of global challenges and provide strategic guidance to the international institutions on how to address them") in defining a stronger and clearer mandate for an expanded summit grouping. There was consistency in the responses among issues, as indicated by the second priority among respondents on the question of summit mandate and mission being to "push for international institutional reform in the IMF, World Bank, United Nations, and other international institutions" (43 percent of U.S. respondents versus 67 percent of those from other major countries) and the third priority being to "return to the original emphasis [of summits] on international economic coordination issues" indicates consistency in the responses among issues.

Form follows function. The compositional shift in the membership of the summit grouping is not just a freestanding political issue. It is intimately linked to the roles and functions, the mandate and mission of summits to address global issues and align the international institutions to deal with them. This is a powerful result that makes clear that summit reform, in both form and function, is required to enhance both representativeness and effectiveness together, as a means of increasing the legitimacy of summits and the international institutions at the same time. Since these are each major components of the international system, these results would appear to define inter-related steps toward improving the capacity of the international system as a whole to deal with global challenges as the top priorities in redefining the mandate of summits.

A third aspect of consequence for the future is the strong response among those from the other major countries to questions regarding the degree to which they viewed U.S. support for summit reform as important to the U.S. "as a vehicle for engaging the rest of the world" and "as a high-profile political step toward changing the perception of the U.S. in the world." If this were not the case, and there were less support for summit reform among Americans (which there is in some of these results), then there would be no foreign policy rationale for the U.S. to support summit reform because U.S. support would not have a positive impact on leaders in other major countries. But this is decidedly not the case. On average, American respondents and respondents from other countries all felt that U.S. support for reformed and expanded summits would be "important" as a vehicle for engaging the rest of the world and as a high-profile political step toward changing the perception of the U.S. in the world. More than that, 85 percent of respondents from the rest of the world favoured "the next president of the United States announcing her/his support for the 2009 summit in Italy to be convened in an expanded group of permanent members," while 67 percent of U.S. respondents favoured this option.

Clearly, beyond its own perceptions of the summit reform issue, the U.S. can reap foreign policy benefits by becoming an active supporter and leader of summit reform because leading figures in other major countries overwhelmingly think that this would directly benefit the U.S. at this moment in history. If this were not the case, whatever the views of the U.S. policy makers on the merits of summit reform itself, there would be no added incentive to support it based on the direct foreign policy benefits of doing so, which these survey results clearly reveal. If the survey results themselves are extended, it seems that U.S. support for summit reform and expansion would be received by the rest of the world as a gesture toward a more engaged, collaborative, cooperative, multilateral approach to global politics in contrast to what might be construed to have been the unilateralist, confrontational, narrow national-interest approach of the recent past. It would be a way of signalling a fundamental shift in the U.S. conduct of its role in the world and of subduing the tendency to create antagonisms that have put the U.S. in a position of generating security threats to itself rather than eliminating them. The facts that the U.S. responses are positive for at least two thirds of almost all the major strategic questions and that in general there is more similarity than difference between the U.S. respondents and those from other countries suggest that U.S. exceptionalism is not so evident in the U.S. group. As Andrew F. Cooper observed, this might "allow the return to responsible multilaterally oriented [U.S.] leadership to be accomplished in a far easier manner than might be anticipated."

Finally, the other major finding is that despite the fact that between 90 and 100 percent of both groups viewed the "recent evolution of the G8" as important, positive, and necessary, less than 25 percent of both groups found the recent evolution into a G8 Plus Five to be inadequate. Nearly 80 percent of U.S. respondents and 85 percent of respondents from other major countries preferred "other changes in the leader-level summit, beyond the 13." This, too, is a major result with consequences for the pathways forward because it implies that the evolution of the G8 Plus Five into a G13 is neither inexorable nor inevitable but rather that some additional countries should be added "beyond the 13," in the view of an overwhelming majority of the 76 officials and experts polled in this survey. Despite the strong and consistent pattern of meeting at G8 Plus Five from Gleneagles in 2005 to St. Petersburg in 2006 to Heiligendamm in 2007, and despite a reporting requirement on the HP scheduled for the summit to take place in Italy in 2009, there may well be additions to the G8 Plus Five grouping, based on the opinions in this survey, when and if summit reform eventually occurs. Whichever happens, G8 enlargement or the formation of a new summit grouping, there is a push by the officials and experts in this survey toward an expanded summit grouping larger than 13.

Pathways Forward for Summit Reform

These implications of the survey results lead directly into a consideration of alternative pathways toward summit reform or alternative future scenarios of how summit reform may or may not evolve. The most likely possibilities would seem to be: a) validation of the G8 Plus Five process at the Italian summit in 2009 and acceptance by leaders there to convene the 2010 summit in Canada at L13; b) G8 enlargement initiated by the host country wherein Italy might convene an expanded G8 summit at 13 or some other configuration in 2009 or the Canadians might do so in 2010, surely after consulting other G8 members and other potential candidate countries to assess their interest in becoming members of an enlarged G8 summit; c) a new U.S. presidential initiative might occur early in 2009, either privately through intermediaries or publicly in an announcement, in support of an enlarged G8 summit or a new summit grouping to be convened in 2009; d) a separate meeting in 2009 at the leaders level on a major global issue, such as energy security or climate change, might occur in an expanded summit grouping, perhaps larger than 13, which might then evolve gradually into a new regular annual summit grouping to act as a global steering mechanism; e) an unexpected expansion and new mandate for summits might well result from spontaneous combustion among leaders meeting for another purpose or because of a sudden global crisis or event; and f) the pattern over the last several years might continue into the future wherein the G8 continues to meet at eight, inviting other countries in for specific issues and for only part of the summit meetings, revealing no consensus at leaders level on summit expansion or reform. These are assessed in turn below.

Scenario A: Validation of the G8 Plus Five Process
[Possible, but Unlikely]

This scenario is possible where the pattern of G8 summits with partial openings to the leaders of the O5 continues until the summit in Italy, when an assessment is scheduled to be made of the HP. Given that this assessment is already on the agenda of the 2009 summit, it forces the issue of permanent membership of the five countries in an expanded summit group to the fore. It could be foreseen that it would be embarrassing for the G8 leaders to say no, and drop the issue of summit expansion and essentially discontinue the pattern by turning the O5 leaders away from future summits. This would be a visible snub, which is hard to imagine G8 leaders would want to embrace. But this does not mean that there is inevitability in the inexorable march toward a G13 or L13.

The respondents to this survey show an overwhelming sense that the G13 is inadequate and more than 80 percent favoured "other changes in the leaders-level summit, beyond 13." This undoubtedly reflects a strand of thinking in relevant governments, beyond the particular officials and experts in this survey. But at the time of the survey there was some indication that the government of Japan in 2008 might interrupt the pattern of inviting the O5 to the Hokkaido Toyako Summit. If this had been the case, the pattern since 2005 would have been broken and there would be considerably less pressure in 2009 to transform the G8 Plus Five to a G13 or L13 on a permanent basis. As a result of this uncertainty at the hands of the G8 host, while it remains possible that eventually the G8 Plus Five process will be validated and transformed into a new summit grouping of 13, it is probably unlikely to occur as an extension of the existing pattern alone.

Scenario B: G8 Enlargement [Possible, but Unlikely]

There is the factor of the convening power of the host country. This power can be influenced both in a negative and a positive way. It is possible that either Italy or Canada in the next two years could choose to convene the summits at 13 instead of eight, or in some other configuration. No summit host would dare to send invitations to an enlarged group of countries without consulting the G8 leaders themselves in the first instance, and the newly invited members in the second, to assure that this governance innovation by the host would be successful. The constraint of "what the traffic will bear" has been a highly influential one in the first decade of the 21st century.

The greatest champion of expansion of the G8 summits has been former Canadian prime minister, Paul Martin. He was the original proponent of transforming the country grouping of the G20 finance ministers, for which he was the inaugural chair as finance minister of Canada, into an L20, leaders-level group. As prime minister of Canada in the early years of 2000, Martin pushed hard in speeches and in private with G8 leaders to get them to accept the idea of meeting at leaders level (see, for example, Martin 2005). But he had no luck, in large measure because of a reluctance on the part of U.S. president George W. Bush to accept the proposal. Later, especially in the run-up to both Gleneagles and St. Petersburg in 2005 and

2006 respectively, British prime minister Tony Blair spoke in public and in private in favour of G8 enlargement. In 2007, upon becoming president of France, Nicolas Sarkozy became a visible and vocal advocate of including the big emerging market economies into the G8. And in 2008 Gordon Brown, Blair's successor, called for G8 expansion in major speeches in both India and in Boston. Still no action resulted.

The consequent conclusion is that the constraint of what the traffic will bear is greater than the convening power of the host country. Whereas it is possible that the conveners in 2009 and 2010 may succeed in realizing transformative change, it seems unlikely that by themselves they will succeed unless there is a major shift in the U.S. position on summit reform, which is indeed possible.

Scenario C: A New U.S. Presidential Initiative [Possible]

The presidential election in the U.S. in November 2008 presents an opportunity for a major shift in the U.S. approach to the world, as the early part of this chapter indicated. The respondents to this questionnaire decisively preferred that the next president of the United States back the idea of convening the 2009 summit as an expanded group of permanent members. This provides not only support for such an initiative by the next U.S. president but also a rationale for it, as indicated earlier, because 85 percent of the respondents from other major countries support this action. This means that a presidential initiative would be perceived by leaders in major countries as a signal of transformative change. In this context, a new president might find support for summit reform to be an attractive initiative to set a new tone and direction, establish a dramatically different approach to engaging the rest of the world, and relate to the embodiment of a "new global order" efficiently without having to communicate with more than a dozen leaders, one leader at a time. It all depends, of course, on who the next president of the U.S. will be, the circumstances that will press upon that person in early 2009, and what the priorities turn out to be. But given the context and the candidates, it is at least a possible option that might be exercised.

Scenario D: Evolution from an Issue-Specific Summit to Summit Reform [Most Likely]

This scenario is more complicated but perhaps even more likely. Energy security and climate change loom as the highest priority global challenges both because of the substance and the process currently under way to develop a post-Kyoto framework beyond 2012. The energy challenges alone are massive. There will be roughly 3 billion more people on the earth in 2050 than today, and already 2 billion people today do not have access to electricity. This means that between now and 2050 the global energy productive system must meet the electricity demands of more new claimants than the current energy system that was developed over the last century already reaches. This is a long-term economic issue of the highest order. Second, the world, including the American public, has come to the view that it is better to invest in reducing carbon emissions now than to have to invest more later, when in any case it may be too late as well as being more expensive. This is a long-term environmental issue of the highest order. Together, energy security and climate change represent the central security issues looking ahead. The scope and scale of these issues, and their global reach and political complexity, provide one of the greatest opportunities for demonstrated, real, and effective global cooperation ever. Hence, an intensive effort by the U.S. to reverse its position on climate change and not only join but lead the global effort to forge a new framework for the future would provide precisely the specific opportunity to demonstrate the new U.S. approach to its role in the world that is needed now.

Crucial in moving this issue forward is the governance mechanism to do so. Indisputably, the United Nations Framework Convention on Climate Change (UNFCCC) is the ultimate forum for finalizing a global agreement among all the states of the world. But the universal membership of the UN makes it too large a grouping to be an effective mechanism for reaching agreement on the fundamentals. And the G8 is too small and unrepresentative a grouping for doing so. Therefore, there have been calls for an intermediate-sized group of major countries to work out a consensus on basic elements of an agreement to forward to the UNFCCC for review, revision and final approval. In the joint efforts of the Centre for Global Studies at the University of Victoria (CFGS), the Centre for International Governance Innovation (CIGI), the Brookings Institution, the Mexican Council on Foreign Relations (COMEXI), and the OECD, energy security and climate change were prioritized as the issue that most needs a larger summit grouping for progress and that it is the issue most likely to leverage summit expansion and reform. Form follows function in this high-profile issue, increasing the likelihood of action.

But the matter becomes more complex. In 2007, the Bush administration convened a conference on climate change, bringing together 16 "major emitter economies"—now referred to as the Major Economies Meeting on Climate Change and Energy Security (MEM)—in August to discuss the post-Kyoto framework. (The 16 consists of the G8 Plus Five plus Australia, Indonesia, and South Korea.) This conference consisted of officials below ministerial level from environmental ministries of the 16 countries. In the run-up to the 2008 Hokkaido Toyako Summit, Japan decided to hold a meeting of the MEM leaders the day after the G8 summit to discuss climate change, which was hosted by Prime Minister Yazuo Fukuda at the end of the summit on July 9. However, before the summit there was much speculation about the usefulness of any such meeting with Bush, as he was well known to be against the carbon emission targets that lay at the heart of the agreement and were endorsed by the candidates in the U.S. presidential race. It is interesting to note that an independent group of scholars working on a Brookings project on "managing global insecurity" came up with a G16 leaders group for global issues that includes the G8 Plus Five as well as Egypt, Indonesia, and Turkey (see Managing Global Insecurity 2008).

But what is more clear, and perhaps more likely, is that there may be a decision to convene an energy security and climate change summit of 13 to 16 or even 20 countries in 2009 to try to forge a draft framework agreement to go to the UNFCCC by the end of 2009, when resolution on a final agreement is scheduled. This would avoid the issues of G8 enlargement or G8 Plus Five validation having to be faced in 2009. The likelihood of an expanded summit for climate change being an attractive and indeed compelling idea for the major countries, and for a new U.S. president, is high. While both candidates will take major steps to reverse the U.S. position on this issue, Democratic candidate Barack Obama has been clearest about the governance innovations he would sponsor, if elected president. The Energy Fact Sheet on his website states that:

> Obama will create a Global Energy Forum—based on the G8+5, which included all G8 members plus Brazil, China, India, Mexico and South Africa—of the world's largest emitters to focus exclusively on global energy and environmental issues. Maintaining a standing international body focused on these issues will give a forum for all of the major emitters—past, present and future—to discuss efforts to combat climate change. (Obama 2008)

Other major countries undoubtedly will push for some intermediate-sized forum in which to negotiate with the U.S. under a new president in 2009, no matter who is elected. If such a summit grouping were formed to deal with energy security and climate change and were successful in doing so, then it would set an example of effectiveness and a precedent for establishing a regular annual summit grouping of a similar size to address global issues and guide the international system of institutions in dealing with them. This is a more complex, convoluted pathway to summit expansion and reform but it ends up evolving out of practice rather than principle, events rather than ideas, and positive success rather than perceived weakness of the G8 as an unrepresentative, ineffective, and illegitimate group to be addressing global issues. The world ends up with a new global steering mechanism, which 80 percent of U.S. respondents to the survey and 94 percent of those from other major countries think the world needs. This may be the most likely scenario for achieving summit reform.

Scenario E: Spontaneous Combustion [Possible]

In contrast to the one-step-at-a-time, slow, evolving progression toward an expanded, reformed, permanent summit grouping that meets annually, as just described, it is also possible that an event, crisis, or opportunity presents itself that vaults summit reform forward in a "big bang" fashion. A simultaneous terrorist attack in the capitals of selected G8 and emerging market countries would be a version of an event that could trigger such an initial meeting that would lead inexorably, perhaps, to permanent summit reform. Or leaders gathered at the inauguration of the next president of the U.S. in January of 2009 might spontaneously come up with the idea that the summit in Italy in 2009 should be the turning point in the history of the G8 and bring to life a new summit grouping for the new global era of the 21st century. Top leaders do not always appreciate being driven by their staff and like reserving spontaneous actions to themselves and among each other. "Spontaneous combustion" of this sort is creative energy that can shape events and institutions. It would not be the first time in history that such a turning point occurred. It is perhaps not the most likely scenario, but it is a possible pathway for reform.

Scenario F: Continuing Stalemate on Summit Reform [Very Possible]

Finally, a very possible scenario looking ahead is that nothing happens. As obvious as the arguments for a larger grouping are, as clear as the weaknesses of the G8 appear to most observers, and as much concern as there is in the world today about the inadequacy of the current system of international institutions to meet global challenges, it is well within the realm of the possible that nothing happens on summit reform in the next couple of years. Every leader of a G8 country is importantly constrained by weak internal support, low polling ratings, and an inability to play a strong leadership role in the international arena. The only wild card in the scenario for 2009 is who will be president of the United States. That could change the dynamic. But it may not.

One of the great divides in U.S. foreign policy in this election year is the difference between an America that draws its strength from its own preoccupations with its national beliefs, values, and ideals and continues to try to form alliances and to project power based on them, and an America that draws its strength from its historic and continuing fusion of pluralism and unity translated into a vision of the world as culturally, politically, and economically diverse, which can nonetheless come together around a common agenda in which compromise and cooperation are both possible and necessary.

History in the end is unpredictable, which is what endows it with both opportunity and responsibility. Time will tell whether processes, issues, events, or leaders will drive summit reform to a breakthrough or whether the continuing stalemate will prevail. Much would seem to depend on the outcome of the U.S. presidential election if the current stalemate is to be broken.

Concluding Remarks

However solid, credible, and consensual the views of the leading figures surveyed in the study conducted for this chapter may be, the truth is that despite the logic of summit reform as a way to increase the representativeness, effectiveness, and legitimacy of the international institutions, steering mechanisms, and system, the leaders simply may not take the steps necessary to effect reform, as clear as those may be. As a consequence, among the options of spontaneous combustion, a U.S. presidential initiative, G8 enlargement, and the validation of the G8 Plus Five outreach process, none of these may actually transpire, although there are reasons why each of them might occur or even should occur. In the end, some combination of continuing stalemate and gradual evolution seems to be the more likely combination of force vectors that will drive the future than more deliberate decisions and dramatic transformative steps. Nonetheless, however much this hybrid scenario of muddling through may appeal to one's sense of realism, the world does indeed seem to be at a historic juncture where new global leadership and governance innovation are called for. A reformist thrust would seem to be the most promising for addressing the global challenges of the 21st century of most interest to most of the world's people. Why is this too much to expect when the case is so clear, at least among those who are directly involved? U.S. leadership seems to be the biggest element that will determine the future of summit reform and global politics.

References

Achebe, Chinua (2000). *Home and Exile*. New York: Anchor Books.

Ahmed, Akbar (2007). *Journey into Islam: The Crisis of Globalization*. Washington DC: Brookings Institution Press.

Dombey, Daniel and Stanley Pignal (2007). "Europeans See U.S. as Threat to Peace." *Financial Times*, 1 July. <www.ft.com/cms/s/0/70046760-27f0-11dc-80da-000 b5df10621.html> (May 2008).

Joffe, Josef (2006). *Uberpower: The Imperial Temptation of America*. New York: W.W. Norton.

Managing Global Insecurity (2008). "Managing Global Insecurity Advisory Group Meeting." Ditchley Park, UK, 13–14 February, Washington DC. Brookings Institution. <www.brookings.edu/projects/mgl.aspx> (www.brookings.edu/events/2008/0213_ditchley.aspx).

Martin, Paul (2005). "A Global Answer to Global Problems." *Foreign Affairs* 84(3): 2–6.

Obama, Barack (2008). *Barack Obama's Plan to Make America a Global Energy Leader*. Chicago. <www.barackobama.com/issues/pdf/EnergyFactSheet.pdf> (May 2008).

Pew Global Attitudes Project (2007). "Global Unease with Major World Powers: Rising Environmental Concern in 47-Nation Survey." Washinton DC. Pew Research Center. <pewglobal.org/reports/display.php?ReportID=256> (May 2008).

Bibliography

Alexandroff, Alan S., ed. (2008). *Can the World Be Governed? Possibilities for Effective Multilateralism*, Waterloo: Wilfrid Laurier University Press.

Bradford Jr., Colin I. and Johannes F. Linn, eds. (2007). *Global Governance Reform: Breaking the Stalemate*. Washington: Brookings Institution Press.

Halperin, Morton H., Jeffrey Laurenti, Peter Rundlet and Spencer P. Boyers, eds. (2007). *The Power and Superpower: Global Leadership and Exceptionalism in the 21st Century*. New York: Century Foundation Press.

Ikenberry, G. John (2002). *American Unrivaled: The Future of the Balance of Power*. Ithaca: Cornell University Press.

Kagan, Robert (2003). *Of Paradise and Power: America and Europe in the New World Order*. New York: Random House.

Leonard, Mark (2005). *Why Europe Will Run the 21st Century*. New York: Public Affairs.

Mazarr, Michael J. (2007). *Unmodern Men in the Modern World: Radical Islam, Terrorism, and the War on Modernity*. Cambridge: Cambridge University Press.

Nye, Joseph S. (2002). *The Paradox of American Power: Why the World's Only Superpower Can't Go It Alone*. New York: Oxford University Press.

Mahbubani, Kishore (2008). *The New Asian Hemisphere: The Irresistible Shift of Global Power to the East*. New York: Public Affairs.

Steel, Ronald (1995). *Temptations of a Superpower*. Cambridge: Harvard University Press.

Appendix: Note on the Summit Reform Survey

Since 2005, Johannes Linn and Colin Bradford have organized an annual seminar series for Washington-based officials from the countries in the G20 finance ministers to discuss under Chatham House rules (with no attribution) the issue of global governance reform, both in terms of the G8 summit and international institutions. These seminars were initiated because there was a need to create a forum for the relevant countries to discuss the opportunities and obstacles to reform in a candid and confidential manner that might help push the reform process forward in practice. These seminars have also included a wide variety of experts, many of whom have experience either as officials in national governments or as officials at the international institutions themselves; they have come from the Brookings Institution and other think tanks and research centres. There has been an especially close involvement with colleagues at the Peterson Institute for International Economics and the CFGS at the University of Victoria, as well as the New Rules for Global Finance Coalition. This seminar series and other research and outreach activities have been consistently supported financially by the CIGI in Canada. In addition, there have been joint activities with the CFGS. The author is grateful to all his official and think tank colleagues for their interest and involvement in these activities over the last four years and to Jim Balsillie and John English and other colleagues at CIGI for their steadfast financial support.

This summit reform survey grew out of this work. Specifically, it resulted from an invitation from Andrew F. Cooper, associate director of CIGI, to prepare a chapter for this book on the role of the United States in the HP of the opening to the G8 Plus Five countries. The idea of doing a survey was driven in part by the overly time-intensive cost of conducting individual interviews and by the U.S. election-year process, which privileged the views of those from other major countries in providing a political rationale for the U.S. supporting the undertaking of summit reform and which depreciated the salience of the views of the Bush administration. As a result, more than 150 Heiligendamm Process questionnaires were sent out individually to officials from G20 countries based both in Washington and in their capitals and to academics, scholars, experts, and researchers at think tanks, universities, and research centres in Washington and elsewhere in the United States and in the G20 countries. Several experts from other countries in this sample participated in the CIGI conference on "Reaching out to BRICSAM: the Heiligendamm Process and Beyond" held in Cancun, Mexico, on 6–7 March, 2008, and a CFGS conference at the Mexican ministry of foreign affairs held on 11 March, 2008, in Mexico City.

In the end, there were 76 respondents, 30 of whom were officials and 46 of whom were experts. Of the 76, 26 were from the U.S. and 50 were from 15 other G20 countries. There was a relatively balanced division among three sets of respondents with 25 government officials from the 15 "other major countries," 21 experts from universities and think tanks in those countries, and 23 U.S. respondents from U.S. universities and think tanks. There was also balance among three other subsets, with 12 officials and 16 experts from seven advanced industrial countries other than the U.S. and 13 government officials from the eight G20 emerging market economies. Only two U.S. officials and five experts from emerging market economies responded. The country distribution was as follows: Canada (10), France (2), Germany (5), Italy (3), Russia (1), and the UK (7), and the U.S. (26) among seven of the G8 countries, and Australia (2), Argentina (1), Brazil (5), Mexico (3), China (2), India (2), Korea (1), South Africa (4), and Turkey (2) among the rest of the G20 cluster of countries not belonging to the G8.

The respondents to this questionnaire were from an involved group of experienced officials, former officials, and experts, most of whom are well known and visible in international affairs. Far from being novices, these individuals included eleven officials from nine G20 capitals, three executive directors in the IMF from three advanced industrial countries, six senior advisers to executive directors in the international financial institutions (IFIs), five former senior IFI officials (Nancy Birsdsall, Jack Boorman, Johannes Linn, David Peretz, and Alex Shakow), one former head of government (Paul Martin, former prime minister of Canada), a former minister (Pedro Malan, former finance minister of Brazil), two deputy ministers (Strobe Talbott, former deputy secretary of state of the U.S., Gordon Smith, former deputy foreign minister of Canada), current senior officials (Shyam Saran, senior advisor to the prime minister of India, Lourdes Aranda, vice-minister of external relations of Mexico, Maurizio Massari, head of policy planning of the ministry of foreign affairs of Italy), several former ambassadors as well is prominent academics and researchers, which included from the U.S. Robert O. Keohane and Anne-Marie Slaughter from Princeton University, Joseph S. Nye and Jeffrey Frieden from Harvard University, and

Stephan Haggard and Miles Kahler from the University of California at San Diego. All the respondents are acknowledged as credible representatives of the international community of officials and experts.

The author is extremely grateful to Johannes Linn, Andrew F. Cooper, Barry Carin, Ralph Bryant, and Jonathan Fried for thoughtful comments on earlier drafts and for excellent comments by participants in the Brookings-CIGI seminar for Washington-based officials from G20 countries on 16 May 2008. In addition, Cooper contributed the idea of asking whether respondents "regard the G8 summits ... [as] the pivotal 'club' for western/like-minded countries" rather than as a global steering mechanism, without which the distinction between enlargement and a new summit grouping would not have been brought out as clearly. Below is an abridged and slightly edited version of the questionnaire used in the summit reform survey with the statistical results discussed in this chapter inserted. Ramin Ostadhosseini, a Brookings research assistant and student at George Mason University, tabulated the data. USR refers to U.S. respondents and OMC refers to other major countries.

Heiligendamm Process Questionnaire

I. *The Role of the G8*

1. Function:
   Do you regard the G8 summits as:
   a global steering mechanism, OR
   the pivotal club for western/like-minded countries?
   Pivotal club: 63% USR / 65% OMC

2. Usefulness:
   Do you think the world needs a global steering mechanism?
   Yes: 80% USR / 94% OMC

3. Performance:
   If so, is the G8 performing the role of a global steering mechanism?
   Yes: 13% USR / 17% OMC
   Is the G8 performing the role of the pivotal club?
   Yes 58% USR / 65% OMC

4. Effectiveness:
   Is the G8 viewed by world public opinion as an effective mechanism for international cooperation?
   Yes: 4% USR / 10% OMC

5. Legitimacy:
   Is the country composition of the G8 viewed by world public opinion as legitimate?
   Yes: 8% USR / 8% OMC

II. *Recent Evolution of the G8 into a G8 Plus 5*
6. G8 + O5:
   How do you view the recent evolution of the G8 into a meeting of leaders from G8 industrial countries plus five "outreach" countries, namely Brazil, China, India, Mexico, and South Africa? [Options: important or unimportant; positive or negative; necessary or unnecessary; adequate or limited]
   Important: 91% USR / 95% OMC
   Positive: 96% USR / 97% OMC
   Necessary: 100% USR / 97% OMC
   Adequate: 23% USR / 24% OMC

7. G8 Transformation:
   Would you favour the permanent transformation of the G8 summit group into an L13 where all 13 countries would be full members of the group?
   Yes: 52% USR / 71% OMC

III. *Beyond the G8 Plus Five*
8. Country Composition:
   Would you favour other changes in the leaders-level summit, beyond the 13? If so, check those that you favour:
   79% USR / 85% OMC
   add a permanent seat for an Islamic country to the L13
   42% USR / 30% OMC
   add a permanent seat for an Arab Middle Eastern country to the L13
   11% USR / 20% OMC
   add X rotating seats to represent smaller, poorer countries to the L13
   42% USR / 18% OMC
   add a permanent seat to the 13 for Nigeria to explicitly represent Sub-Saharan Africa
   16% USR / 20% OMC
   add Y number of seats to the L13 as "variable geometry" to fill with different countries depending on the issue or sector under discussion

32% USR / 30% OMC
add other countries
5% USR / 13% OMC
convert the G8 into an L20 to mirror the G20 finance ministers group of ten industrial countries (the G8 plus Australia and the European Union) and ten emerging market economies (Argentina, Brazil, Mexico, China, India, Indonesia, Korea, Saudi Arabia, South Africa, and Turkey)?
26% USR / 38% OMC
limiting the size of the new leaders-level summit group to 16?
16% USR / 30% OMC

9. European Seats:
   The EU members hold essentially 7 of the 24 seats in the International Monetary Fund (IMF), for example, and 4 of the 8 seats in the G8. Do you think that the EU members should consolidate their seats into one seat in the G8 summits?
   Yes: 72% USR / 50% OMC
   Do you think it is likely EU governments are likely to agree to this option in the near future, say by 2010?
   Yes: 4% USR / 0% OMC

IV. *Summit Mandate and Mission*

10. Summit Mandate:
    Would you favour a stronger mandate and clearer mission for an expanded summit group, such as to:
    limit the focus to geopolitical military security issues?
    0% USR / 4% OMC
    return to the original emphasis on international economic coordination issues?
    43% USR / 33% OMC
    deal primarily with current crises?
    9% USR / 27% OMC
    take on the broad, evolving agenda of global challenges and provide strategic guidance to the international institutions on how to address them?
    78% USR / 81% OMC
    push for international institutional reform in the IMF, World Bank, United Nations, and other international institutions?

43% USR / 67% OMC
focus on a single issue?
9% USR / 6% OMC

11. Potential Effectiveness:
As you look forward toward the future and the challenges facing the
world, how would you rank the *potential* importance of reformed and
expanded summits in addressing global challenges? [Options: very
unimportant; unimportant; possibly helpful; important; very important; crucial]
USR: 4.3 = Important / OMC: 3.8 = Important

V *The United States in a Polarized World*
12. Importance to the U.S.:
How important would you think reformed and expanded summits
could be to the U.S. as a vehicle for engaging with the rest of the world?
[Options: very unimportant; unimportant; possibly helpful; important;
very important; crucial]
USR: 4.3 = Important / OMC: 4.0 = Important

13. U.S. Political Step:
Against the background of historically low ratings for the U.S. in world
public opinion, how would you rank the importance for the U.S. of
actively supporting reformed and expanded summits as a high-profile
political step toward changing the perception of the U.S. in the world?
[Options: very unimportant; unimportant; possibly helpful; important;
very important; crucial]
USR: 3.9 = Important / OMC: 3.9 = Important

14. Next U.S. President:
Would you favour the next president of the U.S. announcing her/his
support for the 2009 summit in Italy to be convened in an expanded
group of permanent members?
Yes: 67% USR / 85% OMC

Enhanced Engagement
The Heiligendamm Process and Beyond

Alan S. Alexandroff

Reform of the G8 is possible, but it is not likely to be accomplished easily or immediately. And if enlargement does occur, it may not be with the G8 institution at all. Reform through enhanced engagement with the outreach countries could result in a wholly new global organization, leaving in place the G8 as it is currently known.

The chapters of this volume chronicle the opportunities and difficulties presented in the efforts to achieve enlargement of the G8. Specifically, they examine the reform process through incorporation of the large emerging economies—the outreach countries—with the developed countries of the G8. They look at the structured dialogue process set up by Germany at the 2007 summit and assess the prospect of the Heiligendamm Process (HP) culminating in membership reform with some or all of the Outreach Five (O5)—Brazil, China, India, Mexico, and South Africa. If it is acknowledged that reform of the G8 is required—and many would suggest that this is an imperative due to what Andrew F. Cooper decries in Chapter 1 as a "double crisis of legitimacy and efficiency," then is the HP an acceptable or possibly even optimal route to enlargement?

The G8 and the Outreach Five

In the face of this double crisis for the G8, the obvious question is why focus on these outreach countries. Andrew Hurrell (2006, 1) has supplied one answer:

One reason is that they all seem to possess a range of economic, military and political power resources; some capacity to contribute to the production of international order, regionally or globally; and some degree of internal cohesion and capacity for effective state action.

Hurrell (2006, 2) suggests a second and further (in this case self-identifying) reason for focusing on the outreach countries: they each "share a belief in their entitlement to a more influential role in world affairs."

This volume hones in on economic statecraft, given that the G8 still concentrates principally on economic issues, although with an agenda that from year to year extends beyond economic matters to encompass environment, development, and even security. These O5 countries have, to a greater or lesser extent, significant economic power, and in addition they have significant diplomatic leverage in the international system. All the chapters measure the economic strength of the O5 and in addition assess in some manner what is called their diplomatic leverage.

Operationalizing economic strength is a fairly easy exercise as Table 14-1 suggests (also see the appendices in Chapter 3). As with the group known as the BRICs (Brazil, Russia, India, and China) and its successor, the N11 (both products of the well-known studies by Goldman Sachs—see Goldman Sachs Economic Group 2007; O'Neill et al. 2005; Wilson and Purushothaman 2003), boundary questions remain even with regard to the questions of economic strength of the outreach countries. For example, does South Africa's status as 27th in gross domestic product (GDP) in terms of purchasing power parity (PPP) separate it from the remaining O5? This is certainly a question raised by Brendan Vickers in Chapter 7. And notwithstanding the strong economic rankings of Brazil as identified in Table 14-1, and commented on by Denise Gregory and Paulo Roberto de Almeida in Chapter 6, there are at least questions raised over Brazil in the face of limited military resources (the same can be said for Mexico and South Africa), although military strength represents principally a measure of diplomatic leverage.

This second category—diplomatic leverage—is both a valuable category used by analysts in this volume and, at the same time, difficult to operationalize. Nevertheless in Chapter 1, Cooper points critically to the measure (or measures) that constitute diplomatic leverage, or, as he calls it, diplomatic agency. He accepts the noticeable lack of economic strength on the part of Mexico, ranking 14th in GDP, and particularly South Africa (again 27th). However, both outreach countries possess, and exercise, a wide array of diplomatic engagements with broad institutional links—global and regional—and leadership participation that represents an influence that

Table 14-1

Measures of Economic Strength of the Members of the G8, the Outreach Five, and Selected Members of ASEAN

	GDP in trillions (PPP) 2007	GDP in trillions[a] 2007	Per Capita GDP (PPP)	GDP real growth rate (%) 2007	Population	Climate Change 2003[b]	Health[c] 2005
European Union	14.38 (1)	16.62	32,300 (36)	3.0	491,018,677 (3)		
G8							
United States	13.84 (2)	13.84	45,800 (10)	2.2	303,824,646 (5)	4,816.2	1,200,000
Japan	4.29 (4)	4.38	33,600 (34)	2.1	127,288,419 (12)	1,231.3	17,000
Germany	2.81 (6)	3.32	34,200 (32)	2.5	82,369,548 (16)	805.0	49,000
Britain	2.14 (8)	2.77	35,100 (30)	3.1	60,943,912 (24)	569.1	68,000
France	2.05 (10)	2.56	33,200 (35)	1.9	64,057,790 (23)	373.9	130,000
Italy	1.79 (12)	2.11	30,400 (39)	1.5	58,145,321 (25)	445.5	150,000
Canada	1.27 (13)	1.43	38,400 (22)	2.7	33,212,696 (39)	565.5	60,000
Russia	2.09 (9)	1.29	14,700 (75)	8.1	140,702,094 (10)	1,493.0	940,000
Outreach Five							
China	7.00 (3)	3.25	5,300 (133)	11.4	1,330,044,605 (1)	4,143.5	650,000
India	2.99 (5)	1.10	2,700 (167)	9.2	1,147,995,898 (2)	1,273.2	5,700,000
Brazil	1.84 (11)	1.31	9,700 (105)	5.4	191,908,598 (8)	298.3	620,000
Mexico	1.35 (14)	0.893	12,800 (84)	3.3	109,955,400 (13)	415.9	180,000
South Africa	0.467 (27)	0.283	9,800 (103)	5.1	43,786,115 (30)	285.4	5,500,000
ASEAN							
Indonesia	0.846 (18)	0.433	3,700 (158)	6.3	237,512,355 (7)	295.0	170,000
Thailand	0.519 (26)	0.246	7,900 (111)	4.8	65,493,298 (23)		
Malaysia	0.357 (31)	0.187	13,300 (81)	6.3	25,274,133 (49)		
Philippines	0.300 (39)	0.144	3,400 (162)	7.3	92,681,453 (15)		
Singapore	0.228 (47)	0.161	49,700 (8)	7.7	4,608,167 (121)	–	5,500

Table 14-1 (*continued*)

	GDP in trillions (PPP) 2007	GDP in trillions^a 2007	Per Capita GDP (PPP)	GDP real growth rate (%) 2007	Population	Climate Change 2003^b	Health^c 2005
Total	2.25 (7)	1.171			425,569,406 (4)		
ASEAN 5 total	2.25 (7)	1.171			425,569,406		
ASEAN 5 % world	3.43%	0.002%			6.37%		
G8 total	30.28	33,045.07			870,544,426	10,299.5	2,614,000
G8 % world	46.15%	57.70%			13.04%	45.63%	6.62%
O5 total	13.647	7651.64			2,823,690,616	6,416.3	12,650,000
O5 % world	20.80%	13.36%			42.29%	28.42%	32.03%
G13 % world	66.95%	71.06%			55.33%	74.05%	38.69%

Notes:
^a Official exchange rate.
^b Carbon dioxide emissions in million tonnes.
^c Estimated number of people with HIV/AIDS.
ASEAN = Association of South East Asian Nations; GDP = gross domestic product; PPP = purchasing power parity.
This table aggregates the G8, the Outreach Five (O5), and then most revealing the G13 (G7/8 plus O5). What is most significant is that the G13 represents almost two thirds of the world's GDP on a PPP basis. It is a significantly greater aggregation than the 46 percent held by the G8. On population the combination is even more revealing. The G8 represents only 13 percent of the world's population. The G13, on the other hand, represents 55 percent of the world's population—more than one half of the world's population. On the broad but not insignificant question of legitimacy and voice, the G13 shows a markedly larger aggregation of power, at least as measured by these economic strength characteristics. It certainly describes, at least in economic strength characteristics, why so much attention focuses on G8 enlargement. The author is grateful for the great assistance of Rachael M. Alexandroff in adapting and supplementing these tables originally created by John Kirton.
Sources: *The Economist* (2008); International Monetary Fund (2008); World Health Organization (2008); Central Intelligence Agency (2008).

prima facie justifies inclusion of these two with the outreach countries. Indeed, Mexico has taken on an energetic diplomatic role in the HP in part because the HP uses the Organisation for Economic Co-operation and Development (OECD) as a secretariat: Mexico is the only O5 country that is a member of the OECD. Mexico, in fact, sees itself as something of a North–South bridge diplomatically and in the enlargement process between the G8 and the O5. South Africa has established an extensive network both in Africa and beyond. But although this qualitative information is a helpful way to further determine the strength of these outreach countries, a task going forward in establishing the outreach group (or what the contributors to this volume call B(R)ICSAM) will be to operationalize this additional category of diplomatic leverage.[1]

With regard to the economic strength of the G8 and the O5, Table 14-1 also reveals a significant contrast in the economic growth rates of the G8 and the O5, but the rankings on GDP growth suggest that, with a few exceptions, the G8, the O5, and the five ASEAN states are major economic powers.

On population, a similar picture emerges with the G8 and O5 states having the largest population, with a few exceptions (Canada, Italy, and South Africa). The rankings in Table 14-1 are affected by the inclusion of Indonesia, Thailand, Malaysia, the Philippines, and Singapore, the top five members of the Association of South East Asian Nations (ASEAN), which allows a comparison of the economic strength measures with the other O5 and G8 members. Some favour including Indonesia as the representative of this regional organization (see both Chapter 2 by Timothy M. Shaw, Andrew F. Cooper, and Agata Antkiewicz, and Chapter 9 by Paul Bowles), not least because it includes a large Muslim state, although not a Middle East one. This economic regional organization represents a challenge, however, in terms of representation at meetings and in particular at summits. While the world is changing—the European Union, ASEAN, the North American Free Trade Agreement (NAFTA), Mercosur, and so on—it is still a leap, albeit an intriguing one, to include a region in a world of states.[2] The economic strength measures of the ASEAN reveal a significant outreach country. As a group, these five ASEAN members rank seventh in GDP, with the fourth largest population of any of the G8 or the O5. Equally revealing are the significant lower rankings of the individual states of the ASEAN.

Views from the G8

Notwithstanding the obvious aggregation of economic strength that arises from enlargement, particularly from the vantage point of the G13 (that is, the G8 plus the five outreach countries), a significant number of G8 members are hesitant to proceed to enlarge the group. It is worth distinguishing two matters in considering G8 reform: first, the views and attitudes of the current G8 members about the effectiveness and purposes of this club of great powers and, second, the proposed process—enhanced engagement via the HP—that is the central feature of this volume.

The views from the G8 capitals differ. As John Kirton suggests in Chapter 3, "there was also a defining divide between an enthusiastic European four and an opposed Pacific four, with Russia for this purpose privately a member of the reluctant Pacific power club." And even within each group opinions vary from national capital to national capital.

The place to start in examining attitudes to enlargement is with those that have championed it. There are the enthusiastic two—France and the United Kingdom—who, through their political leaders, have openly promoted expansion of the G8. French president Nicolas Sarkozy and British prime minister Gordon Brown have suggested that the outcome of the HP should be an expanded G8—in other words, a G13.

Germany, while supportive, has taken a different path. In Chapter 10, Thomas Fues and Julia Leininger examine the German government's motivations. It is apparent that the construction of the HP was in part a creative improvisation of the German government. For the current German leadership under Chancellor Angela Merkel, reform is required but process is key: a successful structured dialogue as established by, and through, the HP is necessary. Reform should first take the form of an HP-like dialogue to show, according to Kirton, "that such a forum would add value and work." Only a successful structured dialogue will open the way to reform.

The remaining European member is Italy. With the Italian election in the spring of 2008, what had been a club of four may only be three or three and a half, according to Kirton. The new Italian government led by Silvio Berlusconi has made it clear that it prefers the traditional G8 grouping of countries with "shared principles" ("G8: Berlusconi to Maintain Summit Format" 2008). However, as the summit host in 2009—when the final HP report will be delivered—Italy will invite the O5 leaders for the entire second day for discussions on the HP's issue areas. In addition, O5 leaders will meet alongside African leaders with the G8 on the third day to discuss development issues (Guebert 2008). This approach signals the inclusion of the O5 again solely on a functional basis.

As for Russia, although it has publicly supported an expansion of the G8 to a G13, privately it has resisted the move, suggesting that a move to a full G8—as opposed to a priority on enlargement to a G13—should be the priority task. This position has not changed with the election of the Russian president Dimitry Medvedev in 2008.

What, then, of the views of the remaining G8 members? The rest, the so-called Pacific four, have expressed varying degrees of hesitation, if not outright opposition, to reform through the HP. Japan is the strongest opponent.

It remained unclear for some time following the 2007 Heiligendamm Summit whether Japan would invite the O5 to attend the Hokkaido Toyako Summit. In the end, Japan encouraged the U.S. to invite the participants in the Major Economies Meeting (MEM) for the final day at Hokkaido. The MEM brings together 16 members—including the major carbon emitters—to discuss climate change. While this group includes the O5, it extends well beyond it. Japan also invited Australia, South Korea, and Indonesia to the G8 summit. These invitations broadened the cast of characters and shifted the focus away from the O5 at Hokkaido.

The Japanese government has suggested that it supports reform without, however, committing to the path of inviting the O5 specifically. It has, like many other G8 members, spoken out in favour of the current size of the G8 and expressed concern that an expansion of the club would hinder an effective summit discussion. Japan has also raised concern over a recalibration that would include South Africa (a question of weight) or, more particularly, China (a question of competition in Asia and possibly a reaction to China's failure to support Japanese membership on the United Nations Security Council [UNSC]).

Canada, as the smallest of the G8, appears to fear marginalization and dilution of influence. As Kirton has suggested, "its instinct was thus toward continuity, incremental expansion, and meeting the demand for expansion through other forums." A number of authors in this volume point out that the hosting lineup of the summit in the next few years—Japan, Italy, and Canada—adds little or no encouragement to enlargement.

As for the United States, the current administration remains dubious about reform, concerned that with the larger grouping, the effectiveness of the leaders summit will be lost (see Colin Bradford's Chapter 13). Indeed, the U.S. was dubious about the HP itself, feeling this structured dialogue was potentially wasted time and effort. It is not yet clear what a new U.S. administration—whether an Obama or McCain administration—will express over expansion.

The current reform scheme—if that is what the HP is—appears to have been built on earlier reform efforts of the G8. In fact, as a great power organization, the G8 is itself a product of reform, since at its initiation in 1975 there were six countries—with Canada attending its first summit the following year, the EU presidency participating as of 1977 and Russia welcomed as a member in 1998. Yet today it is somewhat imperfectly the G8, while reform models have periodically arisen. Thus, much praise has accompanied the emergence—at the finance ministerial level—of the G20 created in 1999. In this forum China, India, Brazil, Mexico, and South Africa are included, as well as a range of middle powers, namely Korea, Australia, Argentina, Taiwan, Hong Kong, Singapore, Indonesia, and Turkey. This expanded model has even been proposed for the leaders-level summit and was contained in the proposal by former Canadian prime minister Paul Martin for a Leaders 20 (L20).

The View from the Outreach Five

The G8 discussion begins with two questions, the first with two parts: First, does the G8 constitute a great power club with adequate authority and influence to act as a significant institution of global management? If not, what membership and enlargement does it need in order to address the issue of legitimacy, if not the effectiveness dimension? Second, does the HP provide a reform path—leaving aside for the moment the composition of the O5? One possibility, as Cooper implies in Chapter 1, is that the HP remain a structured dialogue with no advance to reform.

But this reform process has a strong history. It began when O5 finance ministers joined the G8 ministers to form the G20 in 1999. A further step was taken in 2005 when the O5 finance ministers joined the G7 finance ministers. According to Kirton, "it was elevated to the leaders' level when the O5 came to the G8 summit in 2003 and then regularly from 2005 to 2007. The launch of the officials-level HP thus represents the latest major step forward in this process of partnership between established and emerging powers."

If hesitation is the major response of the G8, notwithstanding the declared enthusiasm of the European three, ambivalence describes the views expressed by the O5. Cooper suggests that "all continue to have a good deal of their international identity shaped by their position either as a developing country or in solidarity with the global South." The O5 support for the developing world and the demands for structural changes and greater equality vary from one member to another, but each refers to its commitment to the developing countries within the international system. Any examination of the O5, suggests Gregory Chin in Chapter 4, sees the trilateral group of Brazil, India, and China struggling over its position with respect to membership in this great power club: "Indeed, Brazil, India, and China are grappling with reconciling their identity as members of the global South and the developing world and their emerging power status—or *de facto* great power, in the Chinese case."

For strong ideological reasons China has approached the G8 with reserve and caution. This reserve is noticeable as well for the HP. Along with a number of the O5 members, the situating of the HP in the OECD—perceived as a club for rich, largely developed countries, with Mexico being a notable exception—only adds to the O5's caution (see Richard Woodward's Chapter 11). Indeed, commentators and Chinese international relations experts originally rejected China's inclusion in the G8. Yet opinion has evolved significantly and, it is presumed, so has the attitude of the Chinese leadership. While the current leadership remains, at least rhetorically, committed to the South and the developing world, it would appear that Chinese opinion makers and government officials support China's integration into the G8. Such membership would identify and reinforce China's great power status. China could influence the "G plus" agenda and leverage its position. But ideologically—subject possibly to having other large emerging economies with it— it could also enable China to propose an agenda and perspective that supported the developing countries.

India and Brazil have retained a strong focus on solidarity with the developing world as well, shaping much of their foreign policy identities. Hurrell (2006, 19) questions, however, as leading nations of the global South continue their economic development, "what happens if that 'developing country identity' comes into conflict with the 'aspiring great power identity'?"[3] In Chapter 6, Denise Gregory and Paulo Roberto de Almeida show that Brazil's rising regional economic clout has forced its leadership to confront this question. So far, Brazil's answer has been to build independent, bilateral linkages with other states while projecting itself as a "responsible developing country, capable of engaging in a serious dialogue with G8 leaders, rather than to be perceived by other developing partners as adhering to a rich club agenda." This foreign policy approach can also explain Brazil's resistance to OECD membership.

In Chapter 5, Abdul Nafey points out that India, like Brazil, sees its great power aspirations focused first and foremost on permanent admittance to the UNSC. G8 admittance takes a back seat, at least publicly. Moreover, India remains a vocal advocate, as Nafey describes it, "of global regimes that redistribute the world's resources on the basis of equity." India sees itself as a strong advocate for the developing world, yet conscious of its growing power and emerging great power status. Nafey concludes by emphasizing the balancing that characterizes all of the O5 countries: as an emerging power, India is not walking out on the G8, but it is also using the G8 as part of an elaborate balancing act. Enhanced engagement with the G8 "is not exclusive.

India is attracted to other groupings and bilateral relations, and it fully appreciates its ascending rank in the evolving global order."

This position of "a foot in both camps" is characteristic of all the O5 members, maybe none more so than South Africa. South Africa has become a strong voice for development and equitable global governance. As Brendan Vickers in Chapter 7 suggests, South Africa is a "leading advocate for greater influence and participation by developing countries in shaping a new paradigm for global governance." It is intent on reversing Africa's marginalization and the marginalization of the South with the objective of having a more meaningful role for the south in international affairs. Yet the G8 and the HP remain contentious. To South African observers, the G8 remains an exclusive club. South Africa fails to have many of the economic strengths that mark the other O5 members. Suspicions remain that its inclusion is designed to solve the G8's problem of including an African representative. In the end there appear to be two views largely in opposition to one another. One view argues that South Africa should use the HP to join an expanded G8. Such a move, if it were offered, would benefit South Africa and possibly the wider African continent, because participation in this great power club would offer important opportunities to advance African issues—development and poverty reduction, trade, aid, and debt relief. The second view argues that, as Vickers suggests, "it would be improper and impolitic." South African membership would undermine its credibility as an advocate for South–South cooperation. Vickers summarizes this tension in views as "South Africa's potential membership of an alluring G8-OECD institutional nexus is fraught with hard political choices and challenges—but opportunities, too."

Finally, there is Mexico. Mexico has taken an active role in the HP and sees it as a means to expand influence and prestige on the global stage. With no evident concern about the OECD, as it is already a member of the organization, Mexico has taken the opportunity to expand contacts with the O5. Mexico hosted the first formal meeting within the HP. Mexico's diplomatic efforts with the other O5 members enabled it to place migration as a priority issue for the group. It sees itself as a bridge between North and South in this G8 plus O5 process, a role it has taken seriously. Mexico's HP sherpa, María de Lourdes Arunda Bezaury, has been a leading voice on the functional necessity to engage Southern partners constructively within the G8 decision-making framework (Williamson 2008). Duncan Wood in Chapter 8 proposes that the "prestige" factor and recognition in some manner of great power status will keep Mexico attuned to the HP and the possibilities for its inclusion in enhanced engagement and the larger reform process.

Prospects for Reform of the G8

It is evident that much ambivalence about reform remains among both the G8 and the O5 members. Although there appear to be clear advocates for an enlarged summit membership—particularly France and the UK—there are many in the G8 who remain unconvinced. And for the O5 there is a variety of reasons that leaders and governments express publicly for stopping short of committing openly to O5 inclusion, leading to the construction of a permanent G13. What is likely or possible? What is the way forward for G8 reform? Or is G8 reform something like reform of the Permanent Five (P5) on the UNSC? Always the bridesmaid; never a bride.

That said, it does seem that G8 reform is not quite the struggle that P5 reform and enlargement pose in global governance. As has been already stated, reform has been a feature of the G8 for much of its existence. Today, officials discuss the prospect of a G13 or even a larger great power organization. What, then, is the way forward? Here are the likely pathways.

Status Quo

The questions over G8 legitimacy—the current membership—have been driving calls for change. As noted above, the collective G8 economic power represents a diminishing share of the global percentage. In areas such as global finance or climate change, it is argued that the G8 cannot lead or manage such critical global governance issues. Yet the chapters in this volume reveal a broad and apparently continuing ambivalence by G8 members, and also among the O5, when it comes to taking the steps to a new organization of equals at the summit level.

Summit-level leadership is the key element of reform. But reform has occurred elsewhere. An evident example is the G20 finance ministers. In the wake of the 1997–99 Asian financial crisis, according to Kirton in Chapter 3, it was created "to prevent financial, economic, and related crises, and to institute the social protections that would make globalization work for all." Kirton examines favourably the growing competence of the G20 and chronicles the widening scope of its agenda. Here is an enlarged organization of the developed and the outreach countries (plus others) that appears to extend effective global governance. But it operates only at the level of finance ministers.

Doubts abound at the summitry level. Notwithstanding the clear process path of the HP, following the final report at the 2009 Italian summit, there may be no momentum to take the G8 to the G13. The explanation and consequences may vary. The G8 may perceive the enhanced engagement through the structured dialogue of the HP useful but may be satisfied with dialogue at the four so-called tables (focusing on innovation and intellectual property, energy efficiency, investment, and development); the G8 may be unwilling to raise the dialogue to the leaders' level. At the leaders' table, the pull of creative discussion and informality and the relatively small crowd may simply have too strong a hold on the current G8 leadership. G8 leaders may be too wedded to the notion that each annual host retain relative independence to shape the discussion and the guest list in his or her way for each particular summit. Such shaping could result in different outreach participants for different subject areas, although a core outreach group—say, China and India and possibly Brazil—could be on the annual outreach list. Such a result would depend heavily on the outreach countries and their willingness to accept the continuing discretion of the G8 leaders and their inability to fashion the summit agenda as equals.

While the G8 members may remain unchanged, with or without the HP's structured dialogue, it is unlikely that great power organization will remain static. The lack of G8 reform in the near term may at least prove a fillip to the outreach countries—whether O5, BRICs, or B(R)ICSAM, or some other configuration—and encourage them to establish their own leaders' forum. Signs of exasperation are slowing emerging. On the sidelines of the 2008 Hokkaido Toyako Summit, the O5 leaders held a preparatory session in Sapporo, culminating in a joint declaration. In it, the leaders espoused a consolidation of their bilateral relations towards collective collaboration with the G8 and multilateral institutions (see G5 2008).

But enhanced engagement, the structured dialogue process of the HP, and the prospect of failure to reform the summit, may lead in other directions. The example of the HP structured dialogue could well encourage critical but functionally specific forums in other areas of global governance. Thus, apart from the UN climate change process, great power organization may become permanent—in this case, the 16 countries that produce 80 percent of the world's carbon dioxide emissions and make up the MEM. The MEM leaders' meeting may or may not become attached to the annual G8 summit, but it may crystallize into a significant climate change forum.

Incrementalism

Given that the G8 has a history of incremental reform, is it possible that such an incremental process may remain vibrant enough to integrate members of the outreach countries into the summit process? The evident candidate for such incremental G8 enlargement is China. Yet, as Chin points out in Chapter 4, the Chinese leadership would be unlikely to proceed if the invitation were extended. As he notes, Chinese experts believe that China's presence would be outmatched by the other G8 members if China were to accede to enlargement by itself. If more than one O5 member were to accede, then it is possible that a larger group—China, India, and Brazil—might be the evident reform step. In the historical path of slow G8 reform the leaders' summit might integrate outreach countries.

Two problems arise however. There is hesitation over China's inclusion as China fails to possess the democratic character presumed a necessary feature of the G8. Yet the Russian case, notwithstanding calls from U.S. presidential candidate John McCain to uninvite Russia, is unlikely to be welcomed by other G8 governments. It is less difficult to envision a China as a member of the G8 with Russia already there. The other difficulty posed by an incremental reform path is that it intersects with the question of when new members get the opportunity to host a summit—a seemingly cherished opportunity for governments. If there is no willingness to stand aside, then the G8 seem to remain in place and questions of the equality of all members will immediately arise.

Big Bang

Another path would consist of a significant reform of the G8. Obviously, one form of reform would use the HP to transform the G8 into a new G13 at the conclusion or near conclusion of the process, much the way the big bang theory posits the universe is an expansion from a much smaller singularity. Or such a reform process might return to an earlier proposal of the L20 promoted by Paul Martin. Such an enlarged G8 group appears to have some continuing attraction in some G8 quarters. But again the administrative and process questions pose obstacles that are not easily overcome: the summit hosting order, the difficulties of maintaining informality in the summit meetings, and the problems in maintaining an agenda focus that is acceptable to the G8 and yet includes the more developmental concerns of the O5. If the G8 agenda is maintained, the O5 countries are likely to become frustrated, and if the agenda is reshaped, the G8 may decide to reform itself although may not necessarily abandon the new G13 or G13 plus.

Each pathway is possible but each poses obstacles and opportunities. There is no certainty over the likely outcome of the HP, but given the contemporary context of global governance and the attitudes, motivation, and behaviour of the G8 and the O5, as revealed in this volume, the following are more probable than less:

- the HP is unlikely to lead to a G13 outcome any time soon;
- such a failure of reform in the short term may well encourage the BRICs or B(R)ICSAM or O5 to consider or establish a new global governance organization and possibly a summit of their own;
- enhanced engagement via structured dialogue may well be maintained and even enlarged and deepened with a more permanent linkage between the functional sections (at least the HP's four) and the summit meetings; and
- while there will likely be no big bang, it is possible—even likely—that the G8 will take steps to integrate as equals the big three of the O5 countries: China, India, and Brazil.

Reform will come but what it will look like remains unclear. Still the HP is likely to be seen at least as an impetus along the road to better great power global governance.

Notes

1 See Chapter 2. The B(R)ICSAM research project at the Centre for International Governance Innovation is a multi-year study of major emerging economies and the various pathways by which these countries have integrated into the world economy. As Russia is already a member of the G8, its role and position in the B(R)ICSAM grouping is limited in this context.

2 Within the G8 framework, there is precedence for regional representation. The president of the European Union (a rotating position) and the president of the European Commission attend the summit, while the EU ministers participate in all G7 and G8 ministerial meetings. By comparison, however, ASEAN has much less central institutionalism.

3 Hurrell (2006, 19) raises this question in the context of Brazil and India, suggesting that they are "in a different category" of emerging economies. "On the one hand, they can be seen—and like to see themselves—as potential major powers, both within their regions and more generally. But on the other hand, they have identified themselves more specifically as developing countries and have understood their foreign policy options through the prism of North–South relations. This has been a persistent theme in the case of India; in the case of Brazil it has been a more ambiguous one, but one that is clearly in the ascendant under the present government. But is the language of Third Worldism and southern solidarity simply a hangover from the past?"

References

Central Intelligence Agency (2008). "The World Factbook." <www.cia.gov/cia/ publications/factbook> (May 2008).

Economist (2008). *Pocket World in Figures*. London: Profile Books.

G5 (2008). "G5 Statement." 8 July, Sapporo. <www.g8.utoronto.ca/summit/2008 hokkaido/2008-g5.html> (August 2008).

"G8: Berlusconi to Maintain Summit Format." (2008). *ANSA*, 8 July.

Goldman Sachs Economic Group (2007). "BRICs and Beyond." <www2.goldman sachs.com/ideas/brics/book/BRIC-Full.pdf> (May 2008).

Guebert, Jenilee (2008). *Italy's 2009 G8: Plans for the Summit*. 31 July. G8 Research Group. <www.g8.utoronto.ca/evaluations/2009italy/2009plans/2009-g8plans -080731.pdf> (July 2008).

Hurrell, Andrew (2006). "Hegemony, Liberalism, and Global Order: What Space for Would-Be Powers?" *International Affairs* 82(1): 1–19.

International Monetary Fund (2008). "IMF Members' Quotas and Voting Power, and IMF Board of Governors." Washington DC. <www.imf.org/external/np/sec/ memdir/members.htm> (May 2008).

O'Neill, Jim, Dominic Wilson, Roopa Purushothaman, *et al.* (2005). "How Solid Are the BRICs?" Global Economics Paper No. 134, 1 December. New Delhi: Goldman Sachs. <www2.goldmansachs.com/hkchina/insight/research/pdf/BRICs_3_12-1-05.pdf> (May 2008).

Williamson, Hugh (2008). "Rich Nations Stall Dialogue with "G5" Powers." *Financial Times*, 2 July. <www.ft.com/cms/s/0/d9724a12-4858-11dd-a851-000077b07658 .html?nclick_check=1> (August 2008).

Wilson, Dominic and Roopa Purushothaman (2003). "Dreaming with BRICs: The Path to 2050." Global Economics Paper No. 99, October. New York: Goldman Sachs. <www2.goldmansachs.com/ideas/brics/book/99-dreaming.pdf> (May 2008).

World Health Organization (2008). "Global Health Atlas." Geneva. <www.who.int/ globalatlas> (May 2008).

List of Contributors

Alan S. Alexandroff is a Research Director at the Munk Centre for International Studies at the University of Toronto. He recently launched the Global Institutional Reform (GIR) Workshop at CIGI, a project designed to evaluate the adequacy of institutional reform proposals for the international system, leading to his edited volume, *Can the World Be Governed? Possibilities for Effective Multilateralism* (WLUP, 2008). In collaboration with Andrew F. Cooper, he is working on a second volume, *Can the World be Governed? Rising States; Rising Institutions.*

Paulo Roberto de Almeida is Professor of International Political Economy at Uniceub-Brasilia, and Associate Professor at Instituto Rio Branco, the Brazilian diplomatic academy. He is also a career diplomat since 1977 and previously served as Minister-Counselor at the Brazilian Embassy in Washington (1999–2003). He holds a Ph.D. in Social Sciences from the University of Brussels and an M.A. in International Economy from the University of Antwerpen. Besides his professional duties, he has engaged in academic activities in Brazil and abroad. Dr. Almeida is also a researcher in economic history and international economic relations of Brazil, and has authored many books in those areas.

Agata Antkiewicz is Senior Researcher and Program Leader at CIGI, where she oversees the Shifting Global Order research theme as well as the BRICSAM and economic governance projects. She holds an MA in Economics, specializing in International Trade and International Relations, from the

University of Economics in Wroclaw, Poland. Ms Antkiewicz's authored or co-authored articles have been published by: *The World Economy, Review of International Organizations, Journal of European Integration, Third World Quarterly, International Studies Review, Canadian Public Policy Journal,* and National Bureau of Economic Research.

Paul Bowles is Professor of Economics at the University of Northern British Columbia. He is a past-President of the Canadian Society for the Study of International Development and is also affiliated with universities in China and Mexico. He specializes in globalization, regionalism and East Asian development. His most recent book is *Globalization and National Currencies: Endangered Species?* (Routledge, 2008). His current research projects include the political economy of China's currency choices and the political economy of labour and globalization.

Colin I. Bradford, Jr. is Research Professor of Economics and International Relations at American University and a Non-Resident Senior Fellow at the Brookings Institution and at CIGI. He has held several positions including Chief Economist at the United States Agency for International Development, Head of Research of the Development Centre of the OECD, Senior Staff of the Strategic Planning Unit of the World Bank, and Associate Professor in the Practice of International Economics and Management at the School of Organization and Management, Yale University.

Gregory T. Chin teaches global politics, comparative politics, and East Asian political economy in the Department of Political Science and the Faculty of Graduate Studies at York University. He is a Senior Fellow at CIGI, and a member of the Advisory Board of the North Korea Research Group at the University of Toronto. He is a member of the Editorial Board of Rowman & Littlefield's New Millennium Books Series, and an academic member of the Editorial Board of the China and International Organization Books Series, jointly published by Shanghai People's Press and Shanghai International Studies University. He has held a visiting fellowship at Peking University (1997–98). His forthcoming book is entitled, *China's Automotive Modernization: Industrial Policy and Rival Firms* (Palgrave, 2009).

Andrew F. Cooper is Associate Director and Distinguished Fellow at CIGI and Professor of Political Science at the University of Waterloo, where he teaches in the areas of International Political Economy, Global Governance,

Comparative and Canadian Foreign Policy, and the Practice of Diplomacy. He has been a Visiting Professor at Harvard University, The Australian National University, and in 2009 a Fulbright Visiting Chair of Public Diplomacy at the University of Southern California. Dr. Cooper's recent publications include, *Global Governance and Diplomacy: Worlds Apart?* (Palgrave, 2008), *Celebrity Diplomacy* (Paradigm, 2007), and *Regionalisation and Global Governance: The Taming of Globalisation?* (Routledge, 2007).

Thomas Fues is Senior Research Fellow at the German Development Institute (DIE). His main research interests are global governance, emerging powers, United Nations and international development cooperation. Recent publications include articles on G8 reform, the role of China and India in the global system, the UN development sector as well as human rights and global governance. In addition to his research tasks, Dr. Fues is responsible for the Global Governance School at DIE as part of the training and dialogue programme "Managing Global Governance" with young professionals from governments and think tanks of emerging economies.

Denise Gregory is a specialist in international relations and business administration, with experience in the areas of foreign trade, integration and international trade negotiations. She was named Executive Director of the Brazilian Center for International Relations (CEBRI) in December 2004. Previously, she acted as Institutional Relations Director of Investe Brasil, and was Chief of Staff to the President of the Brazilian Economic and Social Development Bank (BNDES). Ms. Gregory has also held positions with the Executive Secretariat of the Foreign Trade Chamber (CAMEX), and Department of Foreign Trade Policy within the Foreign Trade Secretariat.

John J. Kirton is a professor of Political Science at the University of Toronto where he is a Fellow of Trinity College. Dr. Kirton is the director of the G8 Research Group, established at the University of Toronto in 1987. He is also a Research Associate of the Centre for International Studies where he leads the Program on Global Health Diplomacy and the G20 Research Group. He has advised the Canadian and Russian governments and the World Health Organization on G7/8 participation, international trade and sustainable development, and has written widely on G7/G8 summitry.

Julia Leininger is Research Fellow at the German Development Institute (DIE) in the Competitiveness and Social Development department. She is also an associate of the Peace Research Institute Frankfurt as part of the PRIF/ Research Associate Project: Democracy Promotion through International Organisations. She has also held research positions with both the German Federal Ministry For Economic Cooperation and Development (BMZ) and the United Nations Development Programme. Her current research activities are in global governance, international institutions, and democracy promotion.

Abdul Nafey is Professor at the Centre for Canadian, US and Latin American Studies, Jawaharal Nehru University (JNU). Before joining JNU, Dr. Nafey taught at the Universities of Delhi and Goa. He was Head of the Centre for Latin American Studies, Goa University in 1989–90. His areas of research include dynamics of democratic development in Latin America, state and civil society, structural adjustment and its consequences, social movements, political and cultural dynamics of Indian diaspora in the Caribbean, regional integration in Latin America, and security and foreign policy dynamics of major Latin American and Caribbean countries.

Victoria Panova is Senior Lecturer in International Relations and Foreign Policy at the Moscow State Institute of International Relations. She is also Regional Director for Russia of the G8 Research Group based at the University of Toronto. Dr. Panova is a member of the National Working Group of the Advisory Council of the Civil G8 project, and was responsible for the substance and organization of the Civil G8 working group on Human Security during Russia's 2006 G8 presidency. Her research focuses on regional conflicts, non-proliferation, terrorism, energy security and sustainability, as well as global governance (notably the G8) in relation to Russian civil society.

Timothy M. Shaw is Director and Professor at the Institute of International Relations, the University of the West Indies St. Augustine. He previously directed the Institute of Commonwealth Studies at the University of London, the Centre for Foreign Policy Studies and International Development Studies programmes at Dalhousie University, where he taught for three decades. Dr. Shaw holds degrees from three continents and is visiting professor in South Africa and Uganda. His latest monograph is *Commonwealth: Inter- and Non-State Contributions to Global Governance* (Routledge, 2007). He is general editor for the International Political Economy series for Ashgate and for Palgrave Macmillan.

Brendan Vickers is Senior Researcher in the multilateral programme at the Institute for Global Dialogue (IGD). Prior to joining the IGD, he was employed as the Deputy Director responsible for International Relations and Trade in the Office of the President of South Africa. He recently completed a PhD with the University of London, focusing on international trade. Dr. Vickers' research interests are: international trade; the WTO; trade law & diplomacy; regional integration; South African foreign policy; and international relations.

Duncan Wood is Director of the Undergraduate Program in International Relations and Acting Head of the Department of International Studies at the Instituto Tecnológico Autónomo de México (ITAM). He is a member of the Mexican National Research System, a member of the editorial board of *Foreign Affairs en Español* and has been an editorial advisor to *Reforma* newspaper and was a non-resident Fulbright Fellow. Dr. Wood's research focuses on the Mexican energy sector, Latin American energy policy, migration and remittances, the political economy of international finance, and Canada-Mexico relations. In 2009 he will direct the Energy Policy Studies Center, to be based at ITAM.

Richard Woodward is a lecturer in the Department of Politics and International Studies at the University of Hull. He has written extensively on different facets of the OECD's role in global governance and his book on the organization will shortly be published by Routledge. Currently he is finalizing his PhD thesis on the governance of the City of London's financial markets since 1997 and is co-writing (with Simon Lee) *Understanding States and Markets: An Introduction to the History of Ideas in Political Economy* (Palgrave, 2009). His other research interests include the financial crime, offshore financial centres, and development in small states.

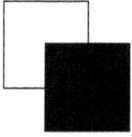

Index

Books in the Studies in International Governance Series

Alan S. Alexandroff, editor
Can the World Be Governed? Possibilities for Effective Multilateralism /
2008 / vi + 438 pp. / ISBN: 978-1-55458-041-5.

Andrew F. Cooper and Agata Antkiewicz, editors
*Emerging Powers in Global Governance: Lessons from the Heiligendamm
Process* / 2008 / xxii + 370 pp. / ISBN: 978-1-55458-057-6

Geoffrey Hayes and Mark Sedra, editors
Afghanistan: Transition under Threat / 2008 / xxxiv + 314 pp. /
ISBN-13: 978-1-55458-011-8 / ISBN-10: 1-55458-011-1

Paul Heinbecker and Patricia Goff, editors
Irrelevant or Indispensable? The United Nations in the 21st Century /
2005 / xii + 196 pp. / ISBN: 0-88920-493-4

Paul Heinbecker and Bessma Momani, editors
Canada and the Middle East: In Theory and Practice / 2007 / ix + 232 pp. /
ISBN-13: 978-1-55458-024-8 / ISBN-10: 1-55458-024-2

Yasmine Shamsie and Andrew S. Thompson, editors
Haiti: Hope for a Fragile State / 2006 / xvi + 131 pp. /
ISBN-13: 978-0-88920-510-9 / ISBN-10: 0-88920-510-8

James W. St.G. Walker and Andrew S. Thompson, editors
Critical Mass: The Emergence of Global Civil Society / 2008 / xxviii + 302 pp. /
ISBN-13: 978-1-55458-022-4 / ISBN-10: 1-55458-022-6

Jennifer Welsh and Ngaire Woods, editors
*Exporting Good Governance: Temptations and Challenges in Canada's
Aid Program* / 2007 / xx + 343 pp. / ISBN-13: 978-1-55458-029-3 /
ISBN-10: 1-55458-029-3